Soft Logic

Other Books by Robert S. Carrow

Electronic Drives

Technician's Guide to Industrial Electronics: How to Troubleshoot
and Repair Automated Equipment

Soft Logic
A Guide to Using a PC as a Programmable Logic Controller

Robert S. Carrow

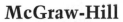

McGraw-Hill

New York   San Francisco   Washington, D.C.   Auckland   Bogotá
Caracas   Lisbon   London   Madrid   Mexico City   Milan
Montreal   New Delhi   San Juan   Singapore
Sydney   Tokyo   Toronto

Library of Congress Cataloging-in-Publication Data

Carrow, Robert S.
    Soft-logic : a guide to using a pc as a
programmable logic controller / Robert Carrow.
        p.   cm.
    Includes index.
    ISBN 0-07-014017-0
    1. Programmable controllers.   2. Microcomputers.   I. Title.
TJ223.P76C37   1988
629.8'9—dc21   97-22481
                                                            CIP

McGraw-Hill

A Division of The **McGraw·Hill** *Companies*

1 2 3 4 5 6 7 8 9 0   DOC/DOC   9 0 2 1 0 9 8 7

ISBN 0-07-014017-0

*The sponsoring editor for this book was Scott L. Grillo, the editing
supervisor was Paul R. Sobel, and the production supervisor was Pamela
A. Pelton. It was set in ITC Century Light by Kim Sheran of McGraw-Hill's
Professional Book Group composition unit, Hightstown, N.J.*

Printed and bound by R. R. Donnelley & Sons Company.

EL1

This book is printed on recycled, acid-free paper containing a
minimum of 50 percent recycled, de-inked fiber.

To all those individuals in industry who have had to work
until 3:00 a.m. to get a machine or process back on-line,
this book is for you. I've been there and done that!

Also, to the memory of my grandparents:
Oliver W. and Elva P. Carrow
and Raymond P. and Winifred A. Toy.

Contents

Foreword:
Personal Computer?
Or a New Era?

In the early 1980s, IBM coined the term *personal computer* to describe desktop computers priced and packaged for the everyday office or casual home user. Based on state-of-the-art Intel 8086 chip technology (sounds funny now, doesn't it?), the PC was originally used for personal computing activities such as basic word processing, printing, and a minimum of clerical activities such as letters and spreadsheets.

From an industrial automation perspective, the PC was first viewed with skepticism. "The PC will never make it to the factory floor" was heard in many circles. The PC was viewed as unreliable and not robust enough to perform the production duties of automation and control. Automation and control in the 1970s and 1980s were dominated by the distributed control system (DCS) and the programmable logic controller (PLC).

In the mid-1980s, the PC began to gain acceptance on the factory floor. First, the DOS-based PC was used to replace proprietary PLC programming terminals that were big and bulky and expensive to maintain. Several companies introduced DOC-based PLC programming software packages offering a higher degree of repeatability and troubleshooting capability. On the DCS side, the PC began to be used as a report generation system and as a "poor person's" data historian. Generating a production report or logging historical data was expensive to do in a DCS, so the PC offered a significant cost advantage over proprietary hardware. During the mid-1980s, a few companies pioneered the use of the PC as a low-cost alternative to proprietary operator interface consoles to the PLC and DCS architectures. The PC continued to gain acceptance on the factory floor as HMI (human-machine interface) and SCADA (supervisory control and data acquisition) systems on top of the control system. At the same time, PCs were being made more rugged and industrialized. Packaging with shock-mounted hard drives, RFI shielding for factory floor noise immunity, and

NEMA 4 waterproofing have made the hardware of a PC every bit as reliable as the control system hardware. Still in the late 1980s, even though there might be several PCs surrounding the control system, the factory floor automation industry was not yet ready to use the PC as the control system itself.

In the early 1990s, after several disappointing revisions, Microsoft released Windows 3.11. The HMI and SCADA markets were quick to jump onto the Microsoft Windows bandwagon. Unparalled ease-of-use advantages and productivity gains were achieved in both the industrial automation and the business sides of organizations. Millions of users added their support. At the same time, many manufacturing companies in the early 1990s began to lay the foundation for plantwide, even worldwide networks of LANs and WANs. The entire foundation for the majority of these networks, certainly on the client side, is Microsoft-based PCs.

Also, in the late 1980s and the early 1990s, PC fans watched the dawning of a new age on the hardware front. Intel began an aggressive release schedule of new processor chips. The original 8086 XT running at 4.66 MHz is laughable by today's standards. In the late 1980s, the 80186 at 12 MHz was released and was quickly outpaced by the 80286 at 16 MHz. The 80386 was then released as the first 32-bit PC system. Intel improved 80386 speeds with clock-doubling techniques that increased the speed of the hardware to 33 MHz and then to 66 MHz. A major advancement, a few short years ago, was the release of the 80486, which combined the processor and the mathematics coprocessor into one chip, significantly increasing the processor execution speed. The rate of advancements in chip technology is now staggering. It seems as though every 6 months there is a faster and cheaper processor. Often this brings about buyers' remorse for not holding out a few more months before buying. The Intel Pentium (80586) and now the Pentium II based PCs are achieving speeds well over 200 MHz! In addition to the advancements in processor technology, both RAM and hard-drive space are now cheaper. Do you remember when a 40-Meg hard drive was a luxury and people wondered "What would you ever need that much memory for?"

While the PC hardware architecture was continuing to get faster, cheaper, and more reliable, Microsoft was busy advancing the operating system. From the 80386 on, the PC became a 32-bit computer. However, the operating system was DOS with a Windows GUI (graphical-user interface). The Windows 3.11-DOS combination was based on 16-bit technology and did not tap into the 32-bit capabilities of the quickly advancing Intel processor technology. After years of development, Microsoft released Windows NT in the early 1990s. The principal Microsoft operating system architect for Windows NT had many years of experience in operating system development as the principal architect of Digital Equipment's mini and midsize mainframe operating system, VMS, as well as other operating systems. Windows NT running on 80486s personal computers rapidly began to propagate into markets traditionally dominated by computer vendors such as Digital Equipment and Hewlett-Packard. Windows NT now owns a commanding share of the business computing, network serving, and database repository marketplaces.

Over the past 5 years, virtually every automated plant has the PC designed into its automation strategy. The PC HMI market and SCADA markets are at an all-time peak. First Windows 3.11 and now 32-bit Microsoft operating systems. Windows 95 and primarily Windows NT, dominate the PC-based industrial automation software marketplace. There are segments of Unix users and VMS users still waving these flags. However, every major study that has been performed shows Windows NT as today's operating system of choice and the operating system of choice for the next 5 to 7 years (infinity in software terms). Evidence of this future dominance is the migration of virtually every major DCS company away from Unix or proprietary operator consoles to those based on Windows NT.

In the industrial automation and control software marketplace, I believe we are on the cusp of a new era. With Windows NT version 4.0, the operating system has caught up with the PC hardware speeds. The PC is now fast enough and reliable enough to handle control applications. Windows NT running on Intel PC hardware is already running in millions of applications and hundreds of thousands of mission-critical applications outside the industrial control market. Software companies in the past have had to solve the problem of real-time capability by adding real-time extension to Unix and other operating systems. Software companies have now added real-time capability to Windows NT. Over the past 3 years or so, the PC has entered the control system arena. This rocks the foundation of traditional control and informational paradigms. The PC and Windows NT bring functionality and capability that are simply not achievable in traditional closed proprietary control systems. Open networking technology, the proliferation of Internet/Intranet technology, and the ability to condense many PCs that used to *surround* the control system into the same PC that has *become* the control system are just too hard to resist. PC-based control offers the benefit of opening up the control system and information architecture and breaks down age-old barriers to information and data handling. It is early in the PC control era, *but this boat has left the dock*. There is no turning back. The PC, running real-time Windows NT, will now dominate the entire plant floor including the control system. PC-based control will literally change the way the automation world deploys control systems and disseminates information throughout the entire company enterprise.

I believe the term *personal* used to describe today's Windows NT/Intel computers no longer fits. The Windows NT-based Intel computer is now so fast and so reliable, is used in such a diversity of applications, and has proliferated into every essence of our daily lives that to call it a *personal* computer is such an understatement that perhaps it is time to change it. The term *PC* might even be considered a negative connotation in the industrial control marketplace. I submit that a more fitting term for today's computer is a *UC*, for *universal computer*. Or even better yet, a *ubiquitous computer*. The ubiquitous computer is, and truly will be, applied everywhere!

CARSON B. DRAKE, Vice President, Gray Matter Systems

Introduction

Automation has changed quite a bit over the last five decades. In fact, the automation of the car industry began in the 1940s, and all industry has been automating processes since. The term *automation* was actually coined from the automobile industry, and that industry is one of the trend setters when it comes to technology. Technology in this case is the use of electronic, microprocessor-based controls and equipment. This automation hardware and software are the essence of this book. This book is intended to be a reference for the multitude of engineers, programmers, and application people who keep the machines and processes running. It should be used to better understand PC-based control, soft logic systems, and industrial automation overall. Many components (software and hardware) used in industry are discussed. Because so many parts and pieces make up any automation application, it is this book's intent to look at as many as possible. To control all of them means that one has to have a basic understanding of each. When and how to use a certain device, what they are, and the sizes and shapes available are often learned by experience. This book will lessen that learning curve.

The term *automation* can be defined in a lot of ways. The dictionary defines *automate* as "to make automatic or have certain parts act in a desired manner at a certain time." To control that event, with respect to the parts, it should be repeatable and consistent. That is the basis for industry's striving to seek the perfect system and better the elements creating the event. Taking the best-available technology and equipment for the time has been industry's approach. This approach still applies today. The automobile industry certainly wasn't the only industry to try its luck at automating, but it is still viewed as that entity which can and does research, develop, and implement new automation and control schemes.

Soft Logic is written so that anyone working in industry can understand the basic concepts. It is also structured for the student or person external to the industry. They, too, can benefit from this book's information on the subject. There are a few formulas and rules of thumb provided, but this book is not a "heavily math-laiden" text. Rather, the information and tables provided will be readily used by the engineer or technician who needs an answer fast. This book will be used over and over by people who have to keep machines running and processes producing!

Each chapter contains its own graphs, charts, and tables. These items alone are invaluable as reference materials. The tables and charts most applicable to soft logic and automation have been included to make finding them (and your answer) easier and quicker. Additionally, a couple of specifications are reprinted. They are the OLE for Process Control (OPC) and Open, Modular Architecture Control (OMAC) and can be found in Chap. 5 on standards and guidelines. Many other standards and industry specifications are discussed in the book also. *Soft Logic* should become the one-stop shop for information on PC-based control systems.

Chapter 1, A World without PLCs, reviews how the term *soft logic* has evolved and how it fully relates to its other synonymous term *PC-based control*. An overview of this whole concept of PCs controlling machines and processes is given. The base technologies are explored, and the challenge is laid down for the reader: WHy is this approach even possible?

Chapter 2, Traditional Control Systems and Operating Systems, provides a review of many technologies, weaving into PC-based control and automation in general Motion control, process control, distributed control systems, PLCs, and related components are discussed. Various operating systems used today and yesterday are also defined.

Chapter 3, Personal Computers, Industrial Computers, and PLCs, is an important chapter. The basics of microprocessor technology, computers, and programmable logic controllers are reviewed. Many things we take for granted in this ever-changing, fast- paced technology are discussed once more (or perhaps for the first time). From relays to present-day software and hardware, each is reviewed from a basic-understanding viewpoint. Computer programming and PLC programming in ladder logic are discussed. ASCII tables, ladder symbols, bit tables, and other figures are included.

Chapter 4, Basic Elements of Industrial Process and Motion Control, covers the systems and application of the PC and soft logic. Understanding what the processes and machines need from the PC-based system will help one to properly apply the systems. Knowing more about the application and what we're trying to control makes designing, programming, and installing a soft logic system much simpler. The ac, DC, servo, stepper, and vector drives are discussed. Open- and closed-loop control systems along with feedback device types are addressed. Additionally, many different sensor technologies are reviewed.

Chapter 5, Standards, Guidelines, and Industry Practices, is the biggest chapter in this book. Because the soft logic discipline is somewhat new and evolving, it is necessary to pull together many standards and guidelines to help define the technology.

Many of these relative standards, guidelines, or industry practices are discussed (some in great detail). OPC, OLE for Process Control, OMAC, RS-274D (CNC control), PLCopen, IEC-1131 and IEC-1131-3, S88 Batch Process Control, Grafcet, and flowcharting are just a few that are included. At the end of the chapter is a complete list of standards organizations with their addresses and phone numbers.

Chapter 6, PC-Based Software, analyzes the various packages which make up the soft logic technology. Application software is reviewed along with dynamic data exchange (DDE) packages. Fault handling, interrupts, and safety issues are discussed. Flowchart application software is reviewed.Chapter 7, PC-Based or PLC-less Control, sits in the middle of the book and strikes at the heart of the subject. PLCs have done the job for years, whereas PCs can do the job now (and their future looks good). *Real*-time systems, *hard* real- time systems, and *soft* real-time systems are discussed. Windows NT is reviewed in this chapter along with the concept of open architectures. Several soft logic points to ponder are listed.

Chapter 8, Connecting the Soft Logic System, is the nuts-and-bolts chapter. In this chapter the reader will learn about the various hardware components and how to put them together. More emphasis is given to wiring, sound wiring practices, and netting a fully operational working *system*. Sheilding, grounding, isolation, RFI, EMI, and electrical noise are all covered. Hardware components such as transformers, switchgear, and filters are discussed.

Chapter 9, Input and Output, is the basis for any soft logic system. Logic is I/O and vice versa. Controlling I/O is the essence of all soft logic systems. Discrete, digital, and analog I/O is reviewed. I/O addressing, I/O hardware, and I/O overall control schemes are discussed.

Chapter 10, Communication Schemes, provides an overview of networks (LANs and WANs), transmission speeds and distances, and protocol. Basic serial and parallel communication is reviewed. Client-server systems and some sample HMI screens are shown.

Chapter 11, Data Collection, Statistics, Quality, ISO 9000, and Soft Logic, appeals to many different readers. Plant managers, quality engineers, process engineers, statisticians, and so on will find one or more parts of this chpater useful. Basic principles of statistics are reviewed and illustrated. QC and QA charts and base discussion are provided. SCADA systems and related charting are discussed. Last, discussion of the base elements of ISO 9000 and its documentation requirements is provided. PC-based control systems are a great help in this area.

Chapter 12, Soft Logic Applications, is the chapter that many readers will find helpful. Piecing together a PC-based system and integrating it as the control of an application are what the business of manufacturing of products is all about. More than 20 applications are provided. Each application note provides the reader with a scope, problem and problem solved, equipment used as the solution, benefits, and an illustration of the particular application. Some application examples include PID set point control, material handling, robotics, process, and other machine control.

Chapter 13, PC-Based Factory Control of Tomorrow, looks at trends in the soft logic industry which will affect automation in the future. Subjects such as the Internet, remote controls, fuzzy logic, and neural networks are analyzed. Virtual reality and artificial intelligence are discussed.

There is an extensive list of acronyms in the Appendix. This list of over 250 acronyms relates not only to PC-based controls and soft logic but also to automation and engineering in general. This is the list we've all been looking for!

The field of soft logic and PC-based control is just getting started. PCs on the factory floor will be commonplace by the year 2000, and beyond that year, they will be there in some form also. Factories want to produce. That is their number one priority. The controls have to be a tool to allow them to produce. The term *zero tolerance* will apply as PC systems are installed. Their reliability will have to be impervious, and I believe in time it will. Now is the time to gain a basic understanding of this discipline and technology so that you can grow with it rather than resist it!

Many thanks go out to the following: GM Powertrain Group, The OPC Foundation, Gray Matter Systems, Steeplechase Software, and my wife, Colette.

Trademarks: Microsoft, MSDOS, iRMX, Intel, UNIX, VMEbus, QNX, and Windows and Windows NT.

ROBERT CARROW

1
CHAPTER

A World without PLCs

It had to happen! Technology and change do force the issues. Factories and workers demand newer and better ways to produce. This will be the case from now until eternity—bigger, better, faster, new and improved—this change is almost a constant. The emergence of the microprocessor over 30 years ago has started us on a path. This path, built around the personal computer (PC), is new and exciting and full of surprises. The programmable logic controller (PLC) had its day, but its useful life may be waning. There was a time when there were no PLCs, and there will come a time when there will no longer be PLCs (except in the Smithsonian Institution).

Everywhere we look, the microprocessor and the PC are there. Every industry has become dependent on these devices. Additionally, commercial, light manufacturing, and even residential markets all utilize PCs today. PCs are in the office, are used by engineering concerns, and are necessary in the medical field. They are everywhere, and they have come of age for heavy, industrial use. Look for the trend to continue as suppliers and end users implement these machines in practically every facet of manufacturing. From the process or machine on the plant floor, to the cell controller, to the plant mainframe, to a system even outside the physical domain of the second-level system, soft logic systems are bringing the highest levels down to the lowest. The lower levels are not less important, but these levels traditionally have had less microprocessor power and capability. However, now with greater capability built into the floor-level machine and the ability to connect virtually anywhere and anytime, the PC-based controller is part of the overall scheme!

The Term *Soft Logic*

The term *soft logic* is very fitting and better than some of the quirky acronyms that have evolved in the computer industry (see the list of common acronyms in the back of this book). The term *soft logic* is coined from *soft*ware and *logic*. The Automation Research Corporation (ARC) is given credit for coining the term. ARC is an industry automation marketing and analysis group whose specialty is controls and electronics for industry. The term is truly appropriate because soft logic packages are actually software which is intended to be used as the application program for the machine or process. Because the application program controls various inputs and outputs for the machine or process, it is designated as an input/output (I/O) or logic controller. This I/O comes in many different forms and is discussed in Chap. 9. Thus the term *soft logic* has been duly and aptly created for this new technology.

Then there is the PLC. This device has been the workhorse of industry as far as I/O and logic controls are concerned. The PLC, or programmable *logic* controller, is that piece of hardware which can be seen in practically every manufacturing plant. It does not move or make many sounds. It has many lights, and although you cannot see the electric wires, they are there. This device has to be programmed also, and thus it acquired its name *program*mable *logic* controller. This was then shortened to *PLC,* and the name is still current.

The Shift from PLC To PC

PCs have become so common in everyday life that the person who fails to keep up with technology will most certainly be left behind. The PC environment emphasizes miniaturization and is proliferating. PCs are packing more power into smaller packages. Costs are decreasing for equivalent capability purchased. The reliability and availability of PCs are incredible. The hardware works well. It is consistent and usually troublefree. Of course, up until now, the PC has not been "abused," as it will be in the manufacturing environment. But this is more a matter of packaging. As long as the internal components are kept clean and are protected, they will function properly. Consider the PLC. It was viewed skeptically when first hailed as the controller for the future in the manufacturing plant. It survived, and now it is the control standard for industry against which the PC will be measured.

Which is more available, the PC or the PLC? The answer is obvious. PC components and spare parts are so readily available that this competition has helped reduce some of the costs, especially of spare parts. The real concern is that whenever a factory process or machine is down, the personnel must stock spare parts or know where to get them quickly. The PC is attractive from the can-I-get-what-I-need? vantage point.

Why Is This Approach Possible?

As you will discover, the programmable logic controller has the combination of hardware and software that closely resembles a personal computer. The PLC's main components are

1. A microprocessor, or central processing unit (CPU)
2. An input and output section
3. An enclosure
4. An application program

5. A power supply
6. Peripheral devices (monitors, keyboards, printers, communication ports, etc.)
7. A real-time operating system (RTOS)

In reviewing the base components of the microcomputer, or PC, we find many similarities:

1. There is a microprocessor, or CPU.
2. The unit is encased or enclosed.
3. It runs a software program.
4. The PC needs a power supply.
5. Peripheral devices are handled in the same manner.
6. An operating system which is not usually associated with real-time operation.

The only real difference in hardware involves the input and output capability of the PC. Couple that with a need to incorporate a hard real-time operating system, and the two devices have very similar structures.

Ironically, in the past, many individuals also recognized this fact and tried to emulate the PLC with the PC. There were always connectivity problems with the input/output interface and/or drivers to the PC. But the real hardship involved the real-time operating system. The PC had none! As you will discover later in this book, operating systems play a vital role in industrial applications. Several operating systems are discussed in this book, and it was not until some recent developments with Windows-based products that PCs have been able to lay claim to be anything close to real-time operation. But that is the essence of the reason why this whole soft logic technology is possible.

Costs of PC versus PLC

As discussed earlier, the shear quantities of PCs and PC parts have made the pricing attractive. The multibillion-dollar PC market overshadows the PLC market tremendously. This is part of the "bad reputation" which the PLC industry is getting. PLC suppliers have been on a supply-and-demand gravy train. If the plant has standardized on the PLC hardware and needs a part, where can the part be gotten? The price may be outrageous, but what is the choice when the plant is losing tens of thousands of dollars per hour when the machine is down? Thus the PLC part price was not the issue, until today. The PC will create, initially, a threat to the PLC market in two respects:

1. There is the threat (or desire) of the end user's wanting to move to an alternative control scheme, that of the PC. Thus PLC suppliers will fear losing the plant and the business.
2. PC components are already much less expensive, so PLCs will have to become competitive quickly.

Both of these issues will cause PLC pricing to begin to fall. There should be a crossover point in the future as PC soft logic systems proliferate and PLCs are displaced. PC pricing will continue to be competitive, and costs should continue to fall, creating PC equivalent capability for the money. Thus the PC industry has a very good headstart compared to the PLC industry. PLC suppliers may have to reduce prices quickly and drastically in the near future.

Proprietary PLC Systems

The term *proprietary* has been used often. In the manufacturing plant, proprietary means that the hardware which is in place has to be supported by and purchased from the same supplier year after year. What if doing business with a particular supplier is a virtual nightmare? Suppliers do not need to support the end user because they know they will get the business anyway—and at their price. All the plant employees have been trained on the proprietary system. The electricians can wire and fix the proprietary system in their sleep. The software engineers can program that PLC in seconds instead of hours. This means a lot to upper management; however, the price tag for this convenience is staggering. And that means more to upper management in the long run. It will always be looking for cost-cutting alternatives, and the PC-based business will catch management's attention.

Unlike the case of PLCs, the fact that PC hardware and software will be more plentiful and transportable is attractive to all levels, managers *and* technicians. The less they are locked into or tied to a particular supplier's hardware, the better. There is a freedom expressed here that can only be appreciated when you have tried to get a spare part at 3:00 a.m.!

Conclusion

This change was inevitable the PC will take over. In this case, industrial and manufacturing environments are the next target. Their controller of choice to date has been the PLC. Other markets and industries will have other needs. However, look for the PC to enter into areas where it was unheard of years ago. This device is getting more powerful with every passing day. Technological advancements are being made with PCs, and PLCs are not getting the development attention (this is another reason why the PLC will lose ground and market share). Studies are indicating that the switch is on and the trend will be to displace the PLC. Many market predictions are made, and all have a similar theme: The PC will emerge the winner in the controller-of-the-future race.

2
CHAPTER

Traditional Control Systems and Operating Systems

Another major factor in the emergence of factory control via the personal computer is the operating system. The operating system (OS) is the heart and soul of the controller. It is the master program that acts as the traffic cop to allow all the competing programs to get their fair shares of time and resources in the computer. This involves sharing memory, disk drives, output devices such as monitors and printers, modems, and of course the microprocessor itself. Obviously, for the operating system to be initialized, the hardware in the form of microprocessor, coprocessor, memory, boards, and I/O devices has to be in place, and there has to be application software. But there has to be an environment in which all these pieces can coexist, prioritizing tasks to keep a factory up and running. Before soft logic, numerous variations of operating systems and control schemes were implemented. This chapter will look at that evolution, compare different control approaches (both old and new), and help to define the operating system for a soft logic system.

The Single Machine versus the Manufacturing Plant

There are many types of business in the world today. Some assemble, others produce raw material, and still others manufacture. Some are large, and most are small. The majority of manufacturing tends to come from the smaller businesses. Sometimes they provide the larger corporations with product and many times provide product directly to the end user. These facilities usually have a machine or process in place, and it needs to be controlled. On a much larger scale, a major manufacturing plant may have several machines and several processes, all under one roof. All these systems have to be individually controlled, and then they must be "tied together." Obviously, this task becomes complicated as more components are added. Yet, to the smaller manufacturer, the task is just as great in orders of magnitude. We look at an example.

ABC Company has an extruder and makes neoprene gaskets, which are attached to automobiles. It supplies these gaskets to an automobile assembly plant which is working with a just-in-time (JIT) manufacturing resource program (MRP). ABC Company is small (there are 15 employees) and has an extruder with a motor and electronic controls attached (see Fig. 2-1). There is no electrician, no engineer, no team of programmers to support this machine. The controls were purchased from three different vendors, and ABC Company *has* to make a shipment of gaskets every day or else it is fined by the automobile assembly plant. This lone machine has to run! ABC's needs may seem simple, but to ABC that machine is its livelihood. It does not have and cannot afford the support infrastructure of the major car maker. Yet this small facility is constantly being asked for data, reports on quality, and other manufacturing information which puts greater demands on everyone. This "ma and pa" operation is commonplace, and this group of companies represents an extremely large market for PC-based controls. However, consider the large assembly plant.

Our large assembly plant, which we call the LAP Company, is also typical but on a different scale. This plant has one extruder of its own but chooses to subcontract the bulk of its gasket needs to ABC company. However, this plant has hundreds of machines and processes (see Fig. 2-2), for it assembles cars. Everything from conveyors and robot welders to paint booths and test stands—this plant has it all. And it all has to work! Millions of parts move through this plant each week. Each part has to carry with it information—Who made it? When? and Was it tested? Besides the enormous task of integrating all the controls for all the machines and processes, there's all these data to be recorded, tracked, and saved. Talk about a complicated setup! Now, it is easy to see why there are so many support people resident at a large manufacturing plant. Yet, their problems are not all that different from those of ABC

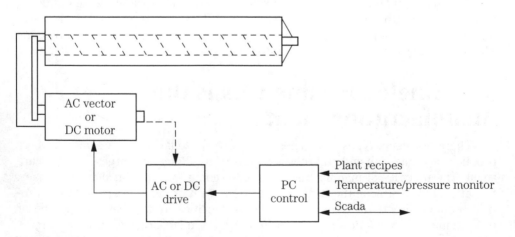

Fig. 2-1   Extruder and PC-based control.

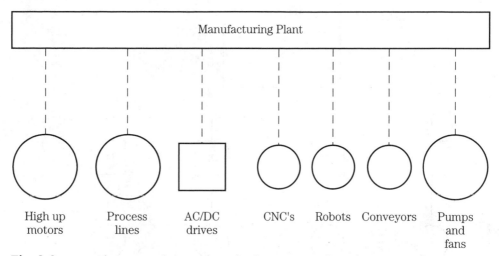

Fig. 2-2   Manufacturing plant with multiple motors and machines.

Company. The machine or process has to work, and the controls have to be reliable, easy to use and support, flexible, and powerful.

The two examples are typical and were not even considered in detail. The point is that PC-based controls and soft logic systems are available to big and little companies. The theory is that everyone should be able to understand them, program them, fix them, and add to them since they are built around a very common piece of equipment, the personal computer. If a machine's controls are down on a Sunday, chances are, there will be a local computer store open which may have the part needed. Additionally, a person somewhat knowledgeable in computers and software may be more readily available than that single PLC guru who only knows ladder logic. Thus this defines the large and small entities which can benefit from PC-based controls. How have they been doing all this in the past?

Traditional Control Schemes

Because there are so many different machines and processes and because free enterprise is the theme in the United States, there are too many controllers and control schemes to be able to address them all. The mere fact that there are hundreds of control suppliers and manufacturers makes grouping controls impossible. Then add the offshore control manufacturers and original equipment manufacturers (OEMs), and there is even greater confusion (this is another sound argument for simplifying the control base with PCs). Therefore, in the next section we look at some more prevalent control schemes for both large and small operations.

A control scheme can be as simple as a switch that starts and stops a motor. Then again, what if there is more than one motor? Now the process has become complicated from a controls standpoint (see Fig. 2-3). Who, what, and where will the brains be that determine which of, when, and why motor 1 or motor 2 should start? Just adding a second component made the control scheme more elaborate. Instead of a maintenance technician's starting the only motor, now we need a controller.

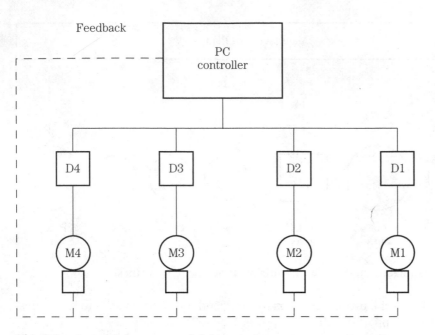

Fig. 2-3   A multiple-motor soft logic system.

Imagine what happens when 40 or 50 motors and hundreds of sensors, gauges, switches, and feedback devices all have to be monitored and controlled! Add the need to send and receive large amounts of data to and from several electronic components, and we now have the makings of a nightmare. It is a possible nightmare because equipment and pieces to the system are added and compatibility is never accomplished. But this is the real situation in the plant today. As controls and technology evolved, equipment was purchased and implemented.

Distributed Control Systems

Which control scheme is best, PLCs, PCs, or the distributed control system (DCS)? Should the control and communication "traffic cop" be housed in a master, single unit, or should the control be local to the process? The answer is that the application and the available funds, many times, dictate the direction of the control scheme. Distributed control is one of those misunderstood terms and is certainly a much broader subject than this book can cover. The prime aspect of a system like this is that one large and powerful PLC shares, or distributes, its controller functions with the lesser subsystem control peripherals.

With soft logic packages gaining in popularity owing to lower installation costs, DCSs and PLC systems should decline in preference. Typically, a PLC-based system is less expensive than a true DCS but does not have the full power and flexibility of the DCS. One important consideration of factory people when designing the control scheme is cost versus downtime. If the control scheme is such that a master device has control of many lesser components (processes, machines, etc.), what are the consequences when (not if, because it *will* happen) the master controller faults, completely fails, or is simply out of service? Can the plant tolerate having all subsequently controlled processes down because the master is down? If not, then the answer is the DCS. Install the control and communication capability at each machine and process such that each controller is in charge of its own local area. Thus if one controller goes down, the rest of the other machines or processes will still be running.

Distributed control systems sometimes are masked by all the other high-technology equipment in a facility. Valves, sensors, electronic drives, and other devices have microprocessors built into their architectures. Sometimes there is a duplication of processing effort. This is not uncommon with today's equipment. Ironically, costs are many times not an issue in the choice of an analog device versus a digital equivalent. So many products have microprocessors as part of the standard package that there is plenty of functionality built into the device. It may be found that the control loop desired is actually part of a manufacturer's standard software. With so many actual independent pieces of equipment becoming the standard with on-board microprocessors and communications capability, DCSs are losing popularity. So much inexpensive computing power can be placed in remote locations in lieu of distinct DCSs today. Even having redundant or "hot" backup controllers in critical processes is an attractive option since the cost versus computing power ratio is so equitable.

Proprietary PLC Systems

The focal point of the soft logic entry into the process control marketplace is the programmable logic controller. The PLC is the incumbent, and the PC-based controller is trying to be elected. Technological advances, reduction of computer hardware and software costs, and more available computer components have led to this "revolution." PC-based, soft logic control will be commonplace for the next decade in industry. But what is a proprietary PLC system?

Many years ago when PLCs burst onto the scene, certain major electrical and controls companies provided industry with their own version of an electronic machine that could control many individual inputs and outputs. These machines had high-speed processors (fast at the time), a dedicated operating system, and their own custom ways of programming. As other pieces of hardware evolved and were added to the existing PLC control scheme, there had to be ways of connecting all pieces to one another. This raised the issue of hardware and software compatibility. The PLC manufacturer had to have the end user purchase the alternating-current (AC) drive or human-machine interface (HMI) from the same source in order to "guarantee" connectivity. Thus, whichever PLC was selected as the first usually became the plant standard. Many other subsequent pieces of equipment had to be purchased from the same supplier. But the problem did not end there—the spare parts in the storeroom had to be for the equipment on the plant floor. If someone changed a controller, I/O rack, or drive, it had to be replaced by one of the same make. Thus, from a spare-parts vantage point, it was hard to justify a change.

Likewise, the human element became a major factor. Electricians and engineers were trained on the equipment that was the plant standard. The software and programming inherent to that particular manufacturer's hardware were often the "only" language known by plant personnel. Managers had to keep these PLC software "gurus" happy because no one else in the plant could troubleshoot the equipment, let alone write a new program for it. Also, once a program was developed for a process or machine, it was often very burdensome to make changes. Flexibility is not a term associated with PLCs. Thus the term *proprietary PLC system* means a whole lot more, especially to upper management.

Programmable logic controllers became the practical option in industry because they offered the manufacturing facility a reliable means of controlling processes. This was accomplished by utilizing the real-time operating system (RTOS) which only the PLC could provide. This RTOS basically had one job—to watch over the inputs and outputs of the machine or process it was controlling and if there was any decision to make (shut down, change, go fast, go slow, turn off or turn on another device, alarm someone, etc.), then it would do just that. *It was a dedicated controller.* There should be no reason for the PLC program to do anything else but control its machine or process. Fast scans, solid ladder logic programs, made for a "bulletproof" machine, and the suppliers of this product recognized this. This RTOS created a monster—what other option would the plant have to change systems, manufacturers, spare parts? It was stuck—until recently. PC-based controls and soft logic have now given the end-user some hope. As the manufacturing world accepts PC-based controls, new and better control schemes will emerge. PLCs and their basics are covered in the next chapter in detail.

Motion Control

As you walk through a factory and see or hear something move, then there is motion. If that motion is to be planned or predicted, then it should be controlled. This controlled motion should be programmable, and this process is called *motion control*. Soft logic and PC-based control systems are very well suited for use in motion control. In fact, as time goes on, virtually all motion control applications will probably be controlled from the PC. This will most likely happen because the basic elements of the motion controller are just like those of the proprietary PLC—readily duplicated by the soft logic system. The machine tool and automotive industries, mainly, have driven this technology in the past and are continuing to do so today. Other industries typically follow suit. Motion control is the essence of the production line, and soft logic will emerge as the control scheme of choice for motion control.

Traditional motion controllers have many looks, require all types of hardware and software, and are usually application-specific. Motion control involves the control of motors—AC, direct-current (DC), servo, stepper, and others—but can involve the control of hydraulic and air-actuated devices. In addition, that motion being controlled can be speed or velocity control (the most common), current control for torque regulation, and position control for servo systems, robots, etc. Additionally, motion controllers can perform much in the way of I/O control. Although this is not their primary function, the ability to watch various inputs and react whenever there is an interrupt is usually built into a motion controller. Thus motion control is no simple, out-of-the-box solution. In fact, there are usually three or four basic pieces of equipment found in a motion control system: the motor, drive or power converter, computer or controller, and some type of feedback device. Figure 2-4 shows a block diagram of the basic system. They all have to connect and work together to yield a functional motion control system.

Motion control is the basis for industrial automation! Sure, the PLCs will control some I/O in a process, or machine vision systems will process graphical images; but unless a product is physically moved out of the door in the factory, there is no true production. Many facets of automation tie directly to motion control: electric motors, electronic drive controllers, reduced-voltage starters, feedback devices, computers, and programmable controllers. Routinely, vision systems interact with motion controllers. As communication capabilities grow, interaction between dissimilar pieces of equipment will grow simpler and more commonplace. Even the basics of electricity, power transmission techniques, and quality control issues relate in some way to motion control.

Mixing software and electronics with mechanics is always interesting. Soft logic systems still have to work within the realm of physics. Simply electronically commanding a 3300-lb hunk of metal to move from point A to point B in 2.25 s does not ensure that it will! Generally speaking, more often we find out why something did not work out as planned after we have implemented the original plan. This says that we are constantly "chalking it up to experience." But a complete automation specialist needs a good understanding of all aspects of automation, attained both through education and through experience.

Other tools of motion control are data collection, process, and motion simulation. Important data can be secured from a motor and its controller. PC-based systems utilizing soft logic are well suited to collect these data. There is a need to predict performance under different conditions, so as to know when to schedule maintenance and document conditions as the product is manufactured. Today, asking the motion

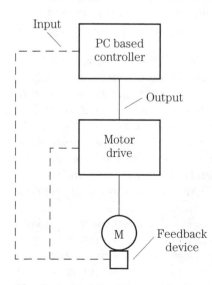

Fig. 2-4 Soft logic motion control system with PC, electronic drive, motor, and feedback device.

control supplier to provide the necessary hardware and software to collect data and statistics is seen as a hardship on the motion controller vendor. This is not the standard product and thus the extra memory, special drivers, and handling of the data create difficulties. Yet this is what the end users and industry need. Soft logic lends itself well to these kinds of situations.

Motion control can be broken down into individual categories: speed, or velocity, control; torque, or current, control; and position control. High-speed microprocessors have allowed the industry to take major steps in types of controls. Given the advancements in power semiconductor technology, designs have become dramatically smaller, faster, and more intelligent. Compared to the CMOS, relay logic controls, and even op amps of yesterday, the technology of today is changing quickly, maybe even too quickly. For example, the motion controller manufacturer introduces a new design or concept and has some success, and then the competition improves on that design. The first manufacturer then makes the next improvement, and the cycle continues. Also the end user of the product tries to standardize on a certain brand of motion controller product by the same manufacturer (seem similar to the proprietary PLC problem?) but to no avail. Everybody is changing so quickly that even spare-parts inventories are obsolete in no time at all. What should be stocked? Now, consider the PC-based system: a common personal computer, well-known operating system, available interface boards, existing (in-stock) I/O, and soft logic software which many can understand.

Basic element

Motion in the factory is mainly actuated by pneumatics (air), hydraulics (liquid), steam, or most frequently electric power. The least common—steam—is sometimes used in larger plants to drive turbines to generate electricity for internal use. Pneumatic, hydraulic, and steam-actuated motion is controllable. However, there are disadvantages associated with each. That is why electronic motion control of electric devices is most common.

Regardless of the motion power source, or prime mover, devices have to be started or stopped, opened or closed, or monitored. These devices can be valves, motors, contactors, lights, sensors, etc. Pneumatic and hydraulic systems tend to require high maintenance. Hydraulic systems tend to leak and are usually dirty. This makes them unsuitable for industries needing clean plant environments, such as the food industry. Pneumatic systems often get water in the air lines and are noisy. Pressure losses equate to poor performance. Nowadays, pneumatic and hydraulic uses in motion control are either specialized or supplemented to machines mainly controlled electrically. Many times a pneumatic or hydraulic solution is appropriate because of costs.

Many older plants have air lines readily available, and a compressor is in place. An air-driven solution is more cost-effective than a new electrical scheme, but perhaps not in the long run. Costs for maintenance and possible loss of production must be considered. Interestingly, the compressor motor is electrically powered.

Machines that are mainly electrically driven will incorporate electric motors. These motors need a power source. This power source is either three-phase or single-phase, AC electricity. Factories start with incoming power in this form. Before this power is fed to any electric motors, it is transformed, filtered, or converted to DC electricity. Some DC power is inverted back to AC power. So in the production world, if the people who make the electricity all took vacations at the same time, factories would virtually shut down.

Motors come in two basic packages, AC or DC, so the controls for those motors should be simple. This is not always the case. As there are different ways to get the desired AC and DC output to the motors, there are also a variety of ways to achieve the desired motion via the controller and its programming. Thus, any soft logic programmer must completely understand the application before developing the code. Being familiar with the motion hardware is a good start. Motors come in many shapes, sizes, and configurations. Common input, or operating, voltages for most three-phase motors in the United States are 208/230, 460, 575, 2300, and 4160 V. Some smaller motors are single-phase and run on 115 and 24 V. If the motor were supplied any of these voltages directly, then it would run at maximum rated speed, or synchronous speed (synchronous with a 60-Hz supply voltage).

As can be seen in Fig. 2-5, controlling the speed of a motor is the start of motion control. From here torque, motor shaft position, and fast reversing become ancillary concerns in controlling the motion of a motor. Let us first look at speed control. Why speed control? Often industry needs to turn down the speed of a motor that normally runs at full speed. This may be true for pump and fan applications where demand is not always a consideration. Additionally, a process may require that different speeds be available for process control. This control must be automatic and sometimes immediate. One means of speed control is through the use of electronic drives. These motion control devices allow for the control of power to a motor. This control can be elaborate and can involve position and precise torque control; these functions are discussed later. And AC or DC motors can be controlled, and many versions of these motors are available. Presently, in industry, there is a gradual movement toward mostly AC systems. The AC drives and AC motors sometimes appear to be more cost-effective, to perform better, and to be more "standard."

AC Drives

The term *drive* means many things to many people. Some may interpret it as the device on the computer into which one might place a floppy disk. Others may consider a drive to be all the mechanisms required to move part of a machine. Some may call this the drive train. Thus, to clarify, when one refers to a drive which electrically changes the electrical input to a motor, it is called an *electronic* drive.

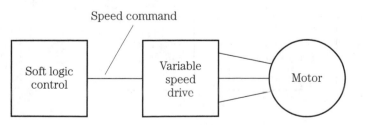

Fig. 2-5 PC controls the speed of an AC motor.

Prior to electronic drives used to control AC motors, the methods for slowing the operation's output were limited. Many were mechanical in nature. One way to slow airflow on a fan is to install dampers downstream of the fan motor. Energy was wasted because the motor was running at full speed. In pumping applications, valves were installed to reduce the liquid flow, all the while the pump motor is running at full, constant speed. Other methods of speed control incorporated other mechanical solutions such as variable-pitch pulleys, fluid couplings, eddy-current clutches, and so on. However, these motion devices could be controlled electrically, and many were. Programmable controllers and even sophisticated motion controllers could be programmed to start and stop many of the aforementioned speed control systems. And the soft logic system can do that and more. But first we give more basic information about drives.

The AC drive has many names in the industry: variable-frequency drive (VFD), variable-speed drive (VSD), adjustable-speed drive (ASD), volts-per-hertz drive, frequency drive, or in many instances simply inverter. Figure 2-6 shows the main components of an AC drive in block diagram form. As can be seen, the drive actually is a converter and an inverter of three-phase power. Also many types of devices are used in the converter and inverter power bridges. These different devices contribute to further naming, or classifying, of AC drives. Examples are pulse-width-modulating (PWM), current-source inverter (CSI), variable-voltage inverter (VVI), six-step inverter (SSI), insulated gate bipolar transistor (IGBT), and pulse-amplitude-modulating (PAM).

One reason that AC drives are so popular is their ability to provide speed control of a standard National Electrical Manufacturers Association (NEMA) design B squirrel-cage motor. This is attractive not only for new installations, but also because of the huge, installed base of existing AC motors which can be retrofitted. The squirrel-cage motor is attractive for many reasons.

First, it is usually less expensive to purchase an AC squirrel-cage motor. It will cost less than a similar-horsepower DC motor because it has no brushes or commutator. It is also smaller for a given horsepower, thus making its metal content lower and again effectively making it less expensive. A motor's enemy is heat buildup, and there must be adequate means of dissipating heat. Sometimes auxiliary fans must be used to provide cooling. These fans are usually cycled on and off by the AC drive. Motor heating must always be considered, as it affects motor construction which affects the cost.

Another advantage of the AC motor over the DC motor is lower maintenance. Since there are no brushes or commutator, there is no need to clean or replace them. The mo-

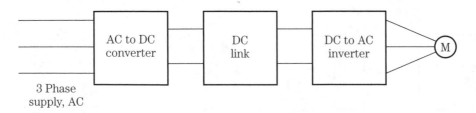

3 Phase
supply, AC

Fig. 2-6   Main components of AC drive: converter, DC link, and inverter.

tor can go into dirty, hostile environments and run, whereas the DC motor and its brush design would falter. These maintenance and downtime costs attributed to a DC motor make it easy to consider the AC motor. Other advantages of using the AC motor include its size and the environment. The AC motor, being smaller, can fit in confined spaces on a machine, and that same AC motor can be used in environments where nonsparking motors are a requirement. The AC motor can be overloaded, within reason. Multiple AC motors can be run simultaneously, and in an emergency the AC motor can be run at full speed, as shown in a bypass scheme in Fig. 2-7. Thus the advantages of the AC motor are so many that nowadays most applications considered ac motors first. So now all that is needed is an electronic means of controlling the ac motor.

The AC drive technology has existed since the early 1960s, but the AC drive did not become popular until the 1970s. This was due in part to the energy crisis at that time. Other factors which influenced the development of AC drives were power semiconductor advancements, the need to increase production and control maintenance costs, and the ability to interface with process control equipment in the plant. Early AC drive designs were awkward, complex, and costly. Thus physical units were large and took up valuable floor space in plants. As microprocessors, logic controls, and advanced power semiconductors became available, AC drives became simplified and smaller.

To understand the application and operation of an AC electronic drive, one must first understand motor speed concepts. In the formula

$$\text{Speed} = \frac{120 \times \text{frequency}}{\text{number of poles}}$$

the value 120 is a constant. For a given motor, the number of poles is constant. Therefore, to change the speed, the only thing that can vary in the formula is the frequency. And this is exactly what a variable-frequency AC drive does. In the equation, if the frequency is normal 60-Hz supplied power, then the motor speed will be the maximum for a given number of poles. This is referred to as the *synchronous speed*. If the frequency is 30 Hz, then the resulting speed is half of full speed.

The number of stator poles relates to the way in which the coils are wound in the stator. This number of poles is fixed and determines the motor's speed in revolutions per minute. Table 2-1 shows the corresponding speed for a given number of poles in a motor. The examples shown are for the most common pole configurations in AC motors.

For the task of driving an actual load, the actual shaft speed of an AC squirrel-cage motor will be slower than the synchronous speed. This is called *motor slip* and is typical of all induction motors. Because the motor is always dynamically correcting itself to maintain speed, when loaded, it lags behind in actual revolutions per minute. The amount is usually 2 to 3 percent of the motor's synchronous speed. For example, an 1800-r/min synchronous speed motor when supplied three-phase power at 60 Hz and with no loading will run at 1800 actual r/min. However, when a load is applied to the motor shaft, the actual speed becomes 1750 r/min. The speed at which a motor can run fully loaded is called the *base speed*. A motor can run above or below its base speed by increasing or decreasing the frequency.

Torque can be said to equate to load which equates to current. Therefore, there are given relationships between speed and torque. Motor slip is a critical element in controlling an AC motor, especially at low speeds. In essence, controlling slip means

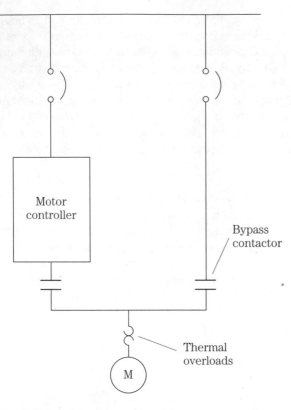

Fig. 2-7   A drive bypass system.

TABLE 2-1   An AC Induction Motor Speed-versus-Pole Chart

Number of poles	Synchronous speed, 60 Hz, r/min	Synchronous speed, 50 Hz, r/min
2	3600	3000
4	1800	1500
6	1200	1000
8	900	750
10	720	600
12	600	500

that the motor is under control. Motors have different values of slip. Some reach 8 percent. Additionally, each design motor carries with it different starting and maximum torque characteristics. The most common design is NEMA's design B, but for special-duty applications NEMA design A, C, or D may be selected for a particular torque output. Note that when a variable-frequency drive is used on a motor other than the NEMA design B, there may be some difficulties in matching the two. Depending on the drive type and the motor parameters, special attention may have to be given to these applications.

As the induction motor generates flux in its rotating field, torque is produced. This flux must remain constant in order to produce full-load torque. This is most important when the motor runs at less than full speed. And since AC drives are used to provide slower running speeds, there must be a means of maintaining a constant flux. This method of flux control is called the *volts-per-hertz ratio*. When the frequency is changed for speed control, the voltage must change proportionally, to maintain good torque production at the motor. The volts-per-hertz ratio nominally is 7.6:1 for a 460-V, 60-Hz system (460/60 = 7.6). The variable-frequency drive tries to maintain this ratio because if the ratio increases or decreases as the motor speed changes, the motor current can become unstable and torque can diminish. This is why variable-frequency drives start to have control troubles below 20 Hz. The flux vector design variable-frequency drive is one solution to maintaining better control of the volts-per-hertz pattern at very low speeds. This drive is discussed later. Another method of increasing the voltage at low speeds to produce adequate torque is to incorporate a voltage boost function, available on most drives. However, if the motor is lightly loaded and voltage boost is enabled at low speeds, then an unstable, growling motor may result. Voltage boost should be used when loads are high at low speeds.

Variable-frequency drives also allow for motor operation into an extended speed range, or overspeeding. Sometimes the application requires that the motor run beyond 60 Hz. Frequencies of 100, 200, even 400 Hz are possible with higher-speed switching inverters. Higher speeds can be achieved, but torque diminishes rapidly as the speed goes higher. High-speed applications include test stands and dynomometers. While this is an attractive feature of the variable-frequency drive, care must be taken when utilizing this function. Many applications cannot tolerate going extremely fast. This can be dangerous.

Alternating-current drives are usually classified by their output. The objective of the AC drive is to vary the speed of the motor while providing the closest approximation to a sine wave. After all, when an AC motor runs directly off 60-Hz power, the signal to the motor is a sine wave (as clean as the local utility can provide). Put a variable-speed drive in the circuit and vary the frequency to get the desired speed. It sounds simple enough, but the industry is continually striving to address all the side effects and to provide a pure system.

As discussed earlier, the variable-frequency AC drive is made up of a converter section and an inverter section (somehow the term *inverter* has stuck). Therefore, there are many converter designs, and the same is true for the inverter section. Generally speaking, the converter section, or the front end of the variable-frequency AC drive, is the DC drive for a DC motor, with some modifications. The DC drive is discussed later in this chapter. The more common designs for the converter utilize diodes or thyristors to rectify the AC incoming voltage to DC voltage. One is called the *diode rectifier*. In Fig. 2-8, the three-phase incoming 60-Hz power is channeled into three legs of the converter circuit, each leg with two diodes. This creates a constant DC voltage. From here this constant DC voltage, through the DC link, goes to the inverter circuit to be changed to variable-frequency AC power to the motor. The diode rectifier is the most popular design because it is simple and the least expensive. Advantages of this type of rectifier include a unity power factor, less distortion

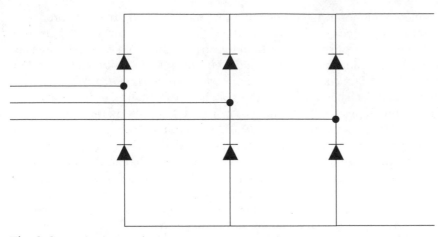

Fig. 2-8 A diode rectifier.

fed back to the supply, and resilience to noise in the converter itself. The biggest drawback to using diodes is the fact that no voltage can return to the source, therefore no regeneration is allowed. Another, separate power bridge must be added to the converter section if regeneration is required. The diode rectifier with a chopper is basically similar to the aforementioned simple diode rectifier. A thyristor is incorporated, usually a silicon-controlled rectifier (SCR), to act as a valve to allow the DC voltage to rise. Once the voltage reaches a predefined level, the valve, or chopper switch, opens to deenergize and then the voltage decreases. This process controls the high and low levels of DC output voltage to the inverter. This design allows for better control of a constant volts-per-hertz ratio while the cost to produce this design is slightly higher than that of a straight diode rectifier.

Figure 2-9 illustrates the robust SCR converter. Like the diode rectifiers, this design is a full-wave type of rectifier. Six SCRs are used to control the gating of the device (12 SCRs for full regeneration back to the supply, as shown). *Gating* is the term given to controlling the SCR's time of conduction by turning the SCR on and off. The SCR cannot be turned on until it has deenergized after being commanded to turn off. This is sometimes referred to as the *zero crossing* of the current. Thus many SCRs have different turn-off times, and it is sometimes necessary to get all six SCRs to match in one drive's circuit in order to ensure proper, smooth gating. The drive's logic circuitry provides the means of control for this gating sequence and thus controlling the output voltage to the inverter.

The SCR, or thyristor-type converter, unlike the diode rectifiers, has some distinct disadvantages and advantages. As speed is decreased, so, too, will the power factor of the system decrease. Distortion fed back to the supply is a major concern. Many times a choke or otherwise special circuit must be added to minimize disturbances. Additionally, these SCRs are more susceptible to line disturbances, which can result in nuisance drive tripping. As long as manufacturers take measures to prevent these problems, this type of rectifier is attractive, especially because it has the ability to regenerate power back to the AC supply simply by gating the SCRs in reverse order.

The heart of the variable-frequency drive is its inverter section. It is the most complex portion of the AC drive and hence is probably the reason that AC variable-frequency drives are sometimes called just *inverters*. There are many designs, and there has been much discussion of which one is best. The answer is that all are, when selected for the right application. Some designs inherently will cost more than others, while other designs may have horsepower limitations or address harmonic distortion. Basically, most lower-horsepower inverters incorporate high-frequency transistors while some higher-horsepower inverters do not. Individual power device costs can be high, and the paralleling of devices to get the higher currents can be expensive.

One of the latest inverter designs is the insulated gate bipolar transistor. This transistor has a combination of features provided by the MOSFET and the bipolar transistor. It has good current conductance with lower losses. It possesses very high switching frequency and is easy to control. Figure 2-10 shows its symbol. This technology has gained much momentum because the IGBT can be used for up to several hundred horsepower.

Other inverters utilizing high-switching-frequency transistors will incorporate MOSFETs, bipolar transistors, or Darlington transistors. The basic advantage of the transistor is that it can be switched from conducting to nonconducting at will. It does not have to wait for a zero-crossing condition, much like its diode and SCR counterparts. Also, since higher current ratings of transistors are now available, higher-horsepower drives are being built, sometimes with transistors in parallel to get the desired output to the motor. These transistors have the ability to switch at several

Dual SCRs per leg (typical for 6 legs)
for regeneration

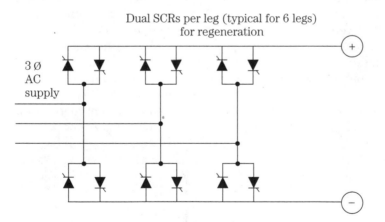

Fig. 2-9   An SCR converter with 12 SCRs for full regeneration back to the supply.

Fig. 2-10   An insulated gate bipolar transistor, or IGBT symbol (basically a switch).

kilohertz. This virtually eliminates audible noise at the motor, which was an earlier impediment to the use of high-switching-frequency transistors. This also means that the current waveform to the motor is close to sinusoidal while the voltage can be modulated much more easily.

Other types of inverters utilize diodes and SCRs. The six-step or variable-voltage inverter needs a chopper in front of the diode bridge or individual SCRs to switch on and off to produce the desired six-step voltage waveform. Each power-switching SCR's conduction time is controlled to get the desired increase or decrease of each individual step, thus changing the frequency output to the motor. Commutation, or the act of turning semiconductors on and off, is accomplished with the aid of an extra circuit, usually of capacitors, to provide power to switch off devices. Transistors and gate-turnoff (GTO) devices do not need this commutation circuitry.

Another type of inverter is the current source inverter (CSI). The equivalent circuit for this inverter is shown in Fig. 2-11. This inverter will normally utilize SCRs as switches to get a six-step current waveform output. Here the conducting time is increased or decreased for each individual step, resulting in a longer or shorter cycle time.

Another type of AC drive inverter is the pulse-width-modulated output version. This type is a constant-voltage-source drive and is very common. Its equivalent circuit is shown in Fig. 2-12. Typically, this inverter is combined with a diode-rectified converter. It can utilize GTO thyristors or, most often, transistors because a PWM inverter requires fast switching devices. Insulated gate bipolar transistors are widely used because they incorporate very high-frequency switching. These devices also have practically eliminated noisy, whining motors. The frequency is out of the human-audible range. The PAM version has its output voltage varied to create either 6 or 18 pulse signals to the motor. This 18-pulse design is good for shaping the motor current more closely to a sine wave and creates less harmonic distortion at the motor. Six-pulse designs tend to promote cogging at low speeds and increased motor heating. Ironically, many would blame the soft logic package if they actually saw the motor cogging. Unless the soft logic controller is solving the speed or current loops, firing the transistors, and monitoring the motor/drive circuit for faults, *it is innocent!*

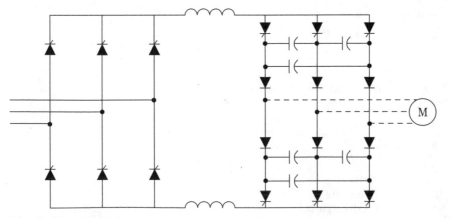

Fig. 2-11   Current source inverter.

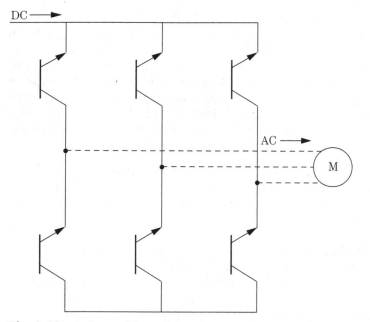

Fig. 2-12   Pulse-width-modulated inverter (IGBT type shown).

AC Drives and Soft Logic

The purpose of the soft logic control system is to control the overall machine or the process. Many times the developer of the control and motion control package is asked (which makes him or her responsible) to recommend, select, and sometimes provide the other components of the motion control system. So why use a particular inverter over another? This is a hard question to answer. Each application dictates what is required. The first issue is to decide whether a DC motor or an AC motor will be used. Will there need to be regeneration? What is the horsepower? Voltage? What is the speed regulation? Torque regulation? Is cost a factor? Is plant floorspace or wall space at a premium? Is a digital or analog drive preferred? What will the maintenance technician find when there is a problem? What kind of duty cycle or loading is predicted? Does the plant have a "clean" voltage supply? Is an efficient drive needed? The questions seem to be endless. Let us look at the issues.

Once it has been decided to use an AC motor for the application, we must choose the horsepower, voltage, and enclosure. Most importantly, can the motor selected run properly with any inverter's output? Is there a good match between motor and drive?

The dos and don'ts of AC drives have been debated by many individuals over the years. Misapplied drives are now and will be a potential problem. Manufacturers of drives may have biased reasons to support or degrade a particular design. The dos and don'ts affect the DC units along with the servo and stepper drive. The best suggestion is to take the time to perform an in-depth analysis of the current equipment available. Also, completely understand the application from a mechanical and electrical vantage point.

One manufacturer's variable-frequency drive (VFD) may be well suited for one application but not for another. There are hundreds of considerations to ponder in selecting a VFD. Section 15, Electrical, of Architectural Specifications usually contains written descriptions of drives to be used on building and construction projects. Get a copy at purchase time or just to achieve a better understanding. Talk to as many technical vendors as possible because the industry is constantly changing. They can advise whether your application is right for their drives and vice versa. Consult the Bibliography at the end of this book for a more in-depth review of certain drive subjects. Here is a list of issues and concerns for AC drives:

1. Determine the complexity of the AC drive circuitry. The greater the number of components, the greater the risk of component failure. Also, consider how long a particular complex drive type has been in production. Reliability is key in an ever-changing industry.

2. Determine whether a digital or analog drive is needed. Although most manufacturers promote digital designs, analog types are simpler. Digital drives offer plenty in diagnostics, protection, and communications.

3. What is the application? What is the speed range, and what is the loading at various speeds? Low speeds under full load are the most difficult for AC drives to control. Similarly, hard-to-start loads may require high breakaway torque. Is speed regulation tight? Typically a drive's slip compensation function can provide adequate adjustment. Check to see if a drive design is retrofittable with a feedback device to gain better speed regulation. Determine whether the load is variable torque or constant torque. Figure 2-13 illustrates the difference between variable torque and constant torque at various speeds. Also, attention may have to be given to the motor

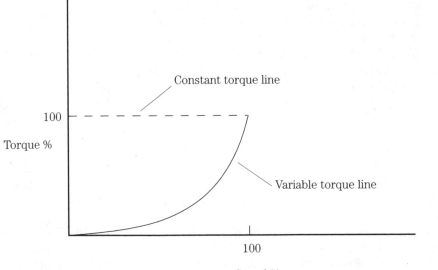

Fig. 2-13   Variable torque versus constant torque. Even the best-designed soft logic system cannot produce more torque if there is none available.

if loads or motor currents are high at low motor speeds. A separate blower for auxiliary cooling may be required.

4. Can the load being driven regenerate? Is braking required, or can the motor coast to a rest due to the friction in the drivetrain? What will happen in an E-stop situation? The drive has no control when it is not being supplied power.

5. How good is the power supply to be furnished to the drive? Some drives are more sensitive than others. Some are sensitive to phase sequence.

6. Generally, AC drives limit the amount of inrush current to the motor, thus lengthening its life while providing softer, smoother starting.

7. Determine how far the drive will be located from the motor. Cable length and cable thickness determine the maximum output current. The longer the cable, the more heat will be generated in the VFD. This is due to a lower capacitive reactance. The Dv/Dt phenomenon, or the derivative of voltage over time, can be tolerated with a filter on the output of the VFD.

8. Does the application require that several motors be run from one inverter? If so, then a current source drive will have limitations, for it is load-dependent. Only a few, if any, motors can be taken off-line when they run the entire set. A voltage source drive is more suitable here.

9. Ground fault and short circuit protection is an issue. Does the drive manufacturer require an isolation transformer? How will the drive handle a ground fault or a motor short circuit? Conversely, what happens to the inverter in an open-circuit situation?

10. The power factor, discussed at length later in this chapter, must be taken into account due to utility penalties. A drive with a constant power factor throughout its speed range is attractive.

11. Harmonic distortion or content is important. Variable-frequency drives create disturbances back to their supply and out to the motor. Determine what your particular system can tolerate. Harmonics is also discussed later.

12. Motor horsepower can sometimes dictate the type of inverter required. Some transistors are not available in higher current ratings. Explore the VFD manufacturer's experience in the high-horsepower area.

13. VFD efficiency is just as important as cost. Analyze each with both the motor and the actual drive. Consider efficiencies at all speeds and mainly for the speeds predicted to be operated. Remember, the VFD is supposed to be an energy-saving device.

14. VFDs are usually air-cooled, some are water-cooled, and some are air-conditioned. Air-cooled drives tend to be noisier. This is due mainly to the cooling fans in the package. Make sure the plant can tolerate higher decibel levels.

15. Ventilation is a concern. A cool drive is a happy drive. In the physical installation of a drive, whether it is an AC or a DC, special attention should be given to the heat generated by the drive. The drive has current running through it, and this heat has to go somewhere. It can dissipate naturally if there is a light-duty cycle. But if loading is heavy, then provisions must be made for cooling or ventilating. First, look at the ambient environment around the drive. Is the room in which the drive will be located warm or hot naturally? What is the temperature on the hottest summer day? Next, is the drive going into an enclosure? Will this enclosure be completely

sealed? Determine if the drive is going to be heavily loaded. Will it run 24 h/day or intermittently? Most of the time, ventilation fans, pulling ambient air into the enclosure and up across the drive, will suffice. How clean is the ambient air? If dirty air is brought into the enclosure, then there is a new potential problem. Dust and dirt may collect on the drive and virtually suffocate it. Eventually no heat will be able to escape from the drive, and the drive will overheat. Most newer drives trip on an overtemperature fault. This protects the drive but is a nuisance because the drive has to cool off before it can be restarted.

Another means of handling drive enclosure heat is by air-conditioning the cabinet. This is a more expensive approach, but sometimes it is the only answer. When the ambient air is too warm or too dirty, then air conditioning makes sense. Many manufacturers specialize in small, compact air conditioners that attach directly to the wall of a drive enclosure. These are self-contained, closed-loop units which keep the inside of the drive enclosure completely cooled. Keep in mind that if the ambient area is dirty, the air conditioner will have to be kept clean in order to operate efficiently. Also, if the air conditioner stops running for any reason, the drives will trip quickly as they are then in a completely sealed enclosure with no way for heat to escape. Many air conditioners today are made to work without any chlorofluorocarbons (CFCs). They are "green" products—environmentally safe. However, they probably will need cooling water supplied to them and will require a drain. They are worth looking into.

16. High-altitude locations can be a problem in a drive installation. Knowing the elevation conditions ahead of time can help prevent drive-related problems. As the altitude increases, so does that air's inability to dissipate heat. Thin air, which is what one might get above 3300 ft above sea level (or approximately 1000 m), cannot hold as much heat as an equivalent amount of air at sea level. Therefore, transferring the heat from the heat source—the drive—is more difficult at higher altitudes. Drives often have derating values for equivalent horsepower, or continuous current output, for a given level of elevation.

17. Typically, high humidity is a problem for a drive if the excessive moisture in the air condenses on the drive's components. Water will conduct electricity, and if enough water forms on the drive, short circuits can occur. The maximum level of moisture in the air is a relative humidity of 95 percent. This again causes nuisance tripping, and likewise there will be downtime until the drive is dried. Another moisture-related problem is harmful, corrosive gases in the air such as acid mist, chlorine, saltwater mist, hydrogen sulfide, and others. Problems can range from slow deterioration of the printed-circuit boards to actual corrosion of the bolts that hold the drive together. Protective coatings on the boards can help, but a better solution is to keep the contaminated air from getting to the drive at all.

18. Long distances between motor and drive can be an important factor depending on the type of drive being used. A voltage source drive tries to maintain a constant voltage in the motor/drive circuit. Long runs of cable can create voltage drops, which can affect the motor's ability to maintain speed under heavier loading. One solution is to increase the gauge, or diameter, of the cable to minimize drops in voltage. This may have to be done if the actual supply voltage is lower than nominal. For instance, if the supply is supposed to be 460 V, most drives can handle a 10 percent range above and below nominal. However, if the supply is lower than the projected 460 V, then a long

run of cable can further reduce that value to the motor in less available volts per hertz. This may limit speed and torque capabilities. Typical distances, though, are less than 300 ft and usually this presents no problems.

On occasion, it is necessary to locate the actual electronic drive farther from the motor than 300 ft. If the drive is a voltage source drive with very high switching transistorized output, then a different phenomenon can occur. This is sometimes called the standing-wave condition. This condition can make for high peak voltages and can possibly damage motor windings. This condition is more prevalent with these types of drives and with very long runs of cable (usually over 300 ft). One solution is to install an output reactor between the motor and the drive. This reactor smoothes out the voltage but adds impedance to the system. This can add to the overall voltage drop, and that fact must be considered in evaluating this option as a solution. Again, if the voltage supply is steady at higher than nominal, then all should be fine at most speeds and load conditions.

Two other considerations pertain to this standing-wave condition: (1) The greater the distance between motor and drive, the higher the impedance output reactor be used. (2) Check the class of insulation in the motor, as it may be better able to withstand voltage peaks without substantial degradation.

19. Often a motor is located very far from the variable-speed drive, even completely out of sight. If a maintenance technician wants to work on the motor, she or he must ensure that there is no electricity possibly going to the motor. One common practice is to install a contactor or disconnect near the motor, in the circuit between the output of the drive and the motor. This is fine from a safety point of view but can be potentially harmful to the drive. For example, often the maintenance technician will go onto the roof of a building where there is a motor driving a fan. The variable-speed drive is located two floors below in a mechanical room. The fan is running along at full speed and full load, and the maintenance technician decides to "kill" power to the motor by opening the contactor at the motor. This could cause a high-energy spike back to the drive and could blow an output device. Rather than assume that all maintenance personnel are trained to never open an output contactor under load, it is more practical to interlock a contact which faults the drive first and then opens the output contactor. This will ensure that there will be no power flowing through the drive and thus will eliminate the possibility of a spike. This contact must be an early auxiliary contact.

20. Do variable-speed drives require isolation transformers? First, what is to be accomplished? Are we trying to minimize noise in and out of the drive at the supply point? Do we need ground fault protection? The isolation transformer can provide all this, but the user should understand the type of drive being supplied before requesting input line reactors.

21. Sometimes output reactors are needed to reduce ringing at the output to the motor with certain types of drives. The major reason, however, to use output reactors is discussed in item 18.

AC Flux Vector Drives

PC-based control systems now allow the industry to exploit the two technologies (drive technology and soft logic). And AC drive technology has progressed to the point where more performance is being demanded of the AC drive and motor. Because the standard, open-loop AC drive has trouble holding speeds as the speed goes lower, a better design has emerged. This drive is called the *flux vector drive*. It takes complete control of the motor slip and the air-gap flux within the AC induction motor. It does this by using special algorithms, high-speed microprocessing, and digital feedback from the motor itself. Often an AC flux vector system (motor and drive controller) can perform much the same as an equivalent-horsepower DC system.

Likewise, soft logic systems have the processing capability to really do some work. Controlling a motor running at 4000 r/min has the look and feel of being a real-time operation. Knowing where the motor shaft is instantly and being able to respond to other machine and process conditions are the challenge of the soft logic system. Because of this capability, tough applications can be attempted with conventional and less complicated equipment. Figure 2-14 shows in block diagram form a traditional positioning system, one which we call the "poor man's servo." With flux vector drives able to deliver *full* torque anywhere in the speed range (even at zero speed) and soft logic systems able to process motor feedback data at tremendous speeds, certain applications are possible.

The flux vector AC drive is key, and the vector component can be defined as a quantity in a definite direction. The drive controller is trying to constantly control the flux angle and the magnitude of flux within the motor's air gap. This is the flux vector being created by the currents supplied. The flux vector drive has incorporated the basic AC power bridge and added some extra control.

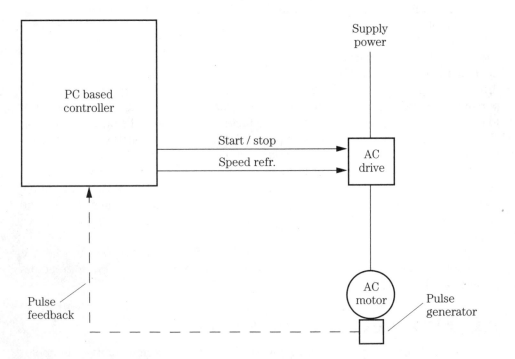

Fig. 2-14   The "poor man's servo."

By attaching a pulse generator to the motor's rotor and feeding this signal back to the drive, the slip frequency can be determined. This signal is compared to the commanded speed. Given the motor slip, a precise speed correction can be made in the form of new voltage output to the motor. This is made possible by utilizing high-throughput microprocessors to crunch the data and create a newly corrected output continuously. Thus, the flux vector drive is constantly correcting as the motor runs. This feedback now makes the flux vector drive a closed-loop drive.

Another factor enters into the equation, however. This is the driven load and the control of the torque to drive it. Control is accomplished by maintaining a constant value of air-gap flux. This means that the volts-per-hertz ratio must be held constant. With rotor speed completely controlled and with the magnetizing and torque-producing currents completely controlled, we now have flux vector control.

As previously mentioned, the microprocessor-based drive has to be programmed with values of motor slip, which is the difference between base speed and synchronous speed, full load and no load, or magnetizing current and other parameters. Once the drive knows what to expect, it can correct for deviations while running. Speed regulation to 0.01 percent of base speed is now possible. This accuracy can be held even at very low speeds while loaded, something that traditionally was the DC drive's sole domain.

Some attention must be given to the AC motor being controlled by the flux vector drive. Its nameplate and test data should be available so the correct parameters can be entered into the drive. Also, the motor physically has to be equipped with a pulse generator and most likely an auxiliary blower for cooling at low motor speeds. Many times it is better to procure the motor from the same supplier as the AC flux vector drive, thus ensuring compatibility. In some instances, a standard AC drive can be converted, or physically modified in the field, to become a flux vector drive. This usually can be avoided if the up-front application evaluation is done.

DC Drives

DC motors are used and will continue to be used in factories and processes. These DC types of applications can be the ones for which soft logic packages may be well suited but could also be the most difficult to control. This is so because of the power and capability of the DC motor and drive. Many process lines utilize several DC motors in a coordinated fashion. This also makes for a more complicated master control scheme. Additionally, there has to be a means of controlling the speed of these DC motors under different load conditions. Some loads are hard to start while others need to have regeneration and/or reversing capability. A DC electronic drive must be able to dynamically change output levels of both voltage and current to a DC motor, in order to control speed and torque. Today's technology utilizes solid-state electronics to accomplish just that.

Direct-current drives can be classified into two groups: transistorized and thyristor, or SCR-based. The workhorse of the DC drive is the SCR-based unit, as it is available in a much larger power range. The transistorized DC drive usually is used in specialized DC motor applications such as running a permanent-magnet motor. In any case, the DC drive controls the speed of a DC motor. The DC drive is less complex than the AC drive. It is actually the AC drive less the link and inverter circuits. Therefore, the DC drive is usually less expensive than its AC counterpart. However, both motor-with-drive packages must be compared, not just the drive alone.

Figure 2-15 shows an equivalent circuit for a three-phase, full-wave power bridge utilizing SCRs. Most often the DC drive will vary the voltage of the motor armature while the motor field has a constant voltage. The SCRs are configured in what is called a *power bridge.* DC power bridges can accept either single- or three-phase AC power or DC (as from a battery source) input supply. The smoothest output from a DC drive would be that of a full-wave, three-phase supplied input to the bridge. Basically, the gating of the SCRs creates pulses of current. The more pulses per second, the smoother the torque output of the motor. Today's DC drive technology allows up to 12 pulses of direct current for every AC cycle (remember the rate is 60 cycles/s, or Hz). That can be 720 pulses per second, which is not bad for a DC drive system.

Typically, the speed of the DC motor is directly related to the voltage supplied. Today's higher-voltage-rated shunt-wound DC motors have 500-V armatures and 300-V fields. Lower ratings are also available at 240-V armatures and 150-V fields. Therefore, if 100 V is supplied (20 percent of 500), then the motor will run at 20 percent of speed, or 350 r/min (when the base speed of the motor is 1750). And at full voltage it is running at full speed. But the real advantage of the DC motor and drive system is that it can deliver 100 percent torque virtually anywhere in its speed range. It will produce as much torque as the load requires, even to the point where it is overloaded with current, enough to damage the motor. This is where motor overload protection must be built into the drive and the motor.

If the armature is the type of feedback circuit used, the DC drive compares the commanded speed reference to the armature voltage that is being produced to run the motor at the given speed. Constant correction of this loop is the DC drive's task. Speed regulations of 3 to 5 percent can be achieved while running in this manner. For better speed regulation, an analog tachometer of usually 50 or 100 V per 1000 motor r/min can be attached to the motor's rotating portion. Regulation below 1 percent is common with an analog tachometer, although impact loading and the age of devices can decrease this accuracy. More common today is the use of a digital tachometer, or encoder, as feedback which can provide motor speed regulation of less than 0.01 percent.

A DC drive with two SCR bridges can regenerate power back to the main input supply. It can also reverse directions. The DC drive can provide 200 percent of full-load current for short periods and even 150 percent for longer periods. These features make it attractive to use in many applications, as it has a simple design. Its rugged design has kept it around for many years and will keep it around for many more. Contrary to the prediction that all DC applications will eventually be replaced with AC drives and motors, there is evidence that this is happening much more slowly than anticipated. Granted, there are several reasons to switch from DC to AC power; however, there are still those applications which require the performance of DC power. And since DC drives themselves have kept pace with digital and solid-state electronics, many extra functions are now possible with the DC drive.

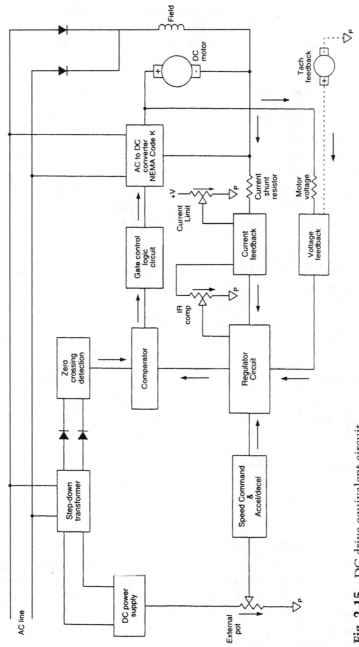

Fig. 2-15 DC drive equivalent circuit.

29

Digital DC drives can accept various inputs and can send certain outputs. Start and stop logic in the form of low-voltage discrete inputs and the ability to accept 0- to 10-V analog signals have become standard on DC drives. Some DC drives also carry a software program which can define application functions and send both discrete and analog outputs, when required, to another computerized device. With microprocessor technology, even high-speed data transmission to other smart drives and host controllers is possible. We are now on the cutting edge of automation with the DC drives of today.

Digital DC drives can diagnose faults when and after they occur. The drive acts as the protective portion of the drive and motor circuit. The DC drive will trip if output current remains at a harmful level for too long. This will stop the motor from being burned up. Thermostats can be included at both the motor and drive heat sinks to monitor excessive levels of temperature in both devices. This is another protective measure which the drive monitors and will alarm accordingly. Also, since most drives are looking at a tachometer feedback signal, they should shut down if that signal, for any reason, goes away. It is better to shut down than to have a motor "run away." The electronic drive can even detect a blown fuse, a short-circuited SCR, and loss of motor field.

Like many digital drives, AC or servo, digital DC drives afford the user the luxury of setting up, or programming the drive to be much faster for the application. By entering numeric parameters into the drive's program, hundreds of drive characteristics can be set. Acceleration and deceleration rates, minimum and maximum speeds, and several other application-dependent parameters can be set simply by pushing a few buttons. The gains, or stability and response of the motor/drive system, can be "tweaked" digitally by entering new values for proportional and integral drive mathematics functions. These are those special parameters that need to be adjusted, usually in the field, for hard-to-start loads and those surprises that were not covered at the engineering review.

The DC drive and motor system needs a means of isolating the motor mains from the drive. This is accomplished by using an M or loop contactor. This contactor must be sized for the current-carrying capacity of the motor and drive.

The DC drive is typically more efficient than its AC drive counterpart. This is so because the equivalent nonregenerative DC drive has only one power conversion section whereas the AC drive has two—the converter and the inverter. This is also true when AC and DC motors are compared. Four-quadrant operation, as shown in Fig. 2-16, is common in DC drives with two bridges of six thyristors each. In four-quadrant operation, the motor can be controlled in the forward direction with positive torque to drive the load or negative torque in that same direction to regenerate the load. The other two quadrants perform similar functions but in the reverse direction. Similarly, an AC drive can become a four-quadrant drive with a matching bridge design on its front end. Four-quadrant means that regeneration and reversing are possible with the motor.

Field weakening and constant horsepower are two problems often attributed to DC drive and motor operation. Field weakening—the running of a DC motor beyond base speed by reducing the stator magnetic field by reducing the current—does not allow for as much usable torque. There are going to be tradeoffs when a given motor

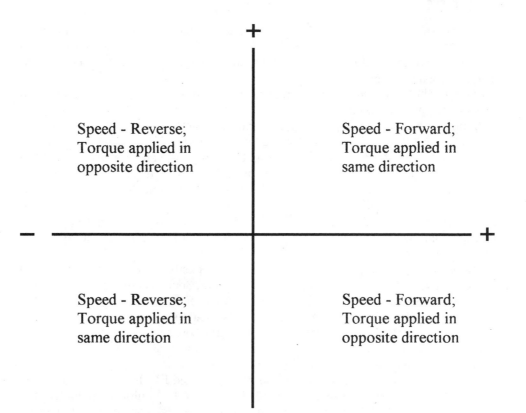

Fig. 2-16   Four-quadrant motion control operation.

is run faster than its base speed. Additionally, any motor has maximum torque limitations. A winding application is a constant-horsepower application.

Specialty Electronic Drives and Soft Starts

There exist other types of electronic power-converting devices which control specific motors. These drives are called *amplifiers* and *power supplies.* Nonetheless, they control the motion of the motor. Some control high speeds while others control shaft position. Again, they usually start with three-phase, 60-Hz supply power. What they do after that is the interesting part. Feedback systems come into the picture and play a major role in the success of a given application. There are several types of specialty drive systems. Servos, steppers, and spindles are the more prevalent types, with soft-start devices being utilized at times to control the voltage to a motor upon starting.

Servo drives

Perhaps, the drive system that is the most versatile and that can be used on the widest variety of applications is the servo. However, it is also potentially the most expensive and most complicated for comparable horsepower. This is a limitation since presently servo systems do not allow for values above 50 Hp. A servo can be defined as an automatic closed-loop control system which uses feedback to electronically control a mechanical motion event.

One of the first rules in "speaking servo" is to discuss power requirements in terms of torque, not horsepower. This should be the rule for all applications, but often people equate power, size, and capability of a motor system to its horsepower or lack thereof. Torque is that force which does the work as the motor shaft rotates. Servo people talk of inch-pounds of torque. Sometimes the analysis is done in foot-pounds of torque, but this is less common as servo systems usually are smaller and foot-pounds of torque will have to be converted to inch-pounds later anyway. The upper limit in servomotor construction is around 800 in • lb. This is due in part to motor construction, the magnets, and the fact that it is less expensive to provide a high-precision gearbox to get the output torque than it is to pay for a larger servomotor and amplifier.

Servo drive systems can be used to control speeds of motors down to a virtual crawl, with turn-down ratios of 10,000:1 and greater. Speed accuracy, or regulation, can be held to 0.01 percent or better. The response of the overall system, or bandwidth is extremely fast. The servo system can also hold to very tight torque accuracy, meaning that as the load changes, so will the servo torque, or current regulator. It will correct quickly and can also provide more than adequate values of stall torque when its amplifier is sized accordingly.

The servo drive can be likened to the AC drive's and DC drive's smart little sister. It is limited in high-horsepower capability but can be equipped to control the actual position of the load it is driving. It has full, fast torque control from full speed down to stall. It can control the acceleration and deceleration rates of its associated motor with ease. Thus it is providing the same control functions as an AC or DC controller and then some.

The servo drive can control a brush-type motor or a brushless motor. This makes for some confusion, especially in terminology. There are brushless AC and brushless DC systems. They are basically the same. The motor is a permanent-magnet type with no brushes. A better description might be that the motor is a brushless synchronous motor with permanent magnets. The brushless AC or brushless DC amplifiers basically take feedback from a motor, which uses no brushes for commutation and linearly amplifies the waveform out to the motor. Servomotor function and commutation are shown in Fig. 2-17. This shows the motor construction and clarification of servomotor commutation. Some servomotors utilize permanent magnets while others are of the switched reluctance type. Whatever the name, it is the function and interactivity with the servo controls and feedback devices which make the servo motor work—and work well.

Note that a servo system is not just the servo motor, amplifier, controller, and feedback device. It is, in actuality, these components working in complete unison with one another quickly. There are several other factors to consider when one looks at the overall servo system.

Bandwidth, the response factor of any drive system, is most important in a servo drive system. Bandwidth is often described as the time a motor controller takes to correct from no load to a loaded condition. It is usually expressed in radians per sec-

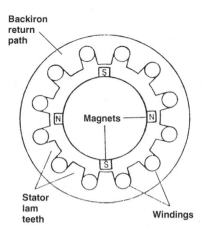

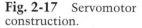

Fig. 2-17 Servomotor construction.

ond. While AC and DC speed control drives have to utilize bandwidth in their control algorithms, a servo system lives and dies by its bandwidth. It is a drive system which is installed by virtue of its performance. It usually costs more initially and is more complicated than a DC or AC drive system. Thus, a higher-bandwidth system is more immune to disturbances and performs or responds better, to produce better. One important factor associated with bandwidth is inertia, particularly load inertia and motor, or rotor, inertia. Other factors which affect system performance and bandwidth are backlash, belting, gearing, acceleration rates, overshoot, and torque ripple.

Figure 2-18 is a block diagram of a servo system with three control loops. The fastest loop is the current loop which calculates the new amperage output to the motor based on actual motor current sensed in the servo amplifier by current transformers (CTs). The next-fastest loop is the speed, or velocity, loop which needs speed feedback from the motor rotating element, or rotor. Either a separately mounted tachometer or a similar device which can provide the appropriate pulses to translate to speed is needed. The slowest loop is that of position. However, good servo systems have position loop update times of 1 to 5 ms so as to hold to some very tight positioning accuracy. Of course, many variables can affect each loop's performance, such as the temperature or the sloppiness of the system mechanics, but starting with a high-response amplifier and controller is paramount.

The type of feedback devices used can vary. In Chap. 4, feedback devices are explored in great detail. As for servo systems, the feedback device is an integral part. Some devices can provide feedback data which can be used to calculate new speed or position requirements. An encoder is able to provide output in the form of pulses which can be used to tell rotor position and to count those same pulses for a given period for speed correction alone. Some are absolute and know where they are upon power-up, while others are incremental. Another device is the resolver, and its feedback must go through an R-D (resolver-to-digital) converter so as to be useful in the controller or amplifier. This R-D conversion also may be a limiting factor in the servo system's resolution. Check the R-D's resolution as to how many bits that conversion solves to. Note that encoder, or tachometer, or resolver feedback can be accepted

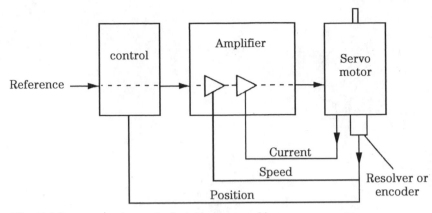

Fig. 2-18   Loops of a typical motion control/servo system.

into a given amplifier or controller, but not all at once. Also, different manufacturers have different standards for their set algorithms and expect certain types of feedback in their products.

The stability of a servo system is dependent on how well the critical components are tuned and matched with one another. The system's critical components are the servomotor, amplifier, power supply, and controller. These components accept some input signals and respond with some output signals. This relationship of signals is referred to as the *gain* of the system. The gain is adjustable and makes the system's performance good or bad. Often called *tuning* a system, adjusting the proportional and integral gains determines performance issues such as smoothness, amount of overshoot, ringing, and oscillation. *Proportional* gain is defined as that adjustment which acts directly and in proportion to its input. Integral gain takes the adjustment a step further and goes through an integrator algorithm to adjust its output on the basis of a timed calculation. Adjusting the gain is one way of getting the most out of a servo system; however, application sizing and pure requirements must be attended to.

If a robot, whose individual axes are servo-driven, tries to move a delicate part from point *A* to point *B*, instability and unwanted mechanical vibrations can be hazardous. The servomotors will overshoot, as shown in Fig. 2-19. This can lead to a condition called *ringing* in which the servo system tries to correct itself but never quite does. In a well-tuned servo system, the critical components have been sized and matched with one another, proper gain values have been programmed, and the user runs the system within the specified operating guidelines. This high-speed, fast-response control is the focus of debate presently in the soft logic community. Can the PC-based controller handle the position, current, and speed loop solving along with the master control?

Matching components in a servo system is always a challenge. There seem to be many answers to the question of which servomotor can be selected for a given application. Careful attention should be paid to the inertia of the load being driven and that of the motor selected. This is called *inertia matching,* and it entails numerous calculations. The actual inertia of each component in the mechanical drivetrain must be calculated. These data are needed to match a servomotor to provide good acceleration and deceleration performance, etc. Sometimes it may be necessary to incorporate a gearbox, as this can greatly reduce the reflected inertia of the load back to the motor. As discussed earlier, inertia through a gear reduction is a square function. Thus, whenever the inertia value is high, a gearbox should be considered.

Likewise, when one is sizing and matching system components, the torque requirements must be considered. Peak torques and accelerating torques must be calculated along with the inertia. Once these values are known, a servo system can be pieced together. It might be better to leave component selection and the lengthy calculations to the manufacturers, as they routinely do this and can prevent obvious problems.

Applications in which servo systems are prominent are found in the machine tool and robotics industries. Grinders, lathes, and milling and boring machines are good places to use servo control to hold position for tight tolerances. The same can be said of robotic applications. It becomes apparent that a servo system can be used for simple speed regulation, but much of its capability is wasted. Most likely the cost of the complete system with all its components dictates where it will be used.

Stepper drives

Some motor and drive applications require a means of positioning inexpensively that does not require high precision. Stepper motor systems allow just that. A stepper drive system is basically similar to a servo system but without the feedback. A step motor system, shown in block diagram form in Fig. 2-20, contains a step motor, an indexer, and the drive. The indexer can be substituted with a programmable motion controller, and the drive can be called an amplifier. For higher-accuracy requirements, a feedback device can be attached to the motor, and better precision can be attained.

Functionally, the step motor system works like this: The indexer gives pulse signals to the drive, or amplifier. The number of these pulses represents the distance to

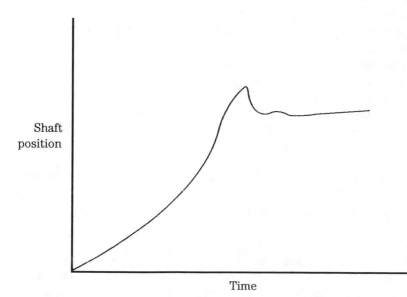

Fig. 2-19   Servomotor overshoot.

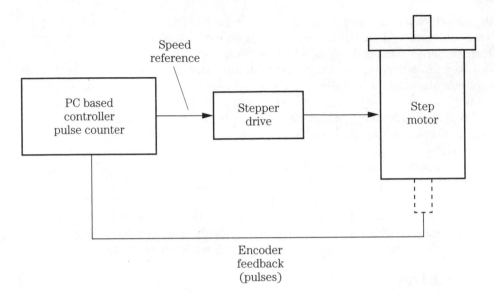

Fig. 2-20   Conventional stepper motor system.

travel, and the frequency of these pulses indicates speed, or velocity. These pulse signals are then amplified and sent directly to the step motor. The motor, constructed specifically to convert electric pulses to discrete moves, turns the load at the desired speed to the predetermined location. The indexer, or motion controller, does not accumulate error or drift; thus for every pulse output, the step motor should move the load to the desired location each time. Of course, closing the position loop with an encoder ensures moves to the exact location every time.

Stepper motors have two windings, or phases, and are located in the stator for maximum heat dissipation. Current is switched on and off in these two phases, which creates an electromagnetic field for rotation. The position of the motor shaft is dictated by the number of current switches and which phase was turned off last. The frequency of the switching dictates the speed of the motor. There is some oscillation in a step motor in each step, and this is more noticeable at low speeds. Microstepping is one method of minimizing resonance due to oscillation. Here the increments are much smaller, thus smoothing the operation. Basically, there are more pieces to the microstep pulse train. A standard of 25,000 pulses per revolution of a motor is very common.

Step motor positioning systems are ideally suited for PC-based retrofit. As seen in Fig. 2-21, the components from the traditional control system can be replaced with those of an equivalent PC-based system.

Spindle drives

In many computerized numerical control (CNC) and machine tool applications, there is usually the need to control the high-speed motor in the system. This is usually the spindle drive; and although it is just a speed-controlled device, its relationships with the other machine components may be critical to the machine's overall

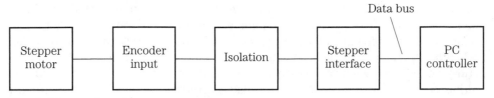

Fig. 2-21 PC-based stepper motor system.

performance. A spindle is often referred to as the *shaft* in a lathe or in a capstan. This spindle, if it is to turn, must be motor-driven. The motor must be controlled by a specialized device called a spindle drive. This drive has a niche in the machine tool industry. Typically, a spindle is required to turn a part at high speeds so as to machine, or work, it. Normally, when the part turns at high speeds, often up to 7000 r/min, the power requirements are constant. Usually, the part spins at high speeds to remove metal from it. In the process it is usually necessary to run at lower speeds and to provide constant torque. These conditions created the need for the spindle system. The duty cycle of the spindle is contingent on the associated motors and drives coordinated with it. As the spindle or part spins at high speed, the other axes of motion are either moving in or out and traversing the part. Depending on the machining, the spindle can slow or remain at a constant speed when it is not doing any work.

In the machine tool environment, smaller, compact designs are needed as space is usually at a premium on the plant floor and on the machine itself. Spindle motors usually have a longer stack, are squarer, and are completely enclosed with a separate fan for cooling throughout the speed range. The industry has, over the years, stressed low maintenance, and therefore no brushes or commutators are incorporated into the design. The most common size of a typical spindle motor will go to roughly 30 Hp and can be handled by AC drive technology. Larger spindle drives have traditionally been left to the DC drive, but this scenario is rapidly changing as AC drive and switching capabilities increase.

Drive technology has also evolved in other ways, especially in the AC inverter realm. Inverters are capable of providing outputs as high as 800 Hz, which is more than 12 times the base speed (60 Hz). The ability to provide constant torque to lower speeds also makes the AC drive attractive to the machine tool user. The emergence of flux vector AC drives has also had an impact on this industry. Enhanced speed and torque regulation from this type of controller has allowed the vector drive to become a standard.

Reduced-Voltage Starters

In most processes, there are pump motors, fan motors, and other motors that have to be turned on and off. Variable-speed control is not necessary. The soft logic system is ideally suited to the proper sequencing and control of these motors. No complex current or position control is required, not even speed control. All that is required is a starter or contactor, rated for the full-load current rating of the motor. But many times a particular motor needs to be capable of starting with lower starting current. It may be necessary to "soft-start" the load so as not to disturb the process. Other reasons to soft-start would be to minimize the inrush current to the motor and to lengthen its winding life. Starting a large motor can demand so much current that the lights in the plant may dim and voltage drops may occur, causing other unwanted disturbances. Thus, when variable-speed control of the motor is not required but the limiting of inrush current is, it makes sense to utilize a reduced-voltage soft-start device. Many times these devices are simply called starters.

Typically, an AC induction motor, when started directly across the line, will require 5 to 6 times its current rating to start a load. This inrush current, after many hundreds of starts and restarts, causes premature wear in the motor. In addition, the other components in the mechanical drivetrain, such as the couplings, belts, and gearboxes, take a beating with every hard start. This shocking of the entire system eventually takes its toll on both the electrical and mechanical parts of the machine. This shock effect is usually undesirable to the driven load. A conveyor motor loaded with product, when shock-started, can actually cause damage to the product, for it might fall over on or even off the conveyor belt.

The electrical supply system must be compatible with the direct starting across the mains, or line starting of the AC motor. Larger AC motors with high current ratings, being started at remote sites where generators are the power source, must be started when there is available power from the generator. This is a matter of coordination and procedure. However, smaller AC motors, many running or starting at once, can cause similar voltage-starving problems. In a facility where there is plenty of available power, there can still be a voltage dip when a large motor is started across the line. What is needed is a device that can start the motor with a reduced voltage and then allow the voltage to increase slowly as the starting procedure advances. This is the reduced-voltage soft start.

The reduced-voltage starter is an electronic power-converting device which contains a power bridge made up of thyristors and a logic circuit. When three-phase power is applied to the bridge and a start contact is closed to the control circuitry, the thyristors begin firing. The control circuit governs how long and at what angle the firing, or gating, of the thyristors takes place. This basically controls the amount of voltage seen at the output of the bridge. The controller is also programmed to know in advance the acceleration, or ramp time, so as to control the voltage as speed increases over time.

Other means of starting an AC motor and limiting the inrush current somewhat are to utilize an autotransformer or to configure the motor windings into a star shape. Either method greatly reduces the inrush current when compared to across-the-line starting; however, they are still not as easy on the motor and drivetrain as the reduced-voltage starter is. Both the star delta method and the autotransformer method incorporate repeated instances in which the motor windings are reconnected to the supply but at an increased, stepped-up voltage. While this is better than shocking the motor windings with 600 percent current, it is still not a soft start.

The autotransformer, having primary and secondary voltages which are close, allows the motor windings to connect to the lower-voltage tap of the secondary. As the motor ramps up in speed, the windings are open-circuited and then are reconnected at a greater voltage level than that before open-circuiting. This procedure is repeated until full speed is attained and the motor windings are transferred to the three-phase, 60-Hz supply. Just as this is a step function procedure, so is the star delta configuration of the motor windings. Opening and closing the circuit as the motor ramps is the mode also in star delta systems. Note that the motor will see far greater values of inrush current than even across-the-line starting, but for substantially shorter periods.

Therefore, for those applications requiring a controlled, reduced-voltage soft start, the starter is the answer. However, the reduced-voltage starter has been misapplied more than once. The reduced-voltage starter can provide some speed control but only on very simple loads. Consult the starter manufacturer before applying it to an application other than soft-starting. Also, remember that the variable-frequency drive can and does provide soft-start capability while also controlling the speed. This is one of its extra benefits.

Braking and Regeneration

One of the most misunderstood topics in motion control and in electronic drive applications is the braking and stopping of an electric motor. Which method is the fastest at stopping the motor? Which is the safest? Does the application require braking? Can the electronic drive provide any braking? Should a mechanical brake be used? And how does the soft logic system enter into the equation? These are good questions with many good answers. We provide some answers.

An electric DC or AC motor moves its desired load and demands that amount of power to do its job. However, when the load drives the motor, then the motor is a generator, a generator of power. Where can this power go? This energy coming from the motor is called *counter-emf,* or back electromotive force. If this counter-emf has a channel to get fully back to the source of supply power, then it is called *regenerative.* If this channel is used to slow or stop a motor and its associated load, then it is called *regenerative braking.* A high-inertia, low-friction load, an overhauling load, a crane, and a hoist are all applications requiring stopping. Thus the choices are controlled stop, dynamic braking of the motor, or regenerative braking of the motor.

Regenerative braking assumes that there is a means of getting the load-generated energy back to the supply mains. It also assumes that this means, or channel, is operating. If a current source AC drive or a regenerative DC drive has faulted and is no longer in control of the motor because it has lost its control power, then regeneration through its power bridges via the firing of SCRs is not going to occur. Thus, it is usually customary to include dynamic braking as a safeguard in those applications needing ensured stops. This involves adding a circuit (contactor-activated), which upon power loss will dissipate the motor-generated energy to a resistor bank. This will stop the motor quickly.

Dynamic braking takes mechanical energy which is fed back through the system as electric energy and dissipates it as heat at a resistor bank. Voltage source drives, diode-rectified drives, and PWM inverters utilize this approach to braking of an electric motor. This method of dissipating regenerative energy is also used to slow a motor so as to provide back-tension or holdback torque, as in winding and unwinding applications. This, of course, is used when regeneration back to the mains is not possible. Note that when a drive which is not fully regenerative tries to control a motor in a generating state, the DC bus voltage rises quickly, and an overvoltage fault will occur. And if the regeneration is tremendous, then most likely devices will "pop."

Obviously, dynamic braking wastes energy as heat. Therefore if the application brakes often and quickly and the loading is heavy, then alternative methods should be explored. The regenerative drive is one. It allows this electric energy to return to the mains. This type of drive must have the appropriate number of power semiconductors and the right type in order to accomplish this. There is a premium for this extra hardware, and it must be decided whether the energy losses in heat outweigh the up-front costs of hardware in a regenerative system.

Another method used as an alternative to dynamic baking is common busing. In this scheme, regenerative power can be used to power another motor which is in a motoring state. This power is resident on the bus for the appropriate use. It can be used only in those instances in which the machine has a motoring component and a generating component. This can typically be found on a line which has an unwind motor and a rewind motor.

To our electric motor, it does not matter whether braking is accomplished via resistors or through regeneration. The motor has become a generator, and that energy is going somewhere. The motor controller must have the necessary logic and means to handle, or divert, this energy. Today's dynamic braking utilizes solid-state components and drive-integrated logic to ensure proper sequencing. The conventional contactor used to remove the armature power supply in a DC system can now be replaced with an SCR.

Remember that we are trying to take this motor-generated current and reuse it as braking torque. Deceleration is a form of regenerating motor energy to achieve slowing and stopping. Deceleration can be described as controlled stopping. It is common to see a holding brake electrically actuated when there is no motion at the motor. Once in normal running mode, these types of brakes should not be used, so the counter-emf dynamic braking through resistors or back to the mains can be optimized.

Another form of braking is DC injection braking, or sometimes it is called simply DC braking. A DC voltage is forced between two of the phases in an AC motor, causing a magnetic braking effect in the stator. This type of braking is commonly found in systems which can tolerate braking at frequencies of 2 to 3 Hz and lower. This type of braking is not used at higher frequencies because the brake energy remains in the motor and could quickly cause overheating.

Harmonic Distortion Attributed to Motion Control

This will most likely emerge as a hot topic in the world of PC-based controls and motion control applications. A controversial topic in power conversion and high-frequency switching is harmonics and harmonic distortion. Harmonic distortion is those nonsinusoidal waves blending unwanted into a system. Why they occur and how to handle them seem to be the hottest topics. If we did not have nonsinusoidal circuits, then we would not have harmonic distortion.

The biggest reason to be concerned with harmonic distortion and PC-based controls has to do with interference and electrical problems in the circuit. As can be seen in Fig. 2-22, electric power is supplied to various pieces of equipment. As sensitive computer and feedback devices are placed onto that circuit, they are subject to that electric power. If, on that supply, there are power-converting components such as drives, then the system's normal sinusoidal waveform can be distorted. This distortion can cause many problems for computers: noise, processing of bad data, microprocessor interruption, hang-ups, screen scrambling, and so on. Let's look at this phenomenon further.

Better defined by the Institute of Electrical and Electronics Engineers (IEEE), the *harmonic* is a sine-wave-based component of a greater periodic wave having a frequency that is an integral multiple of the fundamental frequency. We start with a sine wave and evolve into a nonsinusoidal condition. *Fourier analysis* is the term given to the study and evaluation of nonsinusoidal waveforms. In 1826, Baron Jean Fourier, a mathematician, developed a series of formulas and terms to work with these types of waveforms. There must always be a fundamental component, which is the first term in the sine and cosine series. This is the minimum frequency required to represent a particular waveform. From here there are integer multiples of the fundamental. The component called the *third harmonic* is 3 times the frequency of the fundamental frequency, and so on. In a 6-pulse system, typical of a drive's converter, the real harmonics of concern are the odd-numbered harmonics not divisible by 3. The most critical harmonics to filter usually are the 5th and the 7th. In a 12-pulse system, the lowest producing harmonic is the 11th. What is created from these unwanted waves is the actual disputed issue. Maybe they could be renamed, but the name of harmonics has been attached and will stay. The real issues are, What causes harmonics? and What is the side effect of those distorting waves?

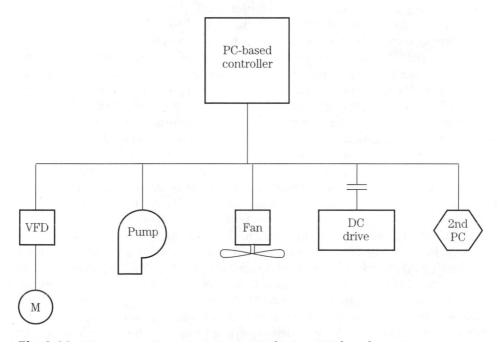

Fig. 2-22 Harmonic effects on a circuit employing a PC-based system.

Harmonic distortion can also be called *electrical noise*. It is said to be garbage, hash, or trash on a given electric line. It is unwanted and undesirable because of the complications it creates with computers and other sensitive equipment now used in many process control environments. More is understood today about what causes the distortion and what can be done to correct the problems. Yet, manufacturers of power-converting devices are always looking at new ways to solve the problem, all the while possibly creating a new set of problems. But, for now, those in the industry are working together to solve the problem.

When static power converters change AC power to DC power and vice versa, there is a disturbance created in both the incoming and the outgoing supply power. This is due to the waveform's being distorted from its original sinusoidal state. This distortion can have detrimental effects on other electronic devices, depending on the severity of the distortion. Studies have given industry standards by which we can at least minimize or predict the harmonic content of a given system and thus take corrective measures. One such standard is IEEE Standard 519. The 1981 version of the standard was referred to for many years, and it was finally revised in 1992. In its new form, the standard has become more than a guideline; it now makes recommendations. This means that the user with a harmonic problem now has some options. Prior to this, a facility had to live with problems due to harmonic distortion. It is important to note here that there is no one single solution to a harmonic distortion problem, and it is not practical to think that just meeting an IEEE standard for allowable distortion levels will keep your plant from having problems. This issue of harmonic distortion definitely takes some study, and usually entails some costs and expenses for correction. Let's face it; loads and things like that change in the plant, thus making it hard to predict future distortion levels.

Harmonic analysis should be neither oversimplified nor taken so seriously that no other productive work is done. Many entities play a role in the analysis. The electric utility has input. The factory or plant, obviously, has a lot to say, especially concerning other sensitive pieces of equipment. The supplier of the phase-controlled converters or rectifiers has much to offer also. So it is important to include all parties along with someone who understands the issue of harmonics and can act as a consultant, or even the mediator, in solving problems and disputes. One fact is clear. There are definite misconceptions about harmonics. For instance, in a factory, when a large electric motor is started on the line, the lights may dim or flicker. Many might imply that this is a harmonic distortion problem, when actually the electric motor's voltage and current demands simply lower the plant's available levels for a brief moment and then the voltage levels recover. This situation does not preclude the possibility that the sine wave was distorted in the area where the lights flickered.

In any electrically supplied installation, there are linear loads and sometimes nonlinear loads. A *linear load* can be defined as a predictable sinusoidal waveform generated by an electrical load. Examples include a facility's lighting system and its other resistor and inductor loads. This is termed predictable because a relationship exists between the voltage and the current whereby the sine wave is "cleaner" and smoother. However, with the advent of rectifier circuits and power conversion devices also came nonlinear loads. Other nonlinear loads have been introduced over time for one energy-saving reason or another. Lighting ballasts, which help to save energy in lighting systems, exhibit a certain hysteresis which contributes to magnetic saturation, thus causing the load to be nonlinear and the wave to be nonsinusoidal. Other nonlinear devices include metal-oxide varistors (MOVs) and electric heating equipment. With these nonlinear loads came waveforms which no longer were nice, clean sine waves. The waves now contain many portions of other waves, thus making the resulting wave notchy and distorted. The challenge now is to identify the problems that this condition causes and what can be done to correct the situation. But first, more basic information is needed.

Harmonic distortion affects many components of the electrical system. Voltage, current, and sometimes both types of waveforms simultaneously can be distorted. Voltage distortion can subsequently affect many other sensitive devices on the same electrical system, whereas current distortion tends to be more local to the distortion-causing load. Consequently, voltage distortion has received most of the attention, and correction has been made. However, this does not mean to imply that current distortion can be ignored; most assuredly it cannot, because the newer standards address it.

Since static power converters have become commonplace in industry, there has been a significant increase in the awareness of harmonic distortion. Variable-frequency drives, uninterruptible power supply (UPS) systems, and electric heating equipment all convert AC to DC power or DC to AC power and by doing so create changes in the sinusoidal supply. This can cause definite interference problems with communication and computerized equipment prevalent in the industrial facility of today. A typical electric circuit in a factory today can have motors, drives, sensitive computers, lighting, and other peripheral equipment on it. Every factory is different, and every circuit within the factory is unique. Thus, a complete analysis must be made of the system in place in order to properly identify the magnitude of the harmonic distortion and the corrective action required. It may be simpler and more cost-effective to place a filter ahead of the only computer in the circuit than to install a more elaborate filter upstream. There is a relationship between the amount of harmonic filtering and the apparent costs involved. This has to be a consideration at some point, along with the ability to predict future load changes on the particular system.

For any harmonic analysis, the point of common coupling (PCC) must be selected. This is an important location in the electrical system, as it is the point where the harmonic distortion measurement will be made. This point is usually at the secondary of a transformer, where many parallel loads of the same electrical system come together to connect to the main power supply. Regarding transformers, in general, we offer a couple of comments. First, many people believe that isolation transformers eliminate harmonics. This is not so. Harmonic currents pass through a transformer. Voltage distortion can be affected by the impedance of the transformer, but this can also be accomplished with a less expensive line reactor, providing it has an equal impedance value. Second, transformers are designed to operate at 60 Hz. The harmonics tend to be present at higher frequencies, thus creating losses in the transformers in the form of heat. A transformer can overheat if subjected to currents containing high levels of harmonics. This has given rise to what is known as the *K* factor element in transformer sizing in converter/inverter applications.

Not only will this power conversion affect the supply power system, but also it will affect the output waveform to a motor. The occurrence is the presence of higher-frequency disturbances that now tag along with the useful voltage and current. Figure 2-23 shows notches in a converted sine wave's current and a voltage spike. Voltage spikes are just as much of a problem to equipment, but for other reasons. The voltage spike can damage hardware. Commutation notches interfere with the electric line, and the depth of the notch is of great significance. Also, the frequency with which these notches are seen is important. Basically, since controllers are changing sine wave AC power to pulses, and this is accomplished by delayed conduction, harmonics are produced. Solid-state devices are the culprits in these rectifier systems, with SCRs and other thyristors being exceptionally notorious for high amounts of distortion because of their intermittent conduction. They appear as a short circuit to the system because they are not dissipating any energy

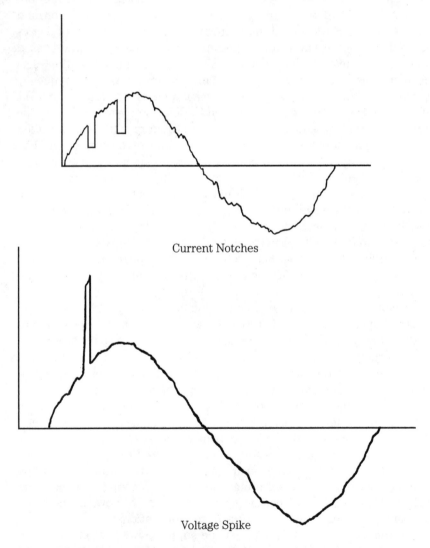

Current Notches

Voltage Spike

Fig. 2-23   Voltage spikes and commutation notches.

when they conduct. They are good for efficiency but bad for harmonics and the power factor.

Distortion limits are classified by the depth of the commutation notch, the area of that notch, and the total harmonic distortion (THD) in terms of voltage. Now limits are also being set on current distortion. What all this means is that manufacturers of power-converting equipment will have to provide filtering where required, so system costs will rise. This is due in part to the fact that the harmonics are not necessarily harmful by themselves, except to other sensitive electronic equipment on the same electrical system.

In summation, harmonics can be and are blamed for a variety of problems in the plant. Blown fuses, burnt-up motors, and hot or burned connectors all point to a potential in-house harmonics concern, not to mention creating havoc with soft logic systems. It is worthwhile to make an analysis and then take corrective action (installing line filters, capacitors, etc.). It is better to determine whether harmonics are present and to what extent than to assume that harmonics are the problem and to proceed down the wrong path, spending time and money wastefully. More importantly, the soft logic system should not be blamed. It actually has the capability to be a tool. Chart recorders could be set up to monitor the electric line, and these data could be fed into a PC-based system which controls a particular machine or process. A correlation could be made as to when notches in the wave occur and when certain equipment is running.

Data required for harmonic analysis

This section can be used as a guideline for implementing an on-line harmonic analysis with a PC-based control system. You will need to be savvy with both computer software and harmonic distortion. If you are that person, then you will enjoy creating a package that will allow the PC to collect data useful in detecting harmonics and measuring the values. This can then be compared to the predicted values that some charts and graphs make, and alas, you have a software program others might want. Just as soft logic systems are becoming more and more accepted, harmonic distortion issues within facilities are hot topics.

Often in considering the installation of a device which can convert AC to DC power and vice versa, it is recommended that the area of the plant where the device is to be located be looked over. Analyze all the equipment on the same circuit. Calculate the total linear and nonlinear loads. Look at the impedances of transformers and reactors in the circuit. Additionally, obtain the short-circuit current data from the utility. Predicted harmonic distortion is easier to correct.

If it seems as though the entire plant could be affected, then all inductive and capacitive elements have to be considered. To all these elements there have to be attributed values of impedance. Any power factor correction systems must be accounted for because typically a power factor capacitor, when affected by resonant oscillating currents, can actually make the power factor worse in the system. Thus, it should be made clear what value of power factor must be held. Also, if the capacitors are switched, it must be made known when the switching occurs.

If symptoms of harmonics seem to exist, then it is best to first ascertain whether there is any rectifying equipment in the plant. Then step by step list and document all the electrical components on a particular circuit. This "plant map" can be invaluable in totaling loads and impedance values, and it will indicate where sensitive equipment is located in the plant and will allow for planned filtering, if required. Concurrently, the utility should be able to provide data relative to the source of power (from them) and the available short-circuit current along with known impedances for upstream circuitry. After all, the power companies are partially driving the requirements of harmonic filtering and power factor correction.

To test for harmonic distortion levels, certain test equipment is required. Along with the proper test equipment, the method of testing must be determined. Needed will be a current transducer, voltage leads, and some type of metering device that allows the user to take measurements of electrical wiring to determine harmonic distortion levels. This device can display, from the readings, waveform shapes or graphs of a selected harmonic. All these data can then be downloaded to a computer for further compilation. Then these data can be compared to allowable limits and acceptable values. Then it can be determined whether corrective action is needed. This corrective action can mean that tuned, harmonic filters or inductors have to be placed in the circuit. This can be expensive, so a good analysis by a specialist is recommended.

Radio-Frequency Interference

Radio-frequency interference (RFI) is not harmonics. Harmonics is the distortion of the sine wave due to power rectification in variable-speed drives. Radio-frequency interference is exactly that—interference to frequencies above the audible by fast switching devices similar to those used in variable-frequency drives. There are filters for shielding the input and output of a VFD so as to minimize the possibilities of interference.

Radio broadcasting frequencies are typically above 150 kHz and below 100 MHz. Whenever current or voltage waveforms are nonsinusoidal, there is always the possibility of radio-frequency interference. Newer switching technology in converter and inverter devices has started to infringe on the high-frequency domain of the radio waves. By the laws of the Federal Communications Commission (FCC), it is forbidden to interfere with these signals. Thus, there are new standards being discussed every day as frequencies of inverters can be seen going higher and higher. Switching frequencies, or carrier frequencies in drives, are approaching 15 kHz with present-day drive technology.

Since drives utilize the switching capability of different transistors, they have come under scrutiny. When current increases so quickly, as is the case with today's power semiconductors, noise can be detected at a radio. Distance from the emitting device, shielding, and filtering are all factors relating to the existence of RFI. Other factors impacting RFI are the horsepower and current rating of the drive, the output and switch frequency, the impedance of the AC supply, and how well shielded the power modules are.

Filtering by means of inductors and capacitors is presently the best way to suppress RFI emissions. This problem, in general, regarding radio-frequency interference and drive equipment is still ambiguous. Emissions and occurrences are rarely proved because they are rarely considered. Enforcing of adherence to the laws and standards has not been paramount. As the occurrences increase, so too will the need to police the issue.

PC-Based Control and Motion Control Fault Handling

Soft logic systems used in any motion control application will be called upon to monitor the electronic drives and motors. Fault information and handling will be critical not only to the real-time machine or process operation, but also to the collection of these fault data for trending and tracing problems with the equipment. Knowing what happened, when, and how often can provide clues to a problem or potential problem. Maybe maintenance of a motor is in order. Maybe some filters need to be cleaned. The PC-based controller serves as a tremendous tool in system diagnostics, troubleshooting, and maintenance.

Electronic drive faults common to AC and DC drives are undervoltage or overvoltage conditions, overcurrent or overload, fuse failure, overtemperature, and if a digital drive, then a microprocessor "ready" check. Undervoltage faults generally mean that either the supply power has been interrupted or the voltage value has dropped below an acceptable minimum. Some drives have ride-through capability, which for a small amount of time keeps the drive in control until the glitch has passed. Conversely, overvoltage faults indicate that the incoming supply has surged to a high level of voltage which exceeds the maximum limit. Overvoltage faults can also mean that the bus voltage has risen to such a high level that components are in danger of burning or blowing, and the drive has to shut down. These trips can also be caused by trying to stop a motor with a load too quickly. The regenerated energy cannot be dissipated quickly enough. Braking resistors may be in order here.

Overcurrent or overload conditions are set for the motor's protection. For a preset amount of time, within limits, output current to the motor is allowed to be above the highest setting. These conditions may exist when starting a load requiring high starting torque. However, if too much time goes by, then there is imminent danger that damage can be done to the motor and the drive will shut down. This may indicate that the motor is stalled or that there is some other type of problem. This needs to be investigated. Another drive fault which mainly protects the drive is overtemperature. Temperature monitors are placed within the heat sinks or bus of the drive. If this temperature gets too high, then the drive shuts down rather than damage itself. This may simply indicate that a cooling fan has stopped running and need to be checked. Other faults common to most drives such as the fuse failure and microprocessor trip are necessary to prevent high levels of current into the drive, which is the fuse's job. As far as the microprocessor is concerned, if it is not ready or has a problem, we had better not start to control a motor. No control is better than bad control in most instances.

There are other fault circuits monitored by drive type. For instance, a DC drive should be checking for loss of field and loss of tachometer signal. An AC drive will not look at field signals because there are none. Likewise, any drive that is dependent on a feedback device from a motor for control of that motor (i.e., AC vector, servo drives, etc.) should always be checking for the presence of that feedback signal. Many times if this signal is lost, the drive assumes that it has some major speed correction to perform and sends a drastic increase-speed command to the motor. This is sometimes called a *runaway motor,* and it is a very dangerous condition, to say the least. If there is a feedback device in the loop, then it must be monitored; and if the signal is lost, then the drive must recognize this and either shut down or go to a minimum speed.

Some drives check control power. Others have a ground-fault sensor to handle these errors. Some drives are phase-sensitive while others are not. Many times motor thermostats are interlocked with the drive to provide extra insurance that the motor cannot overheat (even though the drive is monitoring the output current of a motor). These types of faults vary with the type of drive and the manufacturer. It is best to check with the manufacturers and simply find out what happens when a certain condition exists with the drive and motor. They should have the answers.

It must be kept in mind that the electronic drive is protecting both itself and the motor which it is controlling. When the drive shuts down, it is not trying to put a company out of business; rather, it has detected a problem and that problem needs to be corrected. Sometimes, the drive trips can be a nuisance, especially if they occur often and other computerized equipment stays on-line in the plant while the drives go down. Some devices are more sensitive than others. But filters, snubbers, and capacitor networks can be utilized to correct for nuisance tripping.

Troubleshooting a drive system can be extensive and not always straightforward. The operative word is *system* because troubleshooting the drive may be only half the battle. For example, we may find an overload fault at the drive, but in actuality there may be a problem at the motor or even in the machine which must be found. This is where the fun can begin. A hands-on technician with good mechanical and electrical aptitude is sometimes needed even though the drive is furnishing some data about the problem. All in all, drive troubleshooting is many times application and machine troubleshooting. Because the drive is the least-understood component, it is the easiest and thus the first component to be blamed. So often a drive manufacturer's service representative is called to the job site only to find that the problem was in miswiring, or a motor short, or any number of non-drive-equipment failures. The bill for the service visit still has to be paid. But a good, trained technician, electrician, or operator could do some productive troubleshooting and diagnosis beforehand. This could possibly save costly downtime and service bills.

Having the proper documentation, keeping good records, and proper tools make troubleshooting electronic drives much easier. At least two sets of manuals should be resident at a facility. One set should go in or near the physical drive on the factory floor. The other copy should be kept in an office or company library. Next, if drive parameters have to be set or programmed, then a copy of these should be kept in both places. These settings or values may have to be reentered if there is a dramatic problem with the drive. Also, regarding the issue of entering the drive's program, this should be a limited-access or by-password-only situation. Too many people with the ability to make changes can make for confusion. It is best if only one or two individuals can get into the drive to make changes. As for record keeping, a log, if not a standard feature of the drive hardware, should be kept to track when or if a drive faults and what was done to correct the fault. In this way trends can be determined, and lost production time can be fully tracked. Also, this information will be very useful to the drive manufacturer and/or service person.

The proper tools needed to troubleshoot the drive can be expensive. Tools also should include spare parts, and again nobody wants to purchase and stock expensive items unless it is absolutely necessary. This decision is mainly based on the quantity of drives and the value of lost production time. The expertise of in-house technicians is another factor. Most facilities end up with one or two technicians who become the resident experts on the electronic drive. Many drives come today with a means of getting in and interrogating or making electronic changes. This may be a standard device, or it may be an optional handheld device. It is worth having around. Besides the standard current probes, voltohmmeters, and occasional pot tweaker (yes, some drives out there have many potentiometers which may need adjusting), a digital oscilloscope capable of storing images is always useful. Checking waveforms can help pinpoint problems both into and out of the drive. Also, sometimes it may be necessary to put a strip chart recorder on a drive circuit to monitor line conditions over time. This can help to pinpoint trouble areas. Another tool which is recommended is a digital tachometer, a handheld unit which is handy to measure the speed of a given motor. Since these electronic drives control the speed of the motor, it is sometimes necessary to physically check whether the speed is being controlled. Also the digital handheld tachometer can be useful in determining the speeds of other machine rotating components and other motors. These data can be used to select motors and gear reduction for a given system.

Becoming intimately familiar with the type of drive, its control and fault scheme, and the machine or application is critical to any successful motion control installation. This is true for both the user and the supplier of the drive equipment. Complete training on the product is necessary. And as previously mentioned, good documentation and tools can go a long way toward keeping the drive(s) running. Motion control and soft logic are a natural fit; however, a full book could be written just on PC-based motion control. This book, particularly this chapter, can provide only an overview of motion control. In Chap. 4 more specific discussion of motion control interface boards and applications is provided.

Operating Systems

The power of the newer operating systems today has made it possible to implement PC-based controls on the factory floor, even though for certain simple applications PCs have been used in the factory for more than a decade for some of those processes and machines. This could mean using the disk operating system (DOS) and a 286 computer and kluging together CMOS boards and relays; thus you might have a replica of a programmable logic controller (and it might even work, too). This was usually done whenever a computer wizard was held as an employee and convinced management to let him or her experiment. The concept was great, but it would be a monumental task for anyone. And the forbidden would happen: *The computer wizard would decide to leave the company to start her or his own business!* Who will support the system? But today things are much different.

Operating systems today are much better suited for high-speed factory process and machine control (these are discussed in further detail later in the book). This is so because PC performance has taken a quantum leap in technology. Multitasking operating systems such as Windows and Windows NT have emerged along with 200-MHz processors to lay the foundation for a reliable PC-based control scheme. These systems are often referred to as *real-time* operating systems. They are called real-time because two important functions must occur: information must be processed correctly, and that processed information must be delivered on time. Windows NT comes very close to providing all the capabilities necessary to emulate a PLC. However, many argue that the operating system is not fully there yet.

Windows NT will do other tasks while running a user program. It can choose to service a disk controller or other network card. In these instances, when a large scan or program is being executed, all it takes is the right set of circumstances and a high-speed machine loses its control, or timing. A mess or crash can result. This scenario is an example of a controller's being *nondeterministic*. It is important in any PLC system that the machine or process controller's operating system always be ready for "emergency situations" in which the thousands of lines of code and the constant checking of the hundreds of I/O points can occur without interruption. Obviously, there will always be an exception to the rule. An operating system will not be "bulletproof." The way programs, both logic and computer, are written can allow a system "crash." What happens when a system crashes and the forethought to consider this are probably the best safeguards to preventing crashes (at least to minimize injury in a catastrophe).

Real-time operating systems, Windows, and Windows NT are essential elements of soft logic systems today. All these subjects are discussed in greater detail in Chap. 7. However, some history on operating systems (spanning 20 years roughly) is provided in the following pages. This information is necessary to understand how operating systems have evolved and what users are familiar with.

DOS and MS-DOS

If you own now or have ever owned and operated an IBM or compatible personal computer, then this operating system is the one you grew up with. MS-DOS, the Microsoft disk operating system, has been the mainstay in the personal computer industry for many years. Hundreds of books have been written on this operating system. Thus, this section is intended as an overview.

Sometimes just called DOS as that casual reference to what makes the computer run, MS-DOS is basically the operating system to which all others are compared today. Many parts of it are still utilized in newer operating systems such as Windows, but in a different format. MS-DOS was great for its time and use, but for it to be used as a process or machine controller environment it was *not* practical, for it could not run multiple applications simultaneously. Its other shortcomings were that it was a single-user, single-task operating system. Although many engineers and programmers tried to use it (with some success), it was evident that MS-DOS was not the answer to real-time operating systems. This basically paved the way for programmable logic controllers and their dedicated RTOS architecture to become dominant in the 1980s as the industrial control scheme of choice. But with newer real-time systems available, the prospects for soft logic PC-based systems are very good. But first some DOS history.

The Microsoft disk operating system was designed originally for IBM's personal computer introduced in the early 1980s. IBM compatibles and clones eventually surfaced, and the operating system worked well on those machines as well. All these machines were based on the Intel 8088 microprocessor chip, an 8-bit processor running on a 4.7-MHz clock! Memory was limited, ROM was in BASIC, and expansion cards were few. Monochrome and the color graphics adapter (CGA) were the only two options for video displays. Thus, these items made up the first system, and MS-DOS 1.0, based on CP/M for Z80s and 8088s, was selected to run all of it as the operating system.

Just as it is today, the microprocessor industry and the technology kept advancing. The extended, XT, and the advanced, AT, computers were introduced. The XT's clock rate was still 4.7 MHz, but the AT's "soared" to 8 MHz with the 80286, 16-bit microprocessor chip from Intel. MS-DOS was trying to keep up. Not until version 5.0 did MS-DOS begin to support over 640K of RAM. So much for trying to do anything in real time at this time! Enhanced graphics array (EGA) and super virtual graphics array (SVGA) became the standard for video with higher resolution and better color.

The microprocessor evolution brought next the Intel 80386 chip with clock rates up to 33 MHz. During this period Windows 3.0 was introduced, and MS-DOS began to see its usefulness slip away. The 80486 chip followed next with a built-in mathematics coprocessor. Now mathematics operations could be executed extremely fast and the clock speed was up to 100 MHz. MS-DOS is still accessible to many Windows users today. However, as time goes on and those chips keep getting faster, MS-DOS will become a forgotten operating system. But it was good in its time and should easily make the operating system hall of fame!

iRMX

From the single-tasking, non-real-time world of MS-DOS, we move into a different operating system for the Intel microprocessors—the iRMX operating system. This operating system definitely exploits Intel's high-speed, high-throughput processors. And it is able to do so in real time as its standard. This makes iRMX a natural candidate for soft logic PC-based control systems.

The iRMX operating system is a 32-bit, multitasking operating system that can run many unrelated programs simultaneously, independent of one another. Applications can be programmed in an object-oriented environment. All interrupts, preemptive priority-based multitasking, and predictable response times help to control external events. This multilayer operating system allows users to design and build programs for the 80386, 80486, and Pentium microprocessors. It also has tools for MS-DOS and Windows 3.1 to aid in compiling and linking. This can be generated from the iRMX for Windows operating system which along with iRMX III (the base operating system) and iRMX for PCs (allows execution on PCs using ROM BIOS) makes the iRMX single product that is so powerful to users.

The iRMX operating system is gaining in popularity and use, even though it has been around for several years. It is well suited to soft logic applications in process control. Machine and motion control, automated test equipment, and telecommunications are some other applications which can utilize iRMX's capabilities.

Unix

The Unix operating system actually evolved before MS-DOS. It had many similarities to MS-DOS but was more powerful. Older versions of Unix used abbreviations for commands. The reasons for this were the small memory systems and the slow terminal speeds of the times. Ten characters per second was the speed, and so it was established that abbreviations would make use of the prevailing speeds.

Today, Unix is a popular and powerful operating system that has many real-time qualities similar to those of Windows NT. Unix can support multiple microprocessors while delivering both graphical and text applications. Unix can run a wide variety of platforms—presently more than Windows NT—and offers peer file sharing. The Unix operating system can handle long filenames in advanced file systems along with many other network services. Unix is a great application and database server and is used extensively as a standard for the Internet (Unix E-mail).

Unix is very powerful at functions involving local-area network (LAN) and wide-area network (WAN) connections. Sharing files, printers, modems, and remote applications over a network is a strong point. Getting access to a Unix host will allow the LAN connection to receive all the systems' services and many utilities. The shell, or user interface, utilizes primer commands which are two to three words per line. The format is: Command-Modifier Argument. Much like MS-DOS, the Unix system utilized a hierarchical directory system to store files to disk.

One thing Unix still has is its faithful. Many MIS professionals in corporate America grew up with Unix and still work with it as an operating system. They are comfortable using it as a database server and will continue to use it as long as the package keeps providing new and useful tools. Soft logic packages must have the ability to work with operating systems such as Unix. As PC-based controls become more commonplace, their ability to adapt to whichever operating system is in place, or is preferred, will dictate which soft logic package is implemented.

QNX

The QNX* operating system has been in existence for over 10 years. There are over one quarter of a million users of this message passing microkernel-style OS. QNX offers the unique ability to be used in a wide variety of applications, from commercial and financial projects to engineering and research projects. For the concerns of this book, QNX is a proven operating system in the process control and industrial automation sector. Although QNX is obviously not as prevalent as some other operating systems, it is worthwhile to discuss some of the features of QNX (QNX's real-time microkernel, 32-bit pentium architecture, and networking capabilities).

As operating systems go, QNX has evolved behind the scenes from the other OS giants. Its flexibility, networking capabilities, and robustness make it a desirable and reliable operating system. These are the things which are most important to users. Popular operating systems are fine, but if the OS works for you, the user, and is reliable, then why change? In fact, QNX can be found in medical instrumentation, point-of-sale (POS), and telecommunications installations all around the world. It has been

---

* QNX is a trademark of QSSL.

given the extensive "road test" required of substantial operating systems. QNX's flexible architecture allows it to be scaled from a full-feature disk-based OS down to a full, embedded system, or in other instances up to a large distributed system controlling hundreds of processors. Today, its message passing and handling capabilities plus its interrupt-handling facilities make it a viable player in the PC-based infrastructure of the soft logic system packages.

The microkernel of QNX makes it a real-time player. It has been used successfully in factory automation and process control applications, mainly for this reason. The 10-kbyte microkernel provides for the message and interrupt handling that emulates a real-time executive. The message-passing facility allows communications to take place regardless of whether they reside on the network or are on a separate node. This makes for an operating system which is fully distributed. QNX can be scaled from a large distributed system in charge of many microprocessors down to a disk-based operating system with full features or even into an embedded system. The QNX system has the ability to take hundreds of computers on a network and make them look like a single machine, all possible via the message-passing architecture and its microkernel. Another feature of the QNX system is the way it protects against full-network failures. It does this by utilizing its network distributing messages, over a high-speed Ethernet LAN, to implement redundant, or "hot standby," systems. QNX supports multiple LAN links per node and automatically load-balances network traffic. These capabilities make QNX a very powerful and flexible operating system for use in PC-based systems, especially those which may require several PCs and the need to connect on a network.

VMEbus

VME or VMEbus has been used as an open standard system for almost 18 years. It originated in 1979 around the Motorola system called VERSAbus. They were designed around the Motorola 68000 microprocessor. Two years later, VMEbus was officially on its own as a usable system. One of the most often asked questions about VMEbus is, What does VME stand for? It can mean virtual memory executive, but in terms of operating systems it means Versamodule Eurocards. This evolved from Motorola's agreeing to allow the second sourcing of the MC68000 microprocessor chip with two other companies. At this time Motorola had developed a backplane for the 68000 called the VERSAbus backplane. However, VERSAbus board size was very large and in order to accommodate a smaller package, the Eurocard platform was incorporated. Thus, a backplane with the VERSAbus electrical specifications and the Eurocard mechanical specifications could be employed. Motorola suggested the name VERSAmodule Eurocard (VME). Today VMEbus is in the public domain since VERSAmodule is a trademark of Motorola.

For years, anyone who wanted to go off on his or her own and build a PC-based control system usually took this route. Get an industrial personal computer, or even take a standard PC, get the interface card(s) as required, and make it all work within the VME environment. This could be said to be the beginning of "PLC-less" control!

Using signals patterned from the M68000 bus timing and signals, VMEbus grew into an industrial open-system standard. Powerful and robust computer systems could be built from these modules. Today, VME's boards have data bus sizes of 16, 32, and 64 bits. The VME system board can now contain many other processors than the Motorola 68000 series. They are designed as plug-in boards for backplanes which can handle up to 21 boards. These other boards can be Cpu boards, video/graphics array (VGA) boards, motion control, data acquisition, memory, video, sound, and others. The VMEbus specification provides for the physical dimensions of the backplane, boards, and chassis and addresses the electrical specifications of the bus and necessary communication protocols. Thus, specifying a VMEbus package can be a safe route to end users. System components are readily available, and most interconnect with one another. A "kluged" system does not have to evolve from this.

Unfortunately, many individuals who have some familiarity with soft logic and PC-based control usually compare it to VMEbus. Programming a VMEbus system took some learning and the eventual users of the VMEbus system were not always familiar with the new code. Thus VME was perhaps one of the first PC-based control packages to gain popularity. This explains why so many vendors support and supply peripheral hardware for VME.

A review of VMEbus peripheral hardware reveals that the hardware not only is readily available from electronic parts stores but also is sanctioned by many of the standards' committees. The PCI Mezzanine Card (PMC) carries an IEEE specification as consideration for a low-profile mezzanine expansion bus for VMEbus, Multibus, and others. It has electrical specifications similar to those of the peripheral component interconnect bus (PCI) bus and uses a 32- and 64-bit bus scheme. The VMEbus board is either a single- or double-height board. A single-height board, sometimes called 3U, has one DIN connector with 96 pins on the rear of the board and plugs into the backplane. A double height is physically larger and may carry two 96-pin DIN connectors. It is sometimes called a 6U board. The front edge of a typical VMEbus board will house the RS-232 connectors, indicator switches, and lights. The backplane will have up to 21 slots into which the VMEbus boards can plug. A power supply is then added, and the system is ready for action. There are also provisions for adding I/O interfaces, disk drives, and other external peripherals.

VXIbus, or VMEbus eXtension for Instrumentation, has evolved since the late 1980s. The VXIbus is instrumentation bus compatible with VMEbus, the Eurocard, and standards such the HP GPIB (General Purpose Instrumention Bus). Being an open architecture type system it is useful for automated test stands and data collection systems. The VXIbus expands onto the VME bus so the two bus configurations are virtually identical. Transistor-transistor logic (TTL) and emitter-coupled logic (ECL) trigger signals; a clock, a local bus, and an analog summing bus are among the added features. The VXIbus uses virtually the same pin assignments as the VMEbus, but double-height boards are not as deep. Also, the VXIbus has configuration registers while the VMEbus does not. There are other subtle differences, especially for assignments, but for the most part the two systems are very similar. One should refer to the documentation whenever implementing.

Conclusion

The automation process is very complex. So many factors enter into making an application successful. Soft logic systems and full understanding of their hardware and software are only part of it. Her or his knowledge of both where problem areas might be relating to motion and mechanics and electricity and electronics makes the soft logic engineer valuable. This soft logic engineer (the acronym is SE) will emerge as one of the key individuals in the plant. He or she will know how to program the PC's application program and will fully understand the process or how the machine works. The soft logic engineer must know what peripheral hardware is in place and how it interacts with the PC. All elements have to be known. Thus the soft logic engineer becomes an automation engineer and is vital to the success of that plant and company as was the computer wizard from days gone by (the only person in the building who could program the computer!).

The point is, there is so much to understand and to consider when one is applying controls to processes and machinery. Much is gained by on-the-job experience and actually making those mistakes and learning. This book offers a broader look at PC-based controls and *all* the elements of a soft logic system.

Personal Computers, Industrial Computers, and PLCs

The creation of the microprocessor has changed the way of life on this planet. A multibillion-dollar industry has evolved from that creation, and surely it will become the first trillion-dollar industry. Its effect on all other industries is mind-boggling. Microprocessor chips are everywhere, in everything. That chips are the heart and soul of the personal and industrial computers is obvious, but their presence in other products is not always so apparent. Such is the case of the programmable logic controller. It is actually a dedicated controller housing a microprocessor(s). This chapter will look at all these microcomputer-based devices, their role in process and motion control, an overview of the basis for each of the technologies, and how they relate to soft logic systems.

Computer History

The real origin of the computer is the abacus, which dates back about 5000 years. But the more recent history of computers links the past (the last 150 years or so) with people such as Pascal, Boole, and Babbage. They had a major influence on the beginning of computerization and, by virtue of their names being used in modern-day software and logic, are widely known. Charles Babbage built an analytical engine in the 1830s. He built it to aid machines in making parts more precise. Unfortunately, the industrial world could not comprehend its value, and his concept fell dormant for about a hundred years. Prior to that, Blaise Pascal, a mathematician, invented a mechanical adding machine. Yet another individual, George Boole, made enormous contributions to this technology, and as discussed later, his mathematical principles laid the groundwork for the PLC. Many other people over the years have contributed enormously to this technology; as evidenced by the industry's growth, there are many Booles, Pascals, and Babbages out there!

All these early inventions were created to help people perform tedious calculations more consistently and faster. Those goals drive computer development today. Faster, smaller, and more powerful are the driving forces. Regardless of what the clock speed is at this instant, another faster, more powerful device is being designed. Miniaturization of computers and boards is taking place. If computers were the size of those early units in the 1940s and 1950s, the assembly and production lines would be dwarfed by the computer's hardware (not to mention the extra heat loads). The ENIAC, or Electronic Numerical Integrator And Calculator, built in 1946 was huge. Computers have been getting smaller ever since. This is most evident with the development of the integrated circuit (IC). The IC is a solid-state device which is made up of hundreds of capacitors, diodes, resistors, and transistors on one small chip made of silicon. The IC has allowed more powerful computers to be built at much lower costs. And as usual, the demand that the next-generation microprocessor be more powerful is always present. Throughput is the name of the computer game.

If microprocessors are the heart and soul of computers and PLCs, then switches are the heart and soul of microprocessors. The microprocessor works because of switches. Today's microprocessors can handle millions of switches in an instant. These switches are packaged inside a very small device called the *chip.* Newer and faster methods of switching have continued to evolve. Figure 3-1 shows the evolution of the switch. Computer hardware and switch development continues on a fast track. This is the basis for digital electronics, which evolved from the binary system over the past 25 years. Digital logic is the basis for most modern electronic equipment today. Whether a condition is true or false, on or off, high or low, its state is used to determine how and when an event should be controlled. Various forms of logic exist primarily because they are easy to implement. One is called transistor-transistor logic (TTL) and is widely used in many electronic controllers. By utilizing transistors, input and output circuitry can be used to collect and send various pieces of information in a system. There will also be found in any TTL scheme a network of resistors and diodes and the need for a power supply.

Complementary metal-oxide semiconductor (CMOS) circuitry design evolved out of the TTL scheme. Here, utilizing metal-oxide semiconductor field-effect transistors (MOSFETs), the CMOS digital circuit could achieve better input and output collection, emission, and gating from the transistor. These digital logic hardware schemes preceded the current trend of doing everything in software (the premise of soft logic). One must consider that not all inputs and outputs can be furnished routinely as very low-voltage signals, readily used by a microprocessor.

Computer architectures, or the techniques and components which are the building blocks of any computer system, have changed quite a bit over the past few years. Binary systems abound, but many digital systems employ logic functions consisting of AND logic, OR logic, and NOT logic. These architectures can be used in conjunction with the microprocessor's capabilities. For instance, flash memory is based on NOT logic. This is discussed later in this chapter. AND, OR, and NOT logic can be used in programmable controllers, cellular phones, and even microwave

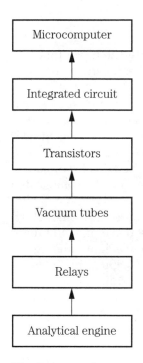

Fig. 3-1 Evolution of the switch.

ovens. The term *logic* is the key. Inputs and outputs have to be accounted for somehow, and they are generally on or off. This is logic. Handling the I/O is the function of the AND and OR operators. Sometimes these operators are referred to as open and closed *gates*. Many times the system, as it determines the status of inputs and outputs, classifies high-voltage readings as being on and low-voltage ones as being off. The NOT operator is sometimes needed to indicate when an event is not happening. Combining the functions of AND gates and NOT gates yields the NAND gate. The same is true for OR and NOT gates. This gives us the NOR gate. While there are a multitude of methods for programming digital devices, it usually has to come to a binary level at some point.

Personal and industrial computers actually comprise many elements, such as hardware, firmware, and software. There is the microprocessor and sometimes a mathematics coprocessor if enormous amounts of numerical data have to be processed. The microprocessors have grown from 8-bit, 16-bit, and 32-bit sizes and will no doubt go well beyond. The microprocessor is dependent on the machine's crystal. The crystal can be likened to the heartbeat of the computer. It oscillates at some high frequency when electricity is applied. This gives the computer clock, or crystal, speeds of 33, 66, 100, and 200 MHz, and again, this speed will be exceeded. This crystal establishes the speed with which the microprocessor can step through the software. The microprocessor's bit configuration and the system's crystal are the two main elements of the computer when it comes to power and throughput.

Processing Basics

As we look at industrial processes and how to automate them, we find that many events are simply "on-or-off" states. Those states could simulate a valve open or closed. Starting and stopping motors use on-and-off logic. The computer takes this basic principle to its extreme. The processor switches on-and-off states, millions of times per second. Therefore, our control scheme is not as complicated as we think. It is just vast. These binary digits, or bits (1s and 0s), are changing their on-and-off status constantly to control the on-and-off status of several pieces of equipment in the plant. Beyond this, the computer multiplies and divides by adding and subtracting at amazing speeds. This allows the machine to make complicated decisions regarding a process.

The bit is the building block. Bits are made into bytes, bytes into characters, and so on. One byte is equal to so many bits. For example, 8 bits equals 1 byte for a given 8-bit machine, 8 bits equals 16 bytes for a 16-bit machine, and so on. Table 3-1 provides at a glance the powers of 2 from 1 to 20. Since the bytes assume the role of a character in a program, there has to be a standard for identifying these characters. This is especially true when characters are transferred from one computer to another. The current standard is the American Standard

TABLE 3-1. Binary Number Decimal Equivalents

Power of 2	Bit number	Decimal equivalent
2^1	1	2
2^2	2	4
2^3	3	8
2^4	4	16
2^5	5	32
2^6	6	64
2^7	7	128
2^8	8	256
2^9	9	512
2^{10}	10	1,024
2^{11}	11	2,048
2^{12}	12	4,096
2^{13}	13	8,192
2^{14}	14	16,384
2^{15}	15	32,768
2^{16}	16	65,536
2^{17}	17	131,072
2^{18}	18	262,144
2^{19}	19	524,288
2^{20}	20	1,048,576

Example: When one is referring to a 14-bit number, the actual total units are 16,384.

Code for Information Interchange (ASCII). This standard allows for 7 bits per character to make 128 unique characters and a further 256 characters with 8 bits per character. The corresponding list for the ASCII standard is shown in Table 3-2. This list shows the binary, octal, decimal, and hexadecimal equivalents for the ASCII characters.

TABLE 3-2. ASCII Character Code Equivalents

Binary	Octal	Decimal	Hexadecimal	ASCII character
0000000	000	000	00	NUL
0000001	001	001	01	SOH
0000010	002	002	02	STX
				EOA
0000011	003	003	03	ETX
				EOM
0000100	004	004	04	EOT
0000101	005	005	05	ENQ
0000110	006	006	06	ACK
0000111	007	007	07	BEL
0001000	010	008	08	BS
0001001	011	009	09	HT
0001010	012	010	0A	LF
0001011	013	011	0B	VT
0001100	014	012	0C	FF
0001101	015	013	0D	CR
0001110	016	014	0E	SO
0001111	017	015	0F	SI
0010000	020	016	10	DLE
0010001	021	017	11	DC1
0010010	022	018	12	DC2
0010011	023	019	13	DC3
0010100	024	020	14	DC4
0010101	025	021	15	NAK
0010110	026	022	16	SYN
0010111	027	023	17	ETB
0011000	030	024	18	CAN
0011001	031	025	19	EM
0011010	032	026	1A	SUB
0011011	033	027	1B	ESC
0011100	034	028	1C	FS
0011101	035	029	1D	GS
0011110	036	030	1E	RS
0011111	037	031	1F	US
0100000	040	032	20	SP
0100001	041	033	21	!
0100010	042	034	22	"
0100011	043	035	23	#
0100100	044	036	24	$

TABLE 3-2. ASCII Character Code Equivalents *(Continued)*

Binary	Octal	Decimal	Hexadecimal	ASCII character
0100101	045	037	25	%
0100110	046	038	26	&
0100111	047	039	27	'
0101000	050	040	28	(
0101001	051	041	29	)
0101010	052	042	2A	*
0101011	053	043	2B	+
0101100	054	044	2C	,
0101101	055	045	2D	-
0101110	056	046	2E	.
0101111	057	047	2F	/
0110000	060	048	30	0
0110001	061	049	31	1
0110010	062	050	32	2
0110011	063	051	33	3
0110100	064	052	34	4
0110101	065	053	35	5
0110110	066	054	36	6
0110111	067	055	37	7
0111000	070	056	38	8
0111001	071	057	39	9
0111010	072	058	3A	:
0111011	073	059	3B	;
0111100	074	060	3C	<
0111101	075	061	3D	=
0111110	076	062	3E	>
0111111	077	063	3F	?
1000000	100	064	40	@
1000001	101	065	41	A
1000010	102	066	42	B
1000011	103	067	43	C
1000100	104	068	44	D
1000101	105	069	45	E
1000110	106	070	46	F
1000111	107	071	47	G
1001000	110	072	48	H
1001001	111	073	49	I
1001010	112	074	4A	J
1001011	113	075	4B	K
1001100	114	076	4C	L
1001101	115	077	4D	M
1001110	116	078	4E	N
1001111	117	079	4F	O
1010000	120	080	50	P
1010001	121	081	51	Q

TABLE 3-2. ASCII Character Code Equivalents *(Continued)*

Binary	Octal	Decimal	Hexadecimal	ASCII character
1010010	122	082	52	R
1010011	123	083	53	S
1010100	124	084	54	T
1010101	125	085	55	U
1010110	126	086	56	V
1010111	127	087	57	W
1011000	130	088	58	X
1011001	131	089	59	Y
1011010	132	090	5A	Z
1011011	133	091	5B	[
1011100	134	092	5C	\
1011101	135	093	5D	]
1011110	136	094	5E	^
1011111	137	095	5F	_
1100000	140	096	60	`
1100001	141	097	61	a
1100010	142	098	62	b
1100011	143	099	63	c
1100100	144	100	64	d
1100101	145	101	65	e
1100110	146	102	66	f
1100111	147	103	67	g
1101000	150	104	68	h
1101001	151	105	69	i
1101010	152	106	6A	j
1101011	153	107	6B	k
1101100	154	108	6C	l
1101101	155	109	6D	m
1101110	156	110	6E	n
1101111	157	111	6F	o
1110000	160	112	70	p
1110001	161	113	71	q
1110010	162	114	72	r
1110011	163	115	73	s
1110100	164	116	74	t
1110101	165	117	75	u
1110110	166	118	76	v
1110111	167	119	77	w
1111000	170	120	78	x
1111001	171	121	79	y
1111010	172	122	7A	z
1111011	173	123	7B	{
1111100	174	124	7C		
1111101	175	125	7D	}
1111110	176	126	7E	~
1111111	177	127	7F	DEL

The basic computer system is shown in Fig. 3-2. The blocks designate the rudimentary elements of any computer system. There must be input devices, output devices, arithmetic and logic processing, and data storage. These are the focal points of development. For industrial applications, special attention is given to the input and output devices. Environment, use, and the user dictate how these packages are applied. Nonetheless, our computer system is a vital cog in the industrial wheel.

Many features of the traditional computer appear in most facets of factory automation. Motion controllers are computers. So, too, are programmable controllers. The microprocessor is utilized in so many ways. Looking at the main elements individually, we find the computer to be a fast-acting, repetitive machine. The input can come from different sources. Direct serial links, magnetic tapes, floppy disks, or operator interfaces can all provide the necessary data which will eventually be processed. The central processing unit (CPU) handles the bulk of the work. It utilizes an arithmetic logic unit (ALU) to "crunch" numbers. Bytes are broken down into bits for processing, and all this work happens at speeds at which electricity can functionally flow. For now, there are resistive and conductor constraints which inhibit processing and transfer speed. This is one of the challenges confronting the computer industry.

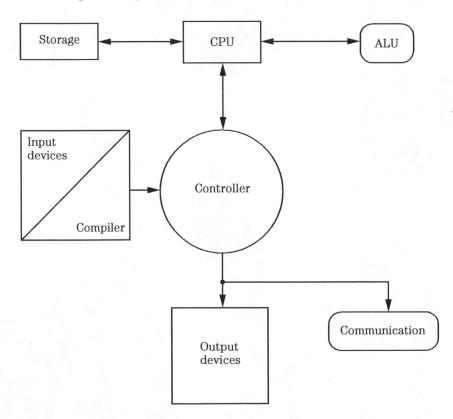

Fig. 3-2   The basic computer system.

Software

This is the facet of the computer industry that is really growing. Application software is becoming more and more powerful. Soft logic is actually a product of this growth and evolution. More and more applications done traditionally with hardware are now possible by using software products. Some may argue that computer hardware is more important than the software. The fact is, there are thousands of applications programs out there, and most are powerful and effective — everything from data acquisition to process simulation to machine control. Without them the hardware is useless. These packages have evolved to icon, or symbol, object-oriented, or graphical high-level programs. They are high-level because they have to be broken down at some point before the computer's processor can run them. This may involve compiling the program, especially if the program is a user-produced or user-changed application. Most of the standard, purchased application programs are already compiled and ready to run.

Prior to the data's being processed, a program or set of instructions must be resident to perform the task. It can be high-level languages which have to be broken down before running or lower-level code which is closer to the electronic, digital machine code ready to be processed. This is software and is placed in the computer's storage. This storage can be random-access memory (RAM). Additional storage called read-only memory (ROM) is available on most computer systems as hardwired programs not so readily changed. Other forms of storage are available, and the next generation of computers will have even newer methods of storage. Software is that powerful part of the computer which makes all applications possible. PLCs have their own versions, as do industrial and personal computers. The intent of this section is not to cover all aspects of software (hundreds of full books have done this) but rather to provide a basic overview. With soft logic and PC-based control systems, certain necessary functions must be built in. Some of these functions are multitasking abilities, deterministic capability, I/O driver and interfaces, real-time packages, and much more. Soft logic software is analyzed in detail in Chap. 6.

Hardware

It is commonly said, "If you can touch it and it is somehow related to a computer, then it is hardware." Microprocessor chips, memory chips, printed-circuit cards, ribbon cable, chip sockets, batteries, light-emitting diodes (LEDs), switches, and integrated circuits are all hardware items. These input devices are hardware, too: the keyboard, disk drives, touch screens, the mouse, scanners, card readers, joysticks, and digitizers. Output devices include printers, monitors, displays, and other computerized devices. There are virtually thousands of different types of input and output devices. Some are actually input *and* output devices such as human-machine interfaces (HMIs). Many are used in the office as well as on the factory floor. Different housings and enclosures have to be considered when they are installed on the plant floor.

A surface-mounted device (SMD) is another advancement in computer printed-circuit board design. This technology allows mounting of the chips, resistors, capacitors, and other small components faster and without too much degradation to the actual board. These SMDs are not the traditional, larger through-the-board components which had to be soldered together, hand-wired, or made into hybrid circuits (sometimes referred to as *breadboard design*). Rather, they are much smaller units, in block form, and are soldered in place to a foil seating. They are then heavily coated with a protective coating which also further solidifies their position on the board. By using SMDs, more components can be placed on a similar-size board than was true years ago. Further, there are actually fewer holes in the board, thus making it stronger. The SMD process is quite fast, and thus many more boards can be produced in a shorter time. Note that these SMDs are small and fragile. They are basically throwaway items, if damaged. They are very sensitive to heat, so board repair and soldering are limited.

Memory

Most microprocessor-based systems utilize some type of memory. Having enough, being able to quickly access it, and ensuring that the resident data stay there are the real issues concerning computer memory. Memory is often mistaken for storage, and storage is mistaken for memory. They are similar but actually two different entities. *Storage* is a place for large amounts of data, other application programs, and other computer files to reside while not in immediate use by the microprocessor. This can be in the form of CD-ROM disks, floppy disks, and magnetic tape (what is best for the plant floor and for use with industrial computers is open for debate). *Memory* is a storage vehicle, but it is *dynamically* involved with the computer's present application. Memory could be classified as hardware because it is resident on a printed-circuit board, since it has to be readily accessed by the microprocessor.

There are several different schemes for computer memory, each with advantages and disadvantages. A computer stores data in its memory within arrays of cells by way of binary, on/off states. These cells must be electrically charged and thus are called *volatile* because if power is removed, the charge is lost and so are the stored data. Many computers rely on volatile RAM. Some go as far as to provide battery backup in case there is an interruption of power. Both static random access memory (SRAM) and dynamic random access memory (DRAM) exist and are volatile. Dynamic random access memory is typically used by the microprocessor as its main memory. This is the more common form of memory in use today. Static random access memory is more complex. It is often associated with cache, or memory, buffers between the main memory and the microprocessor to move data more efficiently and quickly.

Since the memory mentioned so far is volatile, the computer industry has embarked on a trek to find the best, most flexible, and least expensive approach to storing data and not losing them when power is absent. This is nonvolatile memory, and it has evolved many times. The evolution is shown in Fig. 3-3. Volatile memory is also shown along with nonvolatile to achieve a complete look. Nonvolatile memory can permanently store data without the need for constantly updating the electric charge.

These nonvolatile memory devices store data until the data are erased or reprogrammed. The most basic type of nonvolatile memory is ROM. As the acronym suggests, this memory can only be read from. Data can be taken from this memory

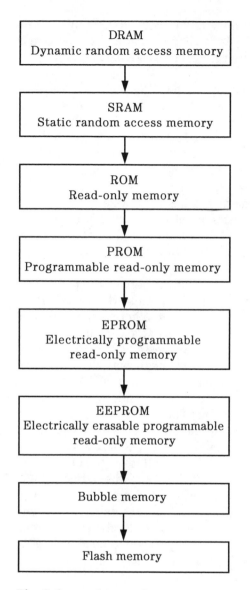

Fig. 3-3   Evolution of memory.

location, but those same data cannot be changed or written over by the active computer and program. ROM is not reprogrammable. Any change to the data and instructions in ROM have to be fully redone. The advantage of ROM is that it is inexpensive and can be mass-produced for products such as video games. The ROM chip is sometimes called a PROM (programmable read-only memory) chip.

A step beyond ROM is the electrically programmable read only memory (EPROM). These devices can be erased and reprogrammed. They have a quartz window on the top of the chip and have to be removed from the socket to be erased. An ultraviolet light has to be directed through the quartz window for several minutes in order to completely erase one. To reprogram an EPROM, approximately 12 V is required to "burn" the new program into the memory device. These EPROMs do get quite warm when software is loaded into them. These EPROMs are used extensively throughout industrial, computerized equipment and are very popular.

The next memory device needing explanation is the EEPROM. This is the electrically erasable programmable read-only memory. These devices require no quartz window, which helps keep costs down, and only a low voltage is necessary to erase the EEPROM. The other nice feature here is that the EEPROM does not have to be removed from its socket for erasure. It can be reprogrammed fully or partially. Because of this capability, it is necessary to have extra capacity for addresses and to aid in decoding when doing portions of a program. The main advantage of EEPROMs is that, for those applications requiring numerous erase/write cycles, they can accommodate upward of 1 million erase/write cycles in a given package. EEPROMs are typically more expensive than PROMs and EPROMs mainly because there can be many more transistors required for error correction. However, their convenience and practicality usually outweigh the added cost.

This brings us to flash ROMs or flash memory. Flash memory has helped to create microcontrollers. Microcontrollers are self-contained units which can handle their own A/D (analog-to-digital) conversion, interfacing to other components, and other instructions necessary to perform some subfunction of the overall process. All this is on one chip. As more and more data have to be processed and more attention is given to external events (I/O) and communications, microcontrollers and flash memory are gaining popularity. Flash memory utilizes AND, NOR, and NAND logic circuits. Each offers some advantage over the other. AND types are mainly low-power and high-speed, with the capability of writing small blocks of code. NOR flash memory devices are similar to AND types but offer random access to memory locations. NAND types are easily erased and consume small amounts of power.

The benefits of using flash memory are many. First, it offers all the erasing and writing advantages of the best EEPROM memory device. Once the device is in its socket, it does not have to be removed. It can be erased and reprogrammed with little effort and power. There is no EPROM eraser or EPROM burner. It also offers upload and download capability at machines, even from remote locations. Just dump the compiled program right into the chip, and away you go. There is no more erasing and burning EPROMs and using express courier to deliver overnight simply for a minor change. Software testing and development can occur faster because the erase/compile/burn process is virtually eliminated. Even the need for software test fixtures is reduced. More immediate testing, on actual equipment and hardware, is at hand. Via the microcontrollers, self-diagnosis and calibration are more practical with flash memory on various machines. Thus, the evolution of memory devices has come to the point, today, where battery backup is not required and we can practically load and reload programming at will. Probably, by the time this chapter is read, there will be a further advancement in memory devices. This is a good segue into firmware.

Firmware can be described in many ways and could be included as software or could be hardware. Because it is the stored instructions and is kept in read-only memory, it could be classified as software. But it also is software stored on a chip and thus could be hardware. That is why it probably got its own name—firmware. A manufacturer's specialized, self-developed code is usually the firmware in a system. The user will not be allowed access to this code.

On-Line in the Factory

Typically, the computer control scheme in the factory is a top-down, distributed arrangement. A main computer, often a mainframe plant computer, controls the scheduling and planning of the entire plant's operations. Some pertinent data are then downloaded to the appropriate smaller minicomputers at the cell or supervisory levels of the plant. From here, all the individual microprocessors controlling the machines, PLCs, and industrial computers on the plant floor receive information. Now, everyone has the assignment for the day, and production can begin. Once production has begun, various exchanges of data take place between devices, and much information is uploaded eventually to the host or plant system for planning and more scheduling.

The plant engineer today wants to arrive at the office in the morning, grab a cup of coffee, go on-line, and find out what is happening in the plant. How is the machinery running? At what speed? How many products have we made? Are we making a good product? Did we have any problems through the night? These are all questions that can be answered right at the computer. Thus, when the boss wants to know something, the engineer does not have to go to the plant floor to interrogate operators or read gauges. The information has been brought to her or his PC.

All this is made possible courtesy of the microprocessor and its ability to move processed data to the proper location. We can monitor our work as we go and adjust the process accordingly. In essence, the throughput of data is proportional to the amount of product manufactured in industry today. Since the machines make the product, the faster all the data are processed, the faster a product is made! The computer lends itself well to the flexibility needed in the factory of today and that of the future. Industrial automation would lose its thunder if plants could not easily change their processes. If expensive and time-consuming hardware changes were required every time a new or improved product was needed, then automation would never have progressed as far as it has today!

The software configurability of any computer allows for the existing hardware to be reused. So retooling is becoming a thing of the past, or at least, retooling times are greatly reduced. Thus, much of the creativity and growth in the computer field is in the software packages that run the machines and computers, as evidenced by soft logic packages. These software packages are so flexible that they can be customized to the machine and the task to be performed. The instructions, or code, must be written in higher-level languages rather than in binary (bit) form, so that plant engineering has the opportunity and ability to maintain the code. Opportunity is the key. Often several computer systems "invade" a particular factory, each with similar hardware but with vastly different software. Plant support people first need a basic understanding of microprocessors and then must be willing to continually learn new programming languages, or instructions. The instructions must also be written so that any operators of the equipment can easily understand them. After all, their job is to run the machine and make product, not to be a computer programmer.

The soft logic system must be as user-friendly as practical and should be self-diagnosing. *User-friendly* in this case means that it should be structured so that any electrician or programmer could look at the software and readily start to program. Likewise, if the machine shuts down the production line, then managers want to know why they are losing money while the line sits idle. Today's machine must be able to quickly, if not instantaneously, tell a maintenance engineer what is wrong, or at least give some indication of the location of the problem so that troubleshooting can begin. This is a big reason why companies tend to standardize on a particular brand of control—because of the complexity and the training involved on new products.

Basic Operation of PLC

Before soft logic and PC-based controllers, there was the programmable logic controller. And before programmable logic controllers there was the *relay*. Control relays and relay logic were the standard of the day between postwar industrial period and the 1970s. This mechanical device was used throughout industry for controlling machines and processes. A typical relay is shown in simplified form in Fig. 3-4. An electromagnetic device, connects a circuit when its other contact portion is electrically activated. When power is removed, the relay returns to its original state. Another type, the latching relay, operates in much the same way except that when power is removed, it remains in its latest position. Both types of relays were used extensively to build control systems in factories. To perform even the simplest of functions, many relays had to be used. There had to be a lot of interlocking between relays. For an event to happen, as shown in the simplified control sequence in Fig. 3.5, multiple relays had to be used. Just to start and stop a motor could take several, interlocking relays. Many wires had to be run from terminal to terminal to perform that simple function. This was a hard-wired approach to control, and relays were up for a large portion of that approach. Relays were bulky devices and so took up valuable factory floor space and required a good wiring plan. Because so many were needed to perform the simplest tasks, one could find an entire enclosure filled

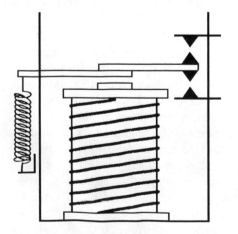

Fig. 3-4   The mechanical relay.

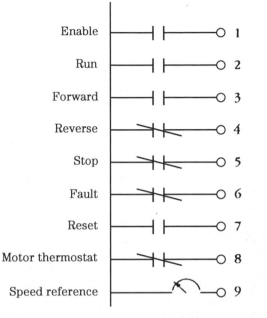

Fig. 3-5 A hard-wired control scheme.

with relays. Sometimes the spring mechanism would get dirty and stick, and it was definitely not self-diagnosing. If the installation was old, chances were that no drawings could be found to help trace the wire. Relays were hard to troubleshoot and maintain, but they were the best answer at the time.

Industry needed an electronic means of sequencing processes, machines, motors, and sensors. This need would mark the beginning of the era of the programmable logic controller. This electronic device has four main components: a processor, an input section, an output section, and a power supply. These can be seen in Fig. 3-6. The input modules could consist of many different sensors such as pressure, temperature, and proximity switches; or these inputs could be from operator pushbuttons. Input data could be in the form of a voltage, usually referred to as an analog signal, or they could be logic or digital data. Output signals from the PLC could trigger motor starters, drives, indicators, alarms, solenoids, lights, and other process devices. These signals were also able to be analog or digital. A program, or list of instructions, would tell the electronic controller what to do, instead of wiring several relays together to get a desired result. Therefore, the control scheme of Fig. 3-5 could be programmed into the PLC and the same result provided.

All programmable logic controllers have a processor, a main central processing unit, and associated memory. While the CPU makes the decisions and is the main device in the PLC, the memory has multiple functions. Memory within the PLC stores messages, programs, and data. Data which will be used by the CPU are stored in data tables. A data table can be broken down into three smaller components: an input image table, an output image table, and a timer or counter instruction storage area. Image tables reflect the status of their respective inputs or outputs. The image table is divided into the smallest units of the memory—bits. Each bit in the image table will

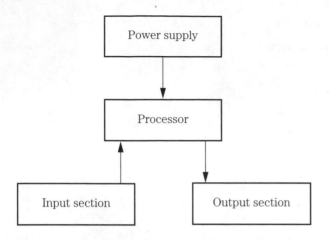

Fig. 3-6   Basic components of the programmable
logic controller.

correspond to an input or output terminal, and the input image table's job is to duplicate the on/off status of the input devices. Whenever voltage is sensed by the input
terminal, this fact is recorded by turning on the appropriate bit, or the bit is "set." If
the terminal senses no voltage, then the bit is turned off or is reset by the processor.
Thus, the processor is constantly looking at these bit settings as the PLC program
executes and decides what to do about that bit's setting. Likewise, the output image
table controls the on/off status of the output device, which is directly wired to the output module terminal. Again, the user program controls the output image table bits.
The timer and counter storage unit keeps track of timing or counting functions in
accordance with the logic of the ladder diagram. The storage of the PLC's program
takes up a large amount of memory. The full instruction set for the PLC is stored here.
Each statement in the instruction set describes what conditions should exist before
any action takes place and then also describes the action which should be taken. The
last area of memory is the message storage area. It begins after the end statement of
the user program. Here, messages can be stored as two characters (alphanumeric)
stored in a word.

The input and output sections of the programmable controller are made up of the
I/O modules and serve four basic functions. These are the termination points for
the field wiring. They also provide necessary isolation to protect the PLC circuitry
from dangerous voltage levels. Additionally, the voltage signal is conditioned at the
input and output modules so that the PLC or field device receives the correct matching voltage needed for proper operation. Last, the input and output units provide a
visual indication of the status of the inputs or outputs. The last component in the PLC
is the power supply. It provides the low-level DC voltage used throughout the PLC's
circuits. This power is required to run the internal clock, to supply voltage for the
LEDs, and to be available for local I/O.

PLC control sequencing and scan sequencing are the next elements in the
PLC's successful operation. As previously described, the processor, power supply,
and I/O are defined. The next step is to work them in conjunction with one another.

When power to the controller is tuned on, the processor begins the scan sequence by scanning the I/O. Data from the input and output modules are transferred to the corresponding image tables. Next, the processor scans the user program, statement by statement. Each statement is checked for a condition, and the image table is read. If a condition is met, then the processor writes a 1 into the corresponding bit location in the output image table. Likewise, if the condition is not met, then a 0 is placed into the corresponding bit location in the output image table. The processor continues this scanning process for all statements in the program. This process is repeated many times a minute, each time setting and resetting bits in the appropriate image tables. Key factors of any PLC include how fast the scan rates are and how many words per scan there are. Many manufacturers of PLCs specify scan times per 1000- or 500-word increments. These scan times can be 1 ms for a 500-word program. This further breaks down to microseconds per basic instruction. To better illustrate how much faster a microsecond is than a millisecond, see Table 3-3 for the mathematical equivalents for these alpha designations and their corresponding powers of 10. PC-based controls can now emulate this functionality by using soft logic software.

PLC Hardware

Typically the industrial-grade programmable logic controller must be "hardened" for the factory floor environment. This can mean placing the PLC within a metal enclosure meeting some NEMA (National Electrical Manufacturers Association) standard or installing a PLC package that is built as a rack-type unit. Various

TABLE 3-3. Various Powers of 10 and Their Alpha Prefix Designations

Power of 10	Alpha prefix
10^{18}	exa
10^{15}	peta
10^{12}	tera
10^{9}	giga
10^{6}	mega
10^{3}	kilo
10^{2}	hecto
10^{1}	deka
10^{-1}	deci
10^{-2}	centi
10^{-3}	milli
10^{-6}	micro
10^{-9}	nano
10^{-12}	pico
10^{-15}	femto
10^{-18}	atto

NEMA enclosure classifications are shown in Table 8.1. The one appropriate for the environment must be selected. The rack-type PLC package is actually nothing more than a metal enclosure with corrosion-resistant paint, protective-coating materials, and a framework such that it can support the mounting of several modules. This rack houses the common bus and slot configuration into which the add-on modules will be seated. These modules have printed-circuit boards attached; and once seated into the backplane, motherboard, or bus, there are usually screws to be tightened so the module cannot become unseated. These boards and modules fit neatly into the rack assembly. This rack and module package is shown in Fig. 3-7 as an exploded view to see how all the individual pieces fit together. The face of each module may have nomenclature which identifies it as a CPU, I/O module, and so on. The face also will have status lights, usually LEDs, to indicate fault and nonfault conditions. There may also be ports for external connections, depending on the module type. The CPU module will be the most pronounced module in the rack, usually having the widest profile. This can be seen in Fig. 3-8, where various modules and pieces of the PLC system are shown.

Within the CPU module there exist many subcomponents. These can be seen in the block diagram for the controller in Fig. 3-9—microprocessors, memory, serial ports, coprocessors, etc. In a redundancy scheme there are two controllers; one is the primary, and one is the backup. Redundancy and "hot" backup control schemes are common. However, when a redundant control scheme is considered, whether PLC or personal computer, duplicate hardware must be incorporated, and this *does* cost more money. In this block diagram, we find the microprocessors, the mathematics coprocessors, and the communication processors. As for the memory, there will be main and shared memory devices in both RAM and EPROM versions. The back portion of the module which is incorporated into the backplane has seated connections for the field bus, primary and secondary, peer-to-peer communications, and so on. On the front, or face, of the module are the coaxial connections for the token-passing network.

The CPU module will have a different set of lights from the I/O modules on its face. These will include message codes for system diagnostics, several communications LEDs, low-voltage and fail alarm LEDs, along with the coaxial connections. The

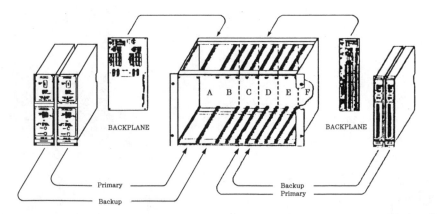

Fig. 3-7   The PLC rack, backplane, and modules.

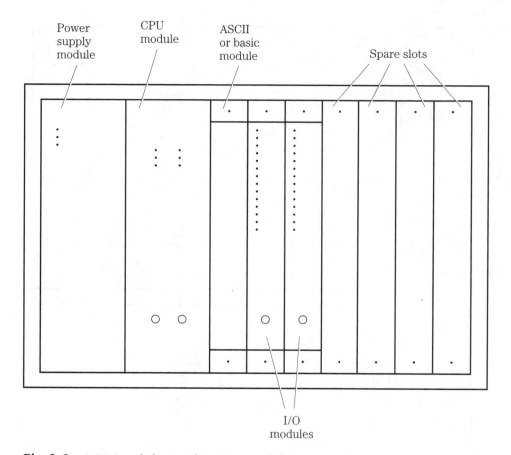

Fig. 3-8   A PLC rack face with various modules.

I/O modules, on the other hand, have many of the same indicator lights, but also contain a status LED for every I/O in use within that module. These I/O modules can be mounted remotely (as they most often are), beside the CPU in a common rack, or below the main controller modules in the rack. The I/O modules tend to be more slender than the CPU modules. Floor standing assemblies can house CPUs, power supplies, and I/O modules along with corresponding racks. With a metal door, this enclosure would give the controller hardware a lot of protection from the factory environment. There is even a filtered ventilation scheme in use to cool the cabinet inside with clean air. It is also shown with a dual-terminal, dual-keyboard workstation. An operator interface always has to be present in a process control system.

Most times in the factory, it is simply not acceptable to lose any data, control, or programming at any time (power outages, electrical noise, etc.) within the process controller. Once it has been decided to give this electronic device control of the entire process—the livelihood of so many people—it is difficult to tolerate any downtime. Downtime can cost thousands of dollars in actual production lost, but also the process may have to go through a lengthy start-up and setup once it is interrupted. Elaborate steps are taken to prevent this. One method is to provide battery backup power in case of electrical supply interruption. This battery backup is mainly

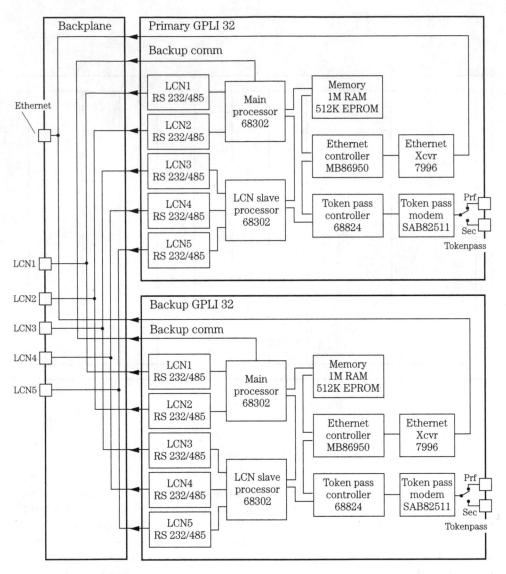

Fig. 3-9   The inner subcomponents of a CPU module.

for the memory. Similarly, read-only memory is used for much of the software and firmware. Another precaution is to incorporate a constant-voltage transformer between the main power supply and the PLC to keep electrical disturbances, or dips, to a minimum. But the most elaborate and most expensive means of ensuring PLC uptime is to install a redundant PLC system. This is often called a *hot backup,* and basically it is a CPU, fully programmed and ready to go on-line should the main CPU fail. This expense is worth it when a production line is producing thousands of dollars in product per day.

The CPU normally is complemented with a supply of input and output modules. The rack's physical size will depend on the number of slots required by the application, for the eventual insertion of all I/O modules and other types of modules. These modules each have a dedicated, specialized function. Those functions can include temperature sensing, motion and positioning modules for motors and servo systems, high-speed counting, ASCII or BASIC modules for two-way serial communication, and PID loop control. But the most prevalent add-on modules are for discrete I/O and analog I/O. Aside from the local mounting of the I/O modules is the remote I/O approach, which is most common. Wiring in the factory is one of the more problematic issues. Routing wire and cable is often difficult. Marking and tracing it later are even more difficult. Remember, these plant electricians are usually under a lot of pressure to get processes and machines running, and one little wiring mistake can be disastrous (short circuits, wrongly applied voltages, etc.). Thus the remote I/O module makes sense. Figure 3-10 shows a PLC system with remote I/O modules. Typically, a coaxial or fiber optic connection comes off the module and is routed to the PLC, thus saving the routing and pulling of hundreds of smaller wires back to the PLC.

Another input scheme uses analog signals. These signals are usually in the form of 1 to 5 V, 0 to 10 V, or 4 to 20 mA. The signal is in the form of direct-current (DC) electricity. These analog inputs can be furnished from potentiometers which are dialed by an operator to an appropriate value which the operator perceives as a setting, maybe for speed or time or any other pertinent function. This signal, upon arrival at the PLC, must be wired into the analog module. The PLC program must then recognize that it has received a 5-V signal. But first it must be determined to what scale that signal must be equal. For instance, if a 0- to 10-V DC potentiometer signal comes into an analog module, what does it mean? The PLC program must be set up to know that 0 V is a message to do nothing while a full 10 V means to panic or to do something in rapid fashion. Likewise, analog outputs can be furnished by the PLC in the same forms: 1 to 5 V DC, 0 to 10 V DC, and 4 to 20 mA. These signals can be used to drive meters with the appropriate values to display accurate and up-to-date readings. An important issue with analog inputs and outputs is resolution. Typical resolutions are 12 bits and higher. This will determine how accurately the analog signal can be scaled. Analog to digital (A-to-D, A-D, or A/D) devices are used to convert the signal to usable processing form. A high-speed, super powerful device will not be of real value to the process if the A/D resolution is low.

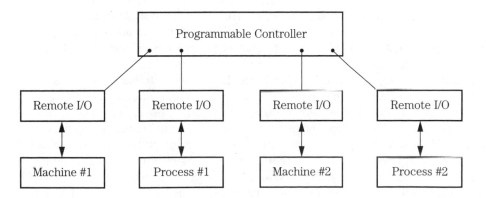

Fig. 3-10 PLC with remote I/O drops.

PLC Modules

Therefore, it is not simply that easy to say that the PLC is just an input and output device. The inputs can have many forms, values, and meanings. The outputs from the PLC can have the same effect and are planned ahead of time by the PLC programmer. They all must be defined, one by one, as to function, timing, and interrelation to other I/Os. A useful document to log and keep track of I/O is shown in Fig. 3-11. These summary sheets can and should be used before, during, and after the controller's program is written. The same must be done for both the discrete I/O and the analog I/O. These hard-copy sheets are extremely useful whether the control system is PC-based or PLC-based. Soft logic systems still control I/O, and there can be hundreds of points to keep track of!

While PC-based communication schemes are discussed further in Chap. 10, there is still common ground between PC and PLC networks. The common mode of communication with most PLCs is via a high-speed network, or bus, rather than discrete wiring or even serial links. This is usually a built-in component of the main CPU control module. There are usually different data transmission speeds set up within the controller. Typical network speeds are 1 to 2 Mbits/s with some more elaborate systems capable of speeds well over 10 Mbits/s. Also different scan rates are assigned for certain critical pieces of information and prioritize those scans. This is necessary because if every bit of I/O had to have the fastest scan and there was an enormous amount of I/O, then a single scan could take too long and possibly could get "hung up" while waiting for some data. Some I/O just is not so critical to the process at every instant in time. For instance, when a high-speed counting routine is performed, these bits must be scanned quickly, whereas the monitoring of a motor thermostat can be looked at less frequently. Remember, we are talking about milliseconds (even microseconds). A motor in a temperature overload condition takes minutes to overheat. A 0.5-s delay in faulting the motor and cutting off power will not destroy the motor.

ASCII and BASIC modules allow the PLC to communicate with other devices. Printers, other PLCs, and computers can receive information from the PLC via a serial communications port by utilizing these type of modules. Drivers which set up the communications ports to send and receive data must be in place or otherwise written, or programmed. This module allows blocks of instructions to be transferred to another device such as a drive controller. The BASIC module must have a certain amount of memory (most of the time backed up by battery), an adequate amount of capacity for a transfer, multiple baud, or transmission rates usually up to 19,200 bits/s, and good diagnostic abilities.

Another module which can be added to a PLC system, into one of the slots in the rack, is a temperature-sensing module. This is a common requirement for temperature watching in many processes. The adage "A watched pot never boils" is appropriate here. Variations of these boards can be used to input thermistor signals from the motor's resistive temperature detectors (RTDs) and most type J or type K thermocouples. A thermistor measures temperature via electric resistance using semiconductor properties, while a thermocouple is a temperature-sensing device which can provide a value for temperature by utilizing a metallic two-wire junction scheme. A simple thermostat, however, just provides a contact closure, many times when two

Analog I/O Summary				
Remarks:				
Project:	Password:	Firmware:	Drawing #	Date:
INPUT NO.				
TAG#				
Description				
Signal				
INPUT NO.				
TAG#				
Description				
Signal				
OUTPUT NO.				
TAG#				
Description				
Signal				
OUTPUT NO.				
TAG#				
Description				
Signal				

Fig. 3-11   I/O summary log.

metals within the unit come into contact with each other. It is important to match the temperature-sensing device with the correct PLC module. Alarms are common with this add-on module, and most are capable of working in a Celsius or Fahrenheit environment.

The position control module has become a means of closing the loop around a speed control device for a motor. Feedback is provided to the position control module in the form of pulses from an encoder or other similar device. This feedback is then utilized in the PLC program, and a quick decision is made by the program as to a response or new output to the motor being controlled. There are many dedicated motion controllers which are more appropriate to controlling motors. However, the module inserted into the rack of a PLC can serve well in motor control.

High-speed counting modules allow for the accounting of parts and production pieces. The modules accept input in the form of pulses from encoders and higher-frequency devices. This type of module is required because under the normal I/O processing and scanning scenario of a PLC, the input speed of such devices is much greater than that of the PLC's microprocessor. Therefore this dedicated high-speed counting module is required for those applications. The counter's data can be incorporated into the PLC program at the appropriate time for action. The data can also be accumulated for later use in reporting and documentation. Bar-code devices, vision systems, and other types of scanners can be used in conjunction with a high-speed counting module.

Some other modules which are available to the factory are even more specialized. They include voice modules to send, record, and receive messages. Another is the radio-frequency module to recognize wireless transmissions and provide the appropriate interface. Even beyond the aforementioned specialized modules, it is possible to mix and match high-speed, high-density I/O modules at the PLC for whatever the application's needs may be. Many of these add-on modules or interface cards are applicable to soft logic, PC-based systems. As the PC hardware replaces the PLC hardware, the need for other functions such as position loops, temperature sensing, and so on is still addressed by these interface modules.

PLC Software and Programming

Programmable logic controllers are really nothing until an application has been defined and the instructions are provided to carry out that application. This is the PLC program. It is, as the name implies, a method of programming the controller to handle the inputs and outputs, or the PLC's logic, conditions, and actions. This is the list of instructions necessary to perform the tasks of the application. Just as the computer must be given instructions to perform its tasks, so, too, must the programmable logic controller. And since there are many manufacturers of PLCs, there exist many different languages and protocols. But first we look at the basis of these languages and instruction sets.

English mathematician George Boole (1847) is credited with the development of a system that utilizes symbols to express logical relationships between entities. This is called boolean algebra, and it has become the standard in computer and digital circuit design. Because this system of algebra incorporates the use of truth values and binary numbers, it lends itself well to the on/off states of electric circuits. That is why digital devices and computers can be given instructions based on what can be predicted by on/off states. Usually a true condition is an on state and is represented by a 1. A false condition is represented by a 0 and is an off state.

In boolean algebra, there exist further postulates which extend beyond ordinary algebra. There are identity elements: In addition, it is 0: $x + 0 = x$, and in multiplication it is 1; $x \times 1 = x$. There also exist certain mathematical laws in boolean algebra that allow for high-speed calculations in digital circuits. The more common and certainly the most familiar are the following: The *associative law* is expressed as $x + (y + z) = (x + y) + z$ and as $x(yz) = (xy)z$. The *commutative law* states that $x + y = y + x$ and $xy = yx$. The *distributive law* combines addition and multiplication: $x(y+z) = xy + xz$.

It is important to have a basic understanding of boolean algebra for boolean logic is often employed in programming a PLC. It and ladder logic are found in many PLCs as the fundamental, low-level program that runs and controls a given process. Of course, a good understanding of the binary (base-2), octal (base-8), decimal (base-10), and hexadecimal (base-16) numbering systems is essential to programming and working with computers and controllers. In working with numbers, especially in the decimal and binary systems, we have learned that the farthest digit to the right is the least significant digit. Likewise, the farthest digit to the left is the most significant digit. This concept comes into play when we are manipulating data and communicating between devices. These functions rely on processing electronically, and there are binary equivalents for everything from numbers to letters. That is why one will hear values expressed as the least significant and most significant bits (binary digits).

As process requirements have become more complex and more extensive calculation is required of the PLC, higher-level languages have emerged. Some are in the form of blocks, which can be still incorporated into the ladder scheme. Each block contains several instructions and is more or less self-contained. This means the programmer simply applies the block to the application program and thus does not have to list, step by step, every equation. This is most critical in performing proportional integral derivative (PID) calculations. PID loops are discussed in detail in Chap. 12. Basically, these are closed loops which aid in the correction of system and process errors. They could not be performed with common boolean and ladder logic. It would be too cumbersome and time-consuming an operation. That is why higher-level languages have emerged. Many even go beyond block diagrams. Today's PLC programming incorporates symbols and coding much as BASIC, C, and other high-level languages do. Many programs are now written with macroprocessors and function blocks. These functions, although having different names and acronyms, yield the same end result when the program is implemented. These differ with each PLC manufacturer, and each is customized to its own microprocessors and types of memory used in the PLC hardware.

Boolean algebra utilizes symbols to represent operators. Once the truth value is known of a particular entity, it can be utilized further in another comparison. For example, there are conditional operators such as AND and OR. The AND function merely implies that a condition, or state, can only be on or off. However, the OR function needs to have one "OR" condition true in order to be on or off. These are sometimes called gates, open or closed states. *Gating* is a term used mainly in electrical and control dialogue in which something is turned on and turned off.

These types of expressions and operators become the building blocks of a PLC program. There are also inverse values for these operators. The NOT versions of these operators are NAND (Not AND) and NOR (Not OR). These and other operators are used to handle the logic in a given control scheme. Representative symbols used in ladder logic are shown in Table 3-4. These common symbols and ladder

TABLE 3-4. Ladder Diagram Symbols

LADDER DIAGRAM	BOOLEAN MNEMONIC
—(+)—	ADD
—(-)—	SUB
—(x)—	MUL
—(÷)—	DIV
—(CMP =)—	CMP =
—(CMP >)—	CMP >
—(CMP <)—	CMP <
—(JMP)—	JMP
—(JSB)—	JSB
—(MCR)—	MCR
—(END MCR)—	END
—| |—	AND
—|⊦|—	OR
—( )—	OUT
—(/)—	OUT NOT
—|⊬|—	NAND
—|⊬|—	NOR
—|| |—	LOAD
—||/|—	LOAD NOT
—(L)—	OUT L
—(U)—	OUT U
—(TIM)—	TIM
—(CNT)—	CNT

diagram abbreviations are used not only in ladder diagrams but also in basic electrical schematics and wiring diagrams. This graphical depiction of the application is called the *ladder logic,* or *ladder diagram.* It can also be called the *relay ladder diagram.* The relay ladder diagram's shortened version is the contact ladder diagram, which condenses the diagram into contacts and outputs. This actually is the hierarchy of events and control for a given PLC application. However, note that programming in logic is really only concerned with conditions and whether these conditions have been met. It differs from relay logic in this way.

The ladder diagram gets its name from its resemblance to a ladder, shown in Fig. 3-12. Lines of the diagram are conveniently called rungs and further help to define where a particular event or sequence of events lies. The rungs should be numbered so as to be able to navigate through the ladder diagram and refer to it when necessary. Comments usually go to the right of the rung, and the rung numbers are placed on the left. Typically an emergency stop rung with the fault logic is at the beginning, or top, of the ladder. There can also be various zones in the ladder diagram. A zone is a certain routine or sequence of events. Each zone should have designations for its beginning and end. Each vertical leg of the ladder is powered such that when a rung completes a circuit, current flows through it. This ladder logic is actually the relay logic of the machine or process and details the events and actions for the relays. How and when do we want electricity to flow through that rung? For instance, in Fig. 3-13, the relay ladder diagram, when the Start pushbutton is selected, power goes to the coil of CR1. Reading the comments to the right of that rung, we find that rung 8 has the normally closed contact of CR1 and rung 9 has the normally open contact. This shows how the green and red lights will be energized or not.

Of course, this is very basic, and there would most likely be many other conditions and actions up and down this ladder. Also, most ladder diagrams for use in PLC programming are shown as a contact ladder scheme, as illustrated in Fig. 3-12. This is the contact ladder diagram equivalent of the relay ladder diagram in Fig. 3-13. The contact ladder diagram is a simplified, quicker form of the relay ladder diagram. Relay ladder diagrams are very useful in the field when one is starting and troubleshooting

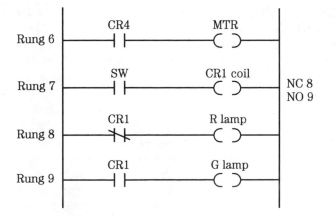

Fig. 3-12 Contact ladder.

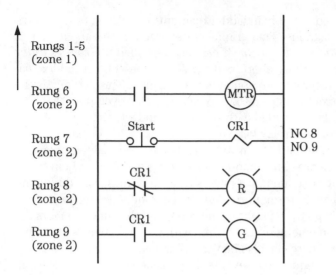

Fig. 3-13   Relay ladder.

equipment. However, the contact ladder diagrams are essential when one is developing the program for the PLC.

The ladder logic contains different components which are common to most PLCs and computerized systems. Addition, subtraction, multiplication, and division are necessary for processing and decision making. Get (for inputs) and put (for outputs) functions are needed to manipulate I/O and for comparisons. As a matter of fact, the ladder many times is the actual program and can be used to run a machine or process. This type of programming contains many necessary functions, or permissives, and the safety interlocks that all those bulky relays provided some 20 years ago. Now the logic is handled electronically. Thus, completely defining all functions of a process or machine operation is just as important. But, at least if a change is made, we do not have to pull and run new wires!

Techniques used in programming a PLC vary from programmer to programmer. Some like to use flags to help locate where they are in the program, especially for troubleshooting. Likewise, a programming tool often utilized is the counter. Many times, after the PLC's central processing unit has counted a predefined quantity of events, an output is triggered. The output could be turned on or off to alert another device or an operator that the desired count has been reached. As discussed earlier, if the actual countable signal is too frequent, then another dedicated counter module must be used. In normal operation, however, the PLC's microprocessor is adequate for counting and logging repeated events.

There are several instructions which allow the programmer to move about within the ladder program. One is the jump command. Once it is activated, the program "jumps" or goes to another location and executes from that point. It is much like a GOTO statement and is even similar to its jump-to-subroutine counterpart. Every PLC manufacturer has its own specific set of instructions, many of which will be similar from manufacturer to manufacturer. However, each has its own "language" and means of programming, making it imperative to have a complete understanding of the

PLC system involved and to obtain all the pertinent documentation. This is why facilities attempt to standardize on control equipment. The relearning and retraining entailed in using a new technology and another manufacturer's control equipment can be very time-consuming. And, frankly, production facilities do not have the luxury of much free time to relearn. So often, technicians are hired for their in-depth knowledge of a particular manufacturer's control equipment, both hardware and software. Thus soft logic and PC-based control systems are fast becoming a PLC alternative because of the prominence of computer hardware and the newer capabilities of microprocessors.

In programming logic, the major concern is all the open and closed input and output devices. There must be a continuous path of true conditions for the appropriate action to be taken. If any logic condition in this path, which can contain any number of conditions, is false, then no action occurs. This can be seen in Fig. 3-14. A pump system works on pressure in a particular line. A pump motor switch is on, this condition is true, and the pump starts pumping. Next, a pressure sensor, or input, is checked for its status. If the sensor is on, then the condition is true and the pump keeps running. However, at condition 3, the pump should keep running if a particular level sensor is off; no overflow is allowed regardless of pressure conditions. When all conditions are met, then the action is allowed. But, as can be seen in Fig. 3-15, whenever one of the conditions is false, the action is not allowed.

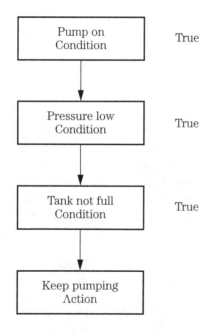

(True is solid line)
(False is broken line)

Fig. 3-14 Pump system—true conditions.

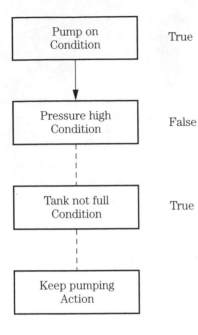

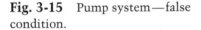

(True is solid line)
(False is broken line)

Fig. 3-15 Pump system—false condition.

These conditions and the checking of these conditions are part of the execution of the PLC program and the scanning of the I/O image tables. The organization of this I/O is achieved with addresses. The processor uses addresses to refer to the words and bits in the image data tables. Each input or output bit has a multidigit address. This address is broken down, typically, like this: The I/O modules in a given rack are part of a module group. This module group is a pair of adjacent I/O modules which occupy a particular slot in the I/O rack. Usually, the first module group is addressed as group 0. Thereafter the module groups increment upward accordingly. These group labels are generally seen on the physical I/O chassis.

The PLC program typically has three elements: the branch instructions, the bit-examining element, and the bit-controlling element. Bit-examining instructions and bit-controlling instructions are the basic elements of a rung. The branch instructions are used whenever parallel sets of conditions are required to enable a given action. The examine on and examine off symbols are shown in Fig. 3-16 and are common to ladder diagram symbology. The examine-on instruction is true when the corresponding bit is set (or "on") and false whenever the bit is reset. Conversely, an examine-off instruction is true whenever the bit in the image table is reset and false when the bit is set. This is the basic makeup of the bit-examining instruction set which is used repeatedly in any PLC program.

At the end of the ladder diagram are the output instruction rungs. They are part of the bit-controlling element of the program. Only one output instruction can be installed on any one rung, and it can be executed only if the preceding conditions are true. These bit-controlling instructions can be used to set memory bits in the output image data table. The processor work area is off-limits to the bit controller instructions. A sample rung with an output energize symbol, sometimes referred to as a coil, is shown in Fig. 3-17. Along with the coil is the bit-examining symbol which precedes the bit-controlling instruction. The latch, or output latch, sets a specified image table bit and is paired with an unlatch instruction. This symbology and rung structure can be seen in Fig. 3-18. Latch and unlatch bits are used basically to protect the program from loss-of-power situations. If power is lost, all latched bits should retain their state prior to the power loss (this is made possible with a processor backup battery).

Whenever the need arises to have several parallel conditions present for a given action to take place, branching instructions are used. This could be compared to the common if-then decision-making scheme of most computer systems. Here, as seen in Fig. 3-19, if either of two parallel conditions is true, then the corresponding action is allowed to happen. Typically a branch has a branch start and a branch end instruction. A nested branch is a rung which has a branch group within a branch group. This can be seen in Fig. 3-20. Too many nested branch instructions can lead to harder debugging and changes down the road, and discretion should be used when going down this path.

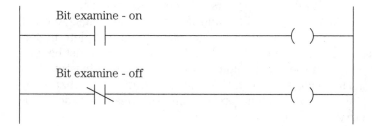

Bit examine - on

Bit examine - off

Fig. 3-16 Examine "on" and examine "off."

Fig. 3-17 A coil.

Fig. 3-18 The latch output. A U may be substituted for L to make an unlatch output.

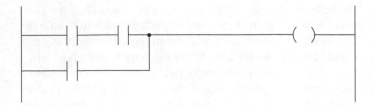

Fig. 3-19   A branch.

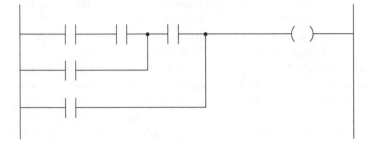

Fig. 3-20   A nested branch.

The actual programming of a PLC is not simple. Many individuals cannot write a good, functional PLC program. It takes many years of experience, and it helps if that experience is with one particular type of PLC and its specific language. Another piece of the equation, just as important to the programming, is a complete understanding of the machine or process. If it can be fully defined as to what must happen when other events happen, then the programmer most likely can get that set of instructions into the PLC. The biggest problem today for programmers is that many functions involving the process or machine are not known ahead of time. Thus changes are made often to the program.

Soft logic control systems and the PC-based software packages many times allow the programmer to continue to build programs in the same ladder diagram environment. This means that the same process or machine instruction set can be developed on the personal computer just as was developed inside the PLC. Image tables, bit examining, bit controlling, and branch instructions can be duplicated on the computer with this software. Many soft logic systems then compile this program for speed of execution in real time.

Connecting PLCs

Many times it is necessary to have multiple programmable logic controllers (even personal or industrial computers for that matter) within a specific zone of the plant. If several machines, processes, or combinations of both are all in need of a controller, then the bigger picture has to be looked at. Will one controller be the master? Will all the controllers be independent? What control scheme is required?

Whether it is a PC-based manufacturing plant or a PLC-based one, the need to link all units together is vital. This is evident today with data, recipes, MRP, and other information-based emphasis on the manufacturing process. *Connectivity* is the buzzword. Connecting many smart, microprocessor-based devices under one roof is sometimes a task unto itself. Every microprocessor wants to be the boss. The engineers of the facility have to determine how to control the overall plant, not just the individual work cells. This is difficult because next year another machine or line might be added. Can it be easily connected then? Soft logic packages have been developed to provide some of this flexibility, because reality in the manufacturing plant dictates that *there will be changes made!*

Multiple PLC- and PC-based control systems can be connected in a wide variety of ways. The communication method is very important, so important that a later chapter discusses various schemes. Some controllers need very little information from outside sources to control a machine or process. Yet, other controllers may not be able to function at all unless they have recipes or instructions on what to do. Different variations of PLC and PC control arrangements have emerged. Besides the stand-alone systems, it is sometimes necessary to tie controllers of "equal strength" together. In doing this, it has to be decided which is the master, as shown in block diagram form in Fig. 3-21, or whether all devices will be equal, or peers (as shown in Fig. 3-22).

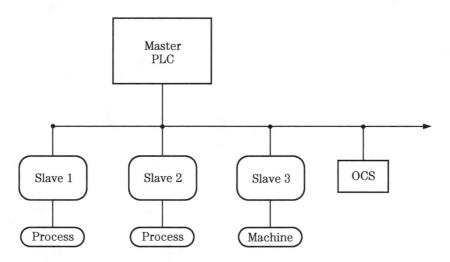

Fig. 3-21 A master-slave controller arrangement.

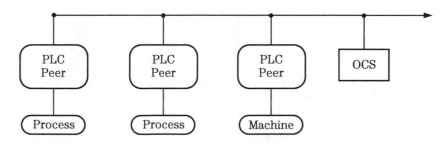

Fig. 3-22 A peer-to-peer controller arrangement.

A variation of the remote I/O drop is the master-slave format. Here, a master controller, or PLC, is in charge of many other slave devices. The key difference between this and an I/O drop is the capability of the slave device. The slave unit will have some processing power and thus does not have to rely on the master for all control and processing. However, the slave does rely on the master controller for instructions, and all communications have to be routed through this master. This approach can even have some implications relative to the distributed control system (DCS). These master-slave arrangements almost always require a redundant master in case the original master fails. If the master is out of service, then the slaves are also down. This approach is generally less expensive than a complete peer-to-peer system.

Figure 3-22 shows the typical peer-to-peer, or PLC-to-PLC, lineup. In this scheme, several PLCs (each able to process on its own) are connected via a high-speed network. In this configuration, each controller is in charge of its own process and is also in charge of its own communications. This means that each device must send, receive, and decipher its own transmission data and then be fully programmed to use those data to control the machine or process to which it is dedicated. In this scheme it is also customary to rotate communication control from device to device. This is known as *token passing*. The peer-to-peer system can keep other sections (peers) running when one of the other peer units has defaulted or is down.

4
CHAPTER

Basic Elements of Industrial Process and Motion Control

Soft logic control systems are personal computer–based systems which yield the same result as any other type of controller in an industrial process or on a motion-controlled machine. The difference is that instead of using proprietary, specialized controllers (often the PLC or process controller), the platform for control should be to utilize open technologies and more standard, off-the-shelf hardware. The manufacturing plant has one major goal—to make product and to make it better. It wants consistent, available, flexible, and reliable control equipment. And the plant will find it or will find ways to make it. With soft logic software proliferating and the increasing capabilities of the packages, more and more PC-based installations are going in every day. Whether it is replacing old controls or putting in an entire new process line, soft logic systems are getting strong consideration.

Whether controlled by a motion controller, a PLC, process controller, distributed control system, or relays (hopefully not too many of these are left out there, but solid-state is somewhat acceptable), a machine or process application still has fundamental needs. There will be starters, switches, lights, sensors, transducers, drives, human-machine interfaces, operator consoles, and displays, and the list goes on. The application will also have specific requirements for proper and safe operation. As this book looks at the various elements of PC-based control, it is necessary to understand some aspects of traditional control systems and the "interworking components" that eventually are controlled by the soft logic system. Several applications are discussed in Chap. 12, but first we give an overview of the basic components used with industrial process controllers and motion controllers.

Controller Systems

The obvious control system that is being replaced by PC-based controllers is the programmable logic controller. In Chap. 3 we reviewed basic concepts of computers and PLCs. There are tens of thousands of programmable logic controller systems in the manufacturing and industrial world. The various types of applications are too numerous to list here because for over two decades PLCs have been able to proliferate, mainly because it has been practically the only controller of choice. But this PLC industry and suppliers of its equipment found themselves each getting deeper into its own proprietary hardware and software. This was accepted by end users because they had manufacturing plants to run and products to make. These controllers were the tools that industry could use to prosper. As time went on, to change suppliers of control equipment became more and more difficult. It was more difficult because each year those people who knew the software, understood how to program and troubleshoot the system, and could make *that* PLC system work for their applications could not afford the time to change and relearn. Thus the phenomenon was perpetuated.

Many manufacturers of specialized process control devices began to offer their own process controllers, smart sensors, and elaborate control schemes. Any process control company could bring in a staff of computer engineers and develop its own dedicated process controller. Many of these looked much like the PLCs, but maybe they were packaged differently or merely specialized for that manufacturer's process or application. Many suppliers of these controller systems found "niches" for their equipment. Some became known for their expertise in steel or aluminum rolling mills. Others could do special cut-to-length applications, while still others could provide elaborate PID control systems. They were all different yet all the same. They all had common elements. They had to have a powerful microprocessor and a real-time operating system to be able to link with input and output modules (analog and digital), to communicate with other computerized equipment, and to reside in a physical package which was suitable for its particular plant environment. A soft logic controller system contains the same basic elements.

The PC-based control package has those common components yet is more available to the end user. This is possible because the personal and industrial computer industries have grown simultaneously with the PLC and process controller industries. However, the PC world has grown to be a much, much larger industry. Certain methods and components are used to create a soft logic controller system for a traditional PLC or process controller application. As is seen in Fig. 4-1, some components cannot be left out (the microprocessor, the I/O modules, the display, etc.). Additionally, other components may have to be added as an essential element to the package. For example, the positioning motor shown in block form in Fig. 4-2 needs an encoder module in order to solve the application. Thus controller systems can look alike but may come in many shapes and sizes. Also many controllers rely on other vital pieces of dedicated equipment.

AC and DC Drives

Many times a PC-based control system has to control the speed of motors via its soft logic. PLCs have been doing this for years. Many machines, pumps, and fans have

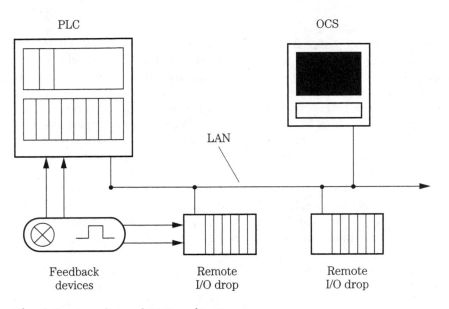

Fig. 4-1   A traditional PLC application.

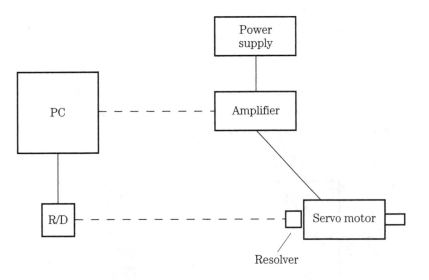

Fig. 4-2   PC-based servo system.

motors that have to be started, speed-controlled, stopped, monitored, and basically controlled by something. This can be done with bit setting and resetting (ONs and OFFs), analog voltage signals (0 to 10 V DC, 4 to 20 mA, 0 to 5 V DC, etc.), and other electric circuits. The associated motor control component is usually some type of starter system (which does not really control speed and torque because, as its name implies, it starts and stops a motor) or an AC or DC electronic drive, often called a motor controller. Electronic drives most often close some type of loop involving the motor. The AC drives can look at voltage or current feedback from the motor, pulses from an encoder, or changes in sine wave from a resolver. All this feedback has to be solved for, quickly, to keep ultimate control of the motor. The DC drive can look at armature voltage and current from the DC motor or digital/analog tachometer feedback. Again, feedback is key to constantly correcting any errors in the control loop. These feedback methods are shown in Fig. 4-3. Soft logic control has the potential to solve these closed loops, process the data fast, and perform all the algorithms needed to replicate an electronic drive. However, present soft logic systems employ interface modules that are dedicated to the handling of motion. These modules correct any errors in speed, current, or torque and handle the gating and firing of the power devices themselves. This process is sometimes referred to as *commutation.*

More and more, soft logic systems are becoming an integral part of motion control. Their role in actual motor control will probably grow as time goes on. The AC and DC drives, as well as the servo and stepper drives, are very sophisticated pieces of electronic control equipment. To better understand the role that a soft logic system does and will play, we look at the basics of these controllers.

The DC motor has been the workhorse of industry for nearly a century. To run that workhorse, a means of changing available three-phase AC power to DC power had to be developed. This became the rectifier, which eventually became the adjustable-speed

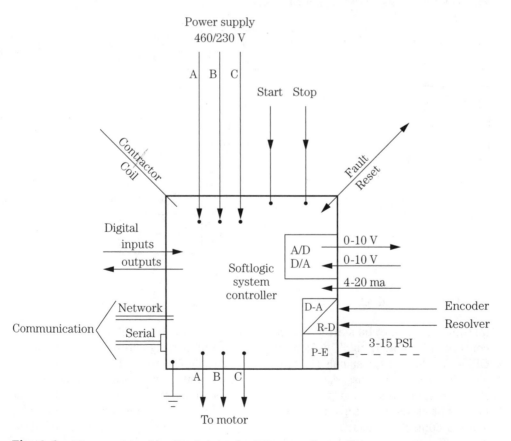

Fig. 4-3 Many types of feedback into the PC controller.

drive for the DC motor. With this basic concept of providing DC power to a plant's machinery and then controlling that power in order to change motor speed, industry grabbed hold of this technology, and it spread. Today, the DC drive is still alive but is slowly being displaced by AC technology. However, with advances in microprocessor-based systems and power electronics, the DC drive can serve a necessary role in manufacturing and production.

A DC drive can control either a shunt-wound DC motor or a permanent-magnet DC motor. The major difference, other than motor construction and performance, lies in the fact that permanent-magnet motors are used most often in applications requiring 5 Hp and below. They are not built beyond that size, whereas shunt-wound DC motors are common from fractions to thousands of horsepower. A PC-based control system could be used to control many small DC motors in a coordinated motion control system (as shown in Fig. 4-4) or in the high-horsepower, single-motor main line machine (as in Fig. 4-5).

The DC drive utilizes basic power conversion techniques to control both the speed and the torque of the DC motor. These approaches had to include means of controlling the speed of the DC motor under different load conditions. Some loads are hard to start while others need to have regeneration and/or reversing capability. Other applications may have constant load changes while the motor is running. A DC electronic drive must be able to dynamically change output levels of both voltage and current to a DC motor, in order to control speed and torque. It must be able to respond appropriately to all types of load changes. Today's technology utilizes solid-state electronics to accomplish just that.

The DC drive's equivalent circuit is shown in Fig. 4-6. The two main components where power must be controlled are the armature and the field of the DC motor. In addition to maintaining proper field voltage and field current, the DC drive must control, or regulate, the voltage and current to the armature of the motor. This can be seen in Figs. 4-7 and 4-8. The torque T is proportional to the armature current, and the speed N is proportional to the voltage. Thus, today's DC drives have fairly sophisticated current and voltage regulators. This attention to the armature will make or break a DC drive's overall performance in a given application. A further look at the DC drive equivalent circuit shows a rectifier circuit. There are different configurations of the rectifier network, and by fixing the firing angle a half-wave (Fig. 4-9), full-wave (Fig. 4-10), or complete three-phase full-wave (Fig. 4-11) rectifier can be configured. The firing angle can be described as the instant in time at which the thyristor is triggered to conduct. Obviously, the immediate differences in these rectifiers lie in the single- and three- phase nature of the power, the component count, and cost weighed against performance.

In the full-wave rectifier circuit shown in Fig. 4-11, the AC sine wave is converted more efficiently and more completely than in the other rectifier schemes. There is a net effect of gaining a positive output from the bridge configuration, even when the input goes negative. This is because the output pulses go positive. In the negative half-cycle, diodes D-2 and D-4 will be forward-biased, and thus the polarity will be positive at D-2. Similarly, in the positive half-cycle, diodes D-1 and D-3 will be forward-biased and thus a positive output is achieved. The thyristor in most of the aforementioned rectifier circuits is the diode; however, there are some SCR-based rectifier networks which are extremely common.

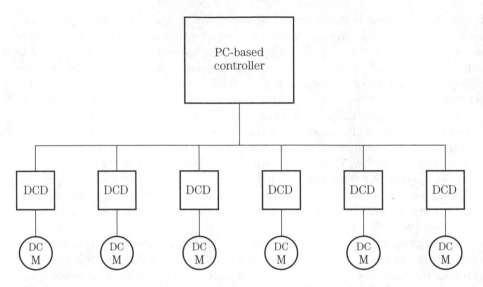

Fig. 4-4   Several DC motors and drives are controlled by one PC.

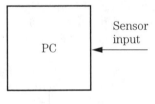

Fig. 4-5
One high-horsepower DC
drive controlled by a PC.

Direct-current drives usually can be classified into two main groups: transistorized DC drives and thyristor, or SCR-based, DC drives. The transistorized DC drive many times is the unit that controls a permanent-magnet motor. However, the most common is the thyristor, or SCR-based unit, because it is available to a much larger power range. This SCR-based DC drive is usually in the form of an SCR phase-controlled circuit. Since the SCR can be given a very small gate voltage compared to the amount of load-carrying capacity it can provide, it is the thyristor of choice in most DC drive designs. In summary, the speed command and DC motor feedback (both voltages in the form of back-emf and motor current) are compared

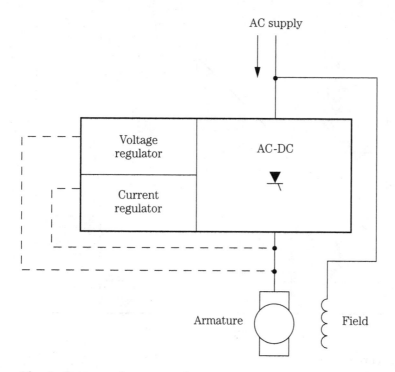

Fig. 4-6   A DC drive equivalent circuit.

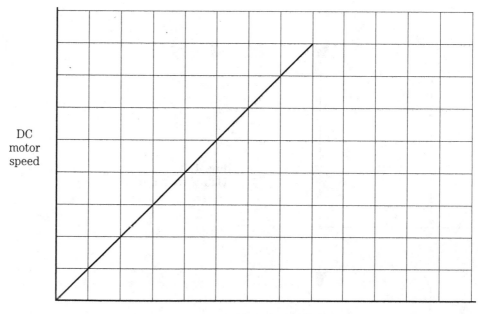

Fig. 4-7   Armature voltage.

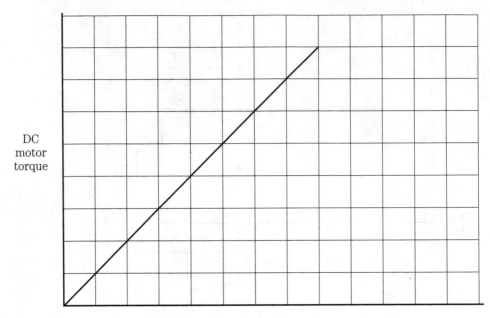

Armature current

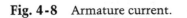

Fig. 4-8   Armature current.

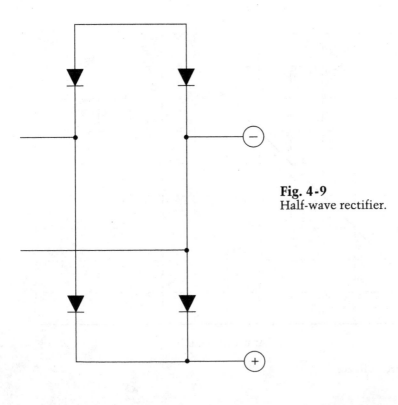

Fig. 4-9
Half-wave rectifier.

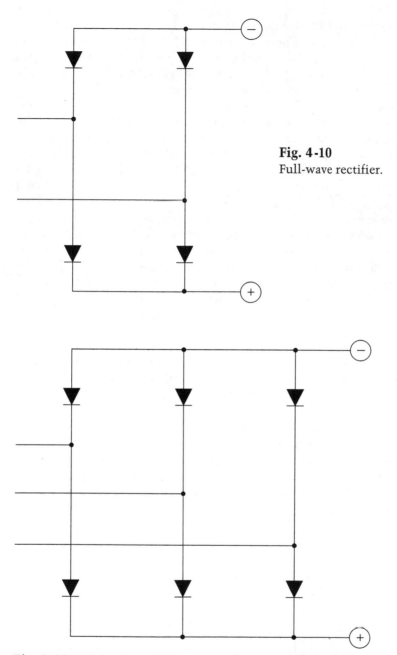

Fig. 4-10
Full-wave rectifier.

Fig. 4-11   Three-phase full-wave rectifier.

in the regulator. This updated value is then compared to the zero-crossing waveform of the SCRs. Then a new firing command is generated, and the cycle is repeated. The number of comparisons per second and the accuracy of these updates are actually the response of the drive system. These criteria separate good DC drive controllers from bad.

Since the transistorized DC drive usually is applied to specialized DC motor applications, such as running a permanent-magnet motor, it is not as common as the SCR-based DC drive. In any case, the DC drive controls the speed of a DC motor via two major power circuits: the armature bridge and the field bridge. Other necessary components are the control circuitry and the feedback circuitry.

The AC motor is the "other" electric motor used in industry. It traditionally was viewed as the lighter-duty variable-torque machine. It could be started and run at full speed by a device called a *starter*. The DC motors and drives were working just fine on tougher applications and machines. But then came the AC drive and variations of it which allowed for enhanced AC motor speed and torque control. The AC drive could actually control a motor so well that the performance of a DC motor and drive was duplicated. Additionally, an AC drive could soft-start (ramp) a motor to its base speed just as a reduced-voltage starter could. But this AC drive could allow the motor to be run at any speed, unlike the starter equipment which has to let the AC motor run at full speed.

Although AC drives were discussed in some detail in Chap. 2, these drives have many other benefits for the application. Many times the AC drive can provide real energy savings as it runs at reduced speeds. Not only will it start and stop the AC motor, but also the AC drive protects the AC motor from dangerous overload conditions and the AC motor can be run directly from the supply power, bypassing the AC drive, in an emergency (this cannot be done with a DC motor). An AC drive provides a good, constant power factor throughout the speed range and can run an AC motor past its base speed. The AC drive technology has also evolved to the point where the drive can be configured into a flux vector drive, thus yielding DC motor–like performance. A block diagram of a typical AC drive and motor along with a master PC-based controller is shown in Fig. 4-12.

There is a movement within industry that reflects the displacing of DC motors and drives by AC motors and drives. This has been ongoing for over 15 years and will continue, especially as the AC drive technology matures. The DC motors will still be used throughout industry for certain applications and by users who simply prefer using DC motors. But as the costs of AC products come down, regenerative bridges become readily available; and as AC drives prove themselves, more and more AC installations will prevail over the DC system.

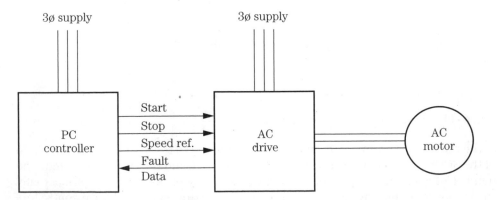

Fig. 4-12   PC-based control of an AC drive and motor.

Likewise, soft logic control systems must gain full acceptance within the motion control community. Users and OEMs must continue to review the technology and explore the capabilities of these emerging PC-based products. Many facets of motion control exist today with multitasking, high-speed microprocessors. There are many soft logic options, interface modules, and associated tools available to the users of motors and controls. Many thousands of AC and DC drives and motors are presently controlled all over the world by PLCs and process controllers. The degree of control is typically simple, but nonetheless these drives are wired to an I/O controller. Thus if a soft logic system can emulate a PLC for process control, then it can certainly do a fine job with any motion a PLC has been controlling.

Servo Drive Systems

Just as soft logic systems are called upon to control AC and DC drives, there is an additional need to control servo motors and stepper motors. These high-performance, closed-loop motion control packages are used mainly for motor shaft position control and fast torque response. These systems do require high-speed processing and high-integrity feedback devices and typically have to be programmed by someone who understands the application well. Many companies offer motion interface cards which allow a soft logic system to basically instruct the motor, or motors, in a coordinated scheme. These instructions typically tell the motor how many revolutions it is supposed to turn, but the actual commutation is done within the high-response motion card. This motion control process has been stated in an oversimplified form, but to better understand servo and stepper motion control, we discuss some of the basics of the industry.

Up to this point we have been concerned with AC and DC drives. Servomotors and step motor drives are actually provided AC or DC power also. They are, however, usually referred to not as AC or DC drives but rather as servos, steppers, DC brushless and sometimes AC brushless packages. These electronic drive systems are the most versatile and can be used on the widest variety of applications. However, they are also potentially the most expensive and most complicated for comparable horsepower. There is as well a limitation in that servo systems typically do not allow for more than 50 Hp. A servo, or servomechanism, in its basic sense can be defined as an automatic device which can control large amounts of power by means of lesser amounts of power. Additionally, a servo system has the ability to automatically correct performance of a mechanism. A servo system can consist of a specific control component, a device to amplify signals, the device or actuator which receives the signal, and some type of feedback. This can be seen in Fig. 4-13. Servo systems are actually any programmable motion control systems, and they can be found in many nonelectronic drive installations such as with hydraulic systems utilizing servo valves.

More appropriate to electronic drive controllers, servo systems mainly comprise a servo motor, amplifier, power supply, and controller (which many times closes the position loop). The permanent-magnet, brushless motors are electronically commutated instead of using the conventional brushes and commutator. The amplifier is sometimes referred to as the drive, and it also can act as the positioner. Actually the amplifier and controller together can equate to an electronic drive. The amplifier

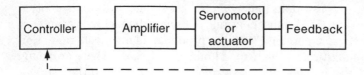

Fig. 4-13　Servo loop feedback.

houses the power devices, and the controller houses the "smarts." The amplifier takes reference and feedback signals and outputs a specific, "amplified" speed and torque signal to the servomotor. The duration and timing of these output signals provide basic position control. The last component is the power supply; and without this device, the amplifier cannot perform. Thus we have all the makings of a servo system. We look further at each of these components.

One of the basic rules in speaking "drive-ese" is to discuss power requirements in terms of torque not horsepower. This should be the rule for all applications, but most often people seem to equate the power, size, and capability of a motor system to its horsepower, and this can lead to misapplications. Torque is the force that does the work as the motor shaft rotates. Servo people talk in inch-pounds of torque. Sometimes the analysis is done in foot-pounds of torque, but this is less common as servo systems usually are smaller and foot-pounds of torque will have to be converted to inch-pounds, or even ounce-inches, later anyway. The upper limit in servomotor construction is about 800 in·lb. This is due in part to motor construction, the magnets, and the fact that, in high-torque applications, it is less expensive to provide a high-precision gearbox to get the output torque than to pay for a larger servomotor and amplifier. Also as the power requirements get higher, high performance in positioning accuracy is not as critical. High-accuracy positioning is a big part of servo application.

Servo drive systems can be used to control speeds of motors down to a virtual crawl, with turn-down ratios of 10,000:1 and greater. Speed accuracy, or regulation, can be held to 0.01 percent or better. The response of the overall system, or bandwidth, is extremely fast. The servo system can also hold to very tight torque accuracy, meaning that as the load changes, so will the servo torque, or current regulator. It will correct quickly and can also provide more than adequate values of stall torque when its amplifier is sized accordingly.

Since a servo system is just that—a system—a motion control system which provides high-performance, closed-loop speed or position control, it has to have several integral components in order to work. The servo drive can control a brush-type motor or a brushless motor. Closed-loop control of a brush-type motor is not done frequently and not done well. Therefore, for our purposes we discuss strictly brushless systems. Yet, this still makes for some confusion, especially in terminology. There are brushless AC and brushless DC systems. They are basically the same. The brushless motor is a permanent-magnet motor with no brushes. A better description might be that the motor is a brushless synchronous motor with permanent magnets. The servomotor is also sometimes referred to as an "inside-out" motor because of the wound stator and permanent-magnet rotor. Some servomotors utilize permanent magnets while others are of the switched reluctance type. Whatever the name, it is the function and interactivity with the servo controls and feedback devices which make the servomotor work.

Servo amplifiers are classified much as their AC and DC drive counterparts—by their particular output. The brushless DC amplifier is a linear amplifier which generates a trapezoidal waveform to the servomotor for commutation. This waveform is compared to the feedback from the motor. Likewise, the brushless AC amplifier generates an AC waveform to the servomotor for commutation purposes which is also compared to the feedback from the servomotor.

The servo system control aspects can be broken down into three distinct areas: speed control, torque control, and position control. In addition, we look at coordinated control, later, as an separate, important entity of servo systems. First, looking at speed or velocity control with a servo system, in Fig. 4-14 we find that the goal is to accelerate to a required speed in a certain time, remain at that speed for a certain time, and then decelerate back to zero speed. Every motion control application will have this type of profile; however, times and speeds will obviously change. The critical accuracies to be held in the servo system for this type of profile relate to the quickness in changing speed states and holding at required states for the desired time, all with load.

As we discuss loading to a servo system, we have actually entered into a second type of control scheme. This can be seen in Fig. 4-15 as the torque profile. Here there is an accelerating torque component to the curve, a running torque component, a deceleration component, and a holding torque component (usually a zero speed). These, again, are based on time. Additionally, they typically relate directly to the velocity profile. This relationship is illustrated in Fig. 4-16. Thus we need torque while we accelerate, run, and decelerate. A servo system's ability to maintain exact control of both velocity (the actual speed desired) and torque (driving the load) is its gauge of accuracy and performance.

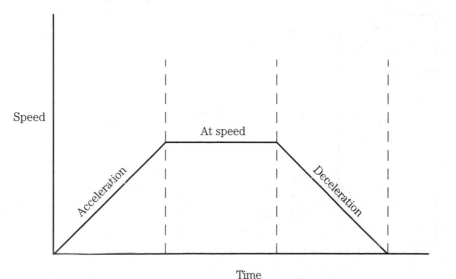

Fig. 4-14   Speed, or velocity, profile.

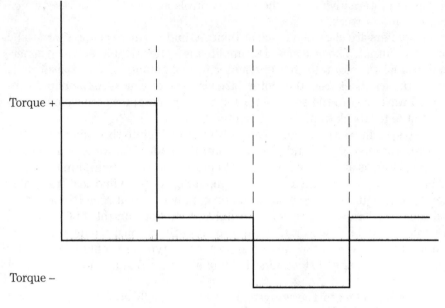

Fig. 4-15 Torque profile.

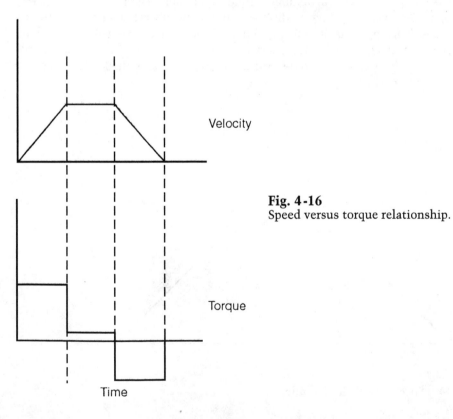

Fig. 4-16
Speed versus torque relationship.

The last control loop is the position loop. While it is not always needed in a servo system with velocity and torque profiles, it is the control loop most often associated with servo control. A typical position profile indicating servomotor shaft position versus time is shown in Fig. 4-17. Depending on the control technique used for the particular application, the drive controller can incorporate velocity or torque inner loops if necessary. Most often these inner control loops are included, but note that for every control loop used, there is a response time needed to perform that function. In servo systems, loop times are usually very critical to the success of the machine. As illustrated earlier, the position loop is the slowest of the three control loops.

A servo system really gets dramatic whenever there are multiple servomotors to control. This is where the controller gets more complicated. It usually comprises a shared bus arrangement for attaching several servos, or axes, to a common "mother board." In this manner, there can be a master controller telling the individual axes what to do, and each individual axis can solve for its own velocity, torque, or position loop (thus saving response time). A multiaxis, coordinated servo control scheme is shown in Fig. 4-18. These types of controllers are common in the machine tool industry where many servo drives and servomotors have to be controlled at the same time. In these types of systems, the component count increases; but some devices, such as power supplies, can be sized for multiple loads and thus reduce the component count somewhat.

Besides the basic controller, power supply, amplifier, and servomotor, the peripheral components in a servo system include the following (some applications may not require all):

- Power cables from servo amplifiers to motors
- Feedback cables from motor to controller
- Isolation transformers (not always needed but recommended)

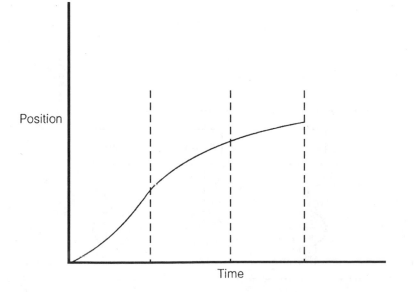

Fig. 4-17   Position profile.

- Power supplies to provide appropriate bus voltage
- Braking resistors to handle regeneration and fast deceleration
- Heat sinks for the amplifiers and power supplies
- Feedback devices, which may be the most critical component (examples include resolvers, Hall effect transducers, encoders, glass scales, and tachometers)

There are several other factors to consider when we look at the overall servo system. One is the system's bandwidth, the response factor of any drive system. Bandwidth is often described as the time a motor controller takes to correct from no load to a loaded condition. It is usually expressed in radians per second; and while AC and DC speed control drives have to utilize bandwidth in their control algorithms, a servo system lives and dies by its bandwidth. It is a drive system which is installed by virtue of its performance. It usually costs more initially and is more complicated than a DC or AC drive system. Thus, a higher-bandwidth system is more immune to disturbances and performs, or responds better, to produce better. One important factor associated with bandwidth is inertia, particularly load inertia and motor, or rotor, inertia. Other factors which affect system performance and bandwidth are backlash, belting, gearing, acceleration rates, overshoot, and torque ripple.

The fastest control loop is the current loop which is solving the new output, in amperage to the motor, based on actual motor current sensed in the servo amplifier by current transformers (CTs) in most cases. It has to be the fastest because the load, a current-dependent component of the system, has always got to be driven constantly and continuously. The next-fastest loop is the speed, or velocity, loop, which needs speed feedback from the motor rotating element, or rotor. Either a separately mounted tachometer or a similar device which can provide the appropriate

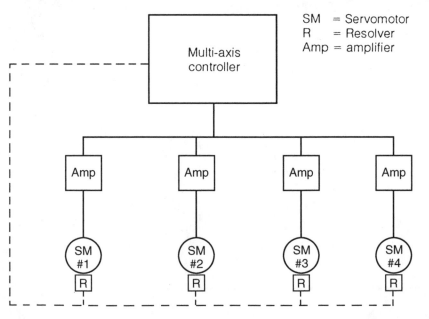

Fig. 4-18 Multiaxis controller block diagram.

pulses to translate to speed is needed. The slowest loop is that of position. However, good servo systems have position loop update times of 5 to 10 ms so as to hold to some very tight positioning accuracy. Of course, many variables can affect each loop's performance such as temperature or sloppiness of the system mechanics, but starting with a high-response amplifier and controller is paramount.

The type of feedback devices used can vary, and for servo systems the feedback device is an integral part. Some devices can provide feedback data which can be used to calculate both new speed and new position requirements. An encoder is able to provide output in the form of pulses which can be used to tell rotor position and to count those same pulses for a given period for just speed correction. Some encoders are absolute, which know where the the motor shaft position is upon power-up, while others are incremental. Another device is the resolver, and its feedback must go through an R/D (resolver-to-digital) converter so as to be useful in the controller or amplifier. This R/D conversion also may be a limiting area in the servo system's resolution. Check the R/D converter's resolution as to how many bits that conversion solves to. Note that encoder, or tachometer, or resolver feedback can be accepted into a given amplifier or controller, but not all at once. Also, different manufacturers have different standards for their set algorithms, and they expect certain types of feedback into their products.

The stability of a servo system is dependent on how well the critical components are tuned and matched with one another. Many times this stability is discovered during the initial start-up of the drive equipment with the actual loads. This is when actual tuning of the gain circuits is best accomplished. As we have seen, any servo system's critical components are the servomotor, amplifier, power supply, and controller. These components accept some input signal and respond with some output signal. This relationship to signals can be referred to as the *gain* of the system. The gain is adjustable and will make the system's performance good or bad. Often called *tuning* a system, adjusting the gain of the system determines such performance issues as smoothness, amount of overshoot, ringing, and oscillation.

The *velocity gain* is the system's speed error multiplied by this gain value to correct the loop. This can be seen graphically in Fig. 4-19. The velocity loop gain provides a means of compensation whenever there is a wide range of load inertia in the system. The *proportional gain* is used in positioning servo systems. This adjustment controls the overall response of the servo system and the magnitude of any positional following error. As is seen in Fig. 4-19, the system positional error is multiplied by the proportional gain. The *integral gain* is more concerned with the positional error at zero speed. Thus this gain is multiplied by the zero-speed position error, and the net effect is that the motor stiffness is improved and the positioning accuracy of the moves is fully controlled. The last gain, *derivative gain,* probably is the hardest to "tweak." This gain controls the dampening and ringing of the servomotor shaft during acceleration. The system positional error due to the position error rate of change is multiplied by the derivative gain.

Another task that a soft logic system presently will have a hard time doing is the tuning of the servo system. It is a straightforward task as long as all the system and machine components are functioning properly. *Proper* in this sense means that mechanical components are tight, basklash is minimal, and everything is electrically

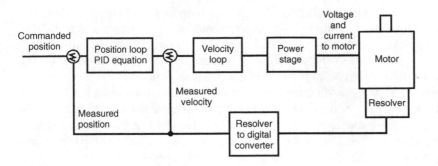

Fig. 4-19   Typical gains in a servo system.

sound. Observing the machine performance with actual loading and making the necessary gain adjustments in discrete increments are the method by which the most can be "gained" from the system. However, advanced application sizing and attention to mechanical details will save time at start-up. A real-life example of a servo system with poorly tuned gains is a robot, whose individual axes are each servomotor-driven, that tries to move a delicate part from point *A* to point *B*. Instability and unwanted mechanical vibrations can cause potential problems. The servomotors can overshoot, as illustrated earlier. This can lead to a condition called *ringing,* in which the servo system tries to correct itself but never quite does. In a well-tuned servo system, the critical components have been sized and matched with one another and have proper gain values programmed, and the user runs the system within the specified operating guidelines.

There are also many other factors to consider when one is designing a servo system. There are many other application requirements which have to be addressed. Following is a partial list:

- What is the load, will it change frequently, and is it of high inertia?
- Is there a shock component associated with the load?
- How fast must the servomotor accelerate? Decelerate?
- What are the complete cycle times? This factors into heat dissipation and actual motor and amplifier size.
- In positioning, what is the positioning tolerance accuracy requested?
- What maximum and minimum speeds are needed from the servomotor?
- Is there known friction in the system?
- What is the load and machine inertia? How does this value match to the rotor inertia of the servomotor? If acceleration is important, then a good match is required. A 1:1 ratio is ideal for load inertia reflected to the motor. A gear reduction scheme may be in order to better match that inertia.
- What inputs and outputs will be required of the servo controller? Discrete and/or analog? (This is handled very well by the soft logic controller.)
- Communications now play an integral role. How will they apply in the application?

Matching the components in a servo system is always a challenge. A PC-based system can be used in many instances. There seem to be many variables for a given application. Careful attention should be given to the inertia of the load being driven, the inertias of the mechanical drivetrain components, and that of the motor selected. This is called *inertia matching,* and it involves numerous calculations. The actual inertia of each component must be calculated and accounted for. These data are needed in order to match a servomotor to provide good acceleration and deceleration performance. The mechanics of these common systems have to be analyzed for every servo or stepper application. Likewise, when one is sizing and matching system components, the torque requirements must be considered. Peak torques and accelerating torques must be calculated along with the inertias. Once these values are known, a servo system can be pieced together. It might be better to leave component selection and the lengthy calculations to the manufacturers, as they routinely do this and can head off any glaring problems. And this may make them responsible for the system's performance and integrity.

Applications in which servo systems and programmable motion control systems are prominent would mainly be in the machine tool and robotics industries. Grinders, lathes, and milling and boring machines are good applications for servo control, in order to hold position for tight tolerances around a part. The same can be said of robotic applications. A servo system can be used for simple speed regulation, but much of its capability is wasted. Most likely the cost of the complete system with all its components dictates where it will be used.

Feedback Devices, Transducers, and Sensors

Sensors and feedback devices in the plant keep the process together. Their proper, reliable operation will make or break any machine application. Compared to computers, electronic drives, and programmable controllers, they are often paid the least attention until they are suspected of being the cause of a problem. At this point everyone asks, How could such an inexpensive component in the factory cause a full machine to completely shut down? These sensing and feedback devices are very important to the uptime and performance of machines. These components provide the valuable information which allows any system to correct itself. Without these feedback devices, automating a plant would not be possible.

Take a look at any piece of automated equipment in the factory. There will be some sort of feedback device providing position, speed, temperature, pressure, or another type of process information. This information is vital to the automated plant's ability to keep producing. Many machines and processes, although it is not always obvious, are using some means of feedback. It might be safe to assume that if there is control, then there is feedback. Most electric motors, if controlled, have a speed sensor, position sensor, or both types of sensors keeping them at speed or in position. Numerically controlled (NC) and computerized numerically controlled (CNC) equipment, being high-precision machines, only function properly with feedback devices. Likewise, any process being monitored or controlled will have sensor technology at work.

Feedback is not always obvious. Many processes are happening around us that we often take for granted. We take for granted that there is some loop closing in that process in order to control it. Take, for instance, the industrial oven or dryer.

Just like the ones in the home, there had better be some device to shut off the fuel to the heater, or else something is going to burn. There is a temperature sensor simply either cycling the heat on or raising and lowering the heat to satisfy the temperature setting. Likewise, some motors are part of an electric circuit which includes a motor controller. Voltage from the motor can be monitored to control the motor's speed. Perhaps the best example of behind-the-scenes feedback is the human operator. How often have we asked, How is the machine being controlled now? The answer comes back: "Our operator, Arthur, goes over to the machine and turns a lever a half turn or so, and the machine is back to where we like it!" Arthur is the feedback device. He is continually correcting the system. This is a prime setting for implementing some automatic sensor or feedback device to perform the same function. The result might even be more consistent.

Open-Loop and Closed-Loop Control

To understand how and when to use sensing devices, it is first necessary to review open-loop control versus closed-loop control. Open-loop control, in its most basic form, does not lend itself well to fully automating anything. Taking a look at Fig. 4-20, we find that an input signal, or command, is given and a direct resultant output is achieved. We do not affect the signals, and we do not know if what we requested actually happened. It might be safe to assume that if an open-loop control scheme is at work, there are no sensors or feedback devices present in that system. If a valve is opened, liquid flows until someone shuts it off. If a switch is thrown to a motor, the motor runs at full speed until someone opens the switch. Then the motor stops. Say we want to fill a tank with hot and cold liquid, maintaining 155°F. However, there is no temperature sensor, and the tank is out of sight of the shutoff valves. We start the process and hope that the correct mix of hot and cold is there and that the tank does not overflow. If we only were using some type of feedback devices.

These all seem like manual systems, not too automatic at all. How does the controller know if the proper function is being performed or how well that function is being performed? It does not. Walk through an older factory. Most processes are handled via an open-loop system and operator intervention. In these cases the operator can be likened to the feedback device. But even operators make mistakes, get delayed, or just are not nearby when an event must happen.

A true closed-loop system can be seen in Fig. 4-21. Note that there is now another component in the diagram which is providing information about the process. This information returns to a summing, or comparison, point for analysis, and then new output is provided based on the comparison with the process input signal, or the "what should we be doing?" signal. This is a cause-and-effect relationship between

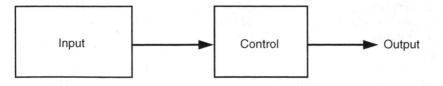

Fig. 4-20   Open-loop control.

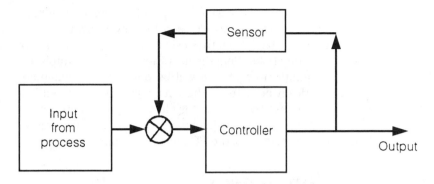

Fig. 4-21   Closed-loop control.

devices. The feedback device tells of any actual error in holding to the prescribed condition, and the controller attempts to correct for that error. A closed-loop control scheme is constantly correcting itself. A good example of a closed-loop system is a cruise control function in an automobile. A speed-sensing device located about the car's wheels lets us know how fast the car is traveling, and that information is fed back to a control point to compare to the desired speed. The more often the error signal is sampled (sent, received, and corrected), the better the overall system accuracy. This we often assume to be the police officer's "lee-weigh" in letting us get away with a couple extra miles per hour!

The PID control scheme is a common closed-loop system. The proportional-integral-derivative control loop is discussed in Chap. 12, but has meaning when it pertains to feedback devices. Without these transducers or feedback devices, there can be no proportional, integral, or derivative loops to control. There is no closing of any loop whatsoever. Once again, open-loop control is the absence of feedback devices. There are two types of closed-loop feedback: negative and positive. Negative feedback will reduce the variable in the controller's routine, which will make a change to the process or machine. The direction of the signal, negative or down in voltage, for instance, will be interpreted by the controller as reason to change the output accordingly. Conversely, for positive feedback, the feedback signal's direction requests an increase to the variable which the feedback represents.

Closed-loop systems are at work in many newer, automated factories and even can be incorporated on many older pieces of equipment. The latter is sometimes difficult to do because the feedback devices will be precise, responsive, and repeatable. This can be problematic to an older piece of equipment with sloppy mechanics and backlash. Sometimes it is better to retrofit much of the machine or start over with many new components when one is making a closed-loop system. Other times, installing the feedback device is the only reason to disturb the system (by putting a feedback device in, Arthur does not have to keep adjusting the machine). However, installing one device may mean that two or three other components have to be changed also. Ideally, it is more predictable and desirable to have all new components, with known mechanical and electrical values and constants, when one is trying to automate a system or process. Given the choice, a designer will always ask to have all new components.

The closed-loop system will contain at least one type of sensor or feedback device. Many applications require more than one. The soft logic system will have to accommodate any and all types of feedback from these sensors. These can be any of several types for many different functions. Some sensors may be used simply for counting while others measure temperature. Some will be photoelectric while another type might simply be electrically actuated. Others may use fiber-optic cabling to transmit information while some use two-conductor electric wire. Whatever the application, there is an appropriate sensing device available and usually a way to handle the sensor or feedback device signal at the PC-based controller.

Speed and Position Sensors

As discussed earlier, motion control would not be possible if it were not for feedback devices. Since motion usually involves a rotating element, or electric motor, the feedback devices are most often directly connected, or coupled, to a motor shaft. Thus as the shaft spins, the sensing device gathers speed or position data or both. Prior to feedback devices in the electric motor control arena, there were attempts to control the motors with the electrical data available. AC motors can provide a form of feedback in the electric circuit called *counter*-electromotive force, or counter-emf. These electrical data can be used by a motor controller to determine how fast a motor is running, with some inaccuracies. Depending on how well the speed has to be regulated for the given motor and application, this means of feedback can be adequate. Similarly, a DC motor, when controlled by a rectifier circuit, can provide armature voltage feedback for speed regulation. As the controller sets the output to the motor, the electric circuit either in the AC or DC situation is monitored to maintain the desired speed.

As speed regulation has to be held better and better, better feedback means must be incorporated into the system. Rather than relying on counter-emf or armature feedback, we might install a simple tachometer. This device attaches to the motor and produces a voltage output to the controller in the form of some many volts per 1000 r/min at the motor. With this information we now have a more accurate way of comparing the actual speed with the commanded speed, and we can correct. There are presently other devices which can provide even more precise information for motor speed control, and their use will only improve the speed regulation in a particular process.

Encoders

One such device to enhance speed and often shaft position is the encoder, or digital pulse tachometer. These are shaft-mounted devices which work on the principle of electric light pulses through a disk with coding, or slots over one revolution of the disk, and utilize a light pickup sensing device to count the light pulses. In this way, data relating to where the disk is and how fast it is turning can be sent to a computer for decisive action. The encoder basically translates mechanical motion to electronic signals. A depiction of this electronic signal is a pulse train and is shown in Fig. 4-22. This feedback device is often called an *optical encoder,* tach (short for

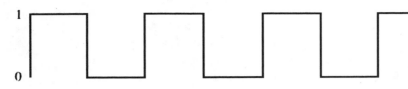

Fig. 4-22   An encoder-pulse train.

tachometer), pulse tachometer, or pulse generator. Understanding what it can do for an application and how it works is more important.

There are two types of encoders. The more common and less expensive is the incremental encoder. The other is the absolute encoder. There are also two versions of each: rotary (the most common) and linear. For discussion purposes we mainly refer to the rotary type. The incremental encoder is made up of the light source, disk, light receptor, grid, and amplifier. As seen in Fig. 4-23, the circular disk has several slots along its perimeter. This disk can be made from glass material with marks imprinted as the slots, or it can be made of metal with precision, machined slots on the outer edge. The light is emitted through the slot and received by the receptor through the grid assembly, and then the signal is amplified and sent to a host for further use. This entire sequence can be seen in Fig. 4-24.

The quantity of slots on a disk is also critical to the application. We often hear encoders specified as having 1024 or 2048 pulses per revolution, most often in powers of 2, which keeps us consistent with binary mathematics for computers and which will aid in the absolute encoder disk design later. This quantity often dictates the resolution, or how accurately the feedback signal begins. If we desire high precision, then we request more pulses per revolution to start. Also, keep in mind that more slots on the disk probably will mean greater expense and a physically larger-diameter disk. Additionally, there has to be a marker pulse somewhere on the disk to use as a reference.

With an absolute encoder package the disk is mainly the big difference. This can be seen in Fig. 4-25. Here the disk has a unique slot design, and it almost looks pretty. But there is a definite reason for the pattern. These slots are actually concentric, becoming larger as they get closer to the center of the disk, and again there is a binary relationship to the pattern. By passing light through all the slots at a given instant, the encoder can provide an exact position. This method of absolute decoding solves for the binary patterns on the disk. These types of encoders are mainly used for positioning applications where position is needed in case there is a power interruption. Also, there does not have to be a "homing" sequence performed to find a starting reference point.

Most encoders employ a quadrature form of decoding. Here, a second channel employs a second light source and receptor. The second channel is physically positioned within the encoder a half-slot distance away from the other channel. By doing this, there will be more available data points, as seen in Fig. 4-26, to work with. This can provide better resolution (i.e., more pulses per revolution). This quadrature approach also allows for the detection of rotational direction—forward or reverse.

These units can be large or small and can be mounted in different ways. Attention should given to applying these devices. Glass disks can sometimes collect a film

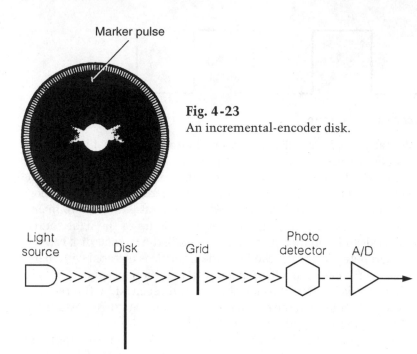

Marker pulse

Fig. 4-23
An incremental-encoder disk.

Light source   Disk   Grid   Photo detector   A/D

Fig. 4-24   The electronics of an optical encoder.

Fig. 4-25
An absolute-encoder disk.

on the surface, thus impeding good light transmission. They also can break. Metal disks, although more expensive, may be a better choice. Protecting the electronics and disks within is achieved by various housing methods. The mounting and housing of the encoder are very critical to its successful and extended use. If it is mounted loosely or misaligned, this condition can cause premature bearing failure on the rotating element of the encoder. Likewise, providing an adequate enclosure around the electronics and the disk will keep them working properly for longer periods.

With such a device providing more accurate speed information and providing that same information faster to the controller, motor shaft speeds can be maintained to even 1 or 2 r/min in a steady-state load condition. Of course, loads tend to change, and this makes our encoder control system work harder at trying to continually make corrections. But that is its purpose as a feedback device. Consider the alternative without the feedback—Arthur? Good, clean, fast feedback is necessary. This is the ongoing battle for true motion control in the automated factory.

Additionally, as the desired accuracy of a particular feedback device increases, so, too, does its cost.

Figure 4-27 shows a sample specification for a digital pulse tachometer which is suitable for harsh environments. Shown are the electrical specifications along with the mechanical specifications. Both are important to the successful installation of the device. The electrical specifications indicate what type of electrical output should be expected. The mechanical specifications show how well suited the particular unit is to the environment and duty cycle.

Mechanically, this particular housing for mill environments is machined anodized aluminum, with the shaft made from type-416 stainless steel. Both metals are corrosion-resistant. The shaft mounting is 20 mm. The shaft rotation contains no backlash. Zero backlash is the absence of mechanical "play" if the shaft were turned. The shaft can turn in both the forward and reverse directions with no effect on the motor to which it is attached. The whole mechanical and physical purpose of the pulse tachometer is to basically ride "free-wheeling" with the motor shaft, adding as little inertia and extra torque as feasible. It has low torque and inertia values. Its slew speed is rated at 5000 r/min. Slew speed is a state in an application where time is made up in a motion profile. In simpler terms, the motor is run at its maximum possible speed for short periods. Bearings are a very important issue with any feedback device attached and expected to run on a motor. If the bearings are a weak link, then the entire process can go down without notice. In this case the bearings have a life expectancy of 20 billion r. The lifetime in hours depends on the speeds at which the motor and tachometer run. The bearings are sealed with grease, thus making them basically maintenance-free. The cover is made of extruded aluminum, and the connectors are MS, or military style, which screw-down for extra protection. The tachometer has good shock and vibration characteristics. All in all, if the tachometer can stand up in a mill environment, then it can stand up in most application environments.

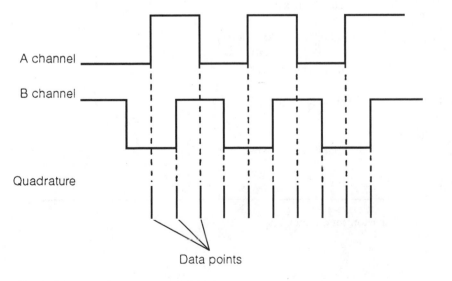

Fig. 4-26 Quadrature-signal decoding.

ELECTRICAL SPECIFICATIONS

Code   -   Incremental, Optical

Cycles per
  Revolution   -   on Code Disc: 60 - 2540 (others available)

Supply Voltage-   12-24 VDC +/- 5%

Supply Current
  (88C30)   -   CMOS - 150 mA max, 125 mA, typical

Output Signal -   Square Wave, Including:
                                  - 2 Channels, phased 90 degrees Inverted Push-Pull Signal
                                  - Differently Driven
                                  - In Quadrature, +/-2 degrees
                                  - With Marker Pulse

Temperature   -   Operating, 40 degrees C to 100 degrees C

Output
  Protection   -   Power Supply Reversal

MECHANICAL SPECIFICATIONS

Housing   -   NEMA 13
                        -          Material - 6061 Anodized Aluminum
                        -          Seal - O-Ring

Shaft Size   -   0.4998" (+.0000, -.0005)
                        -        0.6245" (Optional)
                        -          303 Stainless Steel

Shaft Seal   -   Teflon Graphite

Moment of
  Inertia   -   550 gm-cm squared

Weight   -   12lb.

Fig. 4-27   Specification for an encoder.

Electrically, it is supplied with a low voltage: 12 to 24 V DC. This voltage value must be held within 5 percent plus or minus, or else the output functionality will suffer. The output is a low-voltage pulse in the form of a square wave. This square wave is made up of two channels, 90 electrical degrees out of phase from each other (quadrature). The signal is differentially driven with a marker pulse (home or null). The pulse-to-pulse accuracy is equal to ±2 arc minutes in 1 rms (root mean square). It has a workable frequency range of 0 to 100 kHz, which refers to the clock, or crystal, speed for stable velocity determination. Its operating temperature range is 0 to 70°C, or −32 to 178°F. This means that it can continue to operate at an ambient temperature in this range.

Resolvers

Resolvers are another type of feedback device used primarily in motion control applications. They are different from the encoder and pulse generator in that there are no electronics at the resolver; it is separately excited from a source external to the physical resolver, itself. The resolver is a rotary transformer, with a rotor component and a stator component. It is, in essence, a small AC motor excited by a voltage to itself. When it is attached to the shaft of a motor, alignment is very critical. A flexible coupling can provide some cushion, but this feedback device needs to be mounted as concentric to the motor shaft as possible, to minimize premature failures or bad readings.

The waveshape of the resolver is actually what is being looked at in the circuit. Because the resolver is excited by a sine wave, low-voltage signal, this signal can be decoded within the controller (with power source). This decoding is accomplished through a resolver-to-digital (R/D) conversion. The converter is actually looking at displacement in the returning sine wave to determine shaft location. In this way, the loop is closed to the motor, or rotating device. Accuracies for resolver systems are presented in arc minutes and usually are 6 to 7 arc minutes for most resolvers.

The attractive features about a resolver are the fact that there are no electronics which have to be located at the motor assembly, thus making it more suitable for nastier environments. Also, the resolver is an absolute measuring device. It can retain the exact position of a motor shaft even through a power outage. The feedback from the resolver can be driven great distances, over 1000 ft if necessary, with good resilience to noise. However, it is always recommended that signal wiring be routed separate from any power wiring wherever possible. A single resolver can provide resolution accuracies in some cases up to a 14-bit number, or 16,384 counts. Dual resolver packages can also be utilized and can greatly increase the measurement accuracy in a particular feedback system. In these cases, a fine resolver is geared to a coarse resolver at some ratio. Common ratios are 64:1 and 32:1.

Magnetic Pickups

There are different versions of what are called *magnetic pickups*. This class of feedback device can act much as a resolver; or in other instances a gear, or toothed wheel, can be installed in conjunction with a magnetic pickup sensing device, as shown in Fig. 4-28. In either case, the objective is to get rotating-shaft position data accurately and consistently. The magnetic pickup sensor, working in unison with the toothed wheel, counts the teeth on the gear as they pass. Once set up and properly aligned, this magnetic sensor is fairly reliable. Depending on the environment, the initial cost expectations, and motor/controller application, the magnetic pickup device selected is a critical component. Its selection and application should be fully evaluated.

In addition to motion control sensors in the factory, the soft logic system can be linked to other feedback devices. These devices will be of different types and sizes and can have dedicated functions. These types include temperature, pressure, flow, and ultrasonic. These other sensors will have very similar needs to the motion sensors previously discussed. They will need a good, steady-state power supply. Stable and fast clocks must be incorporated into the control loop. They will be required to network with plant host computers and many other discrete computerized pieces of equipment.

Transducers

A very common feedback device used in gauging, measuring, and detecting displacement is the transducer. A *transducer* usually is defined as a device which converts mechanical energy to electrical output. A better, more appropriate definition is that variations of this device can convert any input energy, including electrical, to output energy. The output energy will, in turn, be different from the known input energy, thus supplying useful feedback information from which closed-loop control and correction can be achieved. There are literally hundreds of different kinds of transducers, and there are just as many ways to provide the input and output to the transducers. Pneumatic, hydraulic, and electrical types are the most common.

Transducers providing an electrical output send sometimes a voltage signal, 0 to 10 V DC, and sometimes a current signal, commonly 4 to 20 mA, with 4 mA being an off condition and 20 mA being full on and any value in between being the range of the transducer. This range signal is generated from a stimulus to the transducer and corresponds to some direct action from which the tranducer's output signal is going. For instance, a process involving the unwinding and rewinding of a material, shown in Fig. 4-29, utilizes a linear displacement transducer, sometimes called a *dancer.* Changes in the dancer position correspond to a voltage drop across a resistor. This voltage output value from the transducer indicates how loose or tight is the web

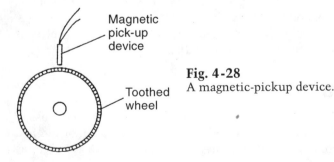

Fig. 4-28
A magnetic-pickup device.

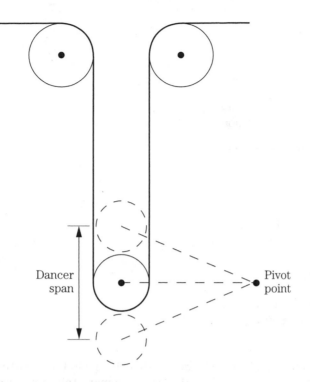

Fig. 4-29 A dancer.

material, and thus a correction can be made by the motor controllers to increase speeds or torques.

Other types of transducers involve the piezoelectric condition which produces motion from an electrical stimulus or, conversely, produces an electric signal from a motion, usually a strain, or load. These types include strain gauges and accelerometers. Another device is the rotary variable-differential transformer (RVDT). This device is a unit employing a rotor-stator relationship to produce voltage. No slip rings are used, as the electrical output results from the electromagnetic relationship of the stator windings and the rotor. It produces a voltage, usually 0 to 10 V DC, whose range varies linearly with the angular position of the shaft. Figure 4-30 shows a typical RVDT's performance curve for output voltage versus input shaft position.

Temperature Control

Many times with process control there is the need to control temperature. Sometimes the temperature can attain extremely high levels. Thus an industrial grade of thermometers has emerged. Temperature-sensing devices which generate electrical output are called *thermoelectric* devices. One common device is the thermocouple which utilizes two metallic components and conducts an electric signal when their junctions are at different temperatures. It is sometimes referred to as a *thermal junction* device. Other temperature-sensing devices use a direct output linear to the measured temperature, whenever feasible. A thermistor is an electric

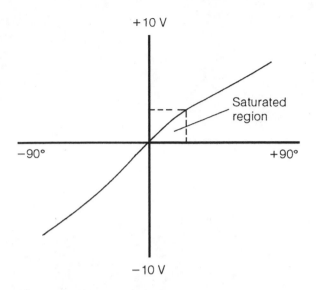

Fig. 4-30   Output voltage versus input shaft position for a rotary variable differential transformer (RVDT).

resistive device which relies on its resistance to vary with a change in temperature. A thermostat is yet another temperature-sensing device which many times utilizes a bimetallic scheme to sense when a predetermined temperature has been met. At this point a single output signal is provided, thus starting or stopping another piece of equipment, such as in a furnace's operation. Temperature-sensing equipment in the factory of today must be able to interface with many higher-level systems. This means that the simple thermometer does not suffice, and thus digital displays, along with microprocessor-based units, come into play for communicating with other devices and for charting and recording of temperature data in a process.

The adage "A watched pot never boils" is appropriate here. Soft logic systems are often employed to monitor the temperature of an oven or process. Variations of the PC-based interface boards can be used to input thermistor signals from motor resistive temperature detectors (RTDs) and most type J or type K thermocouples. A thermistor measures temperature via electrical resistance using semiconductor properties, while a thermocouple is a temperature-sensing device which can provide a value for temperature by utilizing a metallic two-wire junction scheme. A simple thermostat, however, just provides a contact closure, many times when two metals within the unit come into contact with each other. Alarms are common with this add-on module, and most are capable of working in a Celsius or Fahrenheit environment.

Pressure Sensing

The same is true for present-day pressure-sensing devices. They must be rugged for industrial use but also fast-acting and high-precision in order to be useful. These kinds of devices, much like their temperature-sensing counterparts, are installed virtually in line with the fluids which they are measuring or sensing. Thus the integrity of the unit is challenged as it physically sits in the wet and hostile environment. Common pressure ranges go up to 500 mbar (millibars is a unit for measuring pressure), and the accuracy of the pressure sensor is rated by its linearity (or error from steady-state input/output), its hysteresis (or the difference in response to an increase or decrease in the input signal), and its repeatability (or the deviation over many readings which should be the same).

Many times the pressure sensor converts the pressure signal to an electric signal, and other times this conversion is done in an external controller. This is sometimes an overlooked facet of the pressure control loop. This conversion module has to physically reside somewhere, and the application and environment will typically dictate where that location is. Once it is located, the conversion is simple, usually taking a 3 to 15 or 0 to 100 lb/in^2 gage pressure signal (scaling is important) and changing it to a 0- to 10-V DC or 4- to 20-mA electric signal. From here the controller scales the electric signal further for its use, and a resulting output signal is generated.

Flow and Level Control

New technology has allowed many traditional mechanical meters and feedback devices to be fitted with electronics, communications, and electromagnetics. Flow and level control is now a field of several disciplines. In the case of the magnetic flowmeter, the basis for operation—the checking of electrical conductivity in liquids flowing through a pipe—is electromagnetic. Taking the function of determining the flow of a liquid in a pipe, more or less a mechanical occurrence, newer technology has allowed us to perform this function much better. The power source is electrical, and there has to be DC excitation. In addition, the device is worthless unless some meaningful output is transmitted to a central source for processing, such as the PC-based controller. A digital display seems to be always necessary in the automated plant. Response times, the magnetic field, process noise and noise reduction, calibration, maintenance, configuring the memory and display, self-diagnostics, and communications are all important considerations. In addition, installation, grounding, and hazardous locations have to be looked at for potential pitfalls. This type of feedback device is representative of most feedback devices in that it contains much more, today, in the form of electronics than its predecessors.

Specific devices have been developed for the control of fluids. One such device is the magnetic flowmeter. Sometimes called *magmeters,* these magnetic flowmeters measure the flow of liquids in an enclosed pipe. The fluid must be able to conduct electricity in order for the magnetic flowmeter to function properly. These devices have actually been around for over four decades. Today, these magnetic flowmeters are able to handle flows from as little as 0.003 gal/min up to 750,000 gal/min. This range includes some very small pipe and some very large diameters of pipe. In a simplified sense, the magnetic flowmeter is a transducer integral to controlling a hydraulic system. When one is selecting a flowmeter, there are a few critical issues to consider:

1. The flowmeter must provide an obstructionless design. Obviously, the object here is to control the flow as smoothly as possible in a piping scheme. Any

obstruction basically defeats the purpose. Any moving parts in a flowmeter design can pose an obstruction (and a further problem area over time).
2. The output from the flowmeter should be as linear as possible. The signal to a supervisory computer system must be clean, stable, and fast. It should be directly proportional to the velocity of the flow of liquid through the pipe.
3. The flowmeter itself, since it is installed right into the piping system in line with the flowing liquid, must be made of materials resistant to any corrosive chemicals that may be present in the flow. The parts of the flowmeter that come into contact with the fluid are called the *wetted* parts.
4. The flow-measuring device has to be accurate. Not only does the device and its particular design require a wide range in which to be fully accurate, but also it has to be repeatable and consistent and able to adjust output quickly.

The basic operation of a magnetic flowmeter is similar to that of many other controllers and devices discussed throughout this book. The basic operating principle is induction. The fluid, being conductive, flows through a magnetic field. Table 4-1 lists various conductivities of water in many forms. A voltage is produced which is directly related to the flow, regardless of pressure, temperature, densities, or viscosities. In this manner a signal is produced and then supplied to a supervisory system, which determines whether the flow is too much or too little and makes the corresponding adjustment to the device initiating the flow or physically capable of changing the flow (such as a valve).

Although it may seem that a magnetic flowmeter is a fairly simple device in concept, its implementation has many behind-the-scenes activities. These may include the AC excitation, conductivity adjustments, transmitter scaling and configurations, displays and readouts, calibrations, electrical noise reduction, self-diagnostics, and full communications. Besides these issues, material and liner types must be considered along with orienting and properly installing such a device. All must be done correctly for proper operation. Some liquids have lower conductivity rates than others, and special attention may have to be paid here in selecting the flowmeter. Soft logic systems often depend on accurate magnetic flowmeter feedback for a reliable process.

TABLE 4-1. Conductivity of Water

Water type	Conductivity, μS/cm
Boiler feed (condensate)	1.2–20
Circulated coolant	800–8000
Demineralized (industrial)	0.1–0.9
Distilled (in glass)	1.0–7.5
Marine evaporator distillate	5.0–6.0
Mineral waters (soda water)	800–2500
Raw waters	80–900
Rinses (electroplating)	20–70, 750–3000
River and stream waters	80–1000
Ultrapure water	0.05–0.1

Like PC-based, soft logic control, level control has become more exact via electronics. The principles of physics have stayed the same, but now closed-loop control is better achieved through the use of modern technology. Housing the electronics at the feedback device has always been difficult — difficult because fluids and electricity do not get along. Electronic solutions to faster response and higher accuracy drove this industry to find sound ways of housing the electronics, so the devices could reside in the environment which they are monitoring. Many times level control is just an on or off state — is the desired level reached? At other times we need to know how close we are to the desired level. Whatever the requirement, there is a suitable device.

Photoelectrics

PC-based controls often interact with another type of sensors that involve light-detecting electronic devices. This is the field of photoelectrics. These types of sensors and controls are used mainly to detect the absence or presence of an object. Sensing whether an object is present via a light-based device allows plant personnel to control a process and make discrete movements on the production line.

There are three basic elements in any photoelectric system: a light source, a transmitter, and a receiver. Beyond this there are advanced control techniques utilizing logic modules and timers, and there is often the need to amplify output signals to send data to other plant locations. The light source emits a strong beam of light. This beam must be such that it can be distinguished from ambient light and sunlight. Thus, the light is usually in the infrared spectrum and sometimes can be a visible beam emitted from a light-emitting diode (LED). Figure 4-31 shows the basic photoelectric sensing elements.

Once we have a light source, we must have a means to transmit that light signal and a means to receive. The receiving, or light-sensing device, is a light-sensing diode which basically can tell if light is absent or present from the light transmitter. From here the output to another relay or device relative to the receiver's sensing comes into play. Often there is a focal control unit which controls both the triggering of the light source and the actual output signal once the receiver has sensed it. The receiver can be set up to be triggered when it has sensed light, or it can be set up to be triggered when it senses no light. This setup is application- and user-dependent.

Types of photoelectrics include reflective, or proximity, retroreflective, and through-beam. Often the distances that the light must be transmitted dictate which type of photoelectric sensor to use. It primarily issues a contact signal when an object has been sensed (or no object has been sensed). This contact signal is sent to a relay for instant use or later use. A time delay can be incorporated from when the sensor first sends the contact signal to when it is issued to its final destination. For instance, when an object on a moving conveyor is sensed and continues to move, the time delay allows the object to arrive at a predetermined position before the sensor output is received. This way the object can be loaded or unloaded or can have another function performed on it because it is now in position, and the conveyor can keep running without interruption.

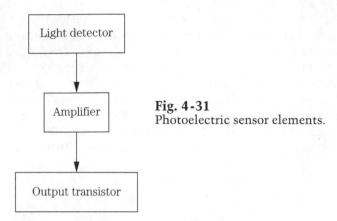

Fig. 4-31
Photoelectric sensor elements.

To select a type of photoelectric sensor, analyze the application. This will greatly aid in the proper selection of the photoelectric device. Distance, as mentioned earlier, is one of the most important issues. How far will the sensor be from the object? What is the object's size, and does that size change? Is the environment dirty, and is there physical room for the wiring? Answer these questions; then the type of photoelectic sensor can be chosen and a control scheme developed.

The through-beam photoelectric sensor is probably the most common. It can be seen in Fig. 4-32 with its elements and action. The light source transmitter and receiver are located opposite each other. Light is sent in a straight line to the receiver. When an object passes between the transmitter and receiver, the beam is broken, thus triggering a contact closure. This type of sensor is popular because it can be used in somewhat nasty environments and has the longest range of all the photoelectric sensors. Alignment is critical between the transmitter and receiver.

The retroreflective photoelectric sensor is shown in Fig. 4-33. Here the transmitter and receiver are placed on the same side, with a reflector opposite. The light beam is transmitted, reflected, and received. Once the beam is broken, the object is detected. These types of sensor systems are relatively inexpensive and have somewhat shorter ranges than the through-beam types. This sensor is easier to install, and alignment is not as critical. Note that the object being detected must not be more reflective than the reflector. This can lead to false triggering.

The easiest to install and perhaps the least expensive photoelectric sensor is the reflective or proximity sensor. However, it is also the most sensitive and can be affected in many ways. It works on the principle of reflectivity of an object, as shown in Fig. 4-34. This means that the sensor must be adjusted for the reflectivity of the object being detected, and all other objects, especially those in the background, must be tuned out. The environment should be relatively clean and the range expectancy not too great.

Applications of photoelectric sensors are many. Photoelectrics in the factory are used for counting, sorting, jam detection, and general inspection. They have many more uses than these, but they do have some limitations. Where they fall short on being able to perform in a particular application or installation, other types of sensing equipment can be the answer.

Other Sensors and Feedback Devices

Ultrasonic or simply sonic feedback devices are used quite extensively in many industrial applications. To be specific, the application and material being sensed must be compatible with sound waves, or else there will be misreadings. For instance, in a metal-stamping press application, sound waves are projected onto the surface of the metal and are bounced back to the receiver. The time it takes for

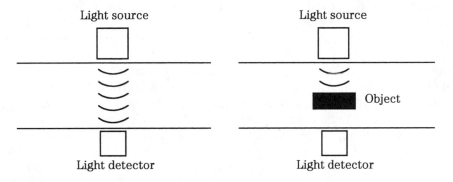

Fig. 4-32   Through-beam photoelectric sensor.

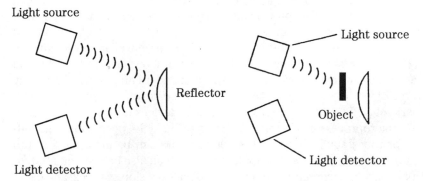

Good beam   **Broken beam**

Fig. 4-33   Retroreflective photoelectric sensor.

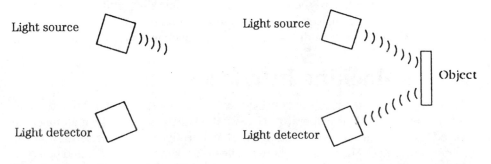

Fig. 4-34   Reflective photoelectric sensor.

the waves to return indicates the distance between the material and the source. This type of device is very good in applications involving solid materials; however, when one is trying to detect materials with porous surfaces, it can be rather difficult.

Machine vision is actually a form of feedback device and sensor system. It uses video imaging to monitor a process and provide real-time output in order to affect the process. Granted, the machine vision system, either on-line or off-line, is an expensive approach to controlling a process. However, there may not be a single-sensor solution available, and thus many sensors and corresponding feedback devices may have to be applied in conjunction with a computerized central station. This can be cumbersome, and the net cost can be equivalent to that of a simple machine vision system.

Likewise, laser technology has allowed for precise measuring and sensing of parts and of processes that were not even possible 5 years ago. The laser beam can work well in nasty environments, and its accuracy is very rarely challenged. On the downside, laser implementation can be expensive, and hopefully this will change in the future. Automatic gauging and weighing systems are also common applications involving sensor technology.

The position control module has become a means of closing the loop around a speed control device for a motor. Feedback is provided to the position control module in the form of pulses from an encoder or other similar device. This feedback is then utilized in the PLC program, and a quick decision is made by the program as to a response or new output to the motor being controlled. There are many dedicated motion controllers in existence which are more appropriate to controlling motors. However, the module inserted into the rack of a PLC can serve well in motor control.

High-speed counting modules allow for the accounting of parts and production pieces. They accept input in the form of pulses from encoders and higher-frequency devices. This type of module is required because under the normal I/O processing and scanning scenario of a PLC, the input speed from such devices is much greater than that of the PLC's microprocessor. Therefore this dedicated high-speed counting module is required for those applications. These counter data can be incorporated into the PLC program at the appropriate time for action. They can also be accumulated for later use in reporting and documentation. Bar-code devices, vision systems, and other types of scanners can be used in conjunction with a high-speed counting module.

Some other modules which are available to the factory are even more specialized. They include voice modules to send, record, and receive messages. Another is the radio-frequency module to recognize wireless transmissions and provide the appropriate interface. Thus the soft logic system has several components. Many of the hardware items, such as the modules, are discussed again in detail in a later chapter.

Human-Machine Interfaces

Another major element in the soft logic system is the device that links the machine or process with the live operator. This traditionally was called the man-machine interface (MMI), but more recently, to be more politically correct, the term *human-machine interface* (HMI) is used. There is a need for data to be exchanged between the PC or programmable controller and the human. What this really means is that there must be a central area for displays and where data entry can occur. Many times this is accomplished with an industrial terminal equipped with a microprocessor. That is the key difference between a monitor or terminal and an HMI. This hardware should be industrially hardened and able to function properly in harsh environments.

Some are mounted and equipped with a keyboard to enter alphanumeric data. These data will be transmitted to the PC-based controller or PLC over a communications wire which can be fiber-optic, coaxial, or simply serial. At the controller there must be a module to accept the data and appropriately route them within the CPU. This can be a LAN controller on the CPU module, BASIC module, or other communication module. Many factories are using flat, sealed screens and keypads as operator interfaces. Some are even using touch-screen devices which virtually eliminate the keypad, as the data can be selected and entered simply by touching the screen at the correct location with a finger.

As for the real power product of the HMI system, the software, it must support soft logic standards, operating systems, and device networks. It should be open to third-party applications and client/server solutions. The HMI software product should have an extensive tool set, on-line configuration capabilities, scalability, and proof statements and should be able to support a number of stations (no longer is it acceptable to have limits here). Many HMIs actually and physically look alike from the outside. All the functions that occur on the inside are the critical ones.

Soft logic plays a key role in the success of an integral human-machine interface. The open-type system and the smooth, quick exchange of data prevail. The HMI is at the center of attention. This is where the process data are extracted by the operator or entered for the program's use. It can be likened to the "first-impression syndrome." If the operator cannot use the HMI or cannot get comfortable with it, then the entire machine or process is off to a poor start. PC-based systems tend to promote this operator-friendliness and are also very flexible, to correct for any unforeseen complications.

5
CHAPTER

Standards, Guidelines, and Industry Practices

By definition, a standard is something which is set up as a rule or base model to which other things like it are compared. By having some basic rules and standards for a controls software platform, its use and implementation can be more universal. Additionally, these rules make for some flexibility and portability to users. Fortunately, soft logic has not burst onto the scene without some prior thought given to standards. Standards which relate to programmable controllers, control languages, batch process control, and other facets of control have been used as a base for the evolution of soft logic. This chapter evaluates many of those which are important to the implementation of PC-based controls. At the end of this chapter is a reference list of standards organizations with addresses, Web sites, and phone numbers.

Many process control and machine control standards have been in existence for some time, some for more than 25 years. Additionally, electrical codes and standards have been around even longer. But as we emphasize regarding PC-based control, it is evident that this technology will evolve over the next few years. It is also important to note that there is no one, single governing standard for PC-based or soft logic control (although IEC-1131 comes very close). Rather, many related standards exist and are evolving to help guide the users, designers, and vendors of these types of systems. The subject of *compliance* will be often discussed throughout the next decade. As users and vendors of control equipment struggle with interpretations and the standards themselves, somebody will be out on the plant floor trying to make a machine work because its program crashed or stopped executing. This chapter discusses the basic elements of many of these standards, their relevance to soft logic, and how they are changing.

PLCopen

PLCopen is not a standards-governing or -setting body. Rather it is a supplier and vendor organization that helps and guides users of programmable logic controllers (PLCs), mainly concerning the IEC-1131 standard. PLCopen is registered in the Netherlands and has offices in the United States (the address is given at the end of this chapter). It was founded in 1992 and has five basic charters: (1) It is *not* a standards-setting or -making body. (2) It will promote the IEC-1131 standard and open environments for PLC-type applications. (3) PLCopen can and will appoint third-party laboratories to perform tests to authenticate or evaluate software and hardware. (4) PLCopen will actively develop concepts for common implementation. (5) Members of PLCopen will commit to use and supply systems which are compatible with IEC-1131. PLCopen's objective is to have one standardized set of programming languages that will allow users to become more proficient and will require less training and retraining. These philosophies are, in part, exactly what the doctor ordered for PC-based and soft logic systems.

Presently, PLCopen has a certification program in place with different levels. These levels are ranked from the lowest class, the *base* level; to the next, called the *portability* level; to the highest, called the *full-compliancy* level. Working groups (WGs) have put into place guidelines for being compliant at each level. At the base level, development environments can be tested for all five languages defined in IEC-1131. At the portability level, it gets a little tougher. As the level's name indicates, parts of a program have to be able to be exchanged between development environments of different suppliers. Last, the final level (another is actually planned) of full compliancy requires that all the elements of the previous levels be met and then some.

Training and retraining are also important issues with PLCopen. The fact that every proprietary PLC carries with it the need to be trained makes the open premise of PLCopen more demanding. If the effort is going to be made to standardize the hardware and software, then training should fall right in line. There is a project called *Mondriaan* which provides for the basis of IEC-1131-3 training and education. A new task force is currently working on specifying new guidelines for training. These can be implemented by independent companies.

The IEC-1131 Standard—Overview

An international language standard for programmable logic controllers (PLCs) has been in existence, in some form, for nearly 20 years. With this ongoing work, this standard has evolved since 1979 to be the guide for much of the development in PC-based control systems. This particular standard is called IEC-1131. The International Electrotechnical Commission (IEC) made the most prominent attempt to define a controls standard for the programmable logic controller.

In 1979, a group of technical experts were given the task by national committees to develop a comprehensive technical standard around programmable logic controllers. The first draft was submitted sometime in 1982 and was in the form of a single document. At that time it was apparent that this subject was far too vast to be covered in a single document. Thus, the task was split up into five distinct sections. The serial number of the standard is 1131, and the five distinct subsections are numbered 1 through 5.

Part 1 (1131-1) is entitled General Information; part 2 (1131-2), Equipment and Test Requirements; part 3 (1131-3), Programming Languages; part four (1131-4), User Guidelines; and part 5 (1131-5), Communications. As one can see, to completely define an industrial control standard, including all these in one document, was a tall order. Thus the IEC standard was broken up into five succinct parts. The section which is most often referred to is 1131-3, the section on PLC programming languages. When discussions involving soft logic or PC-based controls refer to IEC-1131, it is actually a reference to the third section about the programming languages. Thus IEC-1131-3 is the focus of discussion throughout this chapter on soft logic standards.

IEC-1131-3, as a programming standard, specifies the syntax, elements, display methods, and basic rules for industrial control utilizing programmable logic controllers. Since PC-based control schemes utilize the power of the personal computer and not the PLC, the IEC-1131-3 standard can be applied as the building block of any soft logic application software package. In simpler terms, the control scheme remains the same, but the actual hardware types and software platforms are different. And because so much emphasis is placed on the software in a PC-based system, the IEC-1131-3 section on programming languages is most important. After all, software in its basic sense is a list of instructions, or a program, which runs and controls various pieces of hardware. What the soft logic phenomenon has allowed for is the *displacement of control capability from the PLC hardware to the personal computer.* This can be seen in the block diagram comparison shown in Fig. 5-1.

IEC-1131-3—Programming Languages

As programmable controller manufacturers and hardware proliferated, so too did the programming languages. Each manufacturer had its own language and protocol for using its PLC hardware. Some were easier to use than others, and during this period, industry, mainly individual end users, had to make a selection on a PLC make and programming language. Thus the task of selecting one as the common language was nearly impossible. So by applying current software engineering practices and principles, a common language platform was developed to use as a base. It was understood that vendors and manufacturers would not be able to offer the complete, full range of programming languages. However, the languages that would be offered must conform to the standard, based upon established PLC-type languages. Some manufacturers would find it necessary to adapt or, in most cases, probably reimplement their PLC programming software. And rather than having one standard language (making for more arguments than usual), it was decided that four interlinking languages would be established. All would be able to work together under a supervisory, fifth language included in the standard. Additionally, the languages had to be *portable* — able to be used by any programmer, technician, or PLC operator. The standard had to be *recognizable!* Thus standard IEC-1131-3 describes the following programming languages:

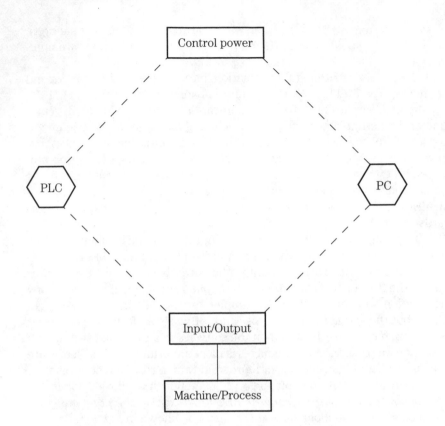

Fig. 5-1 The displacement of industrial process controls.

1. Sequential function chart (SFC)
2. Ladder diagram (LD), also known as ladder logic
3. Function block diagram (FBD)
4. Instruction list (IL)
5. Structured text (ST)

Ladder diagrams and function block diagrams are classified as *graphical* languages while instruction list and structured text are classified as *text-based* languages. Sequential function chart is not a stand-alone language, but rather acts as a governing graphical language by organizing programs written in ladder logic, function block, instruction list, or structured text. By utilizing SFC, one gains sequential control of the entire program. The syntax and basic element of these programming languages are defined such that users find those similarities in all program packages which conform to IEC-1131-3. More discussion follows on the subject of sequential function charts, and an example is shown in Fig. 5-2.

Graphical languages

Perhaps the most recognizable language type when one is discussing programmable logic controllers, graphical languages are employed often. As engineers make that first hand-drawn sketch of their plans, they are actually providing the rough draft of what will eventually be a detailed control scheme. As can be seen in Fig. 5-3, a machine operation is conceived, changed, and then selected as the control segment for that particular phase of the machine's system. Ironically, engineers are not the only people to provide sketches and graphical representations of their plans and ideas. We all do it.

The graphical representation of application programs is commonplace in programmable logic controllers while textual languages are more often associated with the programming of computers. With soft logic comes the need to consider both!

Ladder diagrams and ladder logic

As can be seen in Fig. 5-4, ladder diagrams take on the appearance of a ladder. They are probably the first thing to come to mind in a discussion of programming a PLC. Electrical engineers and electricians should be given much of the credit for the ladder's evolution. They built the standardized set of symbols to represent the electrical sequences of an application's operation. These symbols and more extensive discussion of ladder diagrams can be found in Chap. 3. This graphical language is fully addressed by the IEC-1131 standard and is sometimes referred to as *relay logic.* Hence, the ladder diagram is a diagram of logic symbols representing the actions of relays; thus the term *ladder logic.* Therefore the terms are often used interchangeably even though there may be technical arguments against it.

The ladder diagram works in this manner: All the equipment and devices used in the process or machine have an on/off state. Therefore, a ladder diagram can activate any of these devices based upon the state, or condition, of another. All this is done in some predetermined sequence, from top-down, left-to-right running of the ladder diagram. The process continues until the end and then repeats itself,

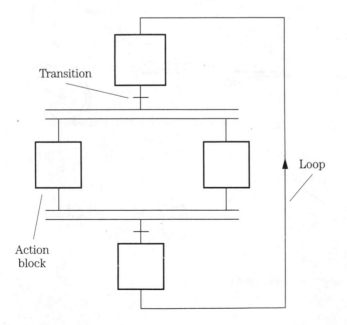

Fig. 5-2 Sequential function chart.

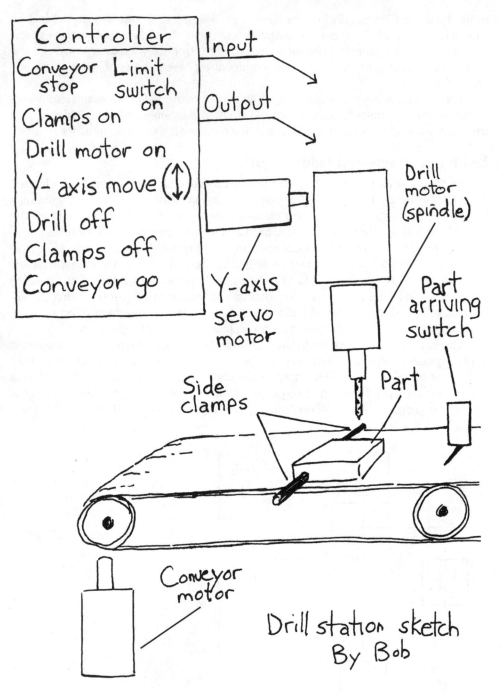

Controller

Conveyor   Limit
   stop   switch
             on
Clamps on
Drill motor on
Y-axis move (↕)
Drill off
Clamps off
Conveyor go

Input

Output

Drill motor (spindle)

Y-axis servo motor

Part arriving switch

Side clamps

Part

Conveyor motor

Drill station sketch By Bob

Fig. 5-3   Engineer's sketch of a machine control idea.

constantly checking the status of every contact as it "scans" the diagram. Ladder logic utilizes normally open (NO) contact symbols, normally closed (NC) contact symbols, and coils used in ladder diagrams and relay logic (see Table 5-1). The steps are the rungs of the ladder and are executed one by one.

With more powerful computers and processors, functions and function blocks have become integral to ladder diagrams. These block routines allow for more complex processing work to be done more simply, easily, and in fewer steps. The IEC-1131-3 standard states, however, that every function must have at least one binary input (ENABLE) and an output (OK). This is to keep the binary data flow characteristics of a ladder diagram in tact. Otherwise this would lead to incompatible function blocks for ladder and function block diagrams.

Function block diagram

Function block diagram (FBD) language is a graphical language which eventually functions as a circuit diagram. Program elements appear as blocks on the screen and are then wired together. The shell of the block receives input and sends output information, all the while processing the I/O as necessary. In this way, the program elements can then execute their respective algorithms and operations in the manner in which the wires dictate. This can be seen in Fig. 5-5. Here, a typical proportional-integral-derivative (PID) routine is represented in block form. Just as engineers and technical people exchange graphical ideas in block form (see Fig. 5-6), so does the overall "look" of function block programming. At a glance and by looking at block titles, one can get the idea or flow of the program.

The IEC-1131-3 standard addresses function block methods and techniques in some detail. This is done to provide the basis for standardization for this common soft logic language. Elements of the standard allow for common object-oriented programming, control using external parameters, and hidden internal arithmetic operations as well as hidden algorithms. Moving data between various control components within a system is a typical use of function block programming. Likewise, function blocks can be utilized serially, one after another, or in parallel, performing operations simultaneously. Additionally, specific routines can be programmed and defined within a function block and, in turn, can be used over and over in a process or machine control master program. An example might be a pulse counter routine for a multiple-motor control program (see Fig. 5-7). Thus, an actual block of code can be

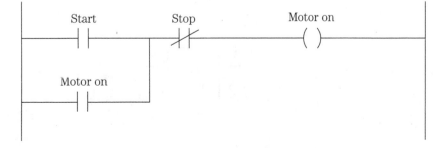

Fig. 5-4 Ladder diagram.

TABLE 5-1. Ladder Contacts and Coils

LADDER DIAGRAM	BOOLEAN MNEMONIC
—(+)—	ADD
—(-)—	SUB
—(x)—	MUL
—(÷)—	DIV
—(CMP =)—	CMP =
—(CMP >)—	CMP >
—(CMP <)—	CMP <
—(JMP)—	JMP
—(JSB)—	JSB
—(MCR)—	MCR
—(END MCR)—	END
——||——	AND
——||——	OR
—( )—	OUT
—(/)—	OUT NOT
—||——	NAND
—||——	NOR
——||——	LOAD
——|/|——	LOAD NOT
—(L)—	OUT L
—(U)—	OUT U
—(TIM)—	TIM
—(CNT)—	CNT

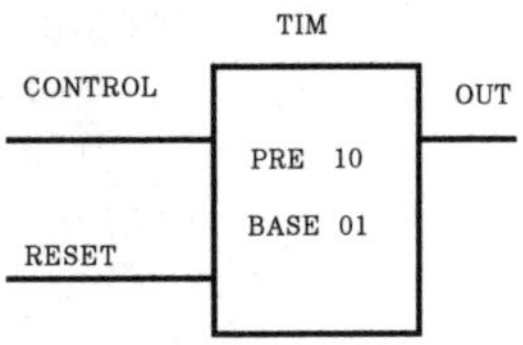

TIM
CONTROL   OUT
PRE 10
BASE 01
RESET

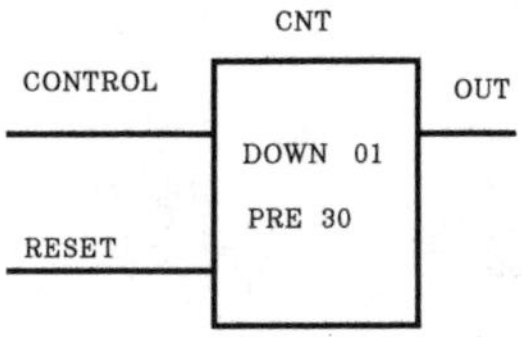

CNT
CONTROL   OUT
DOWN 01
PRE 30
RESET

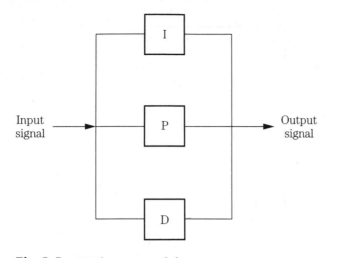

Fig. 5-5   PID loop control diagram.

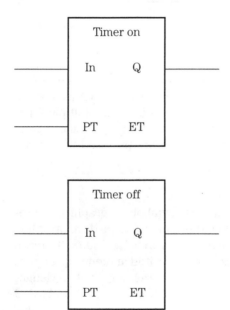

Fig. 5-6   Function block example.

reused (and easily modified) for similar, repeated activities. It can be reused later in the same program, can be used in another process or machine program, or can even be moved to another manufacturer's controller (the intent of the standard, anyway) and reused.

Since function blocks are so common and powerful, they can be manipulated for a wide variety of uses. The data entering the function block can be instructed to be processed in the same manner each time they enter, or the function block can be commanded to change its algorithm based on the data it receives. Data can be stored

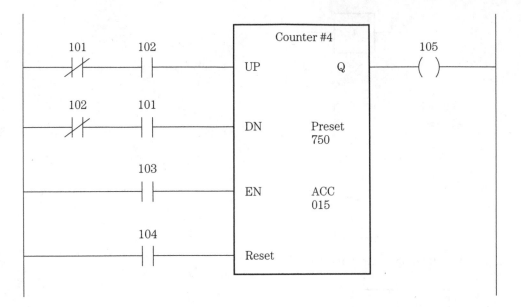

Fig. 5-7   Pulse counter example.

within the function block and retrieved from the function block as desired. These data enter many times in the form of a variable. This means that the data have the ability to be different every time they encounter the function block. Multiple function blocks can be summoned to action by tasks which execute the overall program. Thus, function blocks can be powerful on their own and more powerful when used with others—it is all up to the programmer.

Textual languages

As the name implies, textual languages do not use symbols or graphical representations to build and execute a program. Rather, the code has to be developed line by line. The form can be high or low level, character set, or byte-per-character form. This means that the commonality and usefulness have a limited audience given that the textual language has to relate to PLC devices and that the persons knowledgeable in that particular text, or code, are limited in number. Nonetheless, IEC-1131-3 provides for standardization to this set of languages, addressing structure in the programming and data manipulation. The two PLC languages that are included are instruction list and structured text.

Instruction list

This low-level version of programming has many drawbacks. First, it is similar to assembler language and therefore is not going to be readily recognizable to the plant engineer or electrician (see Fig. 5-8). Computer science experts will probably like it, but its universal appeal is questionable. It performs only one operation per line, such as storing an integer value within a register, which makes it cumbersome to use. Several lines must be written methodically to get the desired results. One apparent advantage of this type of programmable controller language is its ability to process the lines of code quickly since they are in assembler form. This means that certain routines within an application can be programmed in this language to gain fast throughput. Less complicated processes and machines can utilize instruction list programming as long as major changes are not foreseen often. (Who can predict this condition accurately?) This is why IEC-1131-3 has evolved.

Given the fact that there are many PLC programmers who do know instruction list languages, the IEC standard is useful in making the languages portable. With more powerful soft logic application software and more powerful computers, this transporting of code is possible. Per the IEC standard, the structure of instruction list programming will correspond to present instruction list languages in use. The arithmetic operators of instruction list have been addressed as regards standardization, while all symbolic identifiers must be declared before they are used in a program. It is possible to link function blocks in this type of program, and the standard also addresses this. Thus, as PLC packages continue to be implemented with instruction list programs, the IEC-1131-3 will continue to include it for those individuals well versed in it.

Structured text

Structured text (ST) is a step or two above instruction list. It is a high-level language resembling Pascal and containing all the basic components of a modern programming language. Figure 5-9 illustrates a few lines of a structured text program. Common selection branches such as the IF-THEN-ELSE, CASE, and CASE OF and iteration loops such as the FOR, REPEAT, REPEAT-UNTIL, WHILE-DO, and WHILE are included in structured text programming. Structured text also provides boolean and other arithmetic replacement statements and is a natural addition to the present PLC languages. Elements of the sequential function chart can also be expressed in text form in structured text; therefore, structured text can be used on its own, independent of the other IEC-1131-3 languages.

Structured text is well suited for batch-processing applications because there are specific data types, built in, for managing durations, times, and dates. In addition, structured text can be used in developing complex lines, or statements, utilizing a wide range of data types as variables for digital and analog values. Even though structured text is designed for use in "structured programming," it is a more common approach to PLC programming than one might think. It still requires that the programmer be well versed in structure, syntax, and internal implementation, as

```
VAR  XX  ON, XX OFF: TIMER; END VAR
XX ON(IN:= IN, PT:= XX Time):
IF XX ON.Q THEN OUT:= TRUE; END IF;
IF XX OFF.Q THEN OUT:= FALSE; END IF
END BLOCK
```

Fig. 5-8 Instruction list example.

```
IF.....THEN.....ELSE
CASE
WHILE...DO
REPEAT......UNTIL
```

Fig. 5-9 Structured text example.

well as completely understand the process or machine. With IEC committees setting standards for this language type, those who use it should benefit greatly.

Sequential function chart

The fifth language defined in the IEC-1131-3 standard, sequential function chart (SFC) is a higher-order language ranked above the other programming languages, and it enables sequence-oriented problems to be formulated using steps and transitions. The steps represent the actions, which can also be performed in parallel, and the transitions are the conditions which must be fulfilled before moving on to the next step. Features of the SFC language include instructions for steps, transitions, and action blocks which can be used to organize actions. These organized actions form sequential algorithms in the controller. Many SFC elements are actually based on previous standards, such as Grafcet (described later in this chapter). There is also a similarity between sequential function charts and flowcharting.

SFCs offer the programmer the ability to look at the whole picture of the application and organize the program into some order. Once this has been done, the more detailed code (textual or graphical) is developed until the program functions properly for the particular application. With the ability to use the sequential function charts in a variety of lower-order environments, the programmer has the luxury of working within an environment where he or she is most comfortable. This is very important today in traditional, PLC controlled applications. The programmer may often be the electrician or electrical engineer in the manufacturing plant, and there usually will be little time to learn a new software package or environment. SFCs give the application programmer or designer the power to control the lesser parts of the program.

Benefits of Standard IEC-1131-3

Which came first, the standard or the change? Technology is changing, but is it because the standards and industry are demanding these changes? Or is it that technology *will* change, and thus some standards should be set in place before products emerge randomly? The answer is that both demands for standards and change are driving this industry. Besides getting hardware and software suppliers and the end users to finally strive for common ground (actually many will view this standard as "forcing" them to that common ground and therefore will fight the change), IEC-1131-3 was needed for other reasons. Software now can become reusable and transportable. No longer will a project be a one-of-a-kind system. It can be integrated into the complete process or machine environment instead of being the "black sheep" of the factory. Software development can now realize quicker cycles. Ready-tested blocks of code and the ability to reuse them make for much faster implementation. Engineering costs have to be reduced. The software engineer can actually sit down and begin programming in some code or form that she or he is actually familiar with. Another aim of soft logic standard software development is to detect errors as early as possible. It is much more complicated to correct errors detected in later stages. Simulating the running of the program is a valuable tool for the application designer. This means that errors should ideally be detected during the off-line programming phase. IEC-1131-3 takes this into account by making this a full requirement.

There are other important benefits of IEC-1131-3 standardization. The architecture of the application and the configuration of the system will be less problematic to the designers, engineers, and programmers. The IEC-1131-3 standard makes the complete structuring of the particular system and its environment much easier for programmers to navigate within. It also assists them in breaking down the overall control system into smaller, more manageable units. As for system configuration, the entire control system required for solving a particular problem can be simplified. For more complex applications (of which there will be many), it will be necessary to break the application into a number of smaller, more manageable configurations. They each will communicate and function with one another through defined interfaces. A configuration is made up of several resources, each of which should consist of control subsections of a related function or functions. A resource can also administer several tasks. These tasks will be assigned different features and will each consist of programs. These particular programs will be structured into very manageable sections with the function blocks and functions normally used in current programming languages. Functions and function blocks will be able to be called into programs. Function blocks will also have memory. Thus, functions should always provide the same result when supplied with the same input values (hence they will have no memory). Conversely, function blocks cannot be called in a function. The primary difference between function blocks and functions lies in the use of any local data. Function blocks of an equivalent rank shall have memory which retains internal data of this sort. In this way data can be called again later (as in statistical variables). Otherwise, functions will have no internal storage mechanism or facilities for storing status information. Thus, the function's result will depend entirely on its call parameters. It should also be possible to use global variables in these application function blocks. The portability, commonality, and ease of structure should make any programmer a little happier as the demands on these programmers will intensify, proportionately, as more equipment in the manufacturing plant is PC-based or a type of soft logic package!

Flowcharts

Another method of control system programming is *flowcharting*. This is similar in look and function to the sequential function block method described in IEC-1131-3. Both parallel and serial activities must be available in a complete control system, and flowcharting provides this. However, there are subtle differences.

The basis for the flowchart program actually traces back to the roots of computer programming altogether, maybe even back to pure graphical interpretation of machine and process operation. It is usually more effective to express a thought graphically (if one can draw reasonably well). Additionally, as a process grows in complexity, it is necessary to keep the activities in order or to provide the proper flow for all the operations. This methodology became ever so prevalent with the proliferation of computers and the need to program them. So many instructions had to be kept in strict order so that time-consuming debugging could be kept to a minimum. Thus it was established that all programmers should be taught to "flowchart" the program first, on paper (so the changes could be easily erased), to get a feel for how the program would be developed. This sequencing theme has carried through the computer and control industry for over 30 years. Today programming with flowchart methodology has been made easier.

By programming with symbols, a controls programmer can think about the process and what needs to be done and when. The software will do the rest. For every flowchart symbol, the software will interpret another level of code. Thus the programmer does not have to know specific languages such as C to write the program. Additionally, the new soft logic software packages have error checking (while programming) and the ability to compile the program into the bit level for the fastest processing and throughput.

Flowchart programming begins with a basic understanding of the actual flowchart symbols typically used. These symbols are recognizable from the Basic and Fortran courses of yesteryear. The first is the *Start* symbol shown in Fig. 5-10. A program begins execution whenever this element is encountered. Likewise, there is a *Stop* flowchart symbol (see Fig. 5-11), and when the program comes to this point, it stops executing. Next, the symbol for an *action* is shown in Fig. 5-12. It is where the real work is done. Calculations can be made, variables can be changed, and some-

Fig. 5-10   Start flowchart symbol.

Fig. 5-11   Stop flowchart symbol.

Fig. 5-12   Action symbol.

thing can be turned on or off. Machine or process input and output handling comes into play for the action element of a program. Likewise, another important flowchart element is the *decision* symbol, seen in Fig. 5-13. This symbol is sometimes referred to as the *conditional* symbol because the operation of this element involves logic, calculations, and comparisons. Once a decision is made from the internal computation, the program will have the opportunity to advance in one or another direction, as seen in Fig. 5-14. The last symbol typically used is the *connector,* seen in Fig. 5-15. It is used to tie together other parts of the program with the main flow. All the elements of the complete flowchart can be seen in Fig. 5-16. Some soft logic software packages can incorporate more advanced symbology. For instance, reusable subroutines and special functions can have dedicated symbols. This will differ from package to package.

As the flowchart scheme has been initially shown, most of the flow is serial or sequential, as seen in Fig. 5-16. In real life, many operations have to happen simultaneously or in conjunction with one another. Thus, parallel flowcharts or parallel branches of a flowchart can be used to eventually end up at a final point of the branch before the execution can continue. Thus multiple actions can occur, simultaneously if need be.

Flowcharting, or "flo," has an appeal to many programmers. In developing the coded program we have been taught to lay out the flow of the program and use it to aid in the actual coding (the thought is that fewer mistakes will be made and a more efficient program built). At this time, flowcharts are not standardized and are not actually governed by any standard. Thus if a programmer likes this method, then it is available. IEC-1131-3 exists, but it is not accepted completely. Many still view it (1131-3) as another European obstacle. More work with that standard will help give it more universal acceptance. Meanwhile, flowcharting is an accepted method of coding and has been around for many years. Flowcharts are covered in depth in Chap. 6.

S88 Batch Process Control Standard

Another phase in manufacturing is that of batch process control. As with other phases of manufacturing, standards have been developed in order to bring some order and compliancy to this control method. This particular standard has been defined by the Instrument Society of America (ISA) and is called the S88 Batch Process Control Standard. But first, some discussion of batch process control.

A batch is the amount of something made or worked on at one time. This differs from assembly-type facilities and other manufacturing facilities which involve several disciplines and their contribution to the making of a product. Traditional batch processes include mixing or stirring applications, centrifuges, and other chemically related applications. Temperature, pressure, humidity, and flow control become important in batch processes. The handling of material and the quantities of material used are equally important. Thus, the control systems used in batch process control are often complex and in need of some standardization. The S88 committee of ISA came up with a standard which helps to define models, procedures, and process management.

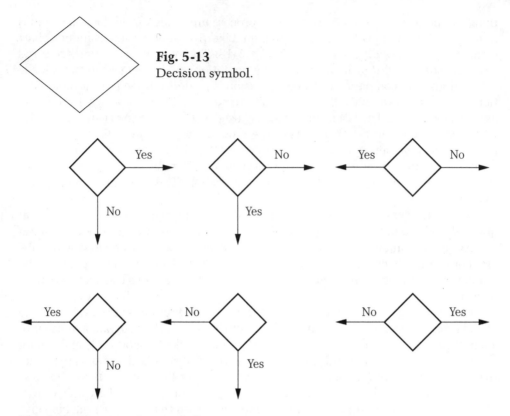

Fig. 5-13
Decision symbol.

Fig. 5-14   Decision leg symbol.

This batch control standard is a good tool and guide for industry. It provides for consistency among end users and suppliers of batch control equipment. It also allows for easier improvements and increased efficiencies. As technology races forward and as hardware changes, there has to be some means for holding vendors of such equipment accountable. This standard attempts to do just that. First, parts of the process such as the process cell, unit, operation, line, phase, and others are defined. Without knowing the exact purpose of each piece of equipment, it is almost impossible to utilize it properly in the process! Then these parts are integrated into models—four as addressed by S88: physical model, activity model, procedure model, and actual process model. In this way manufacturers can analyze their existing batch process and add new equipment much faster and more easily.

The S88 physical model can be described as all the equipment used in the batch process from beginning to end. It does not address the higher levels of the manufacturing company such as the site and area. S88 concerns itself with the lower level, the process control, get-the-task-done level. Typically, the programmable logic controller and related control hardware are at the lower end of the model hierarchy. This is the facet which also concerns soft logic control systems the most. Any relationships between the various controllers concerning their role in the batch process are called the *control activity*. The physical model should define all the equipment needed to perform the process. Each piece of equipment should adhere

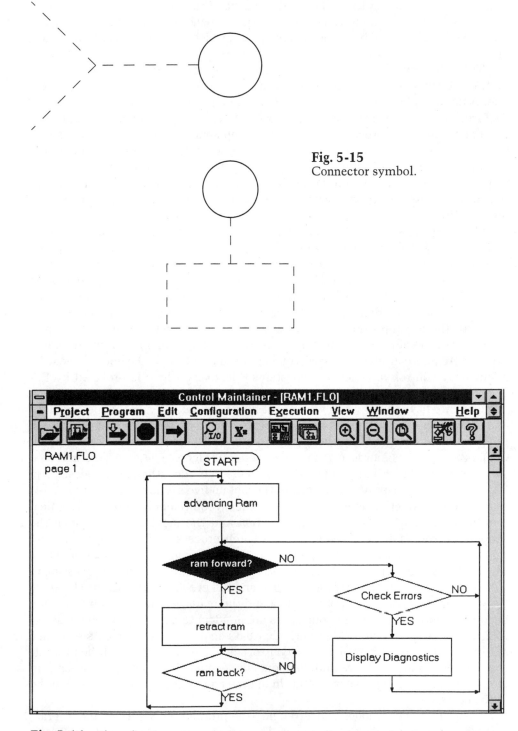

Fig. 5-15
Connector symbol.

Fig. 5-16 Flow diagram. (Steeplechase Software, Inc.)

to guidelines pertaining to the task independent of the product being made. That piece should also be able to run on its own (not depend on another piece of equipment), and there should be ample documentation which sets forth consistent rules of operation.

The batch operation requires process units, process lines, and process cells. A unit, or all the equipment performing a specific operation, is part of the process line. A unit should be able to work on its own, on one batch at a time, and should perform a task which is critical to the process. Several units will make up a process equipment line. The process line is all the equipment needed to produce a single batch. Process lines should have the ability to be changed so as to combine the equipment in required configurations in order to make different products. The process line or lines make up the process cell. The cell is all the equipment, supporting hardware, and production tools necessary to produce a batch. It can include multiple lines.

The S88 procedure model supplements the physical model which deals with the batch equipment. The procedural model deals with the control and action required to make the batch. The procedure is the overall batch plan. For every physical unit model there are unit procedures. These describe the specific function and operation of each unit. Two other key components of the procedural control model are the phase and operation. Soft logic control systems will concern themselves in a major way with these components of the model. An operation, while being made up of phases, must begin and completely end in order to move further in the batch process. Actions caused by the series of steps during a phase of the operation can be affected by control variables and constants. Flexibility which is provided by PC-based, soft logic controls is paramount here.

Once we have the physical equipment hierarchy defined and the methodology and procedures in order, it is time to create and manipulate the process batch recipes. These are the basic elements which make the process a success (or failure). S88 addresses four levels of recipes: general (highest), site, master, and control (lowest). The relationships of each recipe to the others can be seen in Fig. 5-17 with description. Each recipe will contain five sections which are needed to make the product: header, formula, equipment requirements, product specification, and procedure. This recipe information and the moving of it through the proper controllers are the essence of the batch process. Soft logic systems lend themselves well to the handling and processing of this critical information. Once the overall "groundwork" has been laid, it is appropriate to move into process management, production planning, scheduling, and full process supervision. These are the areas in which the collection of data and the management of cell information become important. PC-based controllers are an ideal tool at this stage because of their previous history of SCADA and other data acquisition systems. As soft logic systems become more prevalent as a control scheme in other parts of the process, the need for extra hardware and components declines. Keeping the process control scheme simple pays big dividends in uptime and reliability, not to mention the initial costs.

Last, the process model is inserted into the production equation, and interaction with the other models commences. The process model, comprised of process,

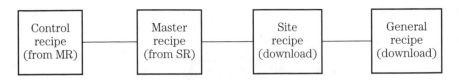

Fig. 5-17   Recipe types.

process stage, process operation, and process action levels, is the last model but not the least. This model is the base model for the procedural, physical, and procedural control models. As they link together, a full and complete system is now in place.

This is a cursory overview of the S88 standard. A copy of this standard can be obtained from the Instrument Society of America at the address shown at the end of this chapter.

OLE (Object Linking and Embedding) for Process Control (OPC)

Another standard important to process control is the OLE for Process Control (OPC). This standard is concerned with embedded objects and how to link them on the factory floor [maybe this explains why this standard carries with it an "embedded" acronym—OLE (object linking and embedding) for Process Control, or OPC]! Some further discussion of OPC can be found in Chap. 10. However, as PC-based controls emerge in the manufacturing plant, the need for more rules and standards increases. Moreover, this standard addresses the integration of plant floor data and information with higher-level computer systems. Following is a reprint (with permission from OPC) of the Introduction and OPC Fundamentals and OPC Overview, sections 1 and 2, from the Final Version of the OLE for Process Control:

Synopsis:

This document is the specification of the interface for developers of OPC clients and OPC servers to enable building of OPC compliant components. The document is a result of an analysis and design process to develop a standard interface for the process control industry to enable development of servers and clients by multiple vendors that shall interoperate seamlessly together. The document includes both an OLE automation interface and a custom COM interface (COM extension library).

Trademarks:

Most computer and software brand names have trademarks or registered trademarks. The individual trademarks have not been listed here.

Required Runtime Environment:

This specification requires Windows 95 or Windows NT 3.51 or later for in process servers. It requires Windows NT 4.0 or later for local or remote servers.

1.   INTRODUCTION

1.1   BACKGROUND

Today manufacturers face the task of integrating plant floor data into their business systems. This task is made difficult because of the almost unlimited number of methods plant floor devices utilized to communicate to other systems.

The current situation in the process control market is analogous to the early stages of the computer industry where two machines from different manufacturers could not communicate (IBM and DEC for example) without many hours of custom programming. Today, a wide variety of computers communicate over vast distances, and diverse networking systems, thanks to standards that have been established. Applications written utilizing powerful Database and Client/Server tools that support these standards allow the application programmer to focus on the task at hand and not the communication underpinnings.

The plant floor must evolve in a similar fashion. Plant floor devices and data can no longer be information islands in a business. Companies today need to have tighter integration of the manufacturing process information.

The information architecture for the Process Industry shown in Fig. 5-18 involves the following levels:

FIELD MANAGEMENT. With the advent of "smart" field devices, a wealth of information can be provided concerning field devices that has not been available in the past. This information provides data on the health of a device, its configuration parameters, materials of construction, etc. All this information must be presented to the user, and any applications using it, in a consistent manner.

PROCESS MANAGEMENT. The installation of Distributed Control Systems (DCS) and SCADA systems to monitor and control manufacturing processes has made data available electronically which had in the past been gathered manually. This data must be provided in a consistent manner to the operators and engineers responsible for making decisions based on that data.

BUSINESS MANAGEMENT. Additional benefits can be gained beyond those typically cited when justifying the installation of control systems. This is accomplished by integrating the information collected from the process into the business systems managing the financial aspects of the manufacturing process. Providing this information in a consistent manner to client applications minimizes the effort required to provide this integration.

To do these things effectively, manufacturers need to access data from the plant floor and integrate it into their existing business systems. Manufacturers must be able to utilize off the shelf tools (SCADA Packages, Databases, Spreadsheets, etc.) to assemble a system to meet their needs. The key is an open and effective communication enabler concentrating on data access, and not the types of data.

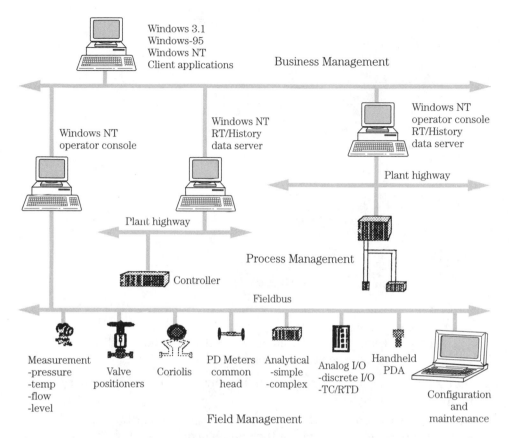

Business Management

Windows 3.1
Windows-95
Windows NT
Client applications

Windows NT
RT/History
data server

Windows NT
operator console
RT/History
data server

Windows NT
operator console

Plant highway

Plant highway

Process Management

Controller

Fieldbus

Measurement
-pressure
-temp
-flow
-level

Valve
positioners

Coriolis

PD Meters
common
head

Analytical
-simple
-complex

Analog I/O
-discrete I/O
-TC/RTD

Handheld
PDA

Configuration
and
maintenance

Field Management

Fig. 5-18 Process control information architecture. (OPC Foundation.)

1.2 PURPOSE

What is needed is a common way for applications to access data from any device on the plant floor, allowing compliant applications to seamlessly access data in a manufacturing environment. Figure 5-19 provides a block diagram of this.

1.2.1 IMPACT ON EXISTING APPLICATIONS

Today, there are numerous existing applications which access plant floor data (MMI's, SCADA, SPC, etc.) that are written by various companies These companies gain access to the data by independently developing "Drivers" for their own packages. This has led to the problems which follow:

- Much duplication of effort
  Everyone must write a driver for a particular vendor's hardware.
- Inconsistencies between vendors' drivers
  Hardware features not supported by all driver developers.
- Support for hardware feature changes
  A change in the hardware's capabilities may break some drivers.

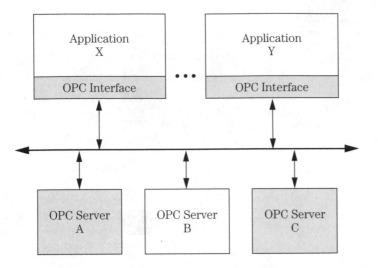

Fig. 5-19 Applications working with many OPC servers. (OPC Foundation.)

- Access conflicts
  Two packages generally cannot access the same device at the same since they each contain independent drivers.

Hardware manufacturers would like to help by developing drivers, but face the problem of which driver to develop.

OLE for Process Control (OPC) draws a line between hardware providers and software developers. It places the burden of data collection and distribution on the shoulders of a single developer. This makes more sense since they know the most about the idiosyncrasies of accessing data from the device in the most efficient manner. The developer's role will be to provide software components for their devices which provide data to clients in a standard manner.

1.2.2 IMPACT ON CUSTOM APPLICATIONS

A growing number of custom programs are being developed in environments like Visual Basic (VB), Delphi, Power Builder, etc. OPC must take this trend into account. Microsoft understands this trend and designed OLE/COM to allow components (written in C and C++ by experts in a specific domain) to be utilized by a custom program (written in VB or Delphi for an entirely different domain). This is why OLE is an integral part of OPC. This model fits the needs of Process Control exactly. Developers will write software components in C and C++ to encapsulate the intricacies of accessing data from a device, so that business application developers can write code in VB that requests and utilizes plant floor data. To achieve this, all the VB programmer needs to know is the interfaces to the OPC objects.

1.2.3 GENERAL

OLE for Process Control (OPC) is designed to be a method to allow business applications access to plant floor data in a consistent manner. With wide industry acceptance OPC will provide many benefits:

- Hardware manufacturers only have to make one set of software components for customers to utilize in their applications.
- Software developers won't have to rewrite drivers because of feature changes or additions in a new hardware release.
- Customers will have more choices with which to develop world class integrated manufacturing systems.

With OPC, system integration in a heterogeneous computing environment will become simple. Leveraging OLE/COM in the environment shown in Fig. 5-20 becomes possible.

1.3 SCOPE

A primary goal in the effort to develop this document was to deliver a specification to the industry in as short a span of time as possible. With this goal

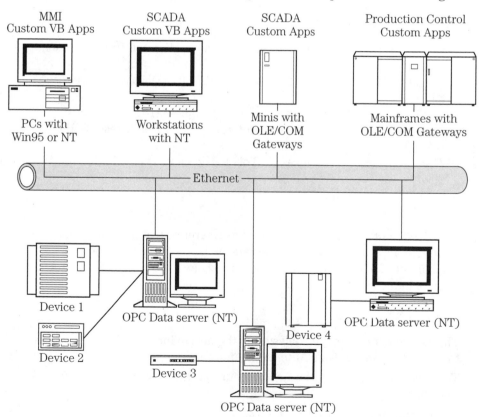

Fig. 5-20 Heterogeneous computing environment. (OPC Foundation.)

in mind, the scope of the initial specification was purposely limited to areas common to all vendors. The intent was that additional functionality could be defined in future releases of the specification. Therefore, the primary emphasis of this release of the OPC specification is on the efficient reading and writing of data between an application and a process control device in the most flexible and efficient manner possible. Functionality such as alarm handling, security, and historical data access is intended to be addressed in subsequent releases of the specification.

Other goals for the design of OPC were as follows:

- Simple to implement.
- Flexible to accommodate multiple vendor needs.
- Provide a high level of functionality.
- Allow for efficient operation.
- A set of OLE Automation interfaces to support clients developed with higher level business applications such as Excel, Visual Basic, etc.
- Current specification does not expressly address remotability. However, it is designed with the latest information from Microsoft regarding the future of distributed OLE in mind.

1.4   REFERENCES

Kraig Brockschmidt, *Inside OLE,* Second Edition, Microsoft Press, Redmond, WA, 1995.

Microsoft COM Specification, Version 0.9, 10/24/95 (available from Microsoft's FTP site).

Microsoft Systems Journal, *Q&A,* April, 1996, pp. 89–101.

OLE Automation Programming Reference, Microsoft Press, Redmond, WA, 1996.

OLE 2 Programming Reference, Vol. 1, Microsoft Press, Redmond, WA, 1994.

1.5   AUDIENCE

This document is intended to be used as reference material for developers of OPC compliant Clients and Servers. It is assumed that the reader is familiar with Microsoft OLE/COM technology and the needs of the Process Control Industry.

1.6   DELIVERABLES

This document covers the analysis and the design for a COM compliant custom interface and an OLE Automation interface.

This document contains the fundamentals and design information for the following:

1. The OPC COM Custom Interface—This section will describe the Interfaces and Methods of OPC Components and Objects.

2. The OPC OLE Automation Interface—This interface will provide developers and end users an interface to access and configure process control data. The OPC OLE Automation Interface facilitates the use of Visual Basic, Delphi, and other products to interface with OPC servers. The Automation Interface is completely independent of the Custom Interface. That is, a single common version of this interface will work for all clients and servers.
3. OPC fundamentals

OPC is based on Microsoft's OLE/COM technology.

2.1 OPC OVERVIEW

This specification describes the OPC COM Objects and their interfaces which are implemented by OPC Servers. An OPC Client (Fig. 5-21) can connect to OPC Servers provided by one or more vendors.

OPC Servers are provided by different vendors. The code written by the vendor determines the devices and data to which each server has access, the way in which data items are named, and the details about how the server physically accesses that data.

Within each Server the client can define one or more OPC Groups (Fig. 5-22).

The OPC Groups provide a way for clients to organize the data in which they are interested. For example, the group might represent items in a particular operator display or report. Data can be read and written. Exception-based connections can also be created between the client and the items in the group and can be enabled and disabled as needed. The "freshness" (time

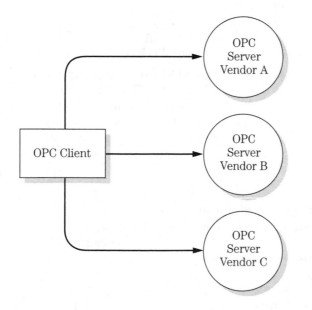

Fig. 5-21 OPC client. (OPC Foundation.)

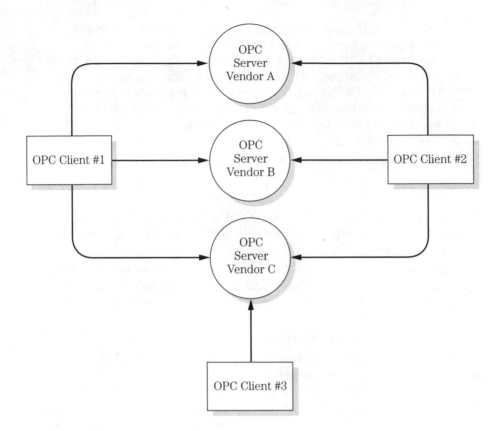

Fig. 5-22   OPC client-server relationship. (OPC Foundation.)

resolution) of the data in the group can be specified.

Within each Group the client can define one or more OPC Items (Fig. 5-23).

The OPC Items represent connections to data sources within the server. Associated with each item is a value, a Quality Mask and a Time Stamp. The value is in the form of a VARIANT and the Quality Mask is similar to that specified by Fieldbus. Note that the items are not the data sources—they are just connections to them. For example, the tags in a DCS system exist regardless of whether an OPC client is currently accessing them.

2.2   WHERE OPC FITS

OPC interfaces can be potentially used in many places in an application. They can be used at the lowest level to get raw data from the physical devices into a SCADA or DCS (Fig. 5-24). They can also be used to get data from the SCADA or DCS system into the application. As will be noted elsewhere, OPC is designed to get data from one server on one network node. However, it should be possible to construct an OPC Server which allows a client application to access data from Servers provided by many different OPC vendors and possibly running on different nodes via a single object.

2.3   GENERAL OPC ARCHITECTURE AND COMPONENTS

OPC is a specification for two sets of interfaces; the OPC Custom interfaces and the OPC Automation interfaces. This is shown in Fig. 5-25.

The OPC Specification specifies COM interfaces, not the implementation of those interfaces. However, it is useful to describe the sorts of architectures that these interfaces are intended for and the implementations that seem most appropriate. Like all COM implementations, the architecture of OPC is

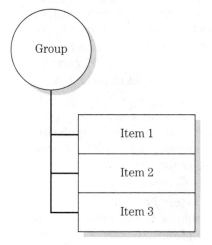

Fig. 5-23   Group-item relationship. (OPC Foundation.)

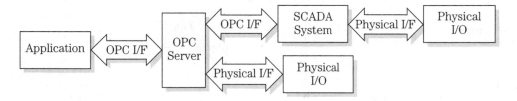

Fig. 5-24   OPC client-server relationship. (OPC Foundation.)

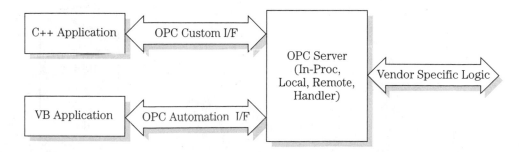

Fig. 5-25   The OPC interfaces. (OPC Foundation.)

a client-server model where the OPC Server component provides an interface to the OPC objects and manages them.

However, there are several unique considerations for the implementation of an OPC Server. The main issue is that it may frequently talk over some sort of non-sharable communications path to the physical devices (for instance a network TCP/IP session or a logical connection over a Serial port). For this reason, we expect that the OPC Server will generally be a local or remote EXE which includes code that is responsible for data collection from a physical device. This vendor-provided server must somehow provide the custom and automation interfaces described later. Although not required, it is expected that in, general, handlers will be used to marshal this interface to provide the additional item level functionality of the Automation Interface. This is the model shown in Fig. 5-26. An additional benefit of this model is that it is easy to remote.

In this figure the implementation is shown using a handler as it is expected that this will significantly improve performance in many cases. Also, the interface between the handler and the server is shown as the OPC Custom Interface. However, the use of a handler as well as the use of the custom interface between the handler and the server is just a suggestion.

It is also expected (though not required) that the server itself will generally consolidate and optimize access to data requested by the various clients to allow more efficient communications with the physical device. For inputs (Reads), data returned by the device will generally be buffered for asynchronous distribution to or synchronous collection by various OPC clients.

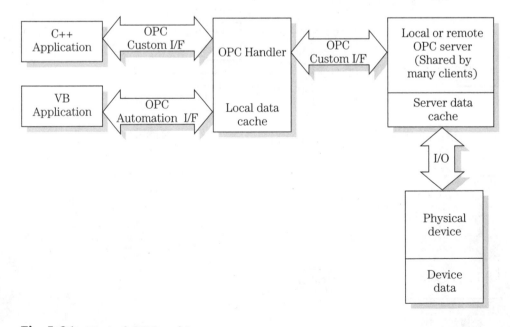

Fig. 5-26 Typical OPC architecture. (OPC Foundation.)

For outputs (Writes), the OPC Server also has the responsibility to update the physical device data on behalf of OPC Clients.

2.4 OVERVIEW OF THE OBJECTS AND INTERFACES

The OPC Server object provides a way to get data from a particular class of data sources. The number and types of sources available are a function of the server implementation.

The OPC Servers provide the capability to define "groups." These groups allow clients to organize the data they want to access. The group can be activated and deactivated as a unit. The group also provides a way for the client to "subscribe" to the list of items so that it can be notified when they change.

Note that all COM objects are accessed through Interfaces. The client sees only the interfaces. Thus the objects described here are "logical" representations which may or may not have anything to do with the actual internal implementation of the server. Figures 5-27, 5-28, and 5-29 represent a summary of the OPC Objects and their interfaces. Note that some of the interfaces are optional (as indicated by [ ]).

2.5 WHICH INTERFACE TO USE?

In general, client programs which are created using some form of scripting language such as VBA will use the automation interface. In general, client programs which are created in C++ and which wish to attain maximum performance will find it easier to use the custom interface.

2.6 THE ADDRESS SPACE AND CONFIGURATION OF THE SERVER

It is important to distinguish the address space of the server (also known as the server configuration) from the small subsets of this space that a particular client may be interested in at a particular time (also known as the "groups"). The details of how these client-specific groups are maintained are discussed throughout this document. The details of how the server address space is defined and configured are for the most part purposely left unspecified. For example the server address space might be:

- Entirely fixed (e.g., for a dedicated interface to a particular device such as a scale).
- Configured entirely outside of the OPC environment (e.g., for an interface to an existing external DCS system).
- Automatically configured at startup by an "intelligent" server which can poll the existing system for installed hardware or interfaces.
- Automatically configured on the fly by an "intelligent" server based on the names of the data items the client applications are currently requesting.

In general, it is expected that this server address space is relatively stable and is managed within the server and that the clients will define and manage

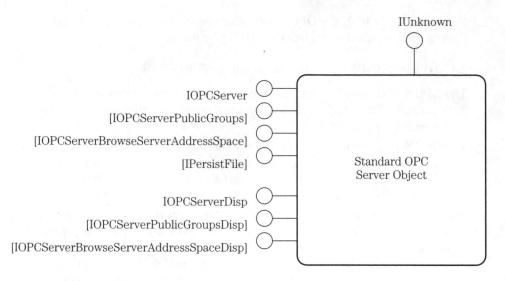

Fig. 5-27 Standard OPC server object. (OPC Foundation.)

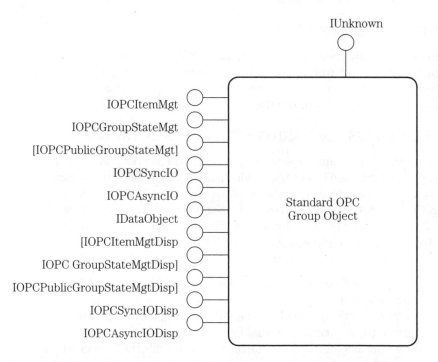

Fig. 5-28 Standard OPC group object. (OPC Foundation.)

the relatively small lists of items called "groups" as needed from time to time. The interfaces described here provide the client the ability to easily define, manage, and recreate these lists as needed through the use of "OPC Groups." The clients will direct the server to create, manage, and delete these groups on their behalf.

2.7 LOCAL VS. REMOTE SERVERS

It is expected that OPC Server vendors will generally take one of two approaches to networking.

1. They can indicate that the client should always connect to a local server which makes use of an existing proprietary network scheme. In this case the "node" of the data might be specified as part of the OPC Item Definition. It is expected that this approach will commonly be used by vendors who are adding OPC capability to an existing distributed product.
2. They can indicate the client should connect to the desired server on the target node and thus make use of DCOM to provide networking. For this reason all of the RPC_E_* error codes should also be considered as possible returns from the functions below.

2.8 APPLICATION LEVEL SERVER AND NETWORK NODE SELECTION

OPC supports the concept of organizing client requests into groups within a server. Such groups can contain requests for data from only one particular server object. Thus, in order to access data, a client application will need to specify:

- The name of the OPC ActiveX server (for use by CoCreateInstance, CoCreateInstanceEx, etc.).
- The name of the machine hosting the OPC Active X server (for use by CoCreateInstanceEx).
- The vendor specific OPC Item Definition (the name of the specific data item in the server's address space).

It is beyond the scope of this specification to discuss the implications of this on the architecture and user interface of the client program.

2.9 UNICODE, NT AND WIN95

All string parameters to the OPC Interfaces are UNICODE. This is because the native OLE APIs are all UNICODE. Microsoft Visual Basic 4.0 is UNICODE

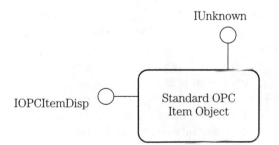

Fig. 5-29 Standard (automation) OPC item object. (OPC Foundation.)

internally and while it normally converts strings to ANSI when calling a DLL it will pass strings directly as UNICODE where a corresponding TYPELIB indicates this should be done (as it will for OPC). See also VB4DLL.TXT supplied by Microsoft with the Visual Basic product.

At the time of this writing, MIDL 3.0 or better is required in order to correctly compile the IDL code and generate proxy/sub software. Microsoft Windows NT 4.0 (or later) is required to properly handle the marshaling of OPC parameters.

Thus, at this time Microsoft Windows 95 will only be able to host in-process OPC servers. In addition, note that in order to implement OPC servers which will run on both Microsoft Windows NT and Microsoft Windows 95 it will be necessary for such servers to test the platform at runtime and in the case of Microsoft Windows 95 to convert any strings to be passed to Win32 from UNICODE to ANSI.

2.10   THREADS AND MULTITASKING

First, note that this specification does *not* require any particular threading model for the server.

The topic of multiple threads and their relationship to OLE is very complex and very important. While these issues are also difficult to summarize, the performance gains for a medium to large-scale server are worth the investment.

FOR OPC SERVERS

For servers, the default handling of threads by OLE is very simplistic. Specifically OLE will use one thread per local or remote server to handle all requests for all clients. An alternate approach is referred to as "Apartment Model Threading" where all OLE calls into an OLE server are guaranteed to be serialized. The apartment model simplifies the issues surrounding multiple client access.

An advantage to this single threaded approach is that it generally simplifies the implementation of servers with respect to reentrancy issues. Since all method calls are serialized automatically by the message loop, methods are never reentered or interrupted by other methods. Another advantage is that it ensures (as required by COM) that all access to an object is done by the thread that created the object.

The major disadvantage of this single threaded approach is that all method calls must run to completion without significant delay. Any delay by a call prevents execution of the message loop and dispatch of additional requests, thus blocking all clients of the server. This means that in general a data read or write will need to be buffered so as not to seriously compromise speed. In particular, this means that physical communications (unless they are very fast) should generally be handled by a separate thread within the server (clearly logic related to data handling by this thread would need to be thread-safe). This in turn makes write verification and error handling for writes more difficult. These issues are reflected in the design of the interfaces, particularly in the areas of "allowed behavior." It will be noted later that the design allows for optional Read and Write modes where the data is read or written directly to the device.

FOR OPC CLIENTS

As noted earlier it is currently a general requirement of COM that an object be accessed only by the thread that created it. This applies both to the actual objects in the server and to any "proxy" objects represented by a marshaling stub or handler. Note that there are ways to partially relax this constraint (e.g., through the use of CoMarshallInterThreadInterfaceInStream()); however, this simply routes all method calls back through the thread that created the object and this involves considerable overhead. In addition, no matter how many threads attempt to access the objects in parallel, they will all be gated by the operation of the dispatch loop in the thread owning the object which will tend to negate any performance improvement.

Note also the general OLE rule that code within asynchronous OLE methods (e.g., OnDataChange) cannot make synchronous or asynchronous OLE calls.

2.11   SYNCHRONIZATION AND SERIALIZATION ISSUES

By "synchronization" we mean the ability of a client to read or write values and attributes in a single transaction. For example, most applications want to ensure that the value, quality, and time stamp attributes of a particular item are in "sync." Also, a reporting package might want to ensure that a group of several values read together as part of a "Batch Report" are in fact part of the same batch. Finally, a recipe download package would want to ensure that all of the values in the group were sent together and that the recipe was not started until all of the values had been removed. These are just a few examples where synchronization is important.

This is an issue at several levels and the short answer is that OPC itself cannot ensure that all of these sorts of synchronization can be accomplished. Additional handshaking and flag passing between the client application and the device server to signal such states as "ready" and "complete" will generally be required. However, there are things that need to be specified about the behavior of OPC servers to assure that OPC does not prevent this sort of synchronization from being done.

It will be seen later that OPC allows explicit reads and writes of groups of items or of individual items as well as exception-based data connections (OnDataChange). Without jumping ahead too far it is possible to make some general observations about these issues and about server behavior.

   1. In general, OPC Servers should try to preserve synchronization of data items and attributes that are read or written in a single operation. Synchronization of items read or written individually in separate

operations is not required. Clearly, data read from different physical devices is difficult to synchronize.

2.   Reads and writes of data items which can be accessed by more than one thread must be implemented to be thread-safe to the extent that data synchronization is preserved as specified in this document. Examples of where this is important might include logic within a server where one thread services method executions while a separate thread performs the physical communications and writes the received data into a buffer area which is shared with the first thread. Another example might include logic in a handler or proxy where a "hidden" RPC thread servicing OnDataChange subscription is writing data into a shared buffer which a thread in the client might be reading.

3.   Threading issues are always important but this is especially true of SMP systems.

By "Serialization" we mean the ability of the client to control the order in which writes are performed.

1.   It is *strongly recommended* that write requests to the same device be handled "in-order" by any server implementation. For example, an application might use a "recipe download complete" flag which is set by the application after the individual recipe items are sent. In this case the data must be transmitted to the physical device in the same order it was output to ensure that the "complete" flag is not set before all the data has actually arrived. Where the server buffers the outgoing data for performance reasons and implements a separate communications manager thread to send these outputs to the physical device (as is often the case), the server implementation must take extra care to ensure that the order of the outputs is preserved.

2.   Where a client can both read values explicitly or receive updates via a callback some attention must be given to defining exactly when a callback will or will not occur. This is discussed in more detail later.

The OPC License Agreement, which appears as Appendix B in the OPC final version, is as follows (reprinted with permission):

NON-EXCLUSIVE LICENSE AGREEMENT

BACKGROUND:

A group of companies have pooled their efforts as part of a task force ("OPC Task Force") to put forth a set of standard OLE/COM interfaces intended to foster greater interoperability between automation/control applications, field systems/devices, and business/office applications in the process control industry. OPC stands for "OLE for Process Control." The specification and related software which has been produced by the OPC Task Force form a set of standard OLE/COM interfaces, based upon the functional requirements of Microsoft's OLE/COM technology, which enables the definition of standard objects, methods, and properties for servers of real-time information like distributed process systems, programmable logic controllers, smart field devices, and analyzers to communicate the information which they contain to standard OLE/COM compliant technologies (e.g., servers, applications, etc.).

AGREEMEN T TO TERMS AND CONDITIONS HEREOF:

Licensee's use of any of the OPC materials constitutes its understanding and agreement with the terms set forth below.

LICENSE GRANT:

The OPC Task Force hereby grants to the licensee ("Licensee") a non-exclusive, worldwide, perpetual, royalty-free license to all OPC specifications, prototype software examples, and documentation ("OPC Materials") set forth in the document or program to which this Agreement is a part and under which Licensee may make, use, sell or lease products and/or product literature which are compliant with such OPC Materials.

WARRANTY AND LIABILITY DISCLAIMERS:

Licensee acknowledges that the OPC Task Force has made a good faith effort to design, engineer, and make the OPC Materials in accordance with sound engineering practices; however, the OPC Task Force does not warrant the OPC Materials or Licensee's use of them against defects or limitations in their design, performance, materials, or manufacture. Similarly, neither shall any company or companies comprising the OPC Task Force, nor other manufacturer or supplier of any component of the OPC Materials, have any warranty obligation for the OPC Materials.

Therefore, the OPC materials and each of its components is provided to licensee "as is," and neither the OPC Task Force, its constituent companies, nor any component supplier shall be liable for any costs, expenses, losses, damages (whether direct, indirect, consequential, incidental, special, or otherwise) or injuries incurred by licensee or other persons as a result of licensee's use of the OPC Materials.

In accepting the terms and conditions of this agreement licensee acknowledges that neither the OPC Task Force, its constituent companies, nor any component supplier makes any warranties, guaranties, conditions, covenants, or representations as to merchantability, fitness for a particular purpose, or other attributes, whether express or implied (in law or in fact), oral, or written.

Further, in accepting the terms and conditions of this agreement licensee acknowledges that neither the OPC Task Force, its constituent companies, nor any component supplier makes any warranties, guaranties, conditions, covenants, or representations as to whether OPC materials infringe the patents, copyrights, trademarks, proprietary

The remaining sections of the OLE for Process Control are available for downloading from the following Web site: WWW. Industry.net/c/origindex/opc. They include:

Grafcet

Sequential function control and sequential function chart (SFC) programming have evolved out of Grafcet. SFCs are used extensively throughout the process industry for batch processing, batch management, supervisory control, and I/O control. This section on Grafcet is not only a good history of the standard but also a good tutorial on sequential function charts. But what is Grafcet, and where did it come from? Why has it emerged as an industrial standard, especially in the United States? Grafcet stands for a derivation and merger of some key words. The g or gr part of the acronym represents the word *graph,* as this high-level programming tool falls into the graphical scheme of things. The remaining letters, afcet, stand for Association Française de Cybernetique Economique et Technique from the French scientific association which developed it. Thus this platform has its origins in France, beginning on or about 1975.

At that time, 40 or so industrial managers, engineers, and scientists from around the French process control community gathered five or six times per year. They discussed process control and batch management. They compared notes. At that time it was decided to begin building models for sequential process control. Seventeen models made up the original set; some were by empirical methods, others came from real experiences, and still others were based on the theoretical model from Petri nets (machine state). The committee eventually decided to make just one custom model, easier than actual ones and more suitable to complex systems and dedicated manufacturing systems.

The basic concepts of this discrete system model, named Grafcet, were very simple. It maintains (1) the step, (2) the action, (3) the transition, and (4) the condition as base elements, and their presence is still felt in programming languages today. Many present soft logic application programs utilize these elements within their own programming environment as tools to build the program. The step represents a partial state of system, in which an action was performed. The step can be active or idle. The associated action is performed when the step is active and remains dormant whenever the step is idle. The transition links the previous step(s) of any transition and the following step(s), represents the fact that the action(s) of the previous step(s) are followed by the action(s) of the following one(s), and determines that there is a changing system state. However, changing is under the control of two conditions: (1) Every step previous to the transition must be active, and (2) a boolean condition associated with the transition must also be true.

These functions are similar to that firing condition of the Petri net. In this case a boolean constraint might be added. All the transitions which can be fired at one time are fired, which makes it a synchronous model. Anytime the conditions are verified for one transition (or several), the previous steps become idle, and the following steps become active. When in conflict at a step, activity has priority over any idleness at that time. This model mixed the ability of the Petri net model for the concurrent modeling and the softness of the boolean function to represent complex decision functions, and included direct delayed signal definition. All the features were deemed necessary to meet industrial requirements.

There were five rules written into IEC-848 concerning the dynamic behavior of this model. (1) The initial situation is characterized by the initial steps which are by definition in the active state at the beginning of the operation. There shall be at least one initial step. (2) Clear a transition. A transition is either enabled or disabled. It is said to be enabled when all immediately preceding steps linked to its corresponding transition symbol are active; otherwise, it is disabled. A transition cannot be cleared unless it is enabled and its associated transition condition is true. (3) There is an evolution of active steps. The clearing of a transition simultaneously leads to the active state of the immediately following step(s) and to the inactive state of the immediately preceding step(s). (4) There is simultaneous clearing of transitions. (5) There is simultaneous activation and deactivation of a step. If during operation a step is simultaneously activated and deactivated, priority is given to the activation.

Further definition of Grafcet, however, indicates Grafcet's platform regarding high-level Petri nets. While Grafcet was being developed, higher-level Petri nets were being developed from ordinary Petri nets. High-level Petri nets combine the formal specification language elements of Petri nets with the high-level programming of Petri nets while maintaining a user-friendly graphical representation. The goal of the project was to make Grafcet a high-level package usable in supervisory-level applications, with batch control management as its focus. The work is based on Grafchart, a Grafcet tool box that has a good application history associated with it (it is tried). Grafcet quickly gained acceptance, and its use spread.

In 1982, Grafcet was accepted as a standard with the French Association called AFNOR. Many PLC manufacturers and software producers chose Grafcet as their I/O language. It soon became widely accepted in industry and a standard required in several contracts and specifications. In 1988 it was adopted by the IEC as an international standard under the name of *Sequential Function Chart* (SFC), with reference to the number IEC-848. Since that time, it has grown in popularity in the soft logic community. PC-based controller packages contain many of the basic elements originally defined by Grafcet.

OMAC (Open, Modular Architectural Controllers) Specification Overview

The main purpose of this document is to make the requirements for an open, modular architecture controller known to the supplier and technology development communities. The expectation is that through awareness and a better understanding of customer needs, such products will become widely available in the marketplace.

Currently, most CNC, motion, and discrete control applications within the automotive industry incorporate proprietary control technologies. There are difficulties associated with using proprietary technologies such as vendor-dictated pricing structures, noncommon interfaces, higher integration costs, and the requirement of specific training for troubleshooting and operation. Controller elements, a modularity concept, and higher-level requirements for various elements of an open modular architecture controller are stated to convey the definitions of open, architecture controller in the context of automotive applications. Satisfying these requirements will enable an open, modular controller to be economical, maintainable, open, modular, and scalable, thus to meet the manufacturing needs in the automotive industry. Expected benefits of having open, modular architecture controllers include reduced initial investments, low life-cycle costs, maximized machine uptime, minimized machine downtime, easy maintenance of machines and controllers, easy integration of commercial and user proprietary technologies, plug and play of various hardware and software components, efficient reconfiguration of controllers to support new processes, and incorporation of new technologies.

OMAC Specification, Reprinted with Permission

Requirements of Open, Modular Architecture Controllers for Applications in the Automotive Industry, Version 1.1

This requirement document is based on the original, modular architecture controller (OMAC) requirement document created by Clark Bailo of GM PowerTrain, Gary Alderson of GM Hughes Information Technology Company, and Jerry Yen of GM North American Operations Manufacturing Center. It has been reviewed by personnel from General Motors Corporation, Ford Motor Company, and Chrysler Corporation. This document is reprinted with permission from General Motors Corporation.

I.   Introduction

The main purpose of this document is to make the requirements for an open, modular architecture controller known to the supplier and technology development communities. The expectation is that through awareness and a better understanding of customer needs, such products will become available in the marketplace. This document describes high level requirements for various elements of an open, modular architecture controller (OMAC). Satisfying these requirements will enable vendors to better address manufacturing needs in the automotive industry.

Currently, most CNC, motion, and discrete control applications within the automotive industry incorporate proprietary control technologies. Even though these proprietary technologies have been proven to be reliable and capable of meeting application needs, there are difficulties associated with using them. Examples of these difficulties include vendor-dictated pricing structures, no common interfaces, higher integration costs, higher costs of extension and enhancement, and the requirement of specific training for operation troubleshooting.

A controller with an open, modular architecture will provide benefits such as reduced initial system cost, simplified integration tasks, easier incorporation of diagnostic functions for the controller, machine, and process, and better integration of user proprietary knowledge. The concept of open, modular control also facilitates the math-based manufacturing strategy being implemented in the automotive industry. Math-based manufacturing requires easily reconfigurable machining operations and the integration of low cost, high speed communications in machining lines for transferring large amounts of data. Flexible, modular controllers are key enablers for making math-based manufacturing easier to implement and cost-justifiable.

II.   Application Needs

The wide range of manufacturing applications in the auto industry impose different capability and functionality demands on equipment controllers. These applications are generally categorized into two major classes:

1. Computer Numerical Control (CNC) type applications requiring coordinated-axis motions and the control of a small number of discrete I/O points such as machining operations, and
2. Programmable logic control (PLC), discrete event-oriented type applications requiring mostly sequential logic solving, with some noncoordinated motions such as transfer line operations.

Within each, the operation requirements can vary greatly. For example, machining applications include all component manufacturing that is general high speed and high volume, and die machining that is low volume but requires long and continuous machining operations. Traditionally, operations in vehicle body assembly, paint chassis, and general assembly are generally discrete event-oriented. More complex operations such as robot control, welding, process monitoring, etc. are controlled by separate, dedicated controllers. PLCs are used mainly for overall coordination of these controllers and transfer of vehicles from station-to-station. However, the complexity of systems in an assembly plant ranges from simple single-station operations to multi-station applications that are linked with local area networks. With the availability of open, modular controllers, the distinction between CNC and discrete applications will become blurred. The modularity and salability of the controller architecture enable easy integration of particular functions for specific applications, hence reduce the need to have controllers with dedicated functions.

Because of the need to support a wide range of applications and the continual pressure to be more cost-competitive, automotive companies are migrating toward controllers that provide agility and flexibility. In the future, it will no longer be acceptable to take the approach of replacing existing controllers with newer and better models when a few new functions need to be added.

Needs of automotive manufacturing applications are examined in the following categories:

Safety and Liability

It is absolutely mandatory for an open, modular architecture controller to meet all safety, reliability, robustness, and environmental requirements currently in place in a manufacturing environment. It should also satisfy all government and company-specific electrical, mechanical, and safety standards in the manufacturing environment. Being an open system, a machine and its controller are potentially more vulnerable to safety violations. However, it is the responsibility of both the controller vendors and machine builders to implement appropriate precautionary procedures to minimize potentially dangerous situations for the products they provide. If a third party is used to perform system integration tasks, verification of the safety-worthiness of the overall system should be the responsibility of the integrator.

Cost

It is critical that the life cycle cost-to-benefit ratio associated with controls be minimized. Some factors affecting life cycle economics are:

- Costs of wiring, interconnections, and making changes in physical equipment configuration;
- Costs of machine downtime due to controller failures;
- Costs of training personnel in operation, maintenance, programming, making changes and upgrades;
- Costs of opportunities lost by not performing upgrades because it is difficult to enhance the functionality of the proprietary equipment without replacing them;
- Costs associated with not having the ability to reuse and easily integrate available and proven hardware and software components, tools, and aids.

These factors must be considered when decisions are made to select controllers for particular applications.

Even though life cycle cost is emphasized, the initial implementation cost of an open, modular control system is still an important factor. It is desirable to have the initial cost lower than that of a proprietary control system for equivalent functionality. One of the purposes of specifying open-architecture controllers is to have the ability to integrate and leverage multi-vendor control solutions. With wider choices of products, lower cost to performance ratio can be achieved for required functions. Control systems should leverage the rapid technology advancements in the general purpose computing industry in order to improve the overall cost to performance ratio.

Flexibility

Because of rapid changes in market demands, manufacturing systems in the automotive industry need to have the flexibility to adjust the product and volume mix. Such adjustments include model changeovers, as well as changes to production schedules due to unexpected interruptions of production and sudden shifts of customer demands. Controllers of these systems must support changes with minimal changeover delay, yet maintain performance requirements. The controllers should also allow users to easily add to or upgrade controller functionality without relying on technology vendors and controller suppliers.

Connectivity

Most machines on the factory floor are generally required to be connected to the manufacturing information system in the plant. Controllers of these machines should allow easy integration of appropriate hardware and software tools to support such connection with minimal cost and effort. It is preferable that off-the-shelf third party components be available to be integrated in the controller for this purpose so that the use of higher cost proprietary technology can be avoided.

Factory floor systems generally have I/O systems associated with them. Controllers for these systems should have flexible architectures so that they can be configured to interact with various I/O systems and/or I/O networks.

Maintenance

In order to minimize downtime of manufacturing systems, controllers should have integrated diagnostic capability and help functions for both the controllers and the machines being controlled to assist in preventive maintenance and troubleshooting activities. Since different diagnostic functions may be needed for different machines and/or applications, controllers should have tools available for users to develop customized diagnostic functions easily.

Training

Retraining the workforce to work with an open, modular architecture controller could be a significant cost issue. The controller architecture should be designed to provide an intuitive, user-friendly environment so that the cost of training can be minimized. It is our belief that, in order to satisfy the application needs stated here, it is necessary to purchase controllers that are economical, maintainable, open, modular, and scalable for automotive manufacturing applications. Particular definitions of these terms are:

- Economical: achieving low life cycle cost;
- Maintainable: supporting robust plant floor operation (maximum uptime), expeditious repair (minimal downtime), and easy maintenance (extensive support from controller suppliers, small

spare parts inventory, integrated self-diagnostic and help functions, etc.)

- Open: allowing the integration of off-the-shelf hardware and software components into a controller infrastructure that supports a de facto standard environment;
- Modular: permitting plug and play of a limited number of components for selected controller functions;
- Scalable: enabling easy and efficient reconfiguration to meet specific application needs, from low to high end;

III.   Controller Descriptions and Modularity Concepts

Functional descriptions of controller elements and the software modularity concept of an OMAC are presented in this section. The controller presented in this document is assumed to have a centralized controller architecture, i.e., controller components are located in a controller enclosure. However, there is no reason why the modularity concept cannot be applied to control systems with components at separate locations connected through a high speed network. The objective of describing a model of the controller is *not* to dictate how an OMAC should be configured and integrated. The main objective is to help explain the view of what an open, modular architecture controller is from the perspective of automotive applications.

Both the openness and modularity of an OMAC are achieved mostly in software modules rather than hardware components. If an appropriate hardware platform is selected, the interchangeability of hardware components should not be a major obstacle. Figure 5-30 illustrates the concept of modularity as various pieces cooperating to perform the different controller functions.

Ideally, the scalability of the controller can be achieved by adding, removing, or replacing modules to the controller architecture. For example, modules for motion, sensing, and network interface can be removed from the controller architecture to meet the requirements of a low end discrete control application. However, all these modules can be integrated to control a complicated, sensor adaptive controlled machining operation.

The modularity concept also allows replacement of a module with another that meets the same interface requirements even if the replacement module may not have identical, detailed internal functions. Instead of replacing a module, the model also allows incremental functional improvements to each module to be implemented either by end users or third party integrator.

Core Modules

The real-time kernel, database, and the graphical-user interface environment form the core of an OMAC, and many of the issues in these areas need to be resolved before an OMAC can be successfully implemented. The graphical-user interface environment is a critical element of the controller

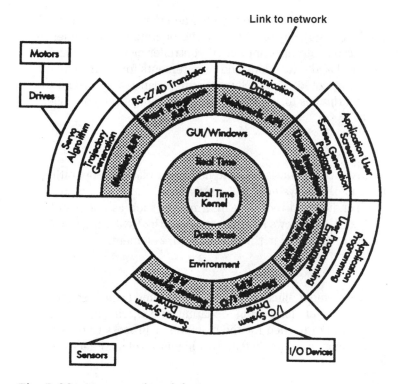

Fig. 5-30 **Concept of modularity.** <small>(Reprinted with permission from GM.)</small>

because an OMAC must maintain a common user interface environment across all applications in order for the scalability to be achieved. An open, modular controller architecture should have the flexibility to allow a controller designer to select the most appropriate operating system kernel for a particular application. In other words, a controller designed to satisfy applications with real-time requirements in the range of seconds may require an operating system kernel that is different from the one implemented in a controller that is used primarily in applications with less than 10 millisecond real-time requirements. However, both controllers must have the same interface environment to the users.

Application Programming Interface Modules

This is an important layer of the controller architecture that allows a plug-and-play concept to be accomplished. With well defined and commonly accepted application programming interfaces (APIs), modules from various vendors can be integrated into the controller infrastructure without extensive reprogramming of the controller. While effort will be required to integrate device-specific software (e.g., device drivers), the overall task should be well defined and straightforward. The API layer is the one that will require the most developmental work, and agreements among component suppliers for needed interface standard. The modules presented in Fig. 5-30 give an illustration of how modules can be linked together and how they can interact with each other through services provided by the operating environment. These modules can also be grouped into eight controller elements, as illustrated in Fig. 5-31, so that the functions and requirements for each element can be more clearly presented. These elements are organized according to functionality, and descriptions for each functional element of the controller are given in Fig. 5-31.

Infrastructure

The controller infrastructure consists of the hardware platform, operating systems, and the underlying system level software that interacts with all other elements by sending and receiving information such as commands, status, and data. The GUI/Windows Environment and the Real Time Kernel modules in Fig. 5-30 are included in the infrastructure element.

Information Base

The Information Base element, illustrated as the Real Time Data Base module in Fig. 5-30, is responsible for storing, updating, and sharing system information and data that are needed for the machine or process to operate properly. This module may also supply data to a higher level manufacturing information system.

Task Coordination

The main function of the Task Coordination element is the coordination of the application tasks being executed in the controller. The Task Coordination element is *not* the task coordination of the operating system. It ensures that proper sequences of machine or process operations are scheduled and executed in the application level, using the scheduling and coordination services provided by the underlying operating system of the controller. It is part of the User Programming Environment module.

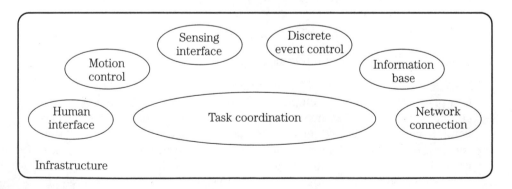

Fig. 5-31   Elements of an open, modular architecture controller. (Reprinted with permission from GM.)

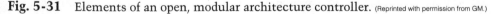

Human Interface

The Human Interface element provides a user with the ability to interact with not only the controller but also the machine or process operations. It is used to input system parameters, program machine and process operations, operate the machine or process being controlled, monitor machine and process performance, display controller and process status, receive and display diagnostic information, etc. The Application User Screens, Screen Generation Package, User Interface API, User Programming Environment, Application Programs, and Programming Environment API modules in Fig. 5-30 are included in the Human Interface element.

Motion control

Path Planning, trajectory generation, and trajectory tracking (servo-loop) are the key functions of a Motion Control element. The RS-274D Translator, Part Program API, Servo Algorithm, Trajectory Generation, and Motion API modules illustrated in Fig. 5-30 are included in this controller element. Encoder inputs and other I/O devices that are needed for servo-loop closure can be a part of this element since they are generally connected directly to the control element. However, this should not be considered as a requirement. If the controller architecture has the ability to handle this critical I/O information in a timely manner, the I/O information that is needed for servo-loop closure can conceivably be provided through the real-time database of the system.

Not all the motion control functions have to be executed by a dedicated motion control board in the controller. Some or all of them can be executed by the main CPU of the controller. However, the motion control application interface between the infrastructure system software and the motion control element should remain the same regardless of the motion control hardware configuration of the controller.

Discrete Event Control

The Discrete Event control element interacts with the environment external to the controller. It includes the I/O System Drive, Discrete I/O API, and portions of the User Programming Environment modules in Fig. 5-30. The element should interact with the multiple-PLC type I/O systems and have the flexibility to incorporate the interfaces to newer buses and I/O systems. It collects input information, executes the discrete logic, enables output devices, and also supplies I/O information to the real-time database for other controller elements to make proper decisions and take appropriate actions.

Sensing Interface

The sensing interface element includes the Sensor Driver and Sensing System API modules in Fig. 5-30. It provides a means to gather information from the environment outside of the controller, and then supplies the information to other elements in the controller for decisions and actions. The category of sensing interface includes more complex sensing devices and systems, such as vision systems and force monitoring systems, that generally acquire and process a large amount of data. Simple sensors such as proximity switches are generally categorized in the Discrete Event Control element.

As indicated earlier in the description of the Motion Control element, sensing inputs necessary for servo-loop closures can be categorized as a part of the motion control element. However, if the core module of the controller, including the real-time database and the operating system kernel, is capable of providing timely services such that information being acquired through the Sensing System module can be provided to the Motion Control module for servo-loop closure, then it is appropriate to categorize these sensing systems in the Sensing System element instead of including them in the Motion Control element.

Network Connection

The Network Connection element ensures that information and data of the processes, machine, and controller are transferred to the plant manufacturing information system when they are requested. It should also support program upload and download when necessary. It consists of Communication Driver and Network API module seen in Fig. 5-30.

IV. Requirements for Controller Architecture

This section contains the requirements for an open, modular architecture controller to meet the goals stated in this document.

Infrastructure

- The controller architecture must incorporate commercially available hardware and software products and be built to industrial standard specifications.
- The controller infrastructure must have the ability to perform all tasks in a deterministic fashion and satisfy specific timing requirements of an application.
- Controller hardware bus structure must be a de facto standard in the marketplace. VMEbus or some other form of PC bus architecture such as ISA, EISA, or PCI is preferred.
- The overall cost of the controller infrastructure must be minimized.
- The controller infrastructure must provide the flexibility for integration of user proprietary technologies.
- The controller infrastructure must provide appropriate, multi-level security access procedures for using and modifying system and application software programs.

Information Base Management

- The information base of the controller must be kept simple.
- The information base management scheme must support built-in

operating and information integrity and ensure that data is valid for all tasks executed in the system. For example, I/O update must be completed before the data is used by other elements in the controller.

- The information base management must support proper authorization and priority schemes.
- The information base must meet the real-time requirements of the system.
- The interface of the information base must be simple and allow data sharing and update from other controller components, e.g., the motion control component of the system.

Task Coordination

- The controller architecture must support both messaging and direct memory access capabilities for information exchange.
- The programming tool for task coordination should have the common look-and-feel of the discrete I/O programming tool. The task coordination functions need to be programmed using IEC-1131-3 or a flowchart type programming language.

Human Interface

- The controller architecture must support a commonly accepted graphical user interface environment that is easily configurable, e.g., Microsoft Windows.
- The controller architecture must support the standard operator interface functions of NC as defined in EIA Standard RS-441.
- The human interface function must include software tools that enable users to customize the interface screen easily for specific needs.
- The environment represented by the human interface must have the ability to emulate existing CNC interfaces for machining operations.
- The human interface must be flexible in its cost structure. In other words, runtime version must be substantially less costly than the development version. Multiple-copy discount and site license options must be available.
- Runtime and development versions of the human interface component must be separated. The executable module of the runtime version must not be burdened with the full functionality that comes with the development system.
- The human interface must have the ability to interface with other elements in the controller, using a messaging scheme, such as DDE in a Windows environment.

Motion Control

- The controller must support standard part programming inputs, such as RS-274D, and other related standards, such as RS-267B Axis and Motion Nomenclature for NC Machines.

- The motion control element of the controller requires an editing and display method that resides underneath the control system's graphical user interface environment and interfaces with the human interface element of the controller.
- The controller architecture must support standard output to server drives, either digital or analog drives.
- The controller architecture must have the flexibility of keeping the trajectory planning and servo control as an entity or separating them.
- The controller architecture must support a wide spectrum of motion control modules, from a simple bus interface card to a full-function motion control module.
- The controller architecture must have a common motion control interface that supports multiple vendor products.
- The controller architecture must allow for easy integration of additional axes when required.

Discrete Event Control

- The discrete I/O system of the controller requires an editing and display method that resides underneath the control system's graphical user interface and interfaces with the human interface element of the controller.
- The IEC-1131-3 standard programming languages must be used to program discrete I/O logic.
- The controller architecture must have the flexibility to allow for the integration of other programming methods that have demonstrated track records of being easy to understand, learn, and use, such as flowcharting and state logic programming.
- The controller architecture must have the capability to interface with various I/O systems, including those commonly used I/O systems on the market, such as Allen Bradley Remote I/O and GE Genius I/O.
- The controller architecture must provide a development environment that allows system integrators to easily develop or modify device drivers for specific I/O systems.
- The controller architecture must provide the capability that allows users to modify I/O logic while the I/O logic is being executed, i.e., the on-line editing function.
- The controller architecture must have the flexibility of integrating special functions such as traces or historical records of discrete I/O events.

Sensing Interface

- Sensing interface must have the flexibility to support one or all four major categories of sensor information:
  1. Coupling tightly with servo control and providing information directly to the servo loop control;

2. Providing discrete information only;
3. Providing sensor and part position information with time stamps for trajectory planning and compensation;
4. Providing other information such as temperature, time, coolant flow, etc.

- The sensing interface must provide a scheme for sensor configuration, initialization, and calibration.
- Sensor data needs to be in pre-defined format that can be processed by the controller.

V. Issues

It is clear that openness in controller architecture brings many advantages, but the openness also creates a set of new issues that need to be addressed. Acceptance of the new technologies and the willingness to have a different way of thinking by plant floor personnel are key success factors for the open, modular controller to realize perceived benefits. Different business practices are required to address retraining of workforce, spare parts inventories, preventative maintenance procedures, repair procedures, etc. Using OMAC also requires users to be more involved in system integration and assume additional responsibilities for keeping systems operational. Users cannot rely on technology providers to take care of all the problems with systems anymore. These are concerns that prevent some people from using the OMAC in their manufacturing applications. However, these real and perceived problems with open, modular architecture controllers can certainly be overcome if proper long-term strategies are developed and acceptable migration paths are established. Efforts should be devoted to developing these strategies instead of resisting the implementations of the OMAC technologies.

VI. Summary

In this document, the concept of an open, modular architecture controller is presented, and the functions of various elements and software modules of an OMAC are described. The high level requirements are stated so that controller vendors, university, and government technology organizations can develop products to meet the needs of the U.S. automotive industry.

RS-274D Standard

The machine tool industry has its own requirements and standards. Computerized numerical controller, numerical controller, milling machines, grinders, lathes, and the like all belong to a specific class of machines. Early on, many of these machines were tape-driven (which was the closest approximation to automatic for the time). Over the years these machines and their requirements have become more demanding—more demanding because these are precision machines making expensive precision parts. A standard has evolved out of this industry, and it is RS-274D. The goal of this standard is to make it somewhat portable between systems—

portable between CAD systems and machines and portable between machines. Industry standard RS-274D is used synonymously with G codes and M codes. Specific variations of RS-274 include D&M, Graves-Humphreys, Paxton-Patterson, and Rhino. A further requirement of soft logic and PC-based systems will be to incorporate some of the machine tool and computerized numerical control (CNC) nomenclature into the package. Machine tool systems are really nothing more than motion control systems specific to the parts machining industry. Soft logic is actually well suited to being an active player in this arena. Some other functions required of the CNC package will include indexer motion control, customization, and enhanced I/O control.

Listed below are some typical RS-274D commands.

Sample G codes:

G00	Fast move
G01	Feed rate straight-line move
G50	Turn off scale
G51 0.01	Apply 0.01 scale factor
G70	Inch units
G90	Absolute coordinates
G93	Reset zero

Sample M codes:

M30   End program, home position, and shutdown

Sample Auxiliary codes:

F	Set feed rate
S	Set spindle speed
X	X coordinate
Y	Y coordinate
Z	Z coordinate

Typically, the commands issued to the CNC machine are stored in an ASCII text file. They can be edited with any text editor or a Windows program Notepad. The CNC program usually has to interface with some other package and/or device. Many times part information is needed for each run. Data acquisition systems inherent to the PC-based environment are adequate for this type of control. Many soft logic system packages are already addressing CNC codes in their offerings. This standard will eventually be required of most PC-based systems.

Standards Organizations

Just as there are several standards, so there are several organizations which exist to control those standards. These organizations vary in their actual roles in the standard, whether in its creation or its maintenance. Following is a list of many of those organizations which are involved in international and domestic standards. Addresses, phone numbers, and Web sites (if available) are furnished.

American Institute of Motion Engineers (AIME)
Kohrman Hall
Western Michigan University
Kalamazoo, MI 49008
(616) 387-6533

American National Standards Institute (ANSI)
11 West 42d Street
New York, NY 10036
(212) 642-4900

Electrical Apparatus Service Association, Inc. (EASA)
1331 Baur Boulevard
St. Louis, MO 63132

Electronic Industries Association (EIA)
2001 Pennsylvania Avenue
Washington, DC 20006-1813
(202) 457-4919

ETL Testing Laboratories, Inc. (ETL)
Industrial Park, P.O. Box 2040
Cortland, NY 13045
(607) 753-6711

Institute of Electrical and Electronics Engineers (IEEE)
445 Hoes Lane
Piscataway, NJ 08854
(908) 562-3803

Instrument Society of America (ISA)
Research Triangle Park, NC
(919) 549-8411
Web site: www:15a.org/index.html

International Electrotechnical Commission
3, rue de Varembé
P.O. Box 131
12111 Geneva 20
Switzerland
Web site: www.iec.ch/home-e.htm

National Electrical Manufacturers Association (NEMA)
2101 L Street, NW
Washington, DC 20037
(202) 457-8400

National Fire Protection Association (NFPA)
1 Batterymarch Park
P.O. Box 9101
Quincy, MA 02269-9101
(617) 770-3000

National Institute of Standards & Technology (NIST)
Building 221/A323
Gaithersburg, MD 20899
(301) 975-2208

National Standards Association (NSA)
1200 Quince Orchard Boulevard
Gaithersburg, MD 20878
(800) 638-8094

OMAC
Open, Modular Architecture Controllers
c/o GM Powertrain Group
895 Joslyn Avenue
Pontiac, Michigan 48340-2920
(810) 857-2075

OPC Foundation
P.O. Box 140524
Austin, TX 76714
Fax (512) 834-7200
Web Site: www.opcfoundation.org

PLCopen America
10229 North Scottsdale Road, Suite B
Scottsdale, AZ 85253-1437
(602) 951-1107
E-mail: dave@hdpug.org

Robotic Industries Association (RIA)
900 Victors Way, P.O. Box 3724
Ann Arbor, MI 48106
(313) 994-6088

Society of Manufacturing Engineers (SME)
One SME Drive, P.O. Box 930
Dearborn, MI 48121
(313) 271-1500

Standards Council of Canada (CSA)
1200 - 45 O'Connor
Ottawa, Ontario K1P6N7, Canada
(613) 328-3222

Underwriters Laboratories (UL)
333 Pfingsten Road
Northbrook, IL 60062

(708) 272-8800

Copies of IEC standards are available from:

International Electrotechnical Commission (IEC)
3, rue de Varembé
P. O. Box 131
12111 Geneva 20
Switzerland
Web site: www.iec.ch/home-e.htm

American National Standards Institute, Incorporated
Customer Service Department
11 W. 42d Street
New York, NY 10036
Telephone: (212) 642-4900

Facsimile: (212) 302-1486

Conclusions

Without standards there is no control. Suppliers go off and develop, build, and promote controller designs that they prefer. Users have to spend extra time learning the differences between suppliers. After the user has made a choice, another standard is set—that of this particular user's plant. The user is attempting to gain some sort of control, at least in his or her own little world or plant. Thus the standardization philosophy means something entirely different here. However, the real issue related to standardization and having a common structure to control is what this chapter has explored. Many controls and corporate-based entities have recognized the need for some sort of commonality among control products. These entities represent both the suppliers and the users. As all groups communicate, the net result should be an environment of uniform structure.

There is a shift in the control marketplace, especially in the PC-based controls industry. The standards may be driving some of this shift, but the end users are finally being heard also. They are the customers, and the customer will get what the customer wants. Therefore, the many different standards of this industry are not only timely but also necessary. People who don't move ahead may see their businesses eventually suffer. An example of this follows.

A manufacturer of programmable logic controllers continues to market the same hardware and software that was developed 2 years ago. The company does not believe that PLCs will become extinct. The directors also do not sit on any standards-producing committees, nor do they acknowledge that their PLC product's software should have to meet a standard that is not fully accepted. This is a dangerous situation for them. As technology changes, so must the hardware and software suppliers within that technology. Obviously, (we hope that) this example would probably never happen! Or does it sound too familiar? The best approach to technology is to continue to educate oneself about new trends and evolving standards and always to strive to learn more about high-technology disciplines.

Standards are necessary in a competitive, changing world. The immediate problems lie in recognizing who sets these standards and whether they are in the best interests of the industrial community. Often an engineer quotes or asks for a particular product and wants compliance to a standard. The supplier may have never even heard of the standard, and the engineer may only know of the standard because he or she heard it was a good idea. Full investigation of a standard and what it really means to all parties is very important. Being prepared with this vital information can make specifying and securing the correct products for a given application easier. One thing seems evident: Time is on the side of the standard(s). If it is a sound program, provides for betterment within industry, and just plain makes sense, then over time the standard will surface *as a viable standard,* fully recognized!

6
CHAPTER

PC-Based Software

Whenever one discusses software for a PC-based system, there are two basic considerations: the soft logic application software and the operating system. The application software developed to run machines or processes needs a good operating system. The operating system allows the application software to do that which it was programmed to do and to be a real-time system. An entire section of Chap. 7 is dedicated to real-time operating systems and their emergence within the controls industry. This chapter mainly concerns itself with soft logic application and development software that is proliferating around the process control and motion control industries.

Just as PLCs, process controllers, and loop controllers all have to be programmed, so do PC-based controllers. Also, with IEC-1131-3 gaining due recognition to help make some semblance of organization and standards for the industry, PC and PLC software languages are the issues. What makes for a good package? Which is better? Which is the most powerful? Which has the greatest capabilities? These and other questions can only be fully answered by the user and her or his needs. The needs and requirements of the application often dictate what is required of the software package. Abilities to interface with many types of I/O and communicate with networks, flexibility in the actual coding, ease of use, and ease of learning are all requirements of the software. Additionally, safety and emergency concerns have to be considered as those sensitive, but real, questions have to asked. What happens if…?

The good news is that the software in use today represents years of development, debugging, and runtime. Do you ever remember running a program or two which got hung up or simply quit running? The software engineers got those bugs out finally and moved on to newer applications. So we are continually the recipients of the latest and greatest software packages. This also seems to be happening faster and faster every year. So it is very important to select the software application package that is the most up-to-date version yet reliable and meets the needs of the application. Obviously, the user's comfort level in the language itself, the documentation, and the support play vital roles, too.

In an earlier chapter, IEC-1131-3 was discussed along with graphical and text-based languages. These have, and will continue to, become the packages that will be offered to end users. Variations of these with features added and features left out are the choices. An end user is not going to write an application in machine code or even in C. The possibility exists for this to be done, but from a practical vantage point manufacturing facilities and their personnel have parts to make and plants to run. The software platform which can be mastered quickly and has more universal appeal, as many soft logic packages can and have, will win out.

Application Software

The application software is the tool which makes our process or machine engine run. Earlier versions of application software were written in a variety of higher-level languages, or code. These higher-level languages were structured such that each instruction represented several machine code instructions. Machine code instructions actually take the program right down to the 1s and 0s for the processor to use. Examples of these traditional higher-level languages included Basic (Beginner's All-purpose Symbolic Instruction Code), Fortran (FORmula TRANslation), Forth, and Cobol (Common Business-Oriented Language). As is evident, there was not a lot to choose from, and each had its own niche in the computer industry—business, science, manufacturing, etc. Over the years, application software has gotten really powerful, flexible, and *user-friendly*. The user-friendliness stems from the ability to program, in an environment which is many times object- or task-oriented, a graphical scheme, which allows users to do more overall, conceptual programming. They don't necessarily get bogged down in coding and scripting. Today's soft logic application software has advanced. Basic has evolved into Visual Basic, and a very common programming language, C and C+, is many times the actual basis to a higher-level graphical system.

Application software for PC-based control systems can be defined as that set of instructions which functions within a real-time operating system and governs the setting and resetting of I/O in order to control a process or a machine. It must also be able to gather and store data and to communicate with a multitude of other smart devices via many different communication schemes. The software must be flexible enough to accept and add modules, in both hardware and software senses, for future changes, as this invariably happens. There has to be a level of integrity built into the software to provide enhanced reliability to the users, programmers, or manufacturing plant in general. It has to work! There must be a good support network in place to also facilitate problem solving and to minimize downtime.

Operating systems and application software go hand in hand. They have to work together, or else the process or machine won't run without the other's interaction. With Windows and Windows NT, operating systems, multitasking, and deterministic operation are possible. The control of a process or machine has to be given top priority in a PC-based system. A predictable and repeatable response is required from the PC. After all, this is what a traditional PLC system provides; therefore, the PC has to deliver the same functionality. This means that if there are other applications running on the PC within the multitasking operating system's environment and they experience some instability, that instability cannot adversely affect the main control application program. Likewise, an application cannot be interrupted by hard-drive crashes or other factors involving the hard drive of the PC system. The application should not be dependent on the hard drive.

Application software comes in many styles and forms. IEC-1131-3 helps to give standardization to this emerging industry. However, software engineers and developers tend to build some interesting routines into packages, and these make for the differences between packages. As users of the software voice their opinions and/or complaints, the soft logic companies will respond with appropriate changes. The customer is *usually* always right!

Dynamic Data Exchange

This is the method by which data are shared between one or more Windows programs. Dynamic data exchange (DDE) allows commands to be sent from one program to the other, as it is the direct communications link between the two application programs. The server is the application program which is the source of the data. The application receiving the data is called the *client*. These data are either pure text or graphical. A client can send commands to a server as long as the server can accept them. The way in which a client and server communicate is much like a telephone call. The client application must initiate and establish the link. Within the programming language of the client is a macro which contains an Initiate command. This Initiate command is basically a query of the server which carries DDE information. This information includes the DDE application name, the DDE topic, and DDE items available to any other applications running concurrently. These three elements, the DDE item, topic, and application name, resemble a telephone number and basically identify to the client which application it needs to communicate with.

Once the dynamic data exchange Initiate command is recognized, Windows opens a communications link between the two application programs. This is referred to as *establishing a link*. Now data can flow freely between the two as required over the channel. This is possible because the link is established, and the client can send execute commands now to the server instead of going through the identification process over and over. The client can terminate the communication link with the server by using a Terminate command, usually a macro. By doing this, all DDE links between the client and server are terminated. A sample screen is shown in Fig. 6-1. It contains several elements which have to be updated every few seconds. Once the link is established, the screen can refresh much more quickly than previously employed methods.

One important point to note when one is working in databases and DDE environments: Numeric values have to be predefined as to their arithmetic notation. For instance, a floating-point (FP) data value can be manipulated via its decimal point. Sign, magnitude, and exponent are values of FP data. Likewise, a non-FP data value is an integer—no decimal point manipulation allowed. Exchanging data into and out of tables will require compatibility.

```
PUMP #1 status:      On                Flow indicator: On

PUMP #2 status:      On                Flow indicator: On

PUMP #3 status:      Off               Flow indicator: On


#1 Inlet temperature: 198 deg          #1 inlet pressure:  8 psi

#2 Inlet temperature: 187 deg          #2 inlet pressure:  9 psi

#3 Inlet temperature: 00               #3 inlet pressure:  00


#1 Outlet temperature: 290 deg         #1 outlet pressure:  8 psi

#2 Outlet temperature: 304 deg         #2 outlet pressure:  9 psi

#3 Outlet temperature: 00              #3 outlet pressure:  00
```

Fig. 6-1   Dynamic data exchange (DDE) screen.

Interrupts, Faults, and Alarms

Just as these occurrences mean critical things to the operating system, they also affect the application program. Often when one is determining the control scheme for a machine or process, it sometimes is necessary to determine which inputs should be "treated with respect." Respect in this case means top priority. How can this bit get the fastest response? Usually, some inputs are dedicated as emergency stop status are attached to a particular scan rate—usually the processor's best. Interrupts are in this class, and they do just what they are called—interrupt the program and the system, because what they have to say is very, very important. Maybe an end-of-travel limit switch has been triggered and a motor has to stop *now*. This could be an interrupt. What an interrupt is *not* is a trigger to lock up an operating system or program. Bit handling and fault handling become jobs of the program and programmer. There are interrupts which can have a lower priority to execution than their other like interrupts, and these are called deferred procedure calls (DPCs). DPCs are the methods used to delay the servicing of a PC interrupt request until a future, more desirable time.

Faults can be interrupts. Some faults are termed *fatal,* and others are called *nonfatal.* Fatal faults should be treated with the highest execution priority and a response (orderly shutdown if desired) provided. Nonfatal faults are the less serious and should be afforded the same luxury of waiting as the deferred procedure call. Depending on the type of application, there could be hundreds of potential faults. One is the nasty general protection fault (GPF). The GPF is an error generated by Windows whenever the central processor encounters an invalid instruction. It is also generated whenever an application program inadvertently writes data to an incorrect portion of memory.

What distinguishes an alarm from a fault or interrupt is the application program. If the application program is still functional during the fault period, then it will send an output, or turn on one or more outputs which may activate horns, sirens, and lights, or send an output to another device. Conversely, if the circuits are such that during a certain fault normally closed contacts are open, a fail-safe routine is present, thus preventing serious damage or injury.

Diagnostics and Fault Handling

The next step in the fault handling process is to correct for the fault, either automatically or by methodical troubleshooting. The first is preferred but not always possible. *Diagnostics* is that word that makes you feel good if the problem is readily identified or if you have no problems at all. However, in the manufacturing environment there is potential for all kinds of catastrophes. A sample fault log for a drive control system and data logger programmed into the PC-based control system is shown in Fig. 6-2. Here we have a snapshot of what can happen prior to the fault. Many times electrical data open many circuits that can be monitored while a system is running. These data must be continually updated into a matrix for use whenever power is off (battery backup is necessary) or a system crashes. If this information can be retrieved, then it might help to diagnose the machine or process condition.

Using fault information properly is quite important. If it is not used at all or if the data are incomplete, then the purpose of the programmed-in routines is not achieved and that code is wasted. Good maintenance and electrical technicians learn to check these data and rely on them for troubleshooting and preventive maintenance.

Prior to the fault handling at the machine or process, there is a stage in which errors and illegal operations occur in the development of the application program. These error messages can occur when one is compiling a program or even running the program during a simulation. A sampling of error messages follows from the Steeplechase Software, Incorporated manual (used with permission):

Driver has no type assigned.

A driver has been created in the symbol table, but no type has been assigned to it. You must choose the driver type.

Device is assigned to an unknown driver \<driver\>

An internal inconsistency in the symbol database has been discovered while compiling the project. Remove the device in question and add it again.

I/O variable assigned to unknown device \<device\>

An internal inconsistency in the symbol database has been discovered while compiling the project. Remove the tag in question and add it again.

Fault #	Fault type	Reset method	Input volts	Output amps	Time	Day
1	Fuse failure	Manual	545	98	1355	7/23
2	Fuse failure	Manual	567	95	1320	7/24
3	Undervoltage	Auto	390	66	0906	8/4
4	Overvoltage	Auto	512	92	0650	8/9
5	Fuse failure	Manual	660	99	1205	9/30
6	Overtemperature	Manual	455	97	1215	10/5

Fig. 6-2   Fault log sample.

No device assigned.

An input or output tag has been defined but not assigned to an external device. Either change the tag to an Internal or assign it to a device.

I/O variable on device <device> is assigned to an invalid point.

An internal inconsistency in the symbol database has been discovered while compiling the project. Remove the tag in question and add it again.

Device has no type assigned.

A device has been created in the symbol table, but no type has been assigned to it. You must choose the device type.

Outgoing flow goes to element inside a parallel branch/merge pair.

The element in question is outside of a branch/merge pair, but the flow leaving it terminates inside a branch/merge pair.

Another <element> has label <label>

Either there are two or more Branch elements with the same label, or there are two or more Merge elements with the same label.

Device has not been configured.

Driver has not been configured.

The specified item must be configured before the project can be compiled.

Device is not assigned to a driver.

All devices must be assigned to drivers before compiling the project.

There are no points of type <input/output type> on device <device>

A tag of type input or output has been assigned to a device that doesn't support that type.

Tag does not have a type.

All tags must have a type specified before the project can be compiled.

Tag is an array with zero length.

An internal inconsistency in the symbol database has been discovered while compiling the project. Remove the tag in question and add it again.

This driver/device requires an I/O driver that is not available on your system.

The project contains references to a device or driver that requires the use of an I/O driver that can't be found. This can be caused when a project is copied from one computer to another. Change the item in question to use an existing I/O driver.

This project requires the driver <driver>, which cannot be found. Project cannot be compiled without changing driver and device assignments.

The project contains references to a device or driver that requires the use of an I/O driver that can't be found. This can be caused when a project is copied from one computer to another. Change the item in question to use an existing I/O driver.

Safety Issues

What if the system or software *crashes?* This question has to be asked. It also has to be answered. What measures have been or will be taken in the event of the eventual system lockup or crash? The program just stops running—what provisions have you made beforehand to avert a crisis or, even worse, avoid injuries and death? It's very difficult to predict everything for any event; however, do a walk-through of the events that take place after a system hang-up. Are fail-safe, emergency stop mechanisms in place, both electrically and mechanically? Make a list and double-check it. Compare it to the logic of the program (especially if you didn't code the program). No one was ever faulted for saving a person's life.

As we evaluate a PC-based system for safety and alarms, actually many facets of the system need to be analyzed. What parts of the process pose the greatest risk? Are there potentially high-temperature and high-pressure conditions? Are secondary and tertiary safety plans available? What is the most expensive component in the machine? Can it be damaged? Can another be made readily available if the main unit is damaged or has to be replaced for any reason? Are other smart devices in the process, such as microprocessor-based transmitters and tranducers, along with drives, able to provide the host PC-based system with fault data? For example, if the drive has blown a fuse, can the PC be told that exact symptom or fault? Or does the PC just get a signal indicating that there has been an external fault and it came from the drive, so we had better turn off the 2000 gal/min water flow quickly?

Thus, it is apparent that faults can be numerous and can tell us much about our soft logic system. When used properly, fault data are invaluable and if interpreted well, can actually signal a bigger problem which might be able to be avoided.

Soft Logic Application Packages

Evaluate them from an application vantage point and from the program writer's personal view. Look at the package from the point of view of logic control, motion control, process control, human-machine interface, and communications decision. Open architectures and plenty of built-in functionality should be part of the package. But look at it from your personnel applications standpoint. Will the software allow you to do certain routines easily, with less code, and will it allow you to fix a problem later? Does it have pretty screens? They do not have to be pretty in the attractiveness sense, but neatness does count; and if a screen is well laid out, then the user can navigate more quickly.

All in all, PC-based software should support many different communication, device, and I/O drivers. Whatever the PLC standard at the plant (governing many times the I/O platform hardware) and communication scheme there, the soft logic program must *fit* right in place. All major PLC network protocols should be supported. On a network level, today's soft logic must work at the device level (DeviceNet, Seriplus I/O, AS-I, SDS, Fieldbus, Profibus, and Interbus, etc.). This simply puts all the application software packages on the same playing field. However, one theme is common: the soft logic package is geared to industry, manufacturing, and process control, not the college student or the inexperienced. It is for those in the trenches making the United States produce.

Flowchart Programming

The following excerpt is from the Steeplechase *PC-Based Control and Flow Chart Programming Handbook for Replacing PLCs on the Factory Floor.* It is reprinted with permission.

5.3   INTRODUCTION TO FLOW CHART PROGRAMMING

Flow charts offer simple, graphical descriptions of processes. They are easily understood because they illustrate a natural, systematic way of thinking. With flow charts, controlling your process becomes as easy as understanding your sequence of operation. The simplicity of flow charts has many benefits. Less time needs to be spent on learning, so more time is available for application development. Relative to relay ladder logic, more people (from various levels in an organization) can follow and understand the process, allowing for faster design cycles, continuous process improvement and easier troubleshooting. This results in less downtime and increased production.

The symbols used in flow charting are straightforward. The most common elements are:

- Start/Stop
- Flow line

- Action
- Decision

Some more advanced elements are:

- Parallel flow
- Subprogram
- Special function
- Connector

Each element has its own function as described in Fig. 6-3.

Start/Stop elements are used to indicate the beginning and end of a flow chart. A flow chart can only have one start element. This is where execution always begins. Stop elements are more flexible. Depending upon flow design, none, one or multiple stops can be employed. For example, a continuously running flow chart might loop back upon itself and never need a stop element. (See Fig. 6-4.)

Flow line elements are simply arrow-shaped pointers that link the flow chart elements together. They direct the program flow along paths according to the conditions encountered. Flow lines can intersect other flow lines. (Also see Fig. 6-4.)

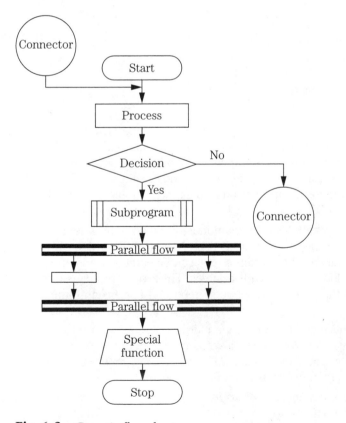

Fig. 6-3 Generic flowchart. (Steeplechase Software, Inc.)

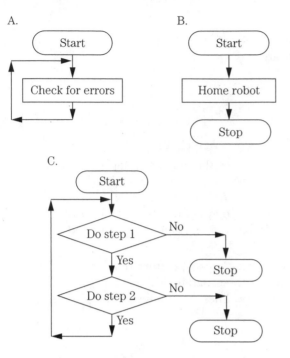

Fig. 6-4   Stop examples. (*a*) Without a stop, this flowchart is continuously executed. (*b*) With a single stop, this flowchart is executed only once. (*c*) Multiple stops allow multiple actions to halt execution. (Steeplechase Software Inc.)

Action elements are used to represent control statements. They contain the action(s) to be taken. This includes I/O or flag evaluation, and setting outputs or flags both conditionally and unconditionally. In addition, mathematical and Boolean operations can be evaluated and executed, or serve as the basis for other operations. Variables and timers are initialized within an action block. (See Fig. 6-5.)

Decision elements are symbolized by diamonds. Boolean expressions are evaluated (True or False), and the result is used to determine which of the two outgoing paths is taken. These expressions can be combinations of discrete and/or numerical I/Os, timers and variables. The structured use of decision blocks is often the difference between good and bad programming. (See Fig. 6-6.)

Parallel flow elements come in pairs. Each pair has one branch (splitting) and one merge (joining) element. They allow the user to define portions of a flow chart that must execute in parallel. All branch flows must reach the merge element before program execution continues beyond it. (See Fig. 6-7.)

Subprogram elements are the flow chart symbol for subprograms. These can be extremely powerful tools for program development. They allow the programmer to develop a hierarchical program structure composed of independent modular sections. Subprograms can call other subprograms. This greatly simplifies programming. Develop and debug each section once and then you have a piece of good reusable code. The same subprogram can be used inside multiple flow charts or multiple times in one flow chart. A good example is a timer. Create a single one but use multiple instances of it, passing the time duration as a parameter. (See Fig. 6-8.)

Parameters can be passed in two ways. The first way is by value (local variable). This makes copies of the parameters and ignores changes in the originals. A second method, passing by reference, again copies the parameters, but changes in the originals are reflected in the copies. Changes made when passing by reference are seen in other flow charts. Passing by value should

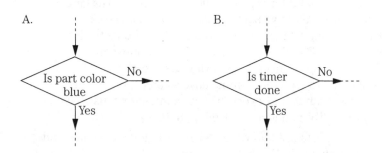

Fig. 6-5   Action block examples. (*a*) Unconditional output. (*b*) Output conditional on input. (*c*) Unconditional internal action. (Steeplechase Software, Inc.)

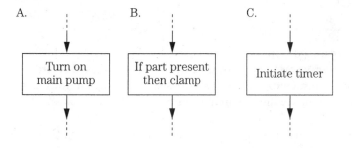

Fig. 6-6   Decision block examples. (*a*) Input test. (*b*) Internal test. (Steeplechase Software, Inc.)

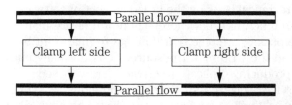
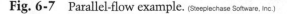

Fig. 6-7   Parallel-flow example. (Steeplechase Software, Inc.)

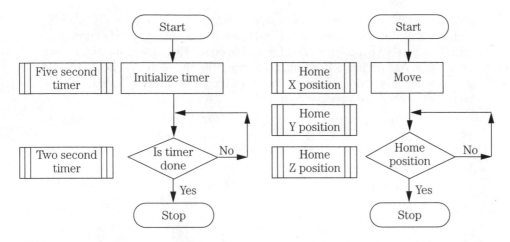

Fig. 6-8   Subprogram examples. (*a*) Here a parameter of 5 s can be passed by value. Since it is by value (copied, ignoring original), another 2-s timer can be started before the first expires. (*b*) Here all three subprograms can call the same subprogram flowchart, sending axis, direction, and appropriate limit switch by reference. (Steeplechase Software, Inc.)

never be done with I/O because actions could be taken on conditions that are no longer true. (See Fig. 6-8.)

Special function elements are catch-all objects for flow charts. They are used to access functions uniquely associated with specific I/O families. They are also applicable to motion and PID functions. (See Fig. 6-9.)

Connector elements are useful for replacing flow lines that cover large areas of a page. They allow for more visually pleasing logic that is easier to follow. There are both "To" and "From" connectors. A "To" connector has the flow line entering it, and a "From" connector has the flow line coming out of it. You can specify labels with connectors, allowing the use of more than one set in a flow chart. Every "To" connector must have a corresponding "From" connector with the same label, and every "From" connector must have at least one corresponding "To" connector. (See Fig. 6-10.)

Additional sample flow charts are shown. Note that the logic is similar but not exactly the same as shown in Fig. 6-11.

Conclusions

Justice can never be done in a technical book on the broad subject of software. It's changing too fast, and there's so much of it out there! There are entire manuscripts written on specific software packages (some that don't go to final print because they've become outdated), and the writers of the source code normally put out gobs of documentation on their products. Application software for PC-based systems is no different. Even though it is specialized for the soft logic industry, every package is a little different. Many times it will come down to the cost to obtain it. Or, could I get it for free? After all, its *only* software. Is it hard to use? Where do I get trained? Who will support me on my first and second questions during development? The answer to these questions is to secure the application software of choice. And if you don't like the package you selected, just wait a few days and there'll be something new and better out there—guaranteed.

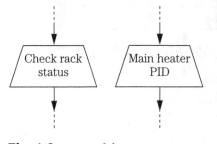

Fig. 6-9 Special function examples.(Steeplechase Software, Inc.)

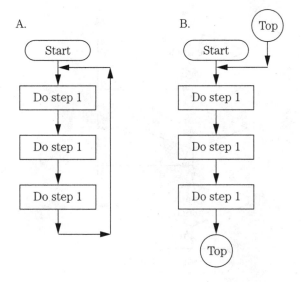

Fig. 6-10 Flowchart examples (*a*) without connectors. (*b*) with connectors. (Steeplechase Software, Inc.)

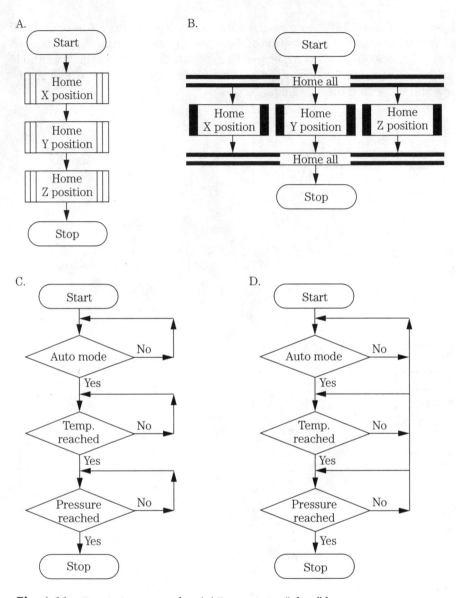

Fig. 6-11 Execution examples. (*a*) Executing a "slow" home by moving X, then Y, then Z. (*b*) Executing X, Y, and Z at the same time. The slowest move dictates total move time. (*c*) Assuming conditions have not changed. (*d*) Confirming conditions have not changed. (Steeplechase Software, Inc.)

7
CHAPTER

PC-Based or PLC-Less Control?

What will be the name of the emerging control platform? In the process and motion control industry, *PC-based* means virtually the same thing as a *PLC-less* system. The PC has replaced the PLC in those instances. In the future, when there are no more PLCs, then it can be called a "world without PLCs." But for now, which is the better controller for a particular application? This question will be asked by every existing PLC user from this point forward. And the answer lies in the question—the application dictates the control scheme, for now.

Consider this dilemma of a manufacturing facility's owners: Is the PC-based technology to the point where we can make the switch? Our plant has standardized on the same PLC hardware and supplier for over 10 years, as seen in Fig. 7-1. However, in that period we lost several PLC technicians, electricians, and programmers who knew our PLC system. This forced us to pay top dollar for new, PLC-savvy employees who eventually left after a short while, also. We spent hundreds of hours and thousands of dollars training new people, but found that many students fresh out of college had no understanding of relay logic and obviously had no or little application experience. They are not training and teaching old technologies anymore (which is what relay technology is). What's a plant manager to do?

Well, obviously the plant manager has to get parts and products out the door! He or she will find a way. It may be expensive to get there and time-consuming to look for good people, but manufacturing has to take precedence. A solution may lie in the emerging technologies of PC-based controls. Personal computers are everywhere. Almost everyone has one or has had one. Computer science is taught in grade schools, and most people are familiar with PCs. Better yet, the hardware and software are available from thousands of sources, and this makes the plant manager happy. The plant manager can take comfort in knowing that a computer part, which has taken the PC-based controller down (in a mock incident), can be found at Radio Shack or a local computer hardware store. What a spare-parts inventory system, and the plant doesn't have to carry that inventory! Still the PC-based technology is emerging.

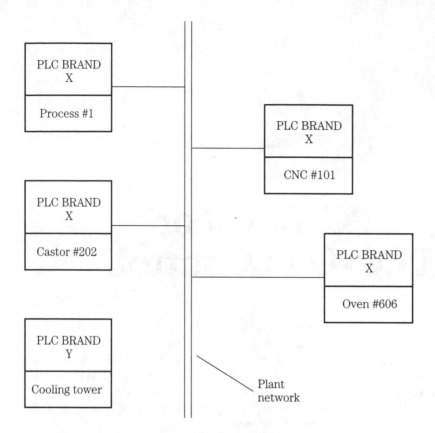

Fig. 7-1   The PLC plant standard, brand X. Yet, there will always be a loner (especially one that doesn't connect to the plant network).

Proprietary PLCs and DCSs or Open-Architecture PCs

The reason PC-based control has evolved to this point is simple: It is the build-it-and-they-will-come syndrome. It doesn't take too many instances of frustration with a proprietary PLC system in a production facility to realize there exists, and to search for, a better way. If support is not readily available (i.e., when the machine has quit running at 1:15 A.M.), or if a part has to be ordered and won't arrive for 6 weeks because there is only one place to get it, then people look for paths of least resistance. After all, they have a plant to run. Their job is *not* to support and sustain a PLC manufacturer with spare-parts business and frequent employee-training sessions. Plus, we all have experienced the other syndrome—technological change. It is more dramatic within the PLC and DCS product area.

Technological change in the PLC arena can have far-reaching effects. First, new equipment usually isn't inexpensive. It may have more capabilities and power as part of the enhanced product. But your plant and process may not need any of that! Second, are the new product and old product (in your plant) compatible? Can parts be interchanged between systems? If not, then the decision to look at another PLC manufacturer's offering or to look at another technology, such as PC-based control, just got simpler. PC-based control offers a more common platform for hardware, even though that technology experiences changes, too.

Real-Time Operating Systems

Of all the issues concerning soft logic and PC-based control, this is the *most important,* without a doubt. PC-based control can be broken down into two segments: soft logic and hard real-time control. Within the industry, experts are debating whether the Windows NT operating system is acceptable for hard real-time control of a machine or process. As it stands right now, Windows and Windows NT are suitable for soft logic applications and for control systems where full interrupt capability is not paramount. Microsoft defines in its White paper, dated June 29, 1995, that a hard real-time operating system is one which must, without exception, provide a response to an occurrence within a specified time. This *must* be repeatable and predictable. This response must also be independent of all other functions active in the operating system. Thus, as defined by Microsoft itself, Windows NT is not a hard real-time operating system. However, it *is* a very fast-responding general-purpose operating system which is not as deterministic as a true hard real-time system. There are those entities out there who are forming a Windows NT "bandwagon," promoting the use of NT as a hard real-time operating system. As time goes on and applications get tried, more will be known about its successes and failures. Currently there is development along the lines of hard real time and the modification of the hardware abstraction layer (HAL). The HAL is the lowest level of Windows NT. It defines the common software interface to the hardware which it is running. This development should lead to hard real-time operation in the Windows NT environment on the PC. Faster response times in the microsecond range instead of several milliseconds will prevail, thus opening the door to many other possible applications which require this kind of system performance.

As mentioned earlier, hard real-time control and soft logic are basically two different control methods for PC-based systems, even though the term *soft logic* is used interchangeably with all types of PC-based control. *Hard real-time control* can be defined as that control package which does function in a like manner to a PLC, with its real-time operating system (RTOS). The programmable logic controller delivers predictable and repeatable results for every scan. The RTOS controls all the operations that run through the microprocessor. There is no way for data to get hung up, an interrupt to get lost, or the operating system to go off and start another task on its own. The dedicated real-time operating system of the PLC allows none of this and is said to be deterministic; its kernel controls all. Each scan returns repeatable, fast, and deterministic information from the control engine. This is exactly how the PLC has operated for many years, as a hard real-time controller with its RTOS, microprocessor, and proprietary hardware (an issue which is helping the PC-based movement). Factory and manufacturing plant personnel still want this type of control from that device in charge of their million-dollar diaper machine or electrostatic vacuum chamber. They know that the PLC will do the job because it has for years, and they can predict its performance.

The same functionality can be delivered from a PC. However, the PC will have to have a real-time operating system loaded onto it. In doing this, the control engine will run as the highest-priority task in the RTOS. All other Windows operations will run as the lowest priority, as a background operating system. By doing this, the user will get control similar to that of the PLC but with the capability to utilize Windows tools and applications. This means that the same PC can be the device used to write the program, act as the operator interface, provide simulations, and run DDE applications. These Windows functions will be lower in priority than the logic control within this RTOS environment. As the control engine of the hard real-time operating system takes over the PC, both processing time and memory are allocated to Windows only as required. Windows will not be able to preempt the real-time control or to write to its memory on its own. By setting up an RTOS on the PC in this manner, deterministic performance for discrete applications and machinery applications requiring 1-ms scan times can be achieved. One is shown graphically in Fig. 7-2.

Here a high-speed film printing line is running at 1600 ft/min and using registration information to control the alignment of color and print. Should the operating system decide to service the hard drive while running at full speed, the printing on the film will most likely get way off-track, and the entire run of film, thousands of feet, could be ruined. Even a slight blip could leave a mark on the film which could mean a full-roll rejection by the customer. Thus, it is critical that the operating system treat the application with the utmost priority. Applications which are best handled by a real-time

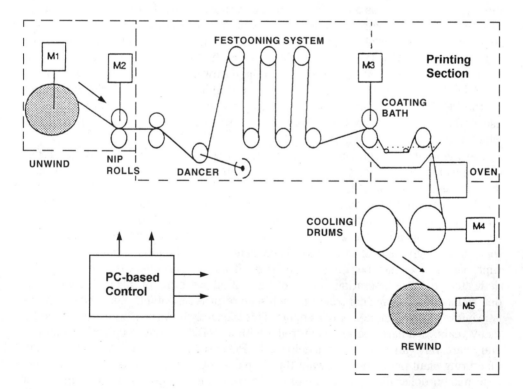

Fig. 7-2   A film printing line.

system should require a high level of safety and reliability, should be able to coordinate many simultaneous events as well as the capture of and response to transient events and to handle several priorities of service and response.

Then again, there are *soft* real-time applications which can tolerate slower response times and a blip or two from the control engine. More appropriately these applications might be called the soft logic applications. However, soft logic is more far-reaching than just a niche control scheme for a simple application such as a conveyor belt. As the hard real-time operating systems work their way into the PC and as microprocessors become more powerful and faster, soft logic probably will stick as the verbal description of the PC-based control scheme for industrial applications.

More about RTOSs

Real-time computer operating systems are in a basic sense the combination of hardware and software, both working together as a system and each useless without the other. These operating systems integrate computers with external processes, machines, and human workers to provide a smooth, proficient, and productive application. All real-time systems should have these basic elements:

1. They should have the capability to prioritize tasks and operations. This is sometimes known as a *priority-based system.* Priority-based systems function in either a preemptive or nonpreemptive mode. In a preemptive system, anytime a ready task has a higher priority than the currently running task, a task switch is made and the higher-priority operation begins to run.

2. They should be multitasking. Real-time systems should be able to process numerous events occurring at random times. These events are said to be asynchronous because they may occur at any given time, and they are potentially concurrent because one event may occur while another is already being processed.

3. Response times of the operating system must be predictable. In a real-time system, the time between an event's happening and the system's responding to the event must be fast and predictable, as would be the case with an end-of-travel limit switch interrupt. If this limit switch interrupt is not acted on immediately, then a machine component which is in motion may slam into something that it is not supposed to hit. The typical response is to perform a task switch to a program that services the event. A task switch saves the state of the current task and starts another task. The saved task state allows the operating system to restart the first task later. In a well-conceived real-time operating system running a critical external process, the speed with which this task switch occurs must be measured in microseconds. The maximum task switch time must be consistently repeatable and predictable.

Windows NT

The major reason that PC-based control has gained momentum is the emergence of Windows NT. Without this leap in technology as far as operating systems go, soft logic and PC-based control would be right back where it was 10 years ago—

a software geek's idea of doing a critical application out of a kluged PC. The PC, years ago, had many limitations, was expensive, and was dangerous (for a multitude of reasons). We should be grateful that Windows happened along and gave us a tool with which to explore a logical alternative. This section provides an overview of Windows and Windows NT product.

Windows NT is supposed to provide the computer world with a crashproof, secure, DOS-free operating system. This is what industry wants. Originally, the hardware demands of a next-generation 32-bit operating system were out of the reach for most. Not many had the required 70 MB of free hard disk space which was needed by the operating system, let alone the 16 MB of RAM required. Today, however, the hardware coming out has the capabilities to run a Windows NT Workstation 4.0. This timing has greatly accelerated the PC-based control business. Standard computer hardware today has 166-megahertz or faster microprocessors, 2+ gigabyte hard drives, and 16 MB or 32 MB of RAM as standard. Windows 95 and Windows NT are the present-day solutions to many applications. The Windows 95 interface is a critical element. Many users are accustomed to this, and it was important to factor in the Windows 95 interface.

Windows NT Workstation 4.0 is the hot operating system for industrial applications today. A lot like Windows 95, users' desktops, task bars, icons, shortcuts, help systems, and window controls all seem identical. The only difference between Windows 95's Explorer and NT's Explorer is the file-attribute display. After installing a bunch of applications, repeating configuration changes, and recreating shortcuts, only a few minor differences clued us in that we'd switched over to NT. The font it uses when running DOS is a little different, and the Ctrl-Alt-Delete keys bring up a Windows NT security dialogue box. There are also differences between the Windows 95 and NT control panels.

Windows NT is compatible with productivity applications running under Windows 95, Windows 3.1, and DOS. In many cases, it can actually get more speed out of the PC, all the while enhancing stability. NT is more flexible than Windows 95, but the most important feature that NT brings to PC-based control systems is its ability to *not* crash, hang up, or interrupt jobs. It can isolate the problem applications by running them in separate virtual engines and isolating their address space, which means you can stop and restart them without crashing or hanging up your system and without leaving garbage in memory that could cause problems later. Windows NT Workstation 4.0 also eliminates the low-resources problem that has beleaguered Windows 3.1 and occasionally has caused problems for Windows 95.

The following numbered paragraphs apply to Windows NT.

1. Windows NT will run 32-bit applications faster if given at least 32 MB of RAM but will most often run slower than Windows 95 (see item 5).

2. Rebooting in Windows NT takes about 1.5 minutes on a 133-megahertz machine; however, the number of times that this has to happen will be fewer due to the reliability of NT.

3. Versions of Windows NT up to and including Version 3.51 use a modified microkernel architecture. Basic operating system services which are used for thread scheduling, multiprocessor synchronization, and other low-level tasks have been implemented in the microkernel. Virtual memory management, process

management, and other operating system services are implemented in a separate top layer of the microkernel. The microkernel itself is isolated from physical characteristics of timers, interrupt controllers, and other hardware devices by services in the hardware abstraction layer. All these modules make up the Windows NT Executive.

4. Windows NT runs slower than Windows 95—the tradeoff for reliability and performance. This is accomplished by placing most of its operating system code and data in ring 3, the same address spaces in which processes run. This increases performance by reducing the overhead often associated with calling API functions.

5. Modern microprocessors allow threads of execution—paths taken through code stored in memory—to run at various privilege levels. Code running at a high privilege level can access data at lower privilege levels, but code running at a low privilege level can't access data in memory marked with higher privilege levels. The NT Executive runs in kernel mode, which is the highest privilege level that the processor offers. The four privilege levels are referred to as rings 0 through 3. The kernel mode is equal to ring 0. Applications typically run in the user mode, which is ring 3. Protection mechanisms are built into the processor to protect the NT Executive from application programs. Every application hosted by Windows NT equals one process, and each process runs in a separate address space where it is physically isolated from other processes. Before transferring control from one process to another, the operating system alters the processor's page tables so that each process sees only its own code and data. In this way, one process cannot access code or data belonging to another process.

6. Portions of NT's operating system, the subsystems, run in user-mode processes simultaneously with application processes. The subsystems provide the environments in which applications run. Much of Windows NT's stability is a direct result of the operating system's architecture. Applications can't interfere with one another because they run in separate address spaces. Operating system code and data in the subsystems are protected from applications because subsystems, too, reside in their own address spaces. The Windows NT Executive shares address space with other processes running, but is protected by the wall between kernel mode and user mode. It's not possible for an application to corrupt code or data stored in the Windows NT Executive because the processor notifies the operating system of memory accesses and prevents invalid memory accesses ahead of time. Any operating system's reliability and resistance to crashes induced by an application are a function of how well it guards itself and the processes it hosts from other processes. Windows NT is an excellent choice for hard real-time projects because of the high level of protection it provides both to the operating system and to its application programs.

7. Whenever the Windows NT application calls an API function in the subsystem, which might happen several hundred times per second, the operating system has to perform a context switch from the calling process to the subsystem process and then back again. Context switches and ring transitions are costly in terms of performance. Ring transitions are shifts from one privilege level to another and are incurred when ring 3 code calls code in ring 0. Ring transitions occur because applications running in user mode use the Windows NT Executive's

kernel-mode local procedure call (LPC) facility to communicate with the subsystems, and because the subsystems must call into kernel mode to invoke services in the Windows NT Executive.

8. Windows NT requires more memory than Windows 95, which neither uses fast LPC nor requires shared memory.

9. Though Windows 95, which runs processes in separate address spaces, is more crashproof than Windows 3.1, a "buggy" application can still overwrite parts of the operating system, causing a system crash.

10. Relative to soft logic, an application running in Windows NT can crash itself, but it can't bring down the operating system, because it can't access memory containing Windows NT code and data.

11. To boost performance and reduce memory requirements, Windows NT 4.0 decided to move many of the operating system's API services out of the subsystem and placed them into the operating system kernel.

12. The architecture of Windows NT should deliver increases in performance, especially in the execution of graphics. All output to the screen is performed through function calls to the GDI. Since the GDI is part of the kernel, applications can call GDI (Graphics Device Interface) functions directly and avoid costly context switches, and video drivers can get to the hardware more quickly.

13. The Windows Manager has been moved to the kernel, eliminating a key bottleneck that limited bandwidth between the Windows Manager and application programs that call Windows Manager services.

14. Now that the bulk of the code and data implementing the OS's subsystem is mapped into the address of every process, there's no longer a need for server threads and shared-memory buffers. Consequently, the system's craving for more memory is lessened. However, this is offset by the much larger footprint of the user interface shell. Windows NT 4.0 uses memory more efficiently than previous versions. But you'll still need at least 16 MB of RAM to achieve acceptable performance.

15. Windows NT 4.0 is built to meet class C2 security standards, just as previous versions were built. The architectural changes will not affect the security subsystem, which like the other subsystems runs in a separate user-mode process.

16. Windows NT is fast becoming the operating system of choice for soft logic and hard real-time applications. Changes to this operating system seem to be leading PC-based systems toward more time-critical applications.

Windows NT and associated products are excellent tools with which to build a PC-based control system for a machine or process. The issue of hard real time and this operating system will prove out over time. Applications tried and successfully run will surface. Applications tried and deemed unsuccessful will surface even more quickly. Industry has a way of spreading the news and the methods for doing things. Controls and tough applications always seem to challenge the best engineer. It is very likely that the evolution of Windows-based products will allow even more time-critical applications to be tried in the future. The reason is that Windows software developers are listening to where industry wants to take this product. Hard real time is just around the corner.

Open Architectures

Many times the terms *open architecture* and *open control* are used interchangeably. Their meanings are synonymous also. In this approach to factory process, machine, and control equipment, the end user has the luxury of mixing and matching hardware and software for personal use. This can mean that the best and most cost-effective components can be selected and married to one another to make a complete, functioning system. Computers, I/O modules, HMIs, and other pieces of equipment can be used, regardless of the supplier in most cases. The idea is to connect to as many different components as possible without extensive and time-consuming interfacing. By utilizing off-the shelf equipment one can "shop around" for the best value, can use existing computer peripherals such as printers, and can implement a system which she or he is comfortable with.

Even having this flexibility as part of the open architecture scheme, the end user must pay attention to the application requirements before going on that shopping spree. There are still pieces of equipment that don't connect up easily (or at all) to one another. Plus, as the computer industry and the technology change, it may be wise to factor in growth, change, or increased production requirements (these always seem to find their way into the picture)! Soft logic control and the application software that is associated with it have made open control systems a possibility. The future of control is headed down (or up) this path. New developments and customer demands will play key roles on where we end up.

Open architecture is taking over with many of the major automobile manufacturers. This is evidenced by the development of a specification dedicated to this type of control: OMAC. Open, modular architecture control (OMAC) is reprinted in Chap. 5 and is quickly becoming a benchmark. Interestingly, whenever the automobile industry mandates a major change in control, it has a ripple effect throughout all industry. The next 3 to 4 years should give us the answer.

Soft Logic and PC-Based Control—Points to Ponder

1. The terms *PC-based controls* and *soft logic* are often used interchangeably and may mean the same thing. However, there are subtle differences. Until the issue of hard real time is solidified, soft logic will not be ranked up there with real-time operating systems. Soft logic for the time being has to be that PC-based control system which can run the slower-response-time applications and can be also termed as a *soft* real-time operating system.

2. Windows and Windows NT go hand in hand with PC-based controls and soft logic systems. Discussion of PC-based controls cannot avoid reference to Windows.

3. A PLC system is basically a microprocessor and a dedicated real-time operating system, many times packaged for harsh environments. A PC-based control system can exactly duplicate the performance of the PLC, provided it gets a similar hard real-time operating system.

4. A soft logic control system functions in this manner: Within Windows NT, the soft logic control engine runs as a high-priority (not the highest) task. It can be interrupted by deferred procedure calls (DPCs). These DPCs are used to service the mouse, network communications, and disk drives.

5. Each microprocessor type has its own hardware abstraction layer, the lowest level in Windows NT. Windows NT can run only if the HAL is compatible with the microprocessor being used.

6. When Windows NT crashes, it is termed *the blue screen,* or *blue screen of death.* This screen, which is blue, displays system diagnostics on the monitor. The question often asked is, Can the application, process, or machine survive a crash or lockup such as this?

7. Should a computer's hard disk crash, the soft logic and PC-based control system should not be affected. If designed properly, these systems should execute directly out of upper memory. Once loaded and running, the RTOS should not have to access the hard drive.

8. Since PCs are becoming as "bulletproof" as PLCs in terms of reliability and integrity, factory floor applications are doable. Factory personnel may raise objections to the way in which the PC-based system is programmed or to what physical package the hardware must possess, but for the most part PCs are fast becoming accepted in this role.

9. What circumstances should exist in order to justify a PC-based system? First, if the present control system is old (over 10 years is close to 8-bit technology), then justification, by virtue of hours saved over waiting for information or having to handle it several times (often by hand or hard copy), is there. Second, if a retrofit or upgrade of a machine is planned, use a PC-based system. Third, as parts for the old system become scarce, use a PC-based system. Fourth, a PC-based solution is now possible (the technology exists) and it can be cost-effective. Fifth, when data in substantial amounts have to be collected, use a PC-based system. Sixth, whenever motion control, SCADA, and process control meet on the same project,
a PC-based system is justifiable.

10. More personnel in any given facility are familiar with PCs than with PLCs.

Conclusions

The choice of controller is governed by what is best for the user, the costs, and the application. Considering the needs of each will allow one or many to make an educated decision. Willingness to exploit the technology is also a requirement. Often we stick with a system only because it works; but in the microprocessor world today, technology is changing very rapidly. The same is true for the electronics industry, too. As new developments and better electronic products are introduced, the system installed several years ago is obsolete (even though it still works). Support and available parts for it will soon become scarce, and then a crisis could be on the horizon. No one relishes the idea of spending money unless it is necessary, but justification can be found to go to the PC-based system. Time will prove this!

8
CHAPTER

Connecting the Soft Logic System

The soft logic system has several basic components. A PC—at least an interface board, wiring, input and output modules (both analog and discrete), I/O racks or boards, housings for various pieces of hardware, often a monitor or HMI—and the *software* should provide a suitable working system. Of course, all those input and output modules will have to connect to something else in the process or on the machine. These "other" components are part of the soft logic system but are not considered the base devices. Figure 8-1 shows a particular machine with the soft logic system base, or primary elements and the secondary elements highlighted. Connecting the base components is this chapter's main concern. Issues relating to the physical components themselves and how to mount properly, wire correctly, and be connected are discussed. The PC-based system comes with manuals for use in setting up the system. Rely on these and keep them in a safe place for future reference. As for the secondary, or external, components, these will come with their own manuals, and these setups should follow the guidelines spelled out in the manuals. Setting up the soft logic system methodically and properly not only will speed up the implementation of the application but also will make troubleshooting later a little easier. So please read on!

Interconnecting the System

The starting piece of equipment in a soft logic system should be the PC. Here is a checklist of questions and issues to address when one is making the selection and applying this main component:

1. Does the computer have to be industrial grade or office grade? The environment and the use (abuse) dictate which is required. Harsh environments call for a PC which is constructed of heavier-gauge metal and requires four-point mounting.

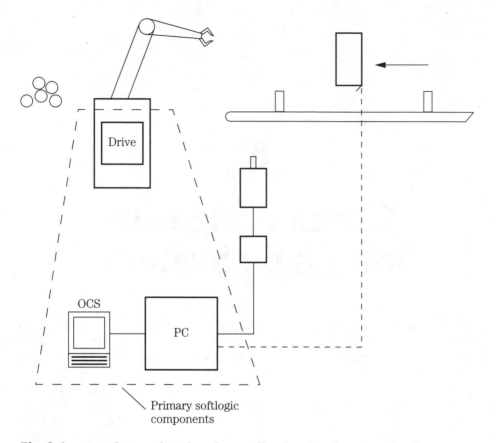

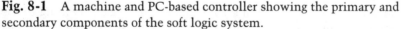

Primary softlogic
components

Fig. 8-1   A machine and PC-based controller showing the primary and
secondary components of the soft logic system.

2. Is the environment so harsh that the PC may have to be mounted within a
separate enclosure? Qualify the environment classification as NEMA 12, NEMA 4,
or class I, II, or III for hazardous use. Thus you can specify to the PC supplier the
proper designation.

3. If a CD-ROM is needed, then finding an industrial-grade machine can be
difficult.

4. Consider placing the PC elsewhere. A cleaner setting will be less expensive
up front, as an office machine can be purchased and installed more easily. The
cleaner environment can also lengthen the life of the system.

5. Consider what might happen in a system crash if the hard drive fails or
something else causes a system to go down. Consider redundant, or backup,
systems.

6. The PC that is purchased must have the fastest processor in it the day that
it is purchased. Don't settle for the next-fastest speed because this factor in PC
design is changing more rapidly than we desire.

7. Check on the memory (RAM) and hard-drive storage requirements. The PC
should have suitable amounts of each (typical values are 16 to 32 MB of RAM and 2

to 3 gigabytes in the hard drive). *Note:* Today's soft logic systems are structured for a 32-bit processor, but a 64-bit is coming in the future and software should be readily upgradable.

8. Make sure all peripherals to the PC such as disk drives and others are not treated as add-ons and have to be configured. The video monitor should be verified to be compliant with working on a real-time operating system.

9. The mouse is usually a better choice over trackballs. Some trackballs use nonstandard interfaces, so be wary of this.

10. Purchase a PC from a quality, reputable manufacturer. *Avoid PC clones.* Support and system integrity will be paramount with any PC-based controller. Confirm that the PC is listed in the approved hardware list for Windows NT.

Once the proper attention has been given to the PC, the remaining pieces of the soft logic system come together relatively easily. As shown in Fig. 8-2, the remaining components are installed and connected where required. Each piece comes with necessary instructions for interconnecting to the PC and the external process or machine. Much of the input and output installation will be a dedicated repetition of the effort for each point of I/O. Ensure that the basic input/output system (BIOS) is the most recent available for the PC. A soft logic system running in real time must have a compatible BIOS, or else serious problems can occur. The actual I/O hardware and application of it in the system are looked at in greater detail in Chap. 9. Refer to that chapter for issues regarding input and output devices.

As these remaining hardware items are connected, attention to sound wiring practices and manufacturing fundamentals will be key to the overall system integrity. If the application has been well conceived and thought out, then the implementation of the system should go well. The software phase comes next, and this will require most of the remaining attention to position the application for start-up. Soft

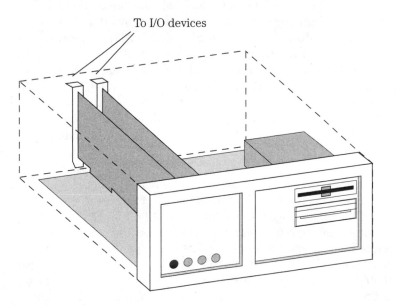

Fig. 8-2   PC-based system and I/O boards.

logic software and operating systems which have been reviewed in earlier chapters now come into play. A successful PC-based system is nearly completed.

Control and signal wiring will make or break the best of PC-based systems. Microprocessors do not like noise or any other problems associated with any electric signal they encounter. Good wiring practices should not be taken lightly. As a matter of fact, problems associated with control and signal wires are harder to diagnose, most of the time are fatal to the process, and sometimes are difficult to prevent. Since PCs and other smart components in the system are microprocessor-based, the information going to and from the control board (which normally houses the microprocessor) either gets to its destination or doesn't. If it doesn't, then the system can experience the hangup, crash, and/or stop. Likewise, if feedback from a secondary or auxiliary device doesn't reach its destination (the signal to the I/O module), other undesirable actions can be taken. Neither of these conditions is tolerable. Therefore, a little common sense along with some practical guidance can go a long way toward making a soft logic installation a success. This section discusses many issues concerning control and signal wiring.

Electrical Noise

Electrical noise has become one of the biggest challenges confronting the automated plant. Often the noise cannot be traced to any one device or source. Many times it is intermittent, which makes finding the problem even more of a chore. Electrical noise, crosstalk, hash or trash, or even sometimes called *garbage,* it is the culprit in many electronic plant shutdowns. The key here is that years ago machines and processes had few components which were microprocessor-based. The microprocessor and the low levels of voltage in the circuitry surrounding it are very susceptible to electrical noise. By now we all know that it is important to save our files when using the computer. We have been trained to do this because all data could be lost in the event of a power fluctuation. With electronic data traveling bit by bit across a conductor at low levels of current, it doesn't take a whole lot of higher-level energy to disturb a bit or destroy it. This is basically what electrical noise will do.

When the subject of electrical noise is discussed, there are many ways to describe it, find it, and handle it. Describing electrical noise is interesting. We have all heard of "trash talking," but this trash talk is a different kind. *Trash* in this case is unwanted disturbances on the electric lines. Actually when discussing noise, we are mostly concerned with noise emissions and noise immunity: Where does noise come from, and how can the control system work adequately if noise is present? A noise emission is defined as electromagnetic energy emitted from a device, whereas immunity is the ability of a device to withstand electromagnetic disturbances.

First, in looking at noise emissions, we find that most electrical noise is made by people. There are natural emissions from the voltage coming off all electrical components. This is sometimes referred to as *thermal noise emission* and it is a law of physics that this type will exist. The good news is that this type very rarely affects the electrical system. Another lesser type is the natural, atmospheric type of noise which is mainly attributed to lightning storms. The last type is the human-made noise, and since it is created by humans, it can be controlled by humans. This type is made up mainly of conductive, inductive, and radiated noise emissions.

Looking at radiated noise, we are concerned with that kind of emission which travels through the air. The other type is that which is actually conducted over a wire. Being able to pinpoint the origin of the noise is obviously going to help eliminate the problem. Identifying all the circuits, isolating them, and locating the point of common coupling are necessary. This is sometimes dependent on how two, and sometimes more, electric circuits have been incorporated into the system. This is called *electrical coupling* and is the common point where the circuits meet. This type of noise emission is many times inductive and sometimes capacitive. Inductive emissions occur when the magnetic field around a live cable affects another cable. This is also referred to as an *eddy-current* phenomenon. Capacitive noise usually occurs when two electric circuits share a common ground.

There are many different types of noise-related phenomena. Being able to distinguish one from the other and taking the proper steps to avoid each are important. These types include harmonic distortion, electromagnetic interference (EMI), ground loops and floating-ground situations, power fluctuations, and radio-frequency interference (RFI). Complete power outages and "brown-outs" can also be included in the category of noise because interruption of service is an issue. If the interruption is short (a cycle or less), then maybe the sensitive equipment will keep running. If it is longer, then relays, most computerized equipment, and other electronic devices will shut down, thus demanding resets of the equipment throughout the plant. This can be costly. Each noise has its own cause, and each exhibits its own effect.

Start with the overall system design and how the control and signal wire shall be run. Steel enclosures should be used whenever there's a choice for mounting electronic hardware needing a "house." It is not safe or a good idea to mount components such as boards on a wall or against something that doesn't protect them from the environmental elements and which, if touched, could cause electric shock. Steel provides shielding from electrostatic, electromagnetic, and magnetic noise. It can also better withstand industrial-type accidents such as forklifts running into it. As for withstanding the actual environment, there are different classifications for enclosures. These are discussed later in the chapter. Try to avoid installing windows in cabinets containing electronic circuits. If a window is unavoidable, particularly in electrically noisy locations, a grounded copper mesh behind the window will provide some protection. A solid-metal door and enclosure offer the best protection from electrical noise.

When low-voltage wire is routed, use steel cable troughs and metal conduit to route wire between control cabinets. As with cabinets, steel cableways provide shielding from electrostatic, electromagnetic, and magnetic noise. Using dissimilar metals for cabinets and raceways can result in eventual corrosion at joints, with eventual degradation of the electrical connection. Steel also provides better physical protection than softer materials. Avoid plastic pipe whenever possible.

Always route power, control, and feedback signal wiring separately. Route different types of wiring through separate conduits or cable raceways. In a typical process or motion control system, there are three major types of wiring: (1) *Power wiring* (which has been discussed previously) is high-voltage (120, 240, 460, and 575 volts and higher) and high-current rating. Such wiring is insensitive to noise but can generate large amounts of it. (2) *Digital* or *discrete signal wiring* is low-voltage

(24 volts, 12 volts, and lower) and low-current and operates very rapidly. It is very sensitive to noise from power conductors but also generates high-frequency noise that can affect analog signal wiring. (3) *Analog signal wiring* (0 to 5 volts direct current, 0 to 10 volts direct current, and 4 to 20 milliamperes) is the most sensitive in the overall system and usually is very low-voltage, very low-current. These are the most likely to have problems. The signal in a 4- to 20-milliampere current is less susceptible to noise.

Another good practice is to avoid tightly bundled cables, even if they are of the same type. Never route power (higher-voltage) wire with control or signal wire. But also try to avoid bundling low-voltage control and signal wires wherever possible. Tight bundling helps couple noise between cables. This is very important for digital and analog signal wiring. Normally, power wiring can be bundled together.

Also, many times it is convenient to use the conduit or metal wireway as a ground point. Do *not* use the wireway as a ground. However, metal cableways should be grounded. Never use a metal cableway as a cabinet or chassis earth-ground connection. Try to use a separate ground connection. Within an enclosure since it is not practical to route the wire in metal conduit and raceway, try to keep analog signal, digital, and power cables as far apart as possible. Avoid parallel runs, and make them cross at right angles to one another.

Shielding and Suppressors

Grounding and shielding are often confused with one another. Shielding is just that—a shield or protection to sensitive wiring. Use shielded cable for low-level analog signal cables. Shielded cable is particularly effective in reducing electrostatic (capacitive) coupling between parallel cables running together in a wiring trough. Shielded cable also provides protection from electromagnetic noise in the RF (radio-frequency) range. Shielded cable is usually not effective against magnetic noise or low-frequency electromagnetic noise. All analog signal wiring should be shielded. This includes motor feedback wiring (encoders, resolvers, etc.) and serial communication wiring if longer than 10 feet. Occasionally digital signal wiring must also be shielded (shielded ribbon cable is available).

In addition to shielding signal and control wire, try to keep any exposed signal wire runs as short as possible. This is common sense but needs to be stated. Keep both exposed signal cables and the bare shield drain cable as short as possible. If there is a possibility of short circuiting, then insulate the bare drain cable with plastic sleeving or tape. Also, avoid excessive terminal strips. Terminal strips have connections, and these connections can loosen or corrode. Any I/O termination can be a troublespot. Use full lengths of wire whenever possible. If terminal strips are used, try to maintain shields through the terminal strip.

As stated earlier, connect shields to ground at *one end only*. Connect shield drain wire to ground at exactly one end. At the other end, insulate the shield with shrink-wrapped tubing or tape to prevent it from short-circuiting to ground or other wiring. Some controls do not provide terminals for shield connections. In such cases, use heavy, solid copper cable or light copper strip to make a shield bus. Remember, shields must not be used as commons, and they are not to be used as returns either. Use them strictly as shields!

Shielding is the most common practice of protecting signal wire from electrical noise. Several techniques can be utilized in routing signal wire and the type of cable actually used. Coaxial cable provides an ample degree of shielding due to its composition. The outer casing protects the inner signal conductor. Coaxial cabling is a safe choice when electrical noise is expected in a system, but not at too high levels. Another common type of signal wiring is shielded wire. This should be used for any analog reference signal. It is shown in Fig. 8-3. Here a three-conductor wire is encapsulated with a shield. This is tied to ground at one end only. This helps keep unwanted noise from getting through to the wires. Another method which helps minimize these intrusions of noise uses twisted wire. Shielded and twisted wire would provide an even better degree of protection.

Another form of shielding is to actually install physical barriers within an enclosure housing multiple electronic components. Often these barriers only have to be sheets of metal just separating compartments inside the enclosure. This should prevent emissions, some natural and some human-made, from getting to the sensitive devices within the enclosure. As suggested, it may be worthwhile to predict this situation ahead of time. Quite possibly the sensitive component or the noise-emitting component can be located from the other external to the enclosure.

Control wiring and signal wiring are also susceptible to noise generated from inductive loads around process equipment and machinery. Contactor coils, solenoids, and relays are examples of inductive loads commonly found in or around an industrial PC-based system's enclosure. Typically, noise suppression techniques are incorporated into these inductive-load networks in order to protect the control and signal wiring. Inductors typically generate large electrical noise transients when contacts controlling them open. These transients can affect low-level control signals or cause malfunctions in high-speed digital (computer) circuits. High-voltage transients can also damage loads, switch contacts, and transistor outputs. A suppressor usually limits peak noise to a voltage slightly higher than the peak voltage applied. Any inductive load that can generate a noise transient near the soft logic equipment

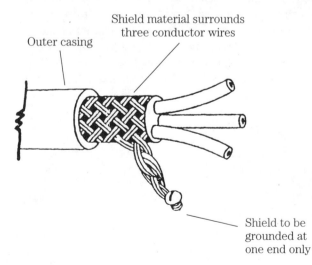

Outer casing

Shield material surrounds three conductor wires

Shield to be grounded at one end only

Fig. 8-3 Shielding.

must have suppressors. It does not matter whether the device is actually controlled by the soft logic. If it is physically close, then it potentially can cause problems. Installing suppressors in parallel with the inductive load and installing them as close to the load as possible are one solution.

There are three basic types of noise suppression devices with rule-of-thumb sizing for suppressing the noise:

Diodes. They are rated 1 ampere for small loads and 5 amperes for larger loads. The peak inverse voltage (PIV) rating should be at least twice the voltage. A heat sink is generally not required for this component.

Resistor/Capacitor (RC) networks. Capacitors should be sized to be approximately 3 times the rms AC voltage. Resistors should be 0.5 watt for small loads and 1 watt for larger ones.

MOVs (metal-oxide varistors). These should be used in conjunction with a resistor/capacitor network, 120- and 240-volt systems.

These noise suppression devices can be used individually or in combination depending upon the voltage and the inductive load. Remember, we are trying to minimize or eliminate noise to control and signal wiring. Higher voltages and ratings associated with power cabling should not be addressed in a similar manner. Use these noise suppression techniques for low-voltage wiring schemes, only. The basic types of applications for noise suppressors are as follows: small and large single-phase AC inductive loads, three-phase AC inductive loads (usually larger than single-phase loads), and small and large DC loads.

Troubleshooting the Soft Logic System

Unfortunately, even when all the shielding, grounding, and noise suppression methods are followed, our soft logic system can still be a problematic application. By following the recommended and proper wiring rules, we certainly minimize most of our noise problems. Radio-frequency interference and harmonic distortion are two other common occurrences which are continually being blamed as culprits in PC-based installations. Some electrical noise problems can be easily traced while others are a mystery. These can be very difficult and expensive to trace in a finished system. Therefore, it is extremely important to design a system with sound practices and integrity to keep problem areas from emerging in the system. Typical symptoms of noise-related electrical malfunctions are as follows:

- CPU faults. No further explanation is given (some controllers can tell us when the fault happened and what some voltage and current conditions were at the time of the fault).
- External faults (interrupt). Something happened in the circuitry outside the PC-based system.
- Complete lockup (freeze). No display, no data recorded, blue screen.
- Scrambled display data on local video display or remote monitor.
- Loss of data in battery-backed memory. This should not happen when the

battery is charged; however, data stored and retrieved from storage can be mixed with "garbage."

- Noise can be found from many sources. The basic types of electrical noise include the following:

    Harmonic distortion is caused by other power conversion equipment in the facility. Anytime AC power is converted to DC power, there is the possibility of line disturbances. This is especially evident with higher-current-capacity devices. Harmonic distortion is such an important issue today that IEEE has dedicated a standard to defining it and providing guidelines on dealing with it.

    Magnetic noise is caused by a changing magnetic field inducing voltages into adjacent wiring or components. A transformer is an example of a device that deliberately uses magnetic coupling.

    Electrostatic is caused by capacitance coupling from a changing electric field.

    Electromagnetic is RF (radio frequencies or "radio waves") transmitted by a device and received (even if unintentionally) by other electrical components.

Sources of industrial electrical noise

There are many sources of electrical noise in an industrial environment:

The AC and DC electronic drives

Relay panels

Welding equipment

The DC and AC motors—especially high-horsepower and when line-started

Lighting systems, especially fluorescent

Generators

Motor starters

Contactors

Some items to check

Here is a checklist of major items to look at:

Are all ground cables large, solid, and routed as directly as possible to earth ground?

Do all inductive loads have suppressors?

Are all shields grounded at exactly one end?

In some cases you may have to experiment with disconnecting an end of common or return cables. Multiple parallel connections of commons are returns (especially if the equipment connects these to chassis ground) and can create large, noisy circulating electric currents called *ground loops*. Ground loops can create hard-to-trace noise problems. If noise is a problem, try disconnecting duplicate returns or commons one at a time to see if the noise lessens. A multipurpose voltohmmeter is useful for tracking down multiple grounds and commons.

With newer techniques in use today to convert AC to DC power and with computerized equipment being so sensitive and prevalent, noise in a facility is more than a nuisance. The absolute best scenario is to install equipment such that the potential for noise problems is all but eliminated. But this is easier said than done, and not everything is known about the subject. This is why consultants and specialists are called into a facility to help diagnose problems. Also, not every installation can be brand new from the ground up. Most installations of electrical equipment are retrofits, modifications, and plant upgrades. Thus electrical noise will probably become an issue at some point.

Whenever noise becomes a problem in an existing installation, these are some initial areas that may be suspect:

In and around any high-frequency switching devices.

Cable shield short-circuited to ground or another shield

Broken shield connection

Faulty noise suppressor

Corroded ground connection

Loose connection

New wiring nearby, especially higher-voltage wiring

New (or portable) electrical equipment nearby

Incoming power from a utility (some problems actually start outside a facility)

Electrical noise is fast becoming the factory problem of the last half of the 1990s. Almost all equipment has microprocessors and this makes that piece of equipment sensitive. Manufacturers of this equipment can add filtering and protection, but this is always added at a price. Therefore, some good research into the application beforehand will probably save downtime and extra costs later.

Transformers

Another component important to the PC-based system is the transformer. Sometimes referred to as the *control transformer,* this inductor has to be considered an integral part because it allows the necessary voltages to flow to the PC. This transformer can also be the unit to provide power for the I/O modules and other process or machine devices. A one-line diagram of components in a soft logic system is seen in Fig. 8-4. One purpose of the transformer is to buffer the AC line from the effects of the conversion equipment and to help keep transients from entering the PC. This type of transformer is referred to as the *isolation transformer.* In some instances, a transformer has to be incorporated on the supply merely to match the line voltage with the system voltage. This has to be done in order for the equipment to function properly, and this transformer is commonly called the *step-down transformer* (usually taking a higher voltage at the primary and stepping it down at its secondary, that is, 460 to 230 volts). In this case the step-down transformer acts as an isolation transformer; thus the line buffer is an inclusive feature.

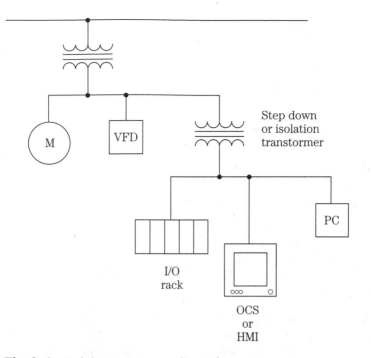

Fig. 8-4 Soft logic system and transformers.

Delta or wye transformer systems which could be grounded or ungrounded are typically used (see Fig. 8-5). The current waveshape is sinusoidal with pulses and consists of the fundamental current (50/60 hertz) and many harmonic currents. To minimize the harmonic currents, a wye configuration is used to eliminate any harmonic current whose frequency is divisible by 3. By using a fourth cable for neutral or ground in a wye system, all current paths will be defined, minimizing voltage unbalances that occur when currents are conducted through an earth ground "conductor."

The harmonics that are caused in a distribution system more often are due to an unbalance between the phase voltages than to the power equipment taking power from that distribution system. To minimize harmonics, the AC line must have equal-voltage waveforms in the positive and negative cycles and must have the same form or shape. Any deviation will create harmonic currents when power is drawn from the distribution system. If a delta configuration is used and one phase is grounded, the equivalent wye circuit is no longer balanced. The resulting line currents will not be equal. This can cause harmonic heating, premature line fuse failure, and failure in the input rectifiers used in some equipment.

Most transformers used today are designed for both linear and nonlinear loads. Incandescent lighting and line-started motors are examples of linear loads. Nonlinear loads are typical of any electrical equipment which has a power switching component associated with it. In addition, nonlinear loads include lighting ballasts (fluorescent lighting), metal-oxide varistors (MOVs), arc equipment, and so on. Thus, nonlinear loads put an additional demand on transformers. This increased demand can be addressed in new installations, but the addition of rectifying and phase-controlled

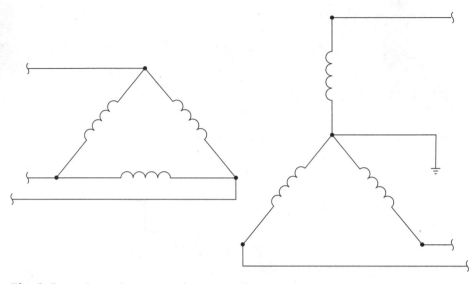

Fig. 8-5   Delta and wye transformer configurations.

converters to existing transformers is a topic in need of investigation. Nonlinear loads demand current from the utility which creates higher frequencies. The waveform or waveshape of the load current is no longer defined by a single frequency. It is a complex shape which contains many frequencies.

When compared to the fundamental waveform we can expect at 60-hertz current, these higher-frequency currents behave differently. High-frequency currents will attempt to flow through the surface area of a conductor. When the cross-sectional area of that conductor becomes too restrictive, the conductor eventually becomes hot. When the conductor is packaged inside layers of wire, as is the case in a transformer, the temperature of the transformer begins to rise and hot spots are created which will ultimately shorten the life of the transformer.

Transformer manufacturers, knowing when nonlinear loads are going to be present, take this into account when sizing the transformer. The rule of thumb is to increase the size of the transformer, sometimes by 10 percent, which in effect derates a transformer with a higher rating. Using a larger transformer does not always guarantee that it will run at a lower temperature. A larger transformer will use wire with a larger cross-sectional area. Increasing the cross-sectional area does not provide a proportional increase in surface area. Harmonic currents can cause hot spots in transformers of any size. This is due to an increase in the eddy-current losses in a transformer, and this loss is difficult to predict. Thus there are two major issues when you are dealing with nonlinear loads.

One procedure to deal with the hot spots within the transformer which is going to run nonlinear loads is to shape the wire so that there is as much surface area as possible to offer the least resistance for the higher-frequency currents. The other method is to attempt to specify the amount of harmonics by use of the *K factor.* Today's transformers are now classified by *K* factor. The *K* factor defines the transformer's ability to handle harmonic currents while operating within its thermal capability. Linear load transformers are classified with a *K* factor of 1. Transformers with a *K* factor of 4 are suitable for moderate levels of harmonic currents. A *K* factor of 13 is suitable for greater levels of harmonic currents while most applications require a *K* factor rating of 6. The *K* factor is merely an attempt by industry to define and address the issue so that equipment lasts longer and catastrophic failures are kept to a minimum.

There are other issues to consider whenever nonlinear rated transformers are used. The associated distribution equipment and switchgear such as circuit breakers must be sized to the transformer rating. However, when oversized linear rated transformers are used, electrical codes dictate that larger, more costly circuit breakers be used. The same can be said for contactors, another electrical device. Therefore, the issue is important as well as costly. Likewise, when you consider line filters to reduce the level of harmonic currents transferred back to the distribution system, other voltage problems can be created with nonlinear equipment. Additional losses can be introduced into the system.

Enclosing the Soft Logic System Components

It is not acceptable or wise to simply start mounting these I/O boards and modules, relays, starters, and other switchgear onto machines or onto the walls in the factory or office building. For one thing, this procedure is not safe. For another, it is unsightly and will probably shorten the life of the electrical product. Many industrial users, especially those without a lot of electrical equipment in the plant, will take the easy route and mount a controller in the most convenient place in the building, which is usually right on the wall. This will drive building code inspectors crazy. However, there exist several alternatives.

Many facilities have dedicated space for electrical equipment. Control rooms which have restricted entry are common in facilities that have a substantial number of electrical products in use. Electrical rooms, mechanical rooms and vaults, and outdoor buildings all can serve as ideal locations for peripheral equipment. However, the PC-based controller usually has to be out near the process or machine. Depending on the environment, it may be necessary to enclose the PC or put it in a control room. In facilities where specific rooms or vaults are not available and wall space may be at a premium, a metal enclosure may be the only alternative—some type of a box, floor- or wall-mountable and made of a metal (preferably steel, as it provides electrical disturbance protection) to withstand the local environment and provide a degree of protection to the workers and the product within. This has become the accepted solution for housing most electrical products in today's factory.

PC-based equipment does not have to be located right next to the process or machine which it is controlling, or even right next to the supply transformer (although keeping the distances short is recommended). Sometimes it is not possible to physically locate it right next to a piece of equipment. This is what wire and cable are used for—to connect the two pieces electrically. Therefore, enclosures can be located away from the traffic and actual production areas in the plant, within reason. It still costs extra to run cable longer distances, but there usually exist logical locations to place enclosures. Once a suitable location is chosen, it is important to select the appropriate enclosure type for the application and for the environment. To aid in this process, there exist standard ratings established by NEMA for degrees of protection, for both indoor and outdoor enclosures. These are shown in Table 8-1.

Switchgear

Any device which functions in a switch capacity for a given circuit is commonly referred to as a *switchgear.* Although it is typically associated in industry with higher-voltage and higher-current rated equipment, it is still worth discussing in PC-based control. The soft logic system by virtue of its I/O control is linked to much of this switchgear anyhow. Switchgear will include circuit breakers, high interrupting circuit breakers, fused disconnects, contactors, starters, and so on. In most processes and machines, there needs to be a way of "killing" incoming power in order to do an emer-

TABLE 8-1. Environmental Protection Classification

Type	Enclosure
1	Intended for use primarily to provide a degree of protection against contact with the enclosed equipment.
2	Intended for indoor use primarily to provide a degree of protection against limited amounts of falling water and dirt.
3	Intended for outdoor use primarily to provide a degree of protection against windblown dust, rain, sleet, and external ice formation.
3R	Intended for outdoor use primarily to provide a degree of protection against falling rain, sleet, and external ice formation.
3S	Intended for outdoor use primarily to provide a degree of protection against windblown dust, rain, and sleet and provide for operation of external mechanisms when covered with ice.
4	Intended for indoor or outdoor use primarily to provide a degree of protection against windblown dust and rain, splashing water, and hose-directed water.
4X	Intended for indoor or outdoor use primarily to provide a degree of protection against corrosion, windblown dust and rain, splashing water, and hose-directed water.
5	Intended for indoor use primarily to provide a degree of protection against dust and falling dirt.
6	Intended for indoor or outdoor use primarily to provide a degree of protection against the entry of water during occasional temporary submersion at a limited depth.
6P	Intended for indoor or outdoor use primarily to provide a degree of protection against the entry of water during prolonged submersion at a limited depth.
7	Class 1, group A, B, C, or D hazardous locations, air break—indoor.
8	Class 1, group A, B, C, or D hazardous locations, oil-immersed—indoor.
9	Class 11, group E, F, or G hazardous locations, air break—indoor.
10	Bureau of Mines.
11	Intended for indoor use primarily to provide a degree of protection against dust, falling dirt, and dripping noncorrosive liquids.
12	Intended for indoor use primarily to provide a degree of protection against dust, falling dirt, and dripping noncorrosive liquids other than at knockouts.
13	Intended for indoor use primarily to provide a degree of protection against lint, dust, seepage, external condensation, and spraying of water, oil, and noncorrosive liquids.

gency stop. In an emergency situation, the master controller (PC-based soft logic system) must have been previously interlocked to some contactors or breakers. *Note:* It is a common practice to run emergency-stop wiring in a separate run to a dedicated relay or trip mechanism. The logic here is that the computer should not have control of the emergency stop. The reasoning is that the processor may not have control, and thus the emergency stop has the potential to never happen. This insurance policy of a dedicated emergency-stop circuit is sound. Many local codes mandate that certain disconnect methods be in place and how and where to implement them. The National Electric Code also goes into great detail on the subject. Consult both local codes and the NEC when in doubt.

Another form of switchgear is the contactor. Contactors are mainly used to isolate power from the source and the destination (see Fig. 8-6). Ironically, the contact symbol is very familiar to you at this point. From ladder logic and I/O control, the contact is the base element in the soft logic system design. A contactor is nothing more than a contact but usually considered of higher voltage and current, which is how it is rated. In the plant, larger contactors can be heard "pulling in" when their coil is energized. The PC-based system is in control of many contactors, some big and others very small. The NEMA sizes for some common starters and contactors are shown in Table 8-2.

Radio-Frequency Interference

Radio-frequency interference (RFI) is not harmonic distortion. Harmonics is the distortion of the sine wave due to power rectification, found, for example, with variable-speed drives. Radio-frequency interference is different. It is interference to frequencies above the audible by fast switching devices, similar to those used in variable-frequency drives. This is where the two are often confused. Obviously, PC-based systems utilize working frequencies in the 166- to 200-megahertz range, internal to the device. RFI is not fingered as a problem so much for PC systems yet, but sound practices should be followed to install the equipment. Proper location of the PC and its enclosure should ensure minimal problems. But as faster clock speeds and throughputs are emerging, the higher frequencies will go. Understanding the potential for problem areas is important.

Radio broadcasting frequencies are typically above 150 kilohertz and below 100 megahertz. Whenever current or voltage waveforms are nonsinusoidal, there is always the possibility of radio-frequency interference. Newer switching technology in converter and inverter devices has started to infringe on the high-frequency domain of the radio waves. By the laws of the Federal Communications Commission (FCC), it is forbidden to interfere with these signals. Thus, new standards are being discussed every day as frequencies of inverters can be seen going higher and higher. Switching frequencies, or carrier frequencies in drives, have reached values of 15 kilohertz with present-day drive technology. Since AC drives utilize the switching capability of different transistors, they have come under the greatest scrutiny. When current increases so quickly, as is the case with today's power semiconductors, noise can be detected at a radio. Walkie-talkies and cellular phones are used more often in the plant by maintenance and engineering personnel; thus RFI can be a problem. Distance from the emitting device, shielding, and filtering

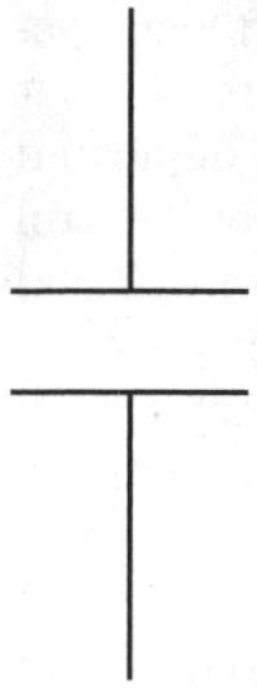

Fig. 8-6   The contactor symbol for use in both logic applications and electric power schemes.

TABLE 8-2. NEMA Starter Sizes

NEMA size	230 volts	460/575 volts
00	1½	2
0	3	5
1	7½	10
2	15	25
3	30	50
4	50	100
5	100	200
6	200	400
7	300	600
8	450	900
9	800	1600

are all factors relating to the existence of RFI. Other factors impacting RFI are the horsepower and current rating of the drive, the output and switch frequency, the impedance of the AC supply, and how well shielded the power modules are.

Filtering by means of inductors and capacitors is presently the best way to suppress RFI emissions. Emission occurrences are rarely proved as they are rarely considered. Enforcing adherence to the laws and standards has not been paramount. As the occurrences increase, so will the need to police the issue. One step is to clearly specify that manufacturers of equipment must adhere to certain levels set forth by the FCC. Then these levels must be measured after equipment installation to see that they are met. By enforcing the issue, proper attention to the matter will be given. Probably one of the best policies is to not locate an industrial PC-based control near a drive, and vice versa. This should eliminate one more piece of noise within the factory.

Power Factor

Power factor is another topic that is often misunderstood. A PC-based system's main components will not affect, and should not be affected by, the power factor of the plant. However, it is worth discussing just to familiarize yourself with the concept. Additionally, several pieces of equipment ultimately controlled by the soft logic system can have an effect on the plant's overall power factor. If you are in charge of the PC-based system being blamed, then you need to know a little about the subject! Similar to harmonic distortion, it is more predictable whenever sine wave power is being monitored; but introduce nonsinusoidal waveforms, and watch out! The power factor is the ratio of the instantaneous, or active, power to the anticipated power. When power is being analyzed as a pure sine wave, all is predictable and understandable. When we deal with nonsinusoidal power, as is the case with drives, the analysis takes on new meaning. Normally, the leading and lagging power factor assumes capacitance and inductance is in the system. This, again, is only valid when sine wave power is evident for voltage and current.

The power factor is actually made up of a displacement factor and a harmonic factor. As seen in an earlier chapter, power in the equation $P = EI$ is the product of voltage E and current I. When voltage and current waveforms are in phase, their zero crossing points are the same. This condition allows for all the available power to be used as productive power. However, when the current is out of phase with the voltage, it is termed *lagging*. The net result is that for this half-cycle, the power is not productive. This is the displacement power factor. The harmonic power factor is of a lesser degree as it basically is the effect of the wave distortion in the same phase sequencing as previously described. The relationship between the displacement power factor and distortion is best illustrated in Fig. 8-7. This relationship is common whenever a converter (such as an electronic drive) is in the system.

Power factor is expressed in terms of VARs, or K-Vars, which is 1000 (kilo) vars. Vars are volt-amperes reactive. This is the reactive power, a product of current rms (root mean squared, a peak average) and voltage rms. Power factor is proportionately equal to the watts divided by the volt-amperes. A diagram commonly used to illustrate power factor is the power factor triangle shown in Fig. 8-8.

Power factor is measured as leading or lagging. Power factor correction comes into play when a predetermined value for a system must be met. Often the utilities demand that certain levels be maintained. A standard circuit for power factor correction can utilize capacitors and inductors to provide a tuned circuit, placed between the supply and the converting/inverting device. This can be an expensive solution, though.

Electromagnetic Interference

Electromagnetic interference (EMI) is not easy to pinpoint and usually does not occur that frequently. This interference occurs when a sensitive device, such as a computer, receives the EMI and trips, faults, or starts acting oddly. Electromagnetic fields can exist around high-voltage, high-current carrying devices such as arc welders, large-horsepower motors, and electric furnaces. This type of interference is best addressed when you locate equipment within the plant. If not, loss of data, bad data, and false contact closures can result.

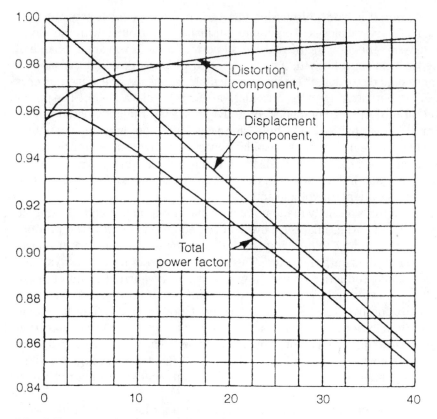

Fig. 8-7 Power factor–distortion relationship.

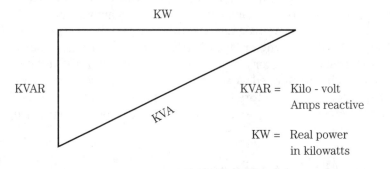

Fig. 8-8 Power-factor triangle formulation.

Grounding and Ground Loops

Ground loops and poor grounding are often sources of electrical noise. A ground circuit is supposed to route higher levels of current to ground rather than destroy valuable electronic components and shock humans. Unfortunately, this is also another route for low level electrical disturbances to travel. This ground route can both send unwanted disturbances out to other sensitive devices and receive unwanted electrical noise. A ground loop exists when there is potential, or emf, between pieces of equipment whose grounds are connected in the same system. A typical ground loop condition can be seen in Fig. 8-9. The best scenario is to ground each piece of equipment directly to its own ground. The trick is not to create a loop condition. This loop will allow unwanted signals from various sources to enter into a completely separate circuit, many times a circuit whose equipment is very sensitive.

Grounding, when done solidly and properly, is a very good practice. However, grounds can become loose over time in environments where vibration and just simple activity around the connection occur. Also, grounds can deteriorate over time, especially in corrosive atmospheres. Checking and inspecting ground wires and all wires in a circuit is good practice. Making sure the connections are constantly solid can prevent damage to devices which normally expect low levels of voltage and can also eliminate disturbances due to ground loops.

When, where, and why should a ground path be found? Grounding is done for mainly two reasons: to protect operators in case of an electrical malfunction and to minimize and protect equipment from electrical noise. However, improper grounding can lead to other problems and, in particular, ground loops. All equipment in a control system has to be properly grounded. All chassis and cabinet grounds should connect to a central ground. Connect all electrical chassis and cabinets to the facility's central earth ground. By *earth ground* we mean the central ground point for all AC power and electrical equipment within a factory. Every facility with electrical equipment has an existing grounding electrode system. Local building codes address grounding requirements, and for further definitions the National Electrical Code can be consulted.

In Fig. 8-10 is shown a typical, good ground system. Figure 8-11 shows a ground system which has multiple controllers. Shown are the proper ground method for these and the improper method which will cause a ground loop. The minimum conductor size for ground wire is no. 6 AWG copper. These conductors should be properly sized to provide full protection in case of an AC wiring fault. Know the current and voltage ratings of all the equipment installed. Also, learn how each piece handles a ground fault. Again, consult your local building and wiring codes. Also, technical manuals show how and where ground terminations are to be made.

For practical reasons, only copper conductors should be used for ground wiring. Aluminum is subject to corrosion and has a high electrical resistance compared to copper. Any ground electrode must be connected to any main ground bus bar. Install a grounding conductor between the grounding electrode and an earth ground bus bar in the AC power distribution panel. The earth ground bus bar is typically a copper bar with threaded holes for connections. Securely attach the earth ground bus bar to the distribution panel cabinet. Do this either by bolting the bus bar to the cabinet or by using a very short piece of copper wire (no. 6 AWG or higher). Bond this securely to clean, bare metal, not a painted surface.

When you lay out or design the wiring scheme for the PC-based system, give the grounding circuit special attention. This may save time later. As a rule, ground connections must not be broken by any switches. The main disconnect switch must never break any ground connection. Each enclosure should have its own ground. Every equipment cabinet must have a ground bus that connects directly to the earth

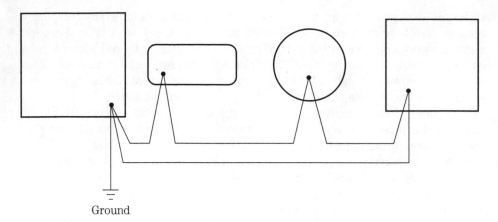

Fig. 8-9   Ground loop.

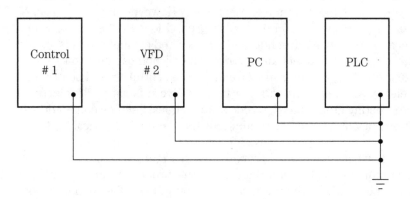

Fig. 8-10   Solid ground system.

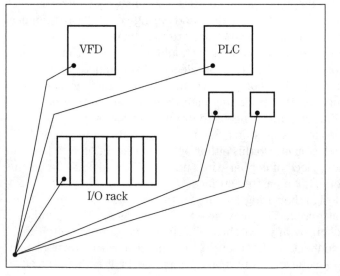

Fig. 8-11
Multiple grounded
controllers.

ground bus bar in the power panel. It can, however, be lighter. Bond it directly and securely to the cabinet. Once again, be sure that all paint is scraped from the bond area. Connect the cabinet ground to the ground bus bar in the power panel using no. 6 AWG or larger cable and ring connectors. This cable should have green (or, in some areas, green with yellow stripe) insulation, and it can be routed through the same cable trough as AC power lines. Keep it as short a run as possible.

Never connect grounds in series. Except where specifically allowed, never connect cabinet ground leads in series (daisy-chained). This approach makes noise signals cumulative, turning several low-level noise signals into one large noise signal. This can result in noise problems and improper controller operation. Instead, use a *star* system, which utilizes individual ground cables going to the system ground. See Fig. 8-12.

A common mistake is to equate the ground circuit to the common or return in the wiring system. This is not correct. The ground is *not* the common, nor is it the return. Sometimes the term *ground* is used interchangeably with *common* or (power) *return*. This is incorrect. Although commons or returns may connect to chassis or earth ground at some point, they should not be used as chassis or enclosure ground connection points.

It is strongly recommended that you use a separate ground cable for each controller in an enclosure. Even if the steel enclosure itself is grounded, it is good practice to do this because copper is much more conductive than steel. Thus electricity, in taking the path of least resistance, will flow through the route we design. Last, the

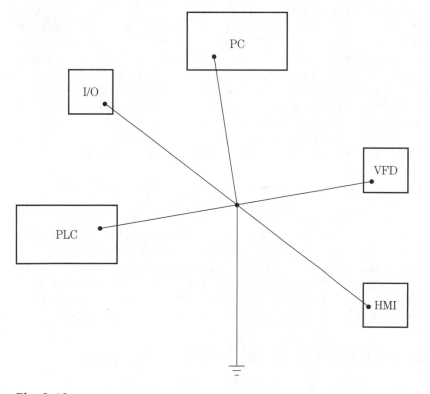

Fig. 8-12   Star ground system.

enclosure may not be a continuous piece. It may not be welded at every seam. This could cause the electrical ground to be unstable or not proper at all. Remember, electricity flows through the path of least resistance, and it will not flow at all if connection is not made.

Power Fluctuations

Since most electronic equipment wants good, clean electrical sine wave energy in a consistent form, we can categorize many power fluctuation phenomena in this section. Alternating current (AC) is nice and convenient, but it is also unforgiving if the supply is disturbed on its way to the recipient. The recipient in the automated factory is usually a computerized piece of equipment. That piece of equipment might have a host of protective devices on the incoming power side. These include fusing, noise suppression, filters, and voltage-matching transformers. Even with some of or all this protection, there can be problems. The problems of this section involve complete power outages, brownouts, sags in voltage or current, oscillations (possibly due to harmonics), and power surges. Each has consequences, and each has its protective circuit—both at some cost and risk to the piece of equipment being protected.

A power outage can have many definitions. Did the lights flicker on and off? If so, is this an outage? Maybe yes and maybe no. If the lights were off for a cycle or two, then this is not a severe outage, or complete loss of power. If the lights and many other electrically driven items went off for several seconds, then that is an outage. Call the utility to find out what happened. Lightning storms are a good culprit in the summertime. Some sensitive equipment can ride through a couple of cycles without power incorporating capacitor networks. Other more-critical, sensitive pieces of equipment have to be placed on a circuit with an uninterruptible power source (UPS) system so as to continue running throughout the outage.

Sometimes the outages occur at the same time of day. This can be an excellent clue in determining whether the occurrence is external to the plant or internal. A chart recorder placed on one of the supply lines will record what happened and when. With this information a determination can be made as to what to do to solve or live with the outage.

Sags in voltage to a piece of equipment can also appear to be an outage of sorts. The end result is the same—the equipment trips and needs to be reset. The cause of the sag is just as important. Is there a large motor in the plant that, when it is started, demands so much current that the overall system sags? Or is there a similar current-needy device somewhere near the plant? If so, then it should be isolated from all other pieces of equipment somehow. Some pieces of equipment can handle lower levels of voltage than nominal for extended periods. This should be prequalified with the supplier of the piece of equipment when these conditions are possible. A brownout is actually a low incoming voltage level over an extended period.

Dealing with Electrical Disturbances

Hash, crosstalk, garbage, harmonic distortion, oscillations, ringing, and notches to the electrical system's waveform are both unsightly and unwanted. They are unsightly because, when picked up on an oscilloscope, they are images we don't want to be see. From an electrical standpoint, they are unwanted. Sensitive pieces of equipment need clean, smooth, low-level waves coming into their circuitry. If not, then erroneous data can be produced, software programs can stop executing, or damage can even occur to components. There are many causes of oscillations, and there are several solutions. Filters, reactors, and capacitor networks can smooth out the waveform on the incoming line, but the best effort should be put into finding the cause and stopping the oscillations there.

Power surges and voltage spikes are types of power fluctuations which are probably the most unwanted. They are truly undesirable because they can destroy electrical components without warning. The best protection against these kinds of fluctuations is fusing or circuit breakers. If fuses are blowing often and randomly, then it may be critical to find the source of the problem rather than to replace fuses constantly. All it will take is one instance, with all conditions just right, to have the surge get past the fuse and take out an important piece of equipment. In addition, if there are spikes in the system, note that transformers and power supplies will be stressed often, and this can lead to premature failure of these components.

The key to dealing with electrical noise is to prevent it. Diagnosing noise and its source later is tough enough. If good wiring practices are followed and attention is paid to the types of equipment to be used together, then some noise problems can be addressed from the start. With so many retrofit projects in plants today and engineers and designers trying to anticipate problem areas, electrical noise is still likely to be present in the system. Being able to test for it and getting the parties responsible are two important steps in solving the problem. There is always a solution. But at what cost, and who should pay?

Here are some steps to follow when you install new equipment or retrofit old machinery in a plant with new. First, know the electrical characteristics of the new pieces of equipment. Find out what types of power conversion devices are used, how fast they switch, and so on. Suppliers of this type of equipment are used to these types of questions and must answer honestly, or else they will have to fix the problem later. Second, make a single line drawing of all the equipment on the electrical system in question. Show both new and old equipment. List all the sensitive pieces of equipment on the circuit, and find out from the operators which ones are the most sensitive. List any filters already in place. Remember, too, when you do this evaluation, that some equipment can be a receiver just as well as a sender when it comes to radio-frequency interference and even electromagnetic interference.

Next, the analysis must take into account the plant's incoming AC supply. If you are going to connect to this source, it is good to know what you are dealing with. Is the supply clean, or is there already a present disturbance? Is the supply stiff, is the short-circuit current level high or low? In other words, can the supply system handle your loading and possible fluctuations? Having a handle on what's coming in can help pinpoint where problems might arise later. Likewise, the plant's grounding system must be measured. Check that the grounds present are proper and whether any show signs of deterioration. This analysis will also aid in the grounding of the new equipment due to be installed. Again, heading off these types of grounding problems will be worthwhile.

After you are satisfied that all the bases are covered, it's time to install the equipment and apply power for the first time. But before you run the equipment in production mode, first test at various key locations for the presence of electrical noise. Check in and out of electrical enclosures, control panels, and even at the sensitive computer stations. Many electrical noise problems will surface right away. Some may not. Be prepared to test the supply and outgoing lines to and from the equipment. Have appropriate test meters and recorders handy. This evidence will be necessary to find the source of the problem. After all, there will be probably only a small window of time to get the equipment back on-line into the production scheme.

Optical Isolation

We have all heard the word *isolation,* but what is it and how is it incorporated? Isolation is, in a basic sense, complete separation of two components in an electrical system such that unwanted noise or signals cannot pass between them. One common means of achieving this is by optical isolation. Since certain diodes emit infrared light, it has become an electronics industry practice to use that capability to isolate expensive electrical components. By using the light emitter in conjunction with a light receptor, no physical connection has to be made. The light receptor is sometimes known as a *phototransistor.* In this way logic commons in low-voltage control circuitry are fully separated, or isolated. This is a safe and effective means of enabling or disabling a circuit. However, it is recommended that when you interface the logic of one manufacturer's product with another's, compatible isolation techniques must be incorporated. This can avoid problems of incompatibility at start-up of the equipment.

With light-emitting diodes (LEDs), it has become a practice in many low-voltage control systems to use optical isolation. Basically, as shown in Fig. 8-13, as the electric current passes through the diode (LED), light is emitted. A light receptor located adjacent to and dedicated just to that particular LED receives the light transmission and keeps the circuit flowing. The attractiveness of optical isolation is that there is built-in circuit protection. No actual electric current flows through this isolation point. Since control equipment is usually expensive and board-level components are not easily replaced (it's now customary to discard the entire board rather than troubleshoot it and replace one or two components), it is extremely important to protect the low-level voltage components from all possible spikes and surges.

Signal Conditioners and Filters

Many times the electrical noise in the circuit cannot be traced to a source and thus eliminated. Fortunately, there exist dedicated modules which can be installed in a circuit and provide the necessary isolation or even filtering so that we can go on to the next problem. Electrical noise and sensitive control or computer equipment don't mix well. Thus a new business of filters and signal conditioners has arisen. Many filtering packages can be purchased off the shelf and installed quickly to eliminate noise. These filter networks many times are a resistor and capacitor in series parallel to the load being filtered. Looking at the resistive-capacitive filter scheme in Fig. 8-14, we see that the values for the capacitor and resistor are selected for the

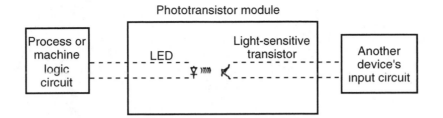

Fig. 8-13   Optical isolation.

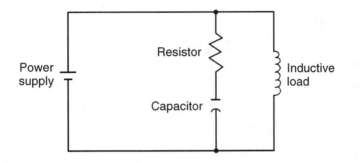

Fig. 8-14   An *RC* filter.

amount of filtering desired, the load, and the actual noise predicted. Often this solution is the least expensive and will work as long as no one inadvertently removes the filter. Many times a single capacitor can provide adequate filtering and dampening in a control circuit, although too much capacitance can make a system very nonresponsive and sluggish. This should be avoided. Another solution is to install metal-oxide varistors (MOVs) in the circuit to accomplish the same result. These solutions are always worth the attempt. At worst, it won't filter enough, and another approach will have to be taken.

Conclusions

Connecting the soft logic system is actually a straightforward process. The PC-based controller and its peripheral components are a working unit. Attention to all the other factors within the manufacturing plant surrounding the successful operation of the soft logic system is paramount. If we put our soft logic control system in its own plant, put in all new equipment, and route each wire in its own conduit, then we might end up with a "bulletproof," high-reliability system. This is the ideal scenario and isn't the norm. However, applying the right practices in designing and installing the PC-based system will return dividends in the form of more uptime and better operation. Connecting the soft logic system entails more than installing a few boards, wiring some I/O, and writing a smooth application program!

9
CHAPTER

Input and Output

PC-based controllers have many types of interface cards available to read and measure external events. These external events are all the inputs, discrete and analog, which are coming from the hundreds of different pieces of equipment in the factory. Sometimes just referred to as *I/O* or *tags,* these events are the ones which the soft logic system must read, track, monitor, set and reset, and control. As discussed earlier, the I/O status is that factor which concerns the soft logic system the most. Placing the correct status of the input or output bit within the image table is what determines the next move or decision by the application program. The only way to update the image table is to get electrical information from outside the PC.

The PC by itself along with the application software cannot work alone. They need to connect to the outside world. This is done via interface boards which are installed within the PC. This scenario is shown in Fig. 9-1 in a block diagram. Here the I/O interface card plugs into the backplane of the PC. From here a network cable is run from the board to the I/O rack(s). At these racks will reside the actual I/O modules to which the electrical wires are run from the individual pieces of equipment. This is better seen in Fig. 9-2. Each individual module is plugged into a board and is fully wired from the device it addresses. The voltage coming into the board or module can be different from that sent to the PC controller.

I/O boards have the ability to detect inputs from thermocouples, voltage sources, current sources, strain gages, and other process equipment. These are all devices which need to have a link to the master soft logic controller. Outside of the PC exists another facet of data acquisition and measurement. These devices are often connected to the PC via some serial interfaces such as RS-232, RS-422, or RS-485. There are also devices which allow an interface to the PC via the GPIB interface, IEEE 488. By having these types of interfaces, the system is capable of total cable lengths in the range of 4000 feet, thus achieving much wider coverage within the plant.

I/O, or more directly the input section of the PC-based controller, provides various functions within the system. The modules provide a point to which the physical wires are connected. Remote I/O also helps to isolate the PC and controller circuitry from dangerous voltage levels associated with industrial sensor measurement. The plug-in

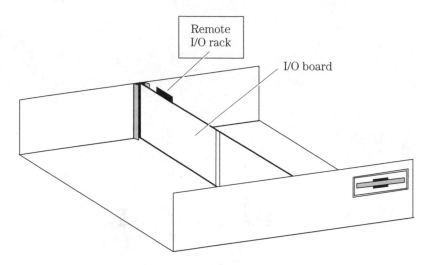

Fig. 9-1   An input/output card plugged into a slot in the PC.

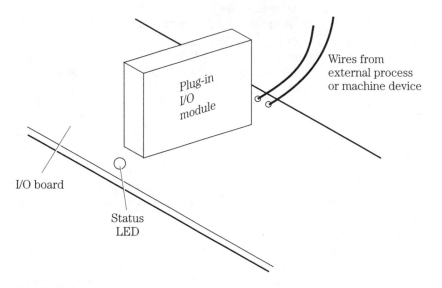

Fig. 9-2   An I/O module, inserted onto the board and wired.

boards usually have a voltage limit for common mode and normal mode. If a higher voltage is allowed to pass through, the internal PC bus can be severely damaged. Thus isolation and protection are at different locations. The remote I/O can be isolated at the sensor, it can be optically isolated at the PC, or it can even get isolation from a serial interface card. Electrical noise and unwanted voltages are somewhat subdued by isolation, but many times it seems that interference finds its way everywhere.

The actual working voltage can also be conditioned at these I/O points so that matching voltages both to the outside equipment and back to the PC are at the proper levels. The last function of the I/O section is to provide at-a-glance indication for present status.

I/O Addressing

I/O addressing takes on the following format (from Fig. 9-3; this figure list relates to Fig. 9-7). As can be seen, the I/O needs to have certain designations attached to it in order to be found by the soft logic controller. This partial listing is from a plant's hard-copy log (which could be typical of a ladder program). As can be seen, one identification tag is broken down this way (not all I/O is addressed in the same way, which is another good reason to keep handy logs): Commonly the I/O has an address number which can correspond to a particular rack, node number, channel element, and subchannel element. All these further define that particular input or output.

Counters and Timers

Another group of I/O tools is the counters and timers. These useful components always seem to be classified together in the world of I/O. Used in a typical PLC or PC-based control scheme, they actually are intermediaries between the master controller and the I/O itself. The counter (or in ladder logic, counter blocks) allows the programmer to count something. It may count inputs from a proximity switch so that it knows when it has met the predefined setting. Pulses from a pulse generator can be programmed to be counted. Optical encoders can supply valuable pulse information about a variety of motion control situations. By getting a trigger, or start, a reset contact, and being told how to increment, the counter block gets the soft logic answer more directly (see Fig. 9-4). The same can be said of the timer block. This block, while typically not needing a trigger from an external input but rather being engaged by the microprocessor itself, actually generates clock ticks to fully time an event. Timers and counters are often provided right on a multifunction analog and digital I/O card. The on-board, internal clock is typically a 1.0-megahertz clock while access to an external clock (the main processor's) can be faster, up to 10 megahertz. Counters and timers many times are concatenated to form a counter/timer of a higher bit count, such as 32, for timed A/D conversions and external frequency generation.

I/O List:

Board No. 1

Point #	Name	Description	Signal	Type	Connections	Wire Marker
100	Pressure Xmitter	Feedwater	4-20ma	Input	T1, T2	FT1
101	Flow Transmitter	Water temp	0-10v	Input	T3, T4	TH1
102	Thermocouple	Tank #3	0-5v	Input	T5, T6	LT3
103	Level Meter	Tank #3	0-10v	Output	T7, T8	LM3

Fig. 9-3 A partial listing of I/O information.

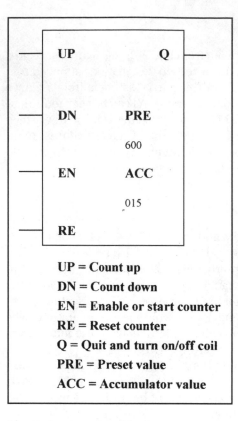

UP = Count up
DN = Count down
EN = Enable or start counter
RE = Reset counter
Q = Quit and turn on/off coil
PRE = Preset value
ACC = Accumulator value

Fig. 9-4   A counterblock.

These dual counter/timers are enabled by the soft logic program control and are clocked by a crystal oscillator source. Typical timer ranges should be no less than 2.5 megahertz and not greater than 1 pulse per hour. This is another great tool in the I/O tool box.

Remote I/O and I/O Drops

A block diagram layout of several I/O drops is shown in Fig. 9-5. This is often referred to as *remote I/O.* This practice has allowed the plant electricians to minimize wire pulls and runs within the manufacturing factory. Time and money have been saved by utilizing remote I/O. These savings are due to the materials monies saved from using less wire and cable and the labor saved from not having to pull or run more wire. Local-area networks and data highways, or buses, have emerged as the best way to date to exchange data over great distances to a multitude of devices. Still there will be prohibitive situations where discrete wires have to be routed.

Connectivity is the buzzword. With so many controllers being scattered about the plant (PCs, PLCs, motion controllers), it is necessary to connect as many as possible. The local-area network got its start and has gained popularity ever since because of this need to link devices. It could even be suggested that wherever there is more than one computing, processing device, there is the need to communicate between them. This need might be to share information on an as-needed basis, to issue instructions, or simply just to monitor. Whatever the reason, different schemes are possible to tie together many controllers and peripherals. One basic scheme is the PC and remote I/O drop(s).

While connecting the PC-based soft logic system and communications are covered in other chapters, there are also multiple control schemes available to end users. These I/O platforms are almost always on an individual, case-by-case, and application-needs basis. These are called *remote racks* or *I/O drops* and usually have a shorter profile. In some instances, depending on the application and use, there might be extra processing power local to the remote rack. But most often, these are racks of I/O which are located closer to the machine or process so as to eliminate long runs of wire. Once these remote racks are wired, then the I/O status data are sent at high speed to the host PLC via a consolidated communication link, many times a single strand of cable.

Master/Slave and Peer-to-Peer Formats

A variation of the remote I/O drop is the master/slave format. Here, a master controller, or PC-based system, is in charge of many other slave devices. The key difference from an I/O drop is the capability of the slave device. The slave unit will have some processing power and thus does not have to rely on the master for all control and processing. However, the slave does rely on the master controller for instructions, and all communications have to be routed through this master. This approach can even have some implications relative to the distributed control system (DCS). These master/slave arrangements almost always require a redundant master in case the original master fails. If the master is out of service, then the slaves are also down with it. This approach is generally less expensive than a complete peer-to-peer system.

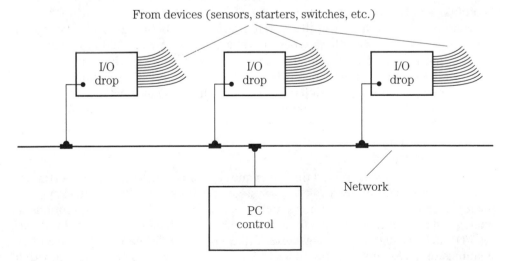

Fig. 9-5   Multiple I/O drops.

The other common I/O control scheme is peer-to-peer, or the PC-to-PC lineup. In this scheme, several PCs (each able to process on its own) are connected via a high-speed network. In this configuration, each controller is in charge of its own process and is also in charge of its own communications. This means that each device must send, receive, and decipher its own transmission data and then be fully programmed to use those data to control the machine or process to which it is dedicated. In this scheme it is also customary to rotate communication control from device to device. This is known as *token passing.* The peer-to-peer system can keep other sections (peers) running when one of the other peer units has faulted or is down.

Digital, Discrete I/O

This is the most common type of I/O found in the manufacturing environment. A typical voltage rating for digital I/O can range from 2.3 to 5 volts DC; thus a low-voltage power supply will be needed for any PC-based control system utilizing I/O. Sink currents for this type of I/O can be 24 milliamperes per channel, while source currents will be 15 milliamperes per channel. Digital I/O boards can be configured to have between 16 and 216 discrete inputs and/or outputs. Many industrialized computers utilize a passive backplane architecture with as many as 20 available expansion slots. Some remote I/O systems can be configured with as many as 2000 data points per serial I/O port. Obviously, with multiple serial ports quite an extensive system can built from a single PC. However, one important tradeoff is that the more I/O, the longer the scan of the program and the longer the execution times. Can the application tolerate these kinds of response times?

Many of these plug-in I/O boards have sampling speeds of up to 100,000 readings per second depending on the A/D converter type and its resolution. By utilizing a direct memory access (DMA) technique within the PC, throughput rates to system memory will be extremely high. For applications requiring a snapshot of transient events, an A/D board with sampling rates of 40 or 100 megahertz should be employed. These cards can handle the short bursts of large amounts of data. It must be recognized, however, that serial interface will be limited to the standard baud rates available with these types of systems. Baud rates of 9600 to 19,200 are still the norm for serial communications. Thus a baud rate of the more common 9600 baud equates to approximately 960 readings, or points per second. As always, the central processing unit will have to handle other system functions besides the serial communications link, and thus the system will slow down even more.

Analog I/O

Analog I/O has to be routed through some type of analog to digital converter before it can be analyzed by a soft logic system. Much like any PLC control system, analog signals have multiple ranges and thus can be scaled. Typical resolutions of analog signals can range from 8 to 20 bits. Speeds which can be measured for analog I/O can be as high as 100 megahertz. Typical plug-in A/D boards will have 8 or 16 channels of analog input. Many times the analog board will come equipped with a few digital channels.

Analog and digital I/O boards have specific features. Many are multifunction cards, and you will pay for that functionality even if you don't need all of it. It sometimes is wise to take a moment to find the board that best suits your application. The most important is the I/O count, or how many and what type of I/O points you get with a one-card footprint. Many have 16 single ended, with 8 differential analog inputs. And 12-bit resolution is common, as are 12-bit D/A or A/D converters (many boards will carry two) with switches on the board for the ranges. An analog output typically is disabled upon power-up and remains disabled until a user program writes to it. The other important feature is samples per second (100,000 per second or more). Some boards come with 4 bits of TTL (transistor-transistor logic) or CMOS (complementary metal-oxide semiconductor) compatible digital input capability, since these types of digital inputs are commonly used.

More on Remote I/O

The remote I/O rack is supplied with a complement of input and output modules. The rack's physical size will depend on the number of slots, required by the application, for the eventual insertion of all I/O modules and other types of modules. Each of these modules has a dedicated, specialized function. Those functions can include temperature sensing, motion and positioning modules for motors and servo systems, high-speed counting, ASCII or Basic modules for two-way serial communication, and PID loop control. But the most prevalent add-on modules are for discrete I/O and analog I/O.

The PC and the soft logic program must be capable of handling hundreds and sometimes thousands of individual, or discrete, inputs and outputs. Discrete inputs and outputs as on/off states, in a typical factory situation, could be described as low-voltage signals of a designated level; for example, an input can be a contact closure or opening of that circuit to indicate that a limit switch has been triggered. This could be the result of a relay sending to the PC a 24-volt or 120-volt signal. The PC, in turn, has its program scanning all the inputs, making note of addresses, ports, or points, and recognizes when a change has been made. This change can be recognized as a change in the on/off status of the particular address.

Another way that the PC recognizes a change at a particular address is by a change in actual voltage coming into that address. If a particular input is said to "go high," then its voltage level has shown an increase to a predetermined value. If it is said to "go low," then the voltage approaches a value of zero. High can equate to on, and low usually equates to off.

Analog signals are usually in the form of 1 to 5 volts, 0 to 10 volts, or 4 to 20 milliamperes. The signal is in the form of direct-current (DC) electricity. In the case of the milliampere signal, a resistor is wired in series, and the voltage is now provided in another form. These analog inputs can be furnished from potentiometers which are dialed by an operator to an appropriate value that the operator perceives as a setting, maybe for speed or time or any other pertinent function. This signal, upon arrival at the PLC, must be wired into the analog module. The PC program must then recognize that it has received a 5-volt signal. But first the scale to which that signal must be equal must be determined. For instance, if a 0- to 10-volt DC potentiometer signal comes into an analog module, what does it mean? The PC program must be set up to know that 0 volts is a message to do nothing while a full 10 volts means to panic or to do something in rapid fashion. Likewise, analog outputs can be furnished by the PC in the same forms: 1 to 5 volts DC, 0 to 10 volts DC, and 4 to 20 milliamperes. These signals can be used to drive meters with the appropriate values to display accurate, up-to-date readings.

An important issue with analog inputs and outputs is resolution. Since typical resolutions are 12-bit and higher, this determines how accurately the analog signal can be scaled. Analog to digital (A to D, A-D, or A/D) devices are used to convert the signal to usable processing form. A high-speed, superpowerful device won't be of real value to the process if the A/D resolution is low. For quick comparison, assigned arithmetic values for each binary designation are shown in Table 9-1. For example an 8-bit number has an equivalent decimal value of 256. This is equal to $2 \times 2 \times 2 \times 2 \times 2 \times 2 \times 2 \times 2$. Soft logic and I/O components are primarily based on the power-of-2 format.

I/O Hardware

There are several manufacturers of I/O products. Many PLC manufacturers carry their own brand of I/O (and thus the end user needs the software driver for

TABLE 9-1. Binary Number Decimal Equivalents

Power of 2	Bit number	Decimal equivalent
2^1	1	2
2^2	2	4
2^3	3	8
2^4	4	16
2^5	5	32
2^6	6	64
2^7	7	128
2^8	8	256
2^9	9	512
2^{10}	10	1,024
2^{11}	11	2,048
2^{12}	12	4,096
2^{13}	13	8,192
2^{14}	14	16,384
2^{15}	15	32,768
2^{16}	16	65,536
2^{17}	17	131,072
2^{18}	18	262,144
2^{19}	19	524,288
2^{20}	20	1,048,576

Example. When one is referring to a 14-bit number, the actual total units are 16,384.

that I/O and can usually get that from the PLC maker). The basic elements of the I/O hardware scheme are the actual modules, the rack to which the modules attach, and the other termination point. Once this arrangement is fully wired to all components, as shown in Fig. 9-6, a functioning I/O system will be in place once the software recognizes what's out there. Different manufacturers of I/O have different color designations for input modules and output modules. Wire sizes are typically smaller gauge to accommodate the tighter terminals. Again, sound wiring practice in these situations is advised because only one critical I/O has to malfunction and a machine can be down. Luckily most I/O packages come with LED diagnostics to indicate a functioning I/O point.

In Fig. 9-7 can be seen several I/O boards, daisy-chained serially to one another. The modules attached to the board all have specific functions and addresses. The hardware scheme for this addressing is shown. In conjunction with Fig. 9-7 is corresponding Fig. 9-3. Here, some of the actual I/O list is shown, complete with I/O type, name, location, and description. As you can see, there will be a correlation between hardware wiring of Fig. 9-7 and the documented listing in Fig. 9-3. This will be atypical for many I/O systems.

I/O Drivers and Software

The I/O used or the plug-in boards provided generally are supplied with the interface programs or samples to aid the programmer. These are often just called the I/O driver, or drivers. In the case of remote I/O, the programming is done in ASCII command strings and should be fairly straightforward to use. Generally, remote I/O is programmed via the serial interface of the PC. Some menu-driven setup and calibration programs are provided as utility software for use with, for example, an analog board. Some drivers are supplied in a C language environment and as a linkable file. Some are supplied in object files for linking to QuickBasic, or Pascal. Sample programs are usually provided with the driver packages. Windows-based drivers are typically provided in dynamic link libraries (DDLs). These libraries work with any Windows 3.0 or newer language which allows DLLs, such as C and Visual Basic.

PC-based controls have to work with any type of I/O. Some soft logic software packages come with drivers built into the source code, while other packages can accept or provide those I/O drivers needed. This means in a bigger sense that a large manufacturing facility can continue to use all the thousands of existing points of I/O on the floor. Whatever the electricians are familiar with and trust can be kept intact.

Conclusions

PC-based control will utilize both plug-in I/O and remote I/O. These schemes and their particular use in a given application depend on many issues. What is the number of points needed for the application? Many may mean doing it one way while a few leads the end users in another direction. What will be the speed requirements of the system and application? If this application is a high-speed line demanding extremely fast processing speeds, then that has to be considered. As

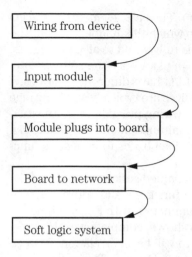

Fig. 9-6 The I/O network.

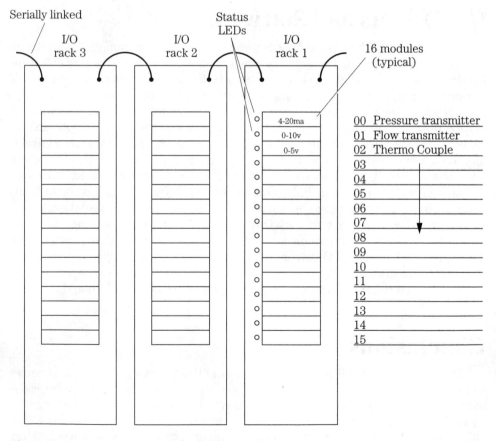

Fig. 9-7 Several I/O devices daisy-chained together.

always, but sometimes overlooked for costs, the environment and its effect on the I/O system must be analyzed. If I/O fails due to high ambient temperatures (typical specification of 0 to 60°C), high humidity (5 to 95 percent relative humidity not condensing), or just plain old nasty dirt and grime, then a more substantial enclosure or device may be required. As is often the case, enhanced performance usually has a price. Plug-in I/O boards, depending on their sophistication and style, can range in price from $1000 to $2000 per board, which in this class might offer the standard A/D with 16-channel input. Other specialty boards could cost more. Costs should be broken down into workable units of cost per I/O point. Remote I/O will typically cost 3 to 5 times that amount.

Many times the I/O in a system is used solely for data acquisition or monitoring purposes only. Temperatures and pressures at many different parts of the process have to be monitored. The input modules used in these data acquisition schemes will most often be analog instead of discrete (on/off, 1/0). The analog signal, 4 to 20 milliamperes or 0 to 5 volts DC, will yield a corresponding value from one of these external sensors. The input module itself will be physically constructed to handle analog signals. To many, data acquisition implies the exchange of numeric data from one smart device to another. This is true, but the origin of much of the data in a process or machine is some I/O module as an analog signal value into that module from a sensor or component out in the process.

Sometimes taken for granted, I/O and the hardware associated with it are an integral component of a working soft logic system. PC-based controllers, application software, and real-time operating systems seem to be getting most of the attention. They're in the limelight while the I/O modules are "in the trenches." Close attention to detail for I/O peripheral components and equipment will only further help to make a system and application successful. Additionally, all those pieces of equipment being started and stopped by all that I/O should be analyzed for the specific application's purposes. Although all that "other" equipment is a vast list (as can be seen by the diagram in Fig. 9-8), individual requirements can be evaluated for each piece. Review some of the earlier chapters of this book for an overview of many you'll encounter. Checking to see whether a particular piece of equipment is compatible with the other electronic equipment in the application is a good start. There is no need to introduce other, new problems with associated equipment. Power-converting type of equipment (AC/DC drives and other wave-changing devices) should be given a close look, especially where it is physically linked to the control system (see Fig. 9-9). Also review Chap. 7 in this book. Too many of these peripheral components now have a microprocessor built in. It seems as though all process and motion control equipment is getting this "smart." In many instances the function of one smart device can or will be integrated into another. Software and even soft logic are providing the ability to do these things.

As you progress through this book, it will become apparent that many facets of soft logic systems *must* work in conjunction with one another, none really able to stand alone. They make up a functioning system, but all the base elements have to be selected and evaluated for the best and most cost-effective use within the application. All industrial automation takes on this theme. All the components rely on one another to provide a working system.

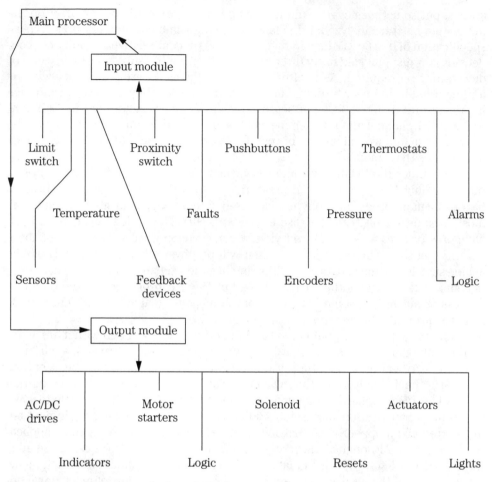

Fig. 9-8 List of frequently found I/O devices.

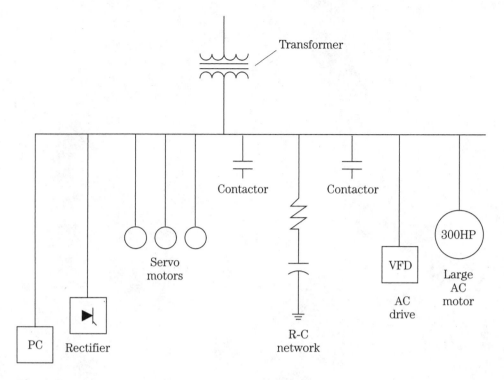

Fig. 9-9 Block diagram of frequently found I/O devices.

10
CHAPTER

Communication Schemes

A big part of any PC-based control system is its ability to connect to the plethora of equipment external to the device itself. Being able to communicate with so many electrical, and smart mechanical, devices in the manufacturing plant is not only important but also required of the PC. No longer can a supplier of electronic equipment claim that a device is "able to communicate" with this or that equipment, only to find out later that the driver or protocol is not compatible. Today it is essential that the communication end of the equipment be almost "bulletproof" in its operation. The tolerance level of electronic equipment for allowing a machine or process to run because information cannot be exchanged is very low. It had better communicate, or else it'll be thrown into the trash dumpster and another supplier's offering will be evaluated.

As PC-based equipment is integrated at higher levels into the factory, it is all the more important to get some common ground between pieces of hardware and the supplier's offerings. That is why there is so much activity with standards committees such as IEC (IEC-1131) and OPC (OLE for Process Control) concerning communication within the soft logic and PC-based industries. These bodies have laid some of the foundation which can be used for comparing like pieces of electronic equipment. Thus end users can rate suppliers of equipment on the same playing field. IEC-1131 has a section, 1131-5, which addresses the communications standards evolving out of the PLC industry. It was reviewed in Chap. 5. Likewise, OPC is a group of companies within the process control industry that deal strictly with communications and data exchange. This group, which has a spokesperson from leaders in the process industry, has provided an extensive specification for object linking and embedding for process control. This specification is reviewed in detail in Chap. 5 also. These are just two examples of the attention being paid to this industry and its needs relative to communications. As time goes on, the communication issue will become more and more important.

Communication in the Soft Logic Factory

Machines must talk to other machines. PC-based controllers must get information from other facets of the process. They must send and receive data which are vital to production. If these data somehow are lost or "hung up" somewhere along the transmission line or if they arrive with unwanted "noise" or trash, then the machine usually stops running. Sometimes the machine or process will appear to be running, but upon receiving bad data it may just sit there. "Why do machines stop running?" Often these unexplainable data transmissions can be blamed. Many times a simple machine reset will clear the problem, but the process may not be able to tolerate the reset and costly downtime will be incurred. This is a most undesirable situation.

Throughout the plant there are signs of communication schemes in place. Not only are they apparent in the machine and process equipment, but also they are part of the plant's host computer, manufacturing systems, and accounting systems. Ideally, these computers should be able to talk to one another. Plant host computers must have current, up-to-the-minute information in order to perform the many tasks of day-to-day business. Communications is the key; moreover, it is the thread tying everything together. Shipping, scheduling, receiving, record keeping, and critical reporting are all dependent on how well data are transmitted throughout the plant.

What constitutes communication in the factory? What wiring is actually critical to communication? There are LAN cables which are usually coaxial or fiber-optic. There is also signal wiring which, as feedback, might be construed as communication between the sensor and controller. Still there are the basic serial and parallel ports which must be considered. Practically, every in and out connection to a control device, with the exception of the power wiring, can be considered communication wiring. This is illustrated in Fig. 10-1 by several wires and cables going in and out of the controller. Each scheme has to be considered for integrity, and each plays a key

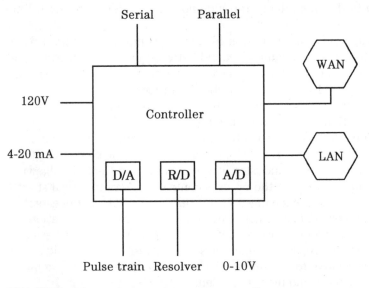

Fig. 10-1 The wires in and out of a controller.

role in the control process. A problem with just one, single wire or terminal can shut down an entire process.

Communication is more than computerized devices exchanging data with one another. It can be the signal coming back from the feedback device on a motor or valve. It can be the 110-volt signal to a relay to stop a process. Communication in the plant can take many forms. In its basic format, communication is usually a lower level of electrical energy moving from location to location. It can be pulsed at a frequency, and it can have a magnitude or amplitude of electrical force (normally voltage). This is the difference between analog and digital communication schemes, shown in Fig. 10-2. In other cases, it can be in the form of higher levels of electric energy (excluding power wiring). It can be video, audio, or electronic in nature. Communication is just another one of those vital phases of industrial automation. Without it, electronic data are confined to a local area, and the best-designed soft logic system will probably fail.

Communication in the plant is more than the telephone call to the plant floor to change production runs. Maybe that is how changes were made in the past. Today's PC-based controls depend on electronic information, in many forms, traveling at very high rates of speed over a conductor, or cable, to and from other smart devices. It sounds simple enough, but with so much happening over those conductors, accidents happen. Transmissions get garbled, and sometimes are lost forever. The machines are only following instructions. They don't think for themselves.

Instead of that physical telephone call to the production manager, the high-speed communications approach works this way: An order comes in which orders entry keys into the plantwide manufacturing system. This immediately shows the manufacturing resource planners (MRPs) and purchasing which parts are on-hand to make the assembly and which parts are short. *Just-in-time* and *made-to-order* are the modes of plant manufacturing nowadays. Soft logic systems fall right into place here. These systems are available to the production people who find that, in order to meet delivery, they must start a new production run immediately. These data are shared with many individuals in the plant and can be referred to as the system-to-human interface. However, there is still a completely separate issue of machine-to-machine interface and human-to-machine interface. All together, this network of data transmissions automates the plant.

Anytime data are transmitted, data must adhere to the rules of that transmission, or the protocol. In any transmission, there are rates of speed at which data are moving over the conductor. Some rates are slower than others. Others are more impervious to noise. But regardless of these factors, there have to be set methods and forms by which data are moved across these conductors. This has to be the case in a simple computer and printer setup on the plant floor. For the computer to transmit good, usable data to the printer, there have to be rules for that transmission. In more elaborate systems, this protocol is extended and more complex. Here, there exist communication networks where tons of data reside on a communication bus, and these are moving at high rates of speed, avoiding collisions. Each bit of data is assigned a register, or address, so that when some piece of equipment needs that particular piece of data, it selects it at the appropriate instant. This type of communication bus is a network and is much more complicated than the serial and parallel communication schemes still prevalent today.

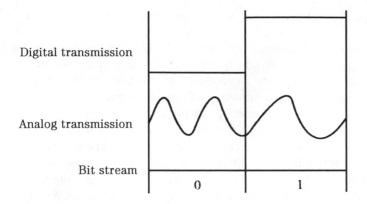

Digital transmission

Analog transmission

Bit stream

0   1

Fig. 10-2   Analog versus digital signals.

Protocol

In any PC-based system, protocol governs the format and timing of data communication, and it is appropriate to look at the individual elements. There is a good deal of handshaking going on. Without this handshaking, data would not transmit in the proper order or even at the proper time. Each manufacturer of a computerized device, capable of data transmission, defines its own protocol. The communication medium is chosen, the rate of transmission is selected as required by the application, and the actual sequencing of bits is determined. The mode of transmission is decided.

There are three basic modes of transmission: simplex, half-duplex, and full-duplex. A simplex channel allows for one-way, or unidirectional, transmission of data. It can send or receive, but it cannot do both. An example is the computer's printer. It is set up to only receive data from the computer. It cannot send data to the computer. The second mode of transmission is the half-duplex mode. Here, communication can occur in both directions. However, this communication must occur in only one direction at a time. This is likened to the serial port from computer to computer. Sometimes one is receiving data, and at other times it will only be sending. This scheme is used in telephone systems extensively. The third communication mode is the full-duplex type. A full-duplex channel can transmit data in both directions simultaneously. This type of transmission is the most versatile and is seen in many network systems today.

Other protocol functions involve the breakdown of a string of bits and what each bit means as it travels to another device. For instance, titles are given to various bits in a transmission scheme. There are start bits, check bits, parity and stop bits, request-to-send bits, and clear-to-send bits. A start bit signals that data are now being transmitted. Parity is that error detection scheme whereby an odd number of transmission errors have been detected. Stop bits are added to every character in a data transmission to signal the end of the character. As these strings of bits travel across a conductor, their order is very important. The receiving device will contain decoding software which, when accepting this initial string of data bits, prepares the device to receive the entire transmission of data. This can get tricky when transmission speeds get faster and microprocessors (at each sending and receiving device) get busier. Now factor in noise and crosstalk, and you've got an interesting situation. That is why it also makes sense to choose the communication medium with care.

Communication Media

The physical material which allows the electronic data to pass from device to device has many names. It is called wire, cable, or conductor. Made from usually copper or aluminum, it is the communication medium and has evolved over the past decade. The outer casing of the metal is usually a plasticized coating, extruded onto the wire as the wire is drawn. Besides the actual material, the communication medium encompasses the full physical form of the bus, or network. Connection methods are critical, as are casing (around the conductor), grounding, and shielding. There are several types of medium. First, there was lighter-gauge, two-conductor wire with another wire used as ground. This evolved into the twisting of the conductors within the casing so as to minimize eddy currents and reduce noise impregnation. Shields were added to this version of conductor and were discussed earlier. The medium has seen a rapid movement to coaxial and triaxial cable. The latest trends in communication media are fiber optics, telephone lines, radio waves, and microwave technology. With these newer means of transmitting electronic data come higher costs and other issues concerning noise, connections, and software. But as time marches on, the costs should come down and experience will teach us the proper methods for implementation.

With each medium type comes added capability. Twisted-pair conductors are typically used for process signals and usually should not be run more than a couple of thousand feet. Transmission rates are limited with twisted-pair wiring. Rates of 100 kilobaud are seen; but usually as the rates increase, other types of medium should be considered. In these cases, it is typical to see coaxial and triaxial cable in use. This communication cable is basically structured so that there are two conducting materials, each sharing the same axial point within the cable (coaxial). The same is true for triaxial cable, but in this case there are three. Whether the coaxial system is set up for broadband (many simultaneous signals) or baseband (one signal at a time) transmission dictates the maximum rate of transmission. Rates of over 10 megabaud are not uncommon with broadband systems.

Fiber-optic cabling has gained acceptance as probably the best noise-resistant communication medium. If we look at the basic method of isolating electronic signals—optical isolation, we find that this principle is sound and useful with fiber-optic cabling. Electrical noise, having no physical way of conducting into the fiber-optic system, is no longer an issue. This cable, per equivalent length of coaxial cable, is lighter and diametrically smaller. However, this still has not made it as cost-effective. The greater the effort to manufacture, or the more complicated the wiring, the higher the cost to purchase. As better manufacturing methods are developed, costs will come down.

Radio wave and microwave technology is coming on strong. Cableless, wireless, and electromagnetic are the hot, new buzzwords. Even more "leading edge" is digital cellular technology. Eventually all cellular telephones will use digital service instead of the present analog in wireless transmissions. This should have far-reaching effects in the LANs and WANs of industry. Communication conglomerates and the television industry are driving a lot of this development. For industrial and factory use, it has a niche in remote areas where physically running the cable is prohibited. This technology will also help make wide-area networking more practical. With satellites and telecommunication schemes gaining in capability and acceptance, the future of communication media is approaching a new frontier.

Transmission Distances

It is often asked, How far can we run the cables for a given application? And there is no single answer. The answer depends on many variables. In the most basic sense, the wire or cable is allowing electrons to flow from one point to another. To get an answer, we have to ask other questions. What electronic data are we transmitting? How critical are the data to the process or machine operation? Do the data have to arrive now, or can they get there when they can? Are they data, or is it some other type of signal? Are there any nonlinear loads in the area (power-converting equipment such as AC or DC drives)? Where will the cable be routed? What size and type of cable are to be used? The run of cable can be for power or signal reasons. Whichever is the case, there are some limitations, and much of the routing methodology is simple common sense. Ask the supplier of any new equipment what is recommended for safe distances, without sacrificing performance. Distances are determined by the type of transmission, the transmitting scheme, and the receiver's ability to accept degraded signals. Obviously, the greater the distance, the more likely it is that electrical noise of some type can be encountered along the way. The shorter the route, the better!

Serial communication has limits. RS-232 lines can typically send and receive safely in a manufacturing environment up to around 50 feet. Beyond this the configuration of the signal must change to a differential form, similar to that of RS-422 or RS-485. With the right drivers, serial configuration, and proper routing, distances greater than 2000 feet are attainable. Normally, though, as distances become too great, coaxial or fiber-optic runs are given serious consideration. This moves the serial link up into the network's (LAN) world. As a base requirement, many devices are expected to connect to a network via a serial interface, over some distance, and then that information is expected to be transmittable over the network, which can carry the data thousands of feet. There are always ways to get the data there.

Networks typically have to transmit over long distances. Sometimes in a large plant these transmissions can be over more than a mile. Good noise-resistant cabling has to be used in these instances. Coaxial and fiber-optic runs are the most common for these kinds of networks. Powerwise, high-voltage cable must be sized according to the amount of current to be carried. In addition, if equipment is sensitive to voltage drops, then this must be taken into account by increasing the diameter or gauge of the wire. Also, line drivers, repeaters, and signal boosters can be used for long-distance transmissions. Use these only when necessary because increasing the components in the circuit potentially creates another area where noise or disturbances can be encountered. If coupling points and junctions have to be made in long runs of cable, make sure that the junction point has good connections and is somewhat sealed to make it as noise immune as possible. The simpler the system, the better.

Transmission Speeds

The rate at which data are transmitted across communication lines is called the *speed of transmission.* Bits per second, or the *baud rate* as it is normally called, are the common unit placed on transmission rates. The baud rate is illustrated in Fig. 10-3. This terminology is used mainly for serial and parallel communication schemes. However, the terminology is appropriate for all data transmission systems (i.e., networks, telecommunications). Common baud rates are 2400, 4800, 9600, and 19,200. These are usable rates; however, there are slower rates such as 1200, 600, 300, and 240 baud (nobody really wants to hear about baud rates this low anymore!). With all the emphasis in the factory on getting data to and from devices quickly, the slower baud rates are becoming extinct. Give us the faster rates! Sometimes they are referred to as kilobaud (19,200 baud is equal to 19.2 kilobaud). At 9600 baud, one character can be sent approximately every millisecond.

Beyond 19.2 kilobaud we start to get into the high-speed lines, mainly used in networking. These transmit at millions of bits per second. Many PLC and PC suppliers offer data bus speeds on their networks that can transmit at several million bits per second. Some of these networks are looked at later.

Serial and Parallel Communication

The traditional, most common means of communication in the office, home, and factory is by serial and parallel methods. Electronic data which are sent and received from one device to another are eventually broken down into individual bits. Since the computer systems are in the midst of creating the electronic data, the data must eventually begin and end as a binary digit, or bit. Transmission of data, one bit after another, over a single conductor is called *serial communication.* This can be seen in Fig. 10-4. There is also the need for a ground wire in this conductor circuit. As a matter of fact, there have to be at least four wires in a serial communications scheme: the ground wire, a signal ground wire, and separate transmit and receive wires. The ground wire, when grounded properly, will help to keep voltage spikes from damaging the low-voltage-level, sensitive communications componentry. Shielded cable can greatly reduce unwanted electrical noise entering the signal conductor.

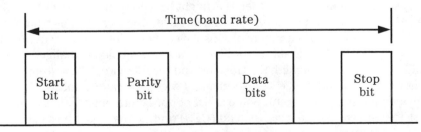

Fig. 10-3 Baud rate illustrated.

Bit 1 x Bit 2 x Bit 3 x Bit 4 x Bit 5 x Bit 6 x Bit 7 x Bit 8 ⟶

Fig. 10-4   Serial transmission.

Acronyms for typical serial ports, or communication connections, define the type of signal configuration. In RS-232, the RS stands for return signal, and it has a certain protocol which must be adhered to. If one of the critical bits is missed or if one device tries to send when it is not supposed to, then both devices just tend to sit there, not performing any function. That is why serial communication from machine to machine in real time is not desirable. A microprocessor must have the available time to handle the transmission and decoding while focusing on the machine's operation. It is more typical to find serial transmissions to and from a machine before it starts running (i.e., to download instructions) or when it stops running (i.e., to upload collected data to a data acquisition system). The connector for a serial communication scheme is typically a 25-pin connector. All 25 pins are available for use, but usually not all are employed. Most often the first few pins are used in the connection.

Variations of serial communication exist. These are the RS-422 and the RS-485 differentiation of RS-232. The basic difference lies in the driver. The signal in an RS-422 scheme is sent in a differential mode, thus allowing transmission over longer distances.

Uploading refers to the sending of electronic data to a host computer, usually for later use in statistical process control and data acquisition systems for reporting. Downloading is the converse. Information to run a machine in a certain way may have to be sent to a machine's memory for use in its program. Obviously, if this were attempted while the machine was executing its program, there would be a greater risk of error and thus potential machine stoppage.

Troubleshooting a serial communication port is pretty straightforward. Hopefully, there will be a documented protocol available. This will allow you to check for certain irregularities. First, compare the bit configuration with what is desired at both the sending and receiving devices. This check should be the first step. The number of data bits, stop bit, start bit, baud rate, and parity should be the same at each device. A device or tool which can assist in serial communication troubleshooting is the serial analyzer. It actually takes the transmission cable right through it and deciphers what has been transmitted. Not every company owns one or desires to afford one (they aren't inexpensive). But if a company's business is built around serial communications, then this might be a good investment. After we check the serial port configuration fully, actual line symptoms can tell us what may be wrong. For example, two characters are displayed when only one is required, it may be a sign that the system is set up for half duplex and should be changed to full duplex. Additionally, if by switching the transmit and receive wires of a system (host and peripheral, or sending device and receiving device) we can establish whether there is any communication present. Some serial ports require handshaking. This is the request-to-send (RTS) and clear-to-send (CTS) routine that some hosts and peripherals go through. By jumpering these pins on the 25-pin connector, we can establish the presence of this scheme. Another check is that of the ground. Earth ground should not be used for the signal. The DC common or signal ground should be used in a serial communication system. Also, make sure that the cable distance is not more than the customary 50 feet for an RS-232C port. If it is, then drivers or optical couplings may have to be incorporated. As for shielding, if any is available with the signal cable, it should be tied to earth ground at one end only. Do not ground both ends. In conclusion, by methodically checking that a serial communication system is set up and installed properly, your problems will be reduced greatly, at least for this portion of the project!

Transmission of multiple bits over multiple lines, simultaneously, is called *parallel transmission.* Parallel transmission requires one wire for each bit of the system in which it is transmitting. This can be seen in Fig. 10-5. It means that an 8-bit system needs eight wires plus a ground wire, a 16-bit system needs 16 wires plus a ground wire, and so on. Parallel transmission is faster than serial but is more costly over greater distances. Transmission speeds are discussed later in this chapter. Typically, ribbon cable assemblies are used in parallel data transmission schemes. While this is a fast and effective means of communication, especially for instances when a small, local terminal is employed, it is not as common as serial communication.

The troubleshooting of a parallel port is not as extensive as that of the serial port. There may be a handshaking procedure to follow, and this must be checked thoroughly. The most common problems in a parallel system occur with incorrect addressing. Making sure the peripheral device is configured properly with respect to the address setting can save troubleshooting time later. Remembering that a parallel port sends data at the rate of a byte at a time rather than a bit at a time will help when you troubleshoot the port. From this vantage point, much else is similar to a serial communication port.

Networks

A network is a communication scheme in which registered, or addressed, data are transmitted over long distances at high rates of transmission speed. Often called

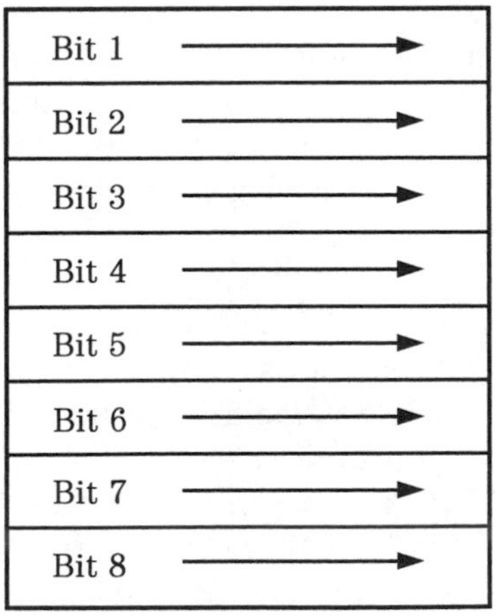

Fig. 10-5   Parallel transmission.

a *data highway* or *information highway,* this communication scheme is preferred in most plants and factories these days. Networks in use today range from the elaborate data highways of the traditional PLC suppliers to low-cost communications links that connect several control devices to the same network, such as DeviceNet. The Internet itself is a network of monstrous proportions and escapes the scope of this chapter and this book (but don't be surprised when factory floor equipment must link up to an Internet server and communicate with another machine, perhaps in Europe!). In this section we look at a few of the more common networks, provide an overview, and discuss general requirements of a network.

The local-area network (LAN) is many times referred to as merely the network. It connects PC-based controllers with other controllers, intelligent equipment, and the rest of the plant. It can even go outside the plant via a wide-area network (WAN). There are several networks that a soft logic computer system can encounter: Profibus (a leading Fieldbus network), Interbus-S, Lonworks' Echelon, and all the others—those proprietary PLCs, DeviceNet, CAN (controller area network), ControlNet, and so on. Process control environments can benefit from these networks, but once they have been selected, the plant scheme is chosen.

A graphical interpretation of a LAN is shown in Fig. 10-6. The need to link multiple computers, PLCs, other processes, smart sensors, and machines has led the communications world to networking. Networking is the practice which allows the connectivity of many dissimilar, computerized devices in the factory or office. These devices may be dissimilar in some respects but are similar in other ways, thus allowing for interconnection. Besides being able to transmit over thousands of feet at millions of bits per second, the network offers good immunity to radio-frequency interference and electromagnetic interference. Additionally, the network is omnidirectional, meaning that data can go virtually anywhere anytime. This type of network is commonly known as the local-area network.

The LAN has gained popularity because it allows for the sharing of data between individual, computer-based devices within a factory, rather than relying on one large high-speed computer. Of course, that large, high-speed computer can attach itself to the LAN and be an active participant, and this is usually the case. But the attractive feature of the LAN is that, within the factory, a programmable controller can have several input/output drops, can be connected to a CNC machine, and can link itself to an operator console across the factory floor, all via the LAN. This is the key to this type of network—all the devices connected are located in the same general vicinity, or locally.

The LAN's main components are the LAN driver, the software, and the actual transmission cabling, its hardware. Coaxial cable and fiber-optic cable are the basic choices in a LAN-based communications arrangement. The television industry has helped make coaxial cable very popular. Fiber-optic cabling is rapidly becoming a challenger to coaxial cable. Reducing its cost will make fiber-optic cable the conductor of choice in time. It is more noise-resilient than coaxial. It works by sending pulses of light through a conductor whose inner walls are basically flexible mirrors, so most of the light is transmitted. A light source unit able to translate electronic data to light pulses and a light receiver able to reverse the decoding are the other necessary components in a fiber-optic network. Prior to coaxial cabling and fiber-optic

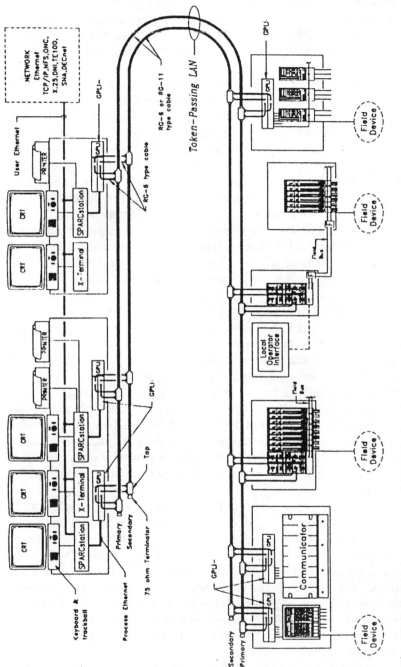

Fig. 10-6 A local area network (LAN) scheme.

cabling, signal wire was lighter-gauge two-conductor wire with a ground wire. This evolved into twisting the wires to reduce the eddy-current phenomena. As shielding and shielding methods of properly tying one end to earth ground became a norm, more noise reduction was achieved. In a nutshell, the signal wiring is probably the most important in an automation sense, and it is also the most sensitive to noise. Therefore, it has become necessary to find ways to clean up the signal and to maintain its integrity during transmission.

Earlier a few, more prevalent networks were mentioned. Interbus-S is a high-performance, high-efficiency protocol which was designed for control systems requiring high speed (appropriate for PC-based systems). This ring-based, distributed device network is well suited for process and machine control. It can service up to 256 network drops and 4096 I/O points in 14 milliseconds. The Interbus-S network communicates at 500 kilobaud, and distances of nearly 8 miles are achievable. Soft logic systems will require an interface card by Phoenix, the IBS PC. Because so many manufacturers offer Interbus-S in their products, a soft logic controller and its open-systems approach to control are ideal for use with this type of network.

Another network is Profibus. Profibus provides fully open, transparent, and interoperable networking between field devices such as AC or DC drives and the PC. This functionality helps make it the leading *field bus* network in the world. There are more than 0.5 million nodes installed, and the list keeps growing. Profibus was introduced 8 years ago and is the network of choice in Europe. Profibus can support a maximum of 125 nodes while data (1 to 244 bytes) can be transmitted in a single message up to 1200 meters (0.75 mile). Transmission rates are from 9600 baud to 12 megabaud, and these are supported via shielded, twisted-pair wire. Profibus-DP is designed for time-critical communications between the PC controller and the field devices. This higher-performance version of Profibus is well suited for soft logic controlled applications.

Lonworks is actually a family of control products used with networks. This technology can handle up to 32,000 nodes on a single network with data able to be transmitted over 2000 meters (1.25 miles) at 78 kilobaud. With a Lonworks network, intelligence is distributed to each of the devices on the network, basically eliminating a central controller. This is a specialized network of engineering tools, chips, and protocols. Lonworks is incorporated into the ASHRAE BACnet protocol for building automation and control.

Honeywell's SDS is a powerful network. It can support up to 64 nodes at 500 kilobaud and up to 8064 I/O points. Distance for cable is dependent on baud rates but can range from 100 to 1600 feet. The Honeywell microswitch interface card is required in the PC-based system. Another I/O network is called Seriplex. This is a very fast network, able to process 510 I/O points in 5.2 milliseconds. Distances of nearly 1 mile are attainable, and an SPLX PC interface board is required with this system.

PLC manufacturers AB and GE offer remote I/O and Genius I/O, respectively. Distances of up to 5000 feet are possible, again depending on the baud rates. Typically 32 nodes can be supported with the addition of interface cards manufactured by each PLC supplier. Modicon has a similar I/O network offering and claims to have the ability to achieve distances of up to 15,000 feet. The I/O products offered by PLC manufacturers have matured considerably over the past decade. Consult the manufacturer of your choice for details when implementing a system.

DeviceNet is a low-cost communications link which allows many field devices to connect to a network and virtually eliminates labor-intensive and expensive hard-wiring. It is an open-network standard, which means that the specification and the protocol are open to all participants. Suppliers do not have to purchase software, hardware, or licensing rights in order to connect. The DeviceNet specification can be obtained from the Open DeviceNet Vendor Association (ODVA). There is a nominal charge. DeviceNet is based on the controller area network (CAN), which is a broadcast-oriented communication protocol. CAN was originally developed for the European automotive industry to replace wire harnesses with lower-cost network cable on automobiles. Thus the CAN protocol has exhibited a fast enough response and the reliability necessary for stringent applications such as controlling airbags and antilock brakes. Since it was found to be extremely reliable for these applications, the network protocol carried over into DeviceNet. Runtime control and the monitoring of devices are accomplished via input and output assemblies. These assemblies are typically data structures of less than 8 bytes in order to keep throughput high. Soft logic and PC-based systems are finding their way into many installations where DeviceNet is already in use.

As PC-based control gains a stronghold on the factory floor, there will be an ever-increasing need to connect to more and more devices. LANs and networks will provide that vehicle by which all devices work in unison for the ultimate goal of the manufacturing facility—to produce. Some typical electrical, software, and mechanical specifications for a network follow. The LAN interface should have software and drivers capable of several thousand I/O points, each with its own tag or name. The update time for this I/O scheme should be milliseconds or better. There should be several ports available, both serial and general-purpose LAN interface type. Data rates, parity, data bits, and stop bits should be software-selectable so as to facilitate configuration of ports. Multiple devices, sometimes up to 50 adjunct controllers, should be able to hang on the LAN (this may involve additional hardware). With regard to the CPU, memory, and clock frequency, these should be the latest, the fastest, and the most reliable and practical.

Another typical electrical consideration is the token-passing scheme. Some standard method is usually incorporated by each manufacturer. Coaxial cable is usually the 75-ohm type with flexible and semirigid trunk connection units. Transmitting levels and sensitivity levels should be 60 to 70 and 14 to 18 decibels, respectively. Repeaters should be allowed, and several repeaters may be needed. EMI and RFI tolerance for a LAN should comply with federal communication standards. Mechanically and environmentally, the LAN hardware must be able to operate in an ambient temperature range found in normal factory environments. This is usually 0 to 50°C (32 to 122°F). This rating does not require additional cooling methods. The relative-humidity tolerance levels should exceed 95 percent, noncondensing (water and electricity don't mix well). Additionally, boards and sensitive components should carry protective coatings to guard against corrosion and chemicals.

Two common LAN architectures are Arcnet and Ethernet. Both have been in use for many years, and each has a niche. Ethernet is the communication scheme of choice with many controllers because it offers the greatest transmission speeds. Rates of 10 megabaud are not uncommon with this method. Arcnet, on the other hand, carries with it speeds of 1 to 2 megabaud. In many instances this is fast enough.

Limitations exist as to how many devices can be added to each, and this should always be considered before a choice of networks is made.

Network technology is gaining momentum. Several different manufacturers of electronic equipment have troubleshooting tools for analyzing a network. They include items such as the LAN "sniffer" and the signal level meter. These devices can detect the presence of network signals. This can be invaluable when you are trying to pinpoint problem areas. Test software is also available and can be used at the start-up of a system and later, if problems arise. The good news, however, is that the network's theory and implementation have minimized the communication problems. Software and LAN drivers are now the most limiting factors. Each plant wants to move enormous amounts of data, quickly. The challenge is now to the LAN programmers. How do they handle all these data? Also, noise is not the problem that it used to be, and with newer transmission media becoming available, the network's future looks promising.

Client-Server Systems

Often it is necessary to share data and thus share disk systems between computers. This is known as the *client-server scheme,* and it is shown graphically in Fig. 10-7. In this scheme the computers are connected, and one computer runs programs resident in the other computer, without having to copy them. The computer used to key in the commands is the client. The other computer is the server, and it typically displays status information of the setup. The client computer can use the disk drives and output devices of the server. In this manner, a pseudo-LAN is achieved. These schemes save time and disk space when properly implemented. The OLE for Process Control (OPC) specification discussed in Chap. 5 addresses the client-server scheme further.

Wide-Area Networks

Wide-area networks connect a number of remote plants or facilities, regardless of the plant's physical location. The WAN can be looked at as an extended local-area network. This can be seen in Fig. 10-8. With telephone transmission facilities gaining more power every day, it is very practical to interface complete, remote factories. These networks do obviously expend tremendous effort in software development, drivers, and implementation. Additionally, the hardware for such a system must be

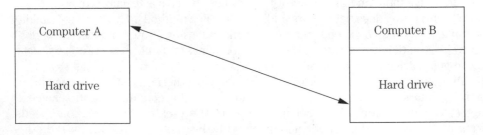

Fig. 10-7 Client-server relationship.

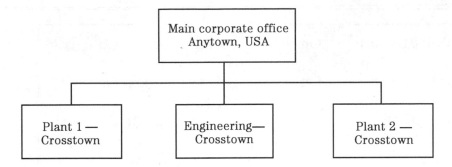

Fig. 10-8   A Wide Area Network (WAN) scheme.

capable of fast action. Costs of a wide-area network are currently on the upside of the scale. To install a system as this, the reasons have to be many and the commitment to a long, deliberate installation must be made.

Modems (modulators/demodulators) preceded WANs as the interconnecting means between facilities. Sending data from a computerized device over the telephone lines to another device has been done for years. Although cumbersome, the modem has been a tool that has kept us in touch with other sites routinely. The telephone and facsimile machine are the other methods. With modem speeds on the increase and the ability to do more with electronic data, satellite plants and remote offices can be linked to the same information and database as are home-based employees. Eventually, the WAN and modem technologies will take us into the home office (or living room). The time eventually has come for plants to link to one another so as to share information more readily.

MMIs, Screens, and Graphics

Soft logic systems exploit the graphical capabilities of the Windows environment. Tools, task bars, views and zooming, icons, screens, drop-down windows, and menus are often provided by the source code of the provider of application software. Rather than program in instruction list or line-by-line code, the soft logic system programmer now can actually enjoy the task. Likewise, the tools are provided to make user-friendly screens at operator consoles or human-machine interfaces. Instead of viewing the traditional screen in the control room, as seen in Fig. 10-9, which lists the text and the present value, the operator can get more of a picture of what is happening. These types of screens are actually easier to read and can be interpreted from farther away. No longer does the operator have to be right on top of the monitor. A graphical screen with the same information as shown in Fig. 10-9 is also shown in Fig. 10-10. Therefore to distinguish between the screen lingo, we will classify screens and graphics as having two parts—one for the application programmer's use in the source code and the other which gets displayed on an operator console for process and machine real-time use.

On the factory floor are several basic versions of display devices. One is classified as a smart device, with built-in microprocessor, and can perform many functions on its own without the help of the host (the HMI and MMI products), while the other

```
PUMP #1 status:      On          Flow indicator: On

PUMP #2 status:      On          Flow indicator: On

PUMP #3 status:      Off         Flow indicator: On


#1 Inlet temperature:  198 deg    #1 inlet pressure:  8 psi

#2 Inlet temperature:  187 deg    #2 inlet pressure:  9 psi

#3 Inlet temperature:  00         #3 inlet pressure:  00


#1 Outlet temperature:  290 deg   #1 outlet pressure:  8 psi

#2 Outlet temperature:  304 deg   #2 outlet pressure:  9 psi

#3 Outlet temperature:  00        #3 outlet pressure:  00


#1 Alarms:  none

#2 Alarms:  none

#3 Alarms:  1

Tank #1 level:  16 ft

Tank #2 level:  12 ft                    DATE:  12/03/98
                                         TIME:  0640
                                         OPERATOR:  RSC
Tank #3 level:  00
```

Fig. 10-9 Old sample data screen.

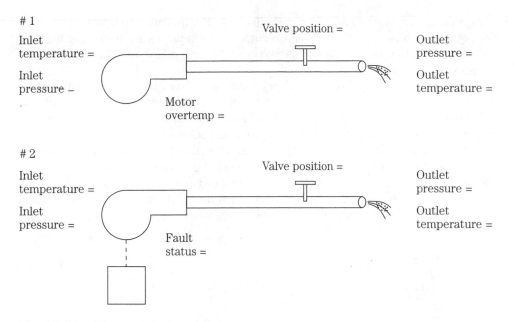

1

Inlet
temperature =

Inlet
pressure –

Valve position =

Motor
overtemp =

Outlet
pressure =

Outlet
temperature =

2

Inlet
temperature =

Inlet
pressure =

Valve position =

Fault
status =

Outlet
pressure =

Outlet
temperature =

Fig. 10-10   New sample data screen.

is the lesser station which is an extension of the PC. A lesser version might be called simply an *operator console,* and it is a data entry and display station, an input/output device to the host PC. Screens have to be downloaded from the PC and refreshed continually. The HMI, on the other hand, is programmed locally, and the screens can be resident in the device itself. With dynamic data exchange packages, only data needed by the screens to be displayed have to provided. An HMI setup is without a doubt going to be the more expensive operator console.

Beyond the monitor and HMI stations, there are other methods of data entry and alarming. Keypads, LEDs, touch screens, and even pushbuttons and lights act as I/O devices to the PC-based system. The basic difference is that obviously no screens can be utilized (except with touch screen devices). Today's factory floor environment actually demands more from an interface. Operators are expected to be more involved with the process and thus need more information, more quickly, than can be furnished over a series of lights, pushbuttons, and analog meters. Despite the fact that these screens are aesthetically pleasing (better to look at), they provide a lot more data in one screen than was done in the past. This makes the application more proficient.

Conclusions

A soft logic or PC-based system must be able to communicate with other electronic devices. It is not so much a strict requirement of PC-based controls but of all devices in the manufacturing and industrial world. Today equipment that doesn't link or connect to other devices will not be selected and will not be used. It's that simple. Too much information exists at the machine or process and has to be sent to the operator, engineer, or manager in the factory. The information is vital to production, quality control, safety, and maintenance. More factories are becoming increasingly dependent on these data and should consider redundancy and backup systems in order to safeguard uptime.

Networks and plant communication techniques have been in place for many years. These networks and communication systems have gotten much better and faster over that period. This has allowed more manufacturers of sensor, drive, and peripheral products to finally focus in on a particular scheme and make their products compliant. This was not the case 10 years ago when the goal was to implant the protocol for a particular brand of PLC. This was costly, burdensome, and often impossible for smaller makers of electronic products. Today, most manufacturers are on a level playing field, all with equal ability and responsibility to provide a networking solution for their products and the manufacturing world.

11
CHAPTER

Data Collection, Statistics, Quality, ISO 9000, and Soft Logic

PC-based control systems, statistics, and quality control programs were made for one another. The PC is the perfect device to collect and manipulate data of all types. Soft logic systems, while coming of age in the motion control and process control areas, have allowed the technologies to merge. Data collection and SCADA (supervisory control and data acquisition) systems can actually be an integral part of the overall PC-based control package. No longer does the SCADA station have to be remotely located from the process; it can be part of the PC-based control system. Displaying the same data and the same screens that traditionally were connected between a SCADA node and the local controller, now able them to be seamlessly connected. No longer are two separate databases and two tag sets required.

Trending

Another facet of PC-based control and process control is trending. Trending allows users to graph real-time and historical data in Windows and Windows NT environments to compare batches. This information could be used in this manner: At a sugar manufacturer called The Sweet Company, consider the case of Red and Ramona. The control operator, Red, is used to reviewing the latest batch run of data collected from the previous night's run of product. Red will compare this with the first batch run in the morning, right from his operator console. If there is any discrepancy at all, Red will alert the process engineers. This analysis by Red is more real-time in application, whereas Ramona, the administrative manager, needs to look at trending information over every day during the last month. Ramona's needs are different from Red's, yet they both have access to the same data. Ramona is looking to see if over a longer period something in the process was drifting out of control.

A good trend batch system can analyze data from differing time ranges. As can be seen in Fig. 11-1, curves from different days and different batches can be displayed on the same chart, thus enabling a good graphical comparison on one sheet. Many trending systems have autoscaling, X-bar formatting, and XY curve plotting abilities. This chapter will look at the base elements of statistics and statistical process control. Quality control, quality assurance, and the total quality management philosophies are also reviewed. Additionally, there will be discussion of various methods of charting and trending. Finally, the chapter will review the 20 sections of the ISO 9000 standard. Soft logic systems are required to provide many of the data on which most of the manufacturing world's quality and statistical programs are based. PC-based control is a vital component to the documentation and success of these programs.

Statistical Process Control and Charting

Statistical process control (SPC) can be defined as running a particular process on the basis that we will correct as we go. In a bigger sense, it is a closed-loop manufacturing system. This can be seen in Fig. 11-2. Using data collected, relative to the process, we continue to correct or to improve the process. The measured data analysis has to be compared to a benchmark or standard requirement in order to take any action at all. Additionally, a process under statistical control should exhibit

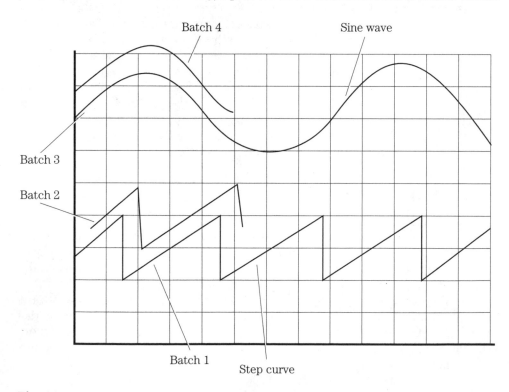

Fig. 11-1   A trend chart.

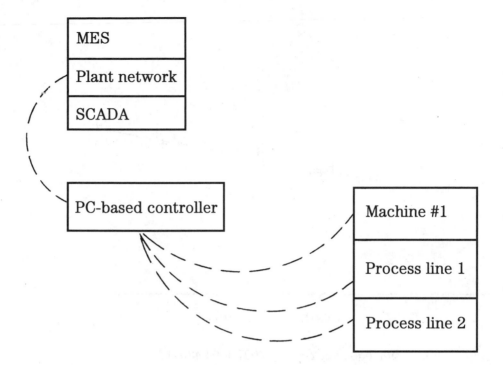

Fig. 11-2   The closed-loop manufacturing environment. The PC is right in the midst of it all.

only random variations, as all other process functions are to be fully corrected or improved as necessary.

Common process functions of a PC-based system monitor are temperatures, line speeds (which usually involve motor speeds), pressures, levels, and other sensors which, when changed, will affect the overall product's outcome. This change might be due to raw materials, used in the process, requiring different temperatures or pressures to make conforming product for whatever reason that particular day. The means of determining whether a change is needed is obviously by not getting to the final product where the impacting change is too late, but by gathering some system data which can be compared to data of runs of good, final product. The data can be evaluated in many forms. One is charts.

Often called *data management,* or *data acquisition,* it is the statistician's dream. Sometimes it's the quality control manager's nightmare. Any way you slice it, the fact remains clear: An awful lot of data is collected these days with high-speed, high-memory-capacity computers. This data has to be provided to upper management in a form which is readable, concise, and clear. Decisions about the process have to be made and sometimes made quickly. These decisions will probably cost somebody time and/or money, so the data had better be right, also. We don't want to spend more money than is necessary. One major tool of the people who compile the data is the control charts. There are many of these types of graphs. We will highlight a few.

There are process capability charts and regression-correlation charts. An example of the regression-correlation chart method is shown in Fig. 11-3. The process

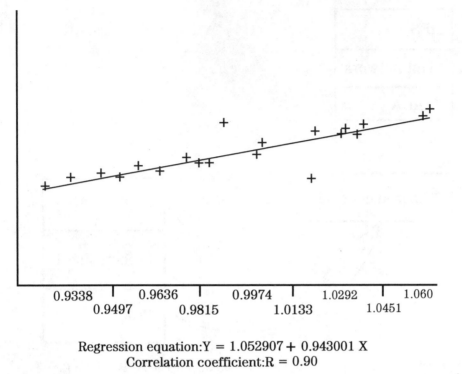

0.9338		0.9636		0.9974		1.0292		1.060
	0.9497		0.9815		1.0133		1.0451	

Regression equation:Y = 1.052907 + 0.943001 X
Correlation coefficient:R = 0.90

Fig. 11-3   Regression-correlation chart.

capability chart can reveal causes of nonconformances. It shows the actual and predicted distribution of the sample. It can be very useful in displaying the out-of-tolerance frequency of the process. The regression-correlation charts plot the relationships of process variables. This can be a valuable tool in analyzing the process.

There are several easy-to-calculate and easy-to-plot charts which can, at a glance, indicate that there are more random occurrences than allowed. These charts will provide the results of on-line sampling to head off a persistent process problem before too much final product is scrap. One commonly used chart is the *histogram,* as shown in Fig. 11-4. This chart is basically a frequency distribution shown in graphical form. It is sometimes called a *bar graph.* Another common SPC/SQC (statistical quality control) chart is the x and R chart (a sample is shown in Fig. 11-5), which is simply the average x and range R of groups of data or most likely measurements. This is one of the more common charts used. Sometimes it is necessary, when the data collected is not showing any coherent relationship, to perform a *scatter plot.* This procedure plots points of data on a graph purely to see if any relationship exists at all. A scatter plot example is shown in Fig. 11-6. To better understand these charts, some basic terms must be defined, some of which relate to statistics and others to QC and process control:

The *control limit* is that region within an upper and lower control level or limit (UCL and LCL). A process is out of control when the values fall outside the UCL and LCL.

The *UCL* is the upper control limit, and the *LCL* is the lower control limit.

Histogram Analysis

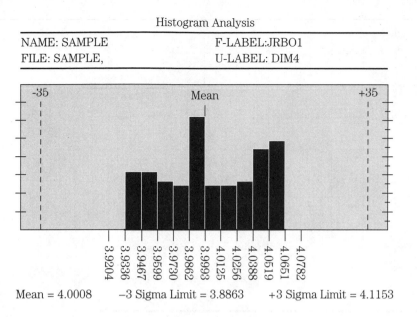

| NAME: SAMPLE | F-LABEL:JRBO1 |
| FILE: SAMPLE, | U-LABEL: DIM4 |

Mean = 4.0008   −3 Sigma Limit = 3.8863   +3 Sigma Limit = 4.1153

Fig. 11-4   Histogram example.

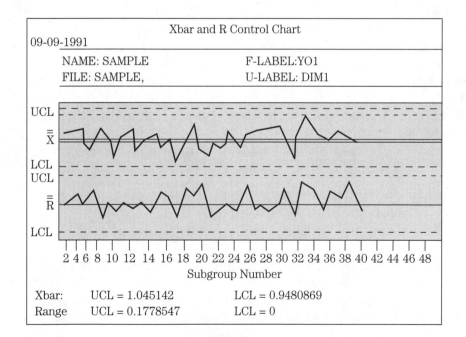

Xbar and R Control Chart

09-09-1991

| NAME: SAMPLE | F-LABEL:YO1 |
| FILE: SAMPLE, | U-LABEL: DIM1 |

Subgroup Number

| Xbar: | UCL = 1.045142 | LCL = 0.9480869 |
| Range | UCL = 0.1778547 | LCL = 0 |

Fig. 11-5   Example of $\bar{x}$ and R chart.

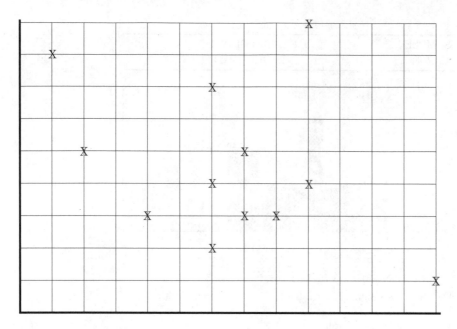

Fig. 11-6   Scatter plot example.

The *range,* sometimes shown as *R,* is mathematically the difference between the lowest and the highest values in a given group of numbers.

A *sample* is a limited number of elements (measurements) taken from a larger source (population). If a sample is selected randomly and if it is of sufficient size, it should display the same characteristics as the population from which it was chosen.

The *mean* is the average value of a collection of values. It is expressed as $\overline{x}$ or x. Its equation is

$$\overline{x} = \frac{x(1) + x(2) + x(3) + \cdots + x(\text{num})}{\text{num}}$$

This is an example. Find the mean of a set of numbers or values as follows: For the numbers 2, 3, 4, 5, 6, and 10, the mean is 30/6, or 5.

The *median* is described in statistics as the middle number or value in a set. Consider the following numbers: 2, 3, 5, 9, 11. The median is 5.

The *mode* is the number or value that appears most frequently. For the numbers 3, 2, 3, 4, 5, 3, 3, 4, 5, 2, the mode is 3.

Metrology is the term used very often in statistical quality and process control. This is the study or science of measurements. So a quality control expert is a metrologist.

Another important term in the quality sector is *percentage defective*. This is most important to the president or owner of the company who wants this value to be at or near zero. The percentage defective is the amount, or percentage, of units in a given lot which does not conform to specification. From here it is time for the statistical analyst to be given the task, from all the data given, of furnishing a *probability*. This probability is the prediction of all the possible outcomes for a given situation based on the initial data given. Some might call it the "best guess"!

A *deviation* is the algebraic difference between one of a set of observed values and their mean or average value.

The *distribution* function describes the probability that a system or set of points will take on a specific value or set of values.

Kurtosis is a means of determining how well a normal curve fits a particular distribution of data points. A sample of a leptokurtic curve is shown in Fig. 11-7 and represents negative kurtosis, or a distribution curve with smaller tails than those in the normal curve. In Fig. 11-8 is shown a positive kurtosis curve, which is also called a *platykurtic curve* because the tails are larger than those in the normal curve.

Obviously, nothing can happen in a charting or graphing sense unless useful data is gathered, crunched, and recorded. In more appropriate words, measurement, inspection, or interrogation data must be collected at the specific point in the process. It is usually transferred over some communications line to a computerized host device. This transfer can be in ASCII form or in dedicated register form so that the receiving device can decode it and then "crunch" it. This phase is mainly comprised of repetitive updating and adding to a matrix so that the final numerical values can be properly calculated. Now the data can be recorded or saved for later use in plotting or further uploading. Once the data has been outputted properly, that all-important decision, usually made by the human manager or operator, is made regarding process correction or modification.

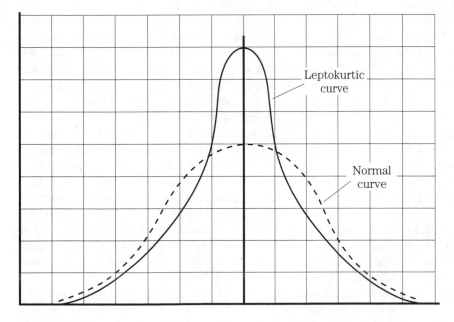

Fig. 11-7   Negative kurtosis.

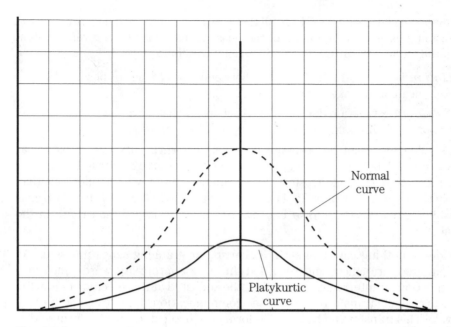

Fig. 11-8   Positive kurtosis.

A Quick History Of Quality Control

Quality issues date back farther than we think. The late 1700s with Eli Whitney's gun contract are an early example. Eli Whitney is credited with one of the first true industrial automation schemes, that of interchangeable parts for firearms. It must be brought to light that he failed miserably at the first production run. He was awarded a contract for several hundred muskets by the U.S. government. His theory of interchangeable parts and subassemblies being mass-produced by different people was tremendous. What it lacked was the ability to change the process, midstream if necessary, to make modifications to it and end up with a 100 percent fit of all parts to one another. This did not happen, as his first run only produced 14 usable muskets (and I wouldn't want to fire one of those first 14 muskets either).

As quality control over the years has gone, surely one or two Roman emperors rejected a chariot, sword, or gift simply because it had a flaw or defect and did not meet their standards. Had a quality program been in place then, the acceptance rates would've been higher (and maybe a few might not have been beheaded)! Quality programs have been in place for years because customers determine if a particular product is acceptable or not. The consequences are predictable if the customer is not satisfied. However, today products are more complex and are sometimes made from many subassemblies which are made by other concerns in the production cycle. Being able to track a part or subassembly from location to location and to provide proper documentation is part of today's quality programs.

Statistical quality control and statistical process control many times are confused, and there is a definite overlap. The confusion arises because a process engineer might collect data for use in changing the actual process, and the quality control engineer might collect similar data for proof that the product is being made to specification. Both need the data, both work for the same company, and both have specific needs for the data. The fact is they could probably share the data, and many times do. The overlap does not end here. Many types of charts can serve a quality control function but can be shown as a process function with different attributes and data. A good example is the Pareto charts. They can be used to plot the number of defective products in a manufacturing process in one instance and the causes of a particular problem in another. The problem could be organizational in nature. Pareto diagrams and charts are discussed later in this chapter.

Early on in the manufacturing sector, quality control meant that routine tests and inspections were administered at different points along the production line. Many of these tests and inspections were done by hand or by eye, definitely allowing room for human error. Acceptance samplings were performed at critical junctures in the manufacturing process. The pass/fail result of the acceptance test dictated whether the part was allowed to move onto the next step. Sometimes all the parts in a particular process are sampled, and this is called a *detailed inspection,* whereas if less than 100 percent of the available parts are checked, it is a *sample inspection.* From here it must be determined what numbers, or inspected values (measurements, sizes, etc.), are critical to product quality and then to against what standard they will be measured to be deemed acceptable. This determines whether the lot is acceptable. This also has a bearing on whether a 100 percent sampling is to be performed all the time or some of the time.

Usually a manufacturing facility's quality program is a set of written regulations or standards to which all manufacturing functions must adhere. The plan is administered by a QC manager who usually reports to upper management and who also interfaces with shipping, engineering, test, and so on. Within the last decade there has been a severe movement in the manufacturing world to enhance and further document a facility's quality control program. This has paved the way for new reporting and created many new jobs, all relating to quality.

Ironically, quality control did not get into full swing until the automotive industry began touting it. The irony here is that the term *automation* grew out of the automotive industry, and so has the need to ensure quality—perhaps because, with so much automated equipment used in the manufacturing processes, more data could be collected. In addition, once an automated piece of machinery starts cranking out parts, it doesn't change its methodology until someone forces the machine to do something. It will make a bad part consistently bad for a long time! Also, as the large automobile manufacturers started to outsource parts and subassemblies, it became necessary to place controls and regulations on the standards for these parts.

During this same era, two individuals, W. Edwards Deming and Malcolm Baldrige, gave us what would be the basis for quality control programs, from the automotive industry to the nuclear industry. The focus of Deming's philosophy was to start with management and change the whole organization from top to bottom, not just to redo a portion of the manufacturing process. Deming-based quality guidelines have some flexibility, whereas the Baldrige plan was more rigid. Documentation is more necessary under Baldrige's plan, and statistical understanding is important to that documentation. Obviously, comparing the two philosophies is more a matter of interpretation, and the intent is still the same—implement a program, satisfy the customer, and continue to improve products and customer relationships.

For many years companies have entered into and gotten out of quality programs for whatever reason. Escalating process and material costs tend to eliminate quality concerns until it is found that the return customer is disappearing. The last decade has presented a renewed emphasis on quality control, and with the emergence of ISO 9000 as a worldwide standard, quality control programs are now a necessity to do business. Virtually gone, we hope, are the temporary fixes to keep somewhat acceptable (and sometimes marginal) product moving out the door. Also, we hopefully don't hear the phrase "That's close enough" used anymore, as exact standards are going to be used as barometers in the manufacturing process.

Quality Control and Quality Assurance

Quality control is that effort in the manufacturing facility to maintain a product to a defined set of standards. This is accomplished by first establishing the set of standards, implementing them, and periodically testing the product to make sure it is living up to the standards. These standards are the specifications by which the product will be manufactured, and since manufacturers must make a profit, quality control is provided at the lowest practical cost. *Quality assurance,* however, is more the pledge by the company and its management that a quality control program is in place.

In order for a quality program to be in place, a manufacturing facility must have a *mission statement.* This simply states that the company puts customers first, desires to make a fair profit, and will continue to strive for perfect product output. From here there must be a documented plan for achieving and maintaining quality for every product made. The degree to which a plan is followed is what sometimes makes or breaks another customer's application of that product. Sometimes company quality plans are turned on and turned off depending on the present clientele, financial situation, and current philosophy of the existing management. It is so easy, and tempting, to ship an electronic product without a complete functional test, so as to get a billable shipment. Electronic testing is a very time-consuming portion of the manufacturing process and is skimped on many, many times. The real "burn-in" occurs on field start-up, and this is truly the wrong time for problems.

True quality control is made up of several subcomponents. First, the quality program has to be fully described. What will constitute a conforming product to the customer's requirements? Next, after manufacturing to a specification, will the performance standard of the product be met? Does it conform to the product specifications and/or the customer's expectations or actual requirements? Another subcomponent becomes preventive maintenance of the program. If bad-product occurrences are frequent, then a way must be found to prevent them. The system must be constantly monitored to minimize, if not completely eliminate, all failures. This portion of a quality program is the performance gauge. To strive for an error-free state is the goal in any quality system. Last, a means of statistically measuring the conformance, or nonconformance, is needed. How do we stack up?

To clearly see if the goals and guidelines are being met, it is often necessary to put the data gathered into charts and graphical representations. This can be statistical quality control (SQC) or just simply looking at causes and effects for various processes or illustrating plant actions so as to gain a better perspective. One such cause-and-effect chart is the *Ishakawa diagram*. An example is shown in Fig. 11-9. This diagram is an effective way to analyze a situation or problem. The problem is shown as the mainline piece, and the causes are shown as limbs which lead to it. It sort of looks like the old way of diagramming a sentence in grammar class!

Another commonly used charting method is by *Pareto analysis*. This is an analysis of the frequency of an occurrence. It is named after an Italian economist, and it helps arrange problems and causes by their importance. It is helpful in establishing priorities for quality control. The Pareto diagram, shown in Fig. 11-10, is often referred to as a *bar graph* which shows the frequency of a given occurrence. Manufacturers often utilize these types of quality control techniques as they are modern-day solutions and philosophies.

There is another important facet of quality management which deals with conformance and nonconformance. A gauge, or measurement, is placed on these areas in the way of direct and indirect costs. These costs can be in actual dollars, time, and labor. The *price of nonconformance* (*PONC*) and the *price of conformance* (*POC*) are two important concepts to help achieve true quality control. *Conformance* is achieved when a product adheres to a documented standard. Nonconformance is the failure to meet the standard. There are costs attributed to both conditions. The price of nonconformance is basically the rework, repair, or replacement time and money values because the standard wasn't met. An example of PONC might be when a printed-circuit board is placed in a fixture for testing, or burn-in, and is suspected to have a defective, or bad, component that requires repair. The board must be tagged bad (time) and troubleshooted to find which component is bad (more extra time); the bad component must

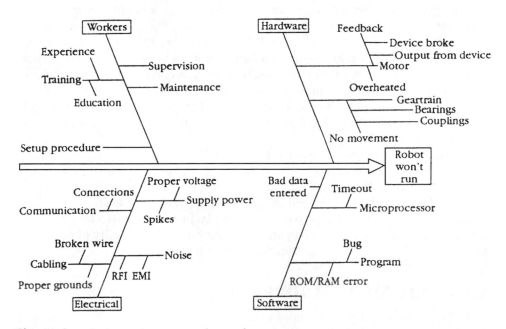

Fig. 11-9 Ishakawa diagram—why a robot system won't run!

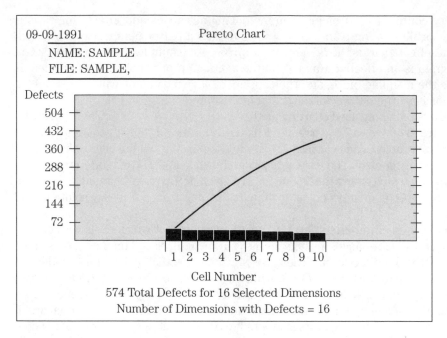

Fig. 11-10   Pareto chart example.

be removed (time); the new component must be purchased (money, and hope it is in stock and doesn't need express delivery), remounted and soldered (more rework time), and finally retested (a full repeat). This nonconformance also interrupts the assembly line, the typical manufacturing cycle, and is basically not favored by many individuals.

Other contributing costs to PONC include, but certainly are not limited to, warranty costs when the product fails in the field, premium freight charges when product has to ship overnight or parts are needed for the product in a hurry, extra paperwork and handling, unplanned overtime, service, or downtime, and returned product. In addition, customer service personnel have to listen to complaints (lost time), situations have to be explained (more time lost), and someone has to make up with the dissatisfied customer (embarrassing). All in all, the price of nonconformance is far greater than the initial rework.

The price of conformance is the better of the two scenarios because it is, hopefully, a lesser and more infrequent charge. This is the cost in time and money to maintain integrity in the part meeting the standard. An example of POC in the electronics industry might be the need to have all the workers who handle a printed-circuit board wear wrist straps to dissipate any static electricity so no stray volts "zap" the board and destroy a component. This ensures the integrity of the board, at least, during this phase of the manufacturing process.

Total Quality Management

Everyone in the corporation must be involved when it comes to quality control, from the president of the company to the individuals having little to do with the manufacturing process or product. This philosophy has changed to include everyone, because at some level and at some point everyone has a role. It used to be that there was just a quality control department and a handful of employees who administered the plan. These individuals were too often not welcomed by their coworkers and were treated as more of a hindrance than an asset to the company. This is not so today. Quality control is everybodys' business. This new *total quality management* (*TQM*) philosophy is being practiced in countless organizations around the country and around the world. From documentation, to design, to maintenance, quality control involvement is not discriminatory. The new quality philosophy now incorporates *teams* of individuals to perform tasks. Employees are now even routinely trained so that more knowledge is shared within an organization. Key elements of the team concept are involvement, concern, knowledge, and shared responsibility. Listening, communicating, evaluating, and keeping good records from every meeting will make the action work. Having an agenda and sticking to it make for quick, efficient, and productive meetings. After all, we *all* dread lengthy meetings.

Many times a team in a particular plant is comprised of members from many different departments in the plant. Manufacturing, engineering, maintenance, shipping, front office, and sometimes outside personnel are often placed on a team. This team is assigned the task of solving a particular problem. Brainstorming, scheduling events, and following up are some of the results of a given meeting. Everyone has a say, and everyone has a vote. This concept encourages the exchange of knowledge within the different groups and disciplines. Sometimes cross-training is a net result of the team philosophy. Also multiple teams can be devised to handle a variety of problems, with some individuals residing on many, overlapping teams. This is an effective way for many individuals to share in the responsibility and to share in the glory and satisfaction of solving a particular problem.

Soft logic systems are included in the TQM scheme of things. Especially with data exchange and data collection, the soft logic system can provide almost instantaneous information about the process or machine it is controlling. With this data in hand, any internal plant arguments concerned with locating a problem area can be solved quickly and efficiently. Everyone can be on the "same page," from the president to the person who pushes the buttons on the human-machine interface panel. Any quality problem at a plant is everybody's problem.

ISO 9000

Manufacturing and business have changed over the past decade. Commerce is carried out on a worldwide basis now, and that means transactions are more complicated. It is not as clear how to satisfy the customer these days (although many can argue that it has been tough for centuries). This is so because dealing in a world market means there can be cultural and language obstacles. Along those lines, different countries have different laws, customs, and standards. Thus, selling a product internationally is more extensive than selling domestically. One fact remains the same, however: A product or assembly can arrive defective or simply can fail to work.

Thus, the paper trail gets a workout. When challenged, a company will maintain that it has a full-fledged quality program and that it tests every piece of manufactured product before the product leaves the factory. However, when an angry customer who is in possession of a faulty or defective component disagrees, who is right? Maybe both parties are right. The customer is right because he doesn't have a good product, and the supplier maintains that she followed the quality guidelines. There is always a solution to any problem, and this one would obviously get solved, but what about a set of standards for every company? One of the more important standards for manufacturing facilities in the world market is ISO 9000.

Soft logic and ISO 9000 were also made for each other. ISO 9000 is heavy in documentation, and soft logic can provide all the data and information ever needed from an application. True, the supplier previously mentioned may indeed have adhered to a quality program. However, to what degree were tests and inspections performed and to whose standards? The term *quality* is easy to use but is frequently hard to substantiate. In the world economy of today, suppliers and customers want proof that a complete quality program is in place, and they want to know exactly how it is implemented. That standard has become ISO 9000, and it evolved from BS S7SO in the United Kingdom.

What exactly is ISO 9000? The initials ISO stand for the International Organization for Standardization, and ISO 9000 has been adopted in many countries around the world as the basis for implementing, controlling, and documenting quality programs. It is not a conformity assessment standard, but rather is a quality management system standard. The ISO organization is based in Geneva, Switzerland. In the United States, there is a U.S. standard which is published by the American Society for Quality Control (ASQC), a member of the American National Standards Institute (ANSI). ANSI, in turn, is the U.S. member body of ISO. Therefore, many important bodies are associated in a major way with the establishment of and full responsibility for these standards. Another important relationship is that of the International Electrotechnical Commission (IEC) and ISO. The two organizations work closely on all matters concerning electrotechnical standardization. This is most important because of the heavy content of electrical and electronic equipment in use today in factories all over the world.

ISO has established a set of standards which are part of the ISO 9000 series. The Geneva standard is approximately 25 pages long while the ASQC's U.S. version comes available in a five-part set, with the ISO 9001-1994 standard being approximately 10 pages long (it is equivalent to ANSI Q91). There are varying degrees of the standard, each requiring a different level of assessment. There are ISO 9001, 9002, 9003, and 9004, with the highest attainable level being ISO 9001. The major differences are that design control and servicing are not requirements of ISO 9002 and design control, servicing, contract review, purchasing, internal quality audits, and corrective/preventive action are not required components of ISO 9003. ISO 9001 requires all the aforementioned items and the main requirements.

There are presently 20 key functions certified under ISO 9001:

Management responsibility	Quality system
Contract review	Design control
Document and data control	Purchasing
Control of purchased product	Process control
Product identification/traceability	Inspection and testing
Control of inspection/testing equipment	Inspection and test status

Control of nonconforming product
Corrective and preventive action
Training
Handling, storage, packaging,
    preservation, and delivery

Quality records control
Internal quality audits
Servicing
Statistical techniques

These include the basic requirements of ISO 9002 and ISO 9003, and the complete set is what makes up ISO 9001. Each of these has a set of rules and standards which must be adhered to. These rules make up the basis for compliance. Actually, it is the act of not adhering to the rules and standards which causes the commotion. This is a state of noncompliance. There are two types of noncompliance:

Major noncompliance is the absence of a documented procedure to address a requirement of the applicable standard; an extensive breakdown or the absence of evidence of a documented procedure required by the applicable standard; an inability to demonstrate compliance with a technical claim relative to matters affecting produce quality. It represents a material risk to produce quality.

Minor noncompliance is a failure to fully satisfy a requirement of the standard with a documented procedure; a breakdown in the implementation of a documented procedure in isolated incidents. It does not represent a material risk to product quality.

The following is an overview of the requirements as they appear in ANSI/ASQC Q9001-1994, and unless otherwise noted, these represent those requirements for certification to ISO 9001, 9002, and 9003:

4.1 *Management Responsibility.* Any quality program starts and ends here. Management shall define a policy relevant to its goals and needs. Responsibilities, authority, and a management representative are to be established throughout the organization. Overall, management will have to be fully committed, make available the resources, and perform periodic reviews of the program.

4.2 *Quality System.* A quality system cannot exist unless it is documented. A quality manual must be controlled and maintained. The manual will be made up of the procedures, work instructions, and the basic quality plan. This section weighs heavily on the implementation of the quality plan itself.

4.3 *Contract Review.* Before any agreement is entered into to manufacture or perform a service, it is important (and logical) to agree on what will be provided. Written requirements should be agreed to by both the customer and the provider. Changes to the contract and written records should be kept. To meet ISO 9003, this requirement is not necessary.

4.4 *Design Control.* This requirement is not necessary for certification to ISO 9003 and ISO 9002. This is so because many manufacturers do not design, but rather build to another's design. Those who do design must keep a complete set of plans and specifications for all products. In addition, design input and output must be well documented. Where and how compliance with regulations and well-defined requirements were established along with proving that the design is safe and will function properly. Design input can also involve other sources, as in technical consultation. Therefore, design review, verification, and validation will occur periodically and shall be so documented. Any and all design changes have to be fully recorded.

4.5 *Document and Data Control.* This is the heart of ISO 9000 certification. Document, document, document. This is the most common source of noncompliance. This requirement states that all procedures shall be documented and controlled and shall be made available. Either hard copy or electronic media may serve as the form by which documentation may be kept. The documentation shall be reviewed and approved, and controlled issues shall be furnished as they are amended. Any and all changes must be recorded. Keeping up with and following a conforming documentation program throughout the whole quality program and especially the ISO 9000 process will practically ensure certification and recertification, at minimal costs.

4.6 *Purchasing.* Given the complexity of many products these days, many components are outsourced. The integrity of the finished product is only as good as the sum of the individual pieces and their integrity. Because many parts are bought from other sources, there has to be a specific way to evaluate suppliers and subcontractors. This requirement addresses both. Again, good record keeping is critical here. Heavy emphasis is placed on documentation which flows with the component from supplier through assembly and so on. Purchased product verification and where the verification occurs are also discussed. For ISO 9003 certification this is not a necessary requirement.

4.7 *Control of Customer-Supplied Product.* This is similar to purchasing, but the customer serves as a supplier also. This requirement provides for the handling of customer-supplied product. Storage, lost, or damaged product is discussed here. Again, recording and documenting the condition and location of product are key to this requirement. For ISO 9003 certification this is not a necessary requirement.

4.8 *Product Identification and Traceability.* It would seem futile to document data relating to a specific part but not be able to locate it or to know which one was used where. That is why this section requirement calls for the tagging and tracing of parts or product through all stages of manufacturing, delivery, and installation. This is extremely helpful in determining where a problem was or could occur.

4.9 *Process Control.* This is that segment of the program which actually furnishes the product—the process itself. There must be control of the process to ensure quality and integrity. The conditions by which control is achieved must themselves be regulated. Most facets of the manufacturing process are covered under this requirement. Production, installation, servicing, and maintaining equipment are all covered, along with the need for written standards regarding each. Workmanship and records on personnel are also addressed. For ISO 9003 certification this is not a necessary requirement.

4.10 *Inspection and Testing.* With a well-documented quality control plan comes the need to prove that product is being manufactured to those standards. This is the actual inspection and testing performed constantly to ensure standards are being met. These procedures must be well documented. Inspection and testing will be performed at three different stages, as required: upon receiving outsourced materials, to product in process, and final inspection. Records shall be kept of all inspections and tests performed. Often this and other technical data and reports generated are used as submittals and follow the part or product.

4.11 *Control of Inspection, Measuring, and Test Equipment.* The inspection and testing phase will only be as accurate and valid as the personnel and equipment used to perform the tasks. Since much of today's testing and inspection equipment is electronic and many times "in line" with the actual process, it is often necessary to perform routine maintenance and calibration to such equipment. These procedures also must be fully defined and documented. With any quality program, consistency and accuracy are always two factors which can improve. The intervals for calibration and maintenance are based on the individual production scheme, environment, and history. Once the actual control procedure is fully defined as to the actual measurements to be made, then the best-suited piece of inspection equipment is selected. This piece of equipment will therein be fully maintained and calibrated, and operators must be fully trained. Calibration records are to be kept. There exists an ISO standard for metrological confirmation that can be very useful in setting up a functioning control procedure (ISO 10012).

4.12 *Inspection and Test Status.* Once any testing or inspections have been made of a particular product, it must be quickly determined whether it is a good or bad product. The term *better-quality* relates to whether the product is conforming to the standard. Once determined, the status of that test or inspection must be made available. This is accomplished many times by tagging or adding to an existing tag of the product in question. Again, full documentation is required here.

4.13 *Control of Nonconforming Product.* The main point in this section is to prevent nonconforming product from being used further in the manufacturing process. This involves review by authorities who can provide adequate disposition of the nonconforming product. Nonconforming product can be reworked, accepted with approval or concession, scrapped, or downgraded for use in another application. Sometimes the disposition is spelled out in the contract, but complete records of nonconforming product are very critical. Also, any reworked product has to be 100 percent reinspected.

4.14 *Corrective and Preventive Action.* This requirement is not necessary for ISO 9003 certification. The goal of this requirement is to eliminate, if possible, the causes of nonconformities. Corrective action includes investigation into how nonconformities happen, the handling of complaints, and determination of the corrective action needed. Another component of this requirement is preventive action and reviewing with management the documentation pertaining to this action.

4.15 *Handling, Storage, Packaging, Preservation, and Delivery.* This section covers a lot of ground, and perhaps these functions represent the larger portion of customer complaints. Documenting the control and procedures of these functions is good, but implementing their successful application is another matter. All handling, storage, packaging, preservation, and delivery of any product are the manufacturer's responsibility. Clear and consistent procedures, when followed, can enhance the success rate. Each of these functions is looked at closely by the ISO standard. Good record keeping is also a must.

4.16 *Control of Quality Records.* Obviously, since so much of the ISO 9000 requirement involves staunch record keeping and extensive documentation, it is no wonder that one key section should be devoted to its control. Maintaining control of quality program records ensures integrity and also proves that documents exist. The quality records must be orderly, legible, and easily accessed by authorized personnel. Today, quality records can be on many forms of media, with electronic multimedia being a convenient means.

4.17 *Internal Quality Audits.* This is optional for ISO 9003 certification. Much like a full-scale quality audit by customers or third parties, an internal quality audit is sometimes necessary. Periodically, it may be necessary to perform one just to reemphasize the importance of and need for the plan itself. Areas of weakness and noncompliance may surface with corrective action being the result. ISO requires documentation of periodic internal audits, results recorded, and corrective action so noted. There exists a good bit of information on quality auditing, some of which is available through ASQC.

4.18 *Training.* This requirement is mentioned near the end of the ISO 9000 standard but, along with service, is extremely critical. They are critical because unless people know and understand their jobs, role in the quality plan, and equipment around them, quality control is hopeless. After all, quality starts and ends with people—trained people. This requirement calls for the supplier to determine the areas most in need of training, then to implement a training program, maintain it, and keep records of who is being trained. Levels of experience also serve as gauges of proficiency and where training needs exist. With so much electronic, high-technology equipment in the production cycle (and even local to the quality program for testing and inspection), it is a given that training and retraining must occur.

4.19 *Servicing.* The intent of this section is to provide a service plan, implement it, and document when the circumstances for service in the contract exist. Many times this is not a contract requirement and therefore is not necessary for ISO 9003 and ISO 9002 certification. However, skilled, trained, and knowledgeable service personnel can salvage the worst products and projects. After all, a product is being purchased to work, and many times it's the service personnel who make it work.

4.20 *Statistical Techniques.* This requirement is mandatory, but each supplier has options as to which forms and methods shall be implemented regarding statistical information. Trending, charting, graphing, and just simple gathering of test data have to be analyzed and then presented in some form so as to get the point across. Clear procedures for handling these statistics must be documented, and the needs should be identified.

The requirements of ISO 9000 are spelled out but are not fully black and white. That is why an external audit is conducted. Auditors are looking for compliancy. They are not looking for noncompliancy! There will be ambiguous points, and some situations may involve explanation during the audit. The aforementioned standards are a basis by which companies around the world can compete on equal terms and common ground. In a world economy this is needed.

ISO 9000 certification has an erroneous enigma associated with it that (1) it is very expensive to attain and (2) there is a high probability that many "dirty laundry" issues will surface. The process of the audit is to find those areas of standards compliancy. If a certain deficiency doesn't pertain, then it's not an issue. Likewise, if a function is found to not be in compliance, then there is probably good reason to correct the situation. Certainly, if a company has not much of a quality program and is seeking certification, then the proposition will be an expensive one. However, with documentation in place and compliancy the norm, ISO certification can be relatively inexpensive with few hidden, or unexpected, costs.

The key to a successful and lasting quality program is constant focus. Sure, a company can get certified and feel as if the pressure is off, but the pressure is not off! Customers will demand the same or better quality from an ISO 9000 certified organization. More appropriately, the surveillance period is the mechanism by which ISO 9000 certified companies can be checked for compliance. That documentation has to be in order!

Documentation and document handling are perhaps the most significant overall ISO 9000 requirement. They must be addressed and must be done! Keeping up with the documentation and record keeping as you go is the best policy. Letting this get behind just compounds the problem of getting it done and documenting true and actual data as it happened. After the initial investment of time and money, it would be a shame to lose certification because of a lack of diligence in procedure and documentation. Most probably this letdown might be seen in the product quality also.

PC-based systems have emerged as an ally to the quality program. Hard data in the hands of a capable quality engineer is hard to beat. The next decade will demand even greater standards for quality. Those standards will further translate to much better and even more documentation. Soft logic systems capable of delivering such quantities of information in a timely manner and effectively will be in great demand. This author's opinion is that PC-based controls are going to become more prominent over the next 5 to 10 years.

To order a copy of the ISO 9001-1994 standard (approved in August 1994), which is a revision of the first edition (ANSI/ASQC Q91-1987) or to inquire, simply call or write to the address below. There are also other adjunct ISO related documents which are also useful if they pertain to your program. There are ISO 8402, which gives definitions; ISO 10013, which provides quality manual instruction; and a set of others. A complete set can be purchased from:

American Society for Quality Control
611 East Wisconsin Avenue
Milwaukee, WI 53202
1-800-248-1946

Conclusions

Because soft logic systems are tools which allow a manufacturing plant to gain better control of its process, they have to be maintained. Topics such as statistical process control, statistics, quality control and assurance, ISO 9000, SCADA systems, and others mentioned in this chapter all relate in a major way to PC-based control. The maintenance of the soft logic tools is not so much a keep-it-clean-and-shiny, keep-it-oiled issue but rather a soft-maintenance issue. Keeping up with technology, updating the soft logic system where required, and keeping abreast of the international and domestic standards are the soft-maintenance concern. Gaining control of a process or machine is a temporary situation. Many elements have to be watched and sometimes changed in order to keep the products moving out the door. Gaining complete control is probably never truly attainable because everything is constantly changing (product demand, laws, rules, regulations, standards, quality of materials used, shortages of materials, environmental changes, speeds of production, interruptions in production, and so on). How often have you heard, "…Ever since we replaced that control component with that other component, our process has never been the same!" Hopefully, that comment is made in the positive sense—that production is better. But the point is that PC-based control systems give to the manufacturer flexible tools and intelligence to affect the process or machine's performance, especially as changes occur in the world marketplace.

The elements of the statistics and SCADA systems provide the numbers by which the manufacturer can determine the next move to make in business. Wherever there is a shortcoming or problem area in the plant, the control systems can help pinpoint it. Just as the PC-based control system pinpoints the problem, it can be changed to correct for the problem (via the software in many cases). Likewise, if there are big changes in the world marketplace, external statistics will be evaluated. Maybe the demand for product is drifting (this happens to every company in time), and the time is now to retool and refocus the manufacturing plant. Well, the good news is that with flexible PC-based control systems in place, changes can be made quickly. With much of the PC-based system made up of software, the changes do not have to involve the hardware and retooling changeovers of yesteryear (not in all cases, but certainly computerized systems have yielded this luxury). Those corporations able to respond the fastest will not only survive but also will continue to grow.

Perhaps, soft logic systems were created with the statistical quality and process control personnel in mind. After all, the microprocessor has changed so much of the way we do business that a PC-based control system on the plant floor makes quite a bit of sense. Combining the control element with the data collection element is logical. As always, the fewer components needed to get the job done, the better!

12
CHAPTER

Soft Logic Applications

Many of the applications described in this chapter will look familiar—familiar to the extent that some have been accomplished utilizing older, relay-style, dedicated motion control, or even PLC equipment. Those components have been replaced by personal computers and industrial computers. The remaining pieces—motors, drives, sensors, feedback devices, networks, HMIs—and all other required pieces are still in the picture, but their master controller is a PC-based system. Basic application concepts will be provided in some applications along with specific concerns and benefits of the soft logic control scheme.

The applications shown in the following pages will give the reader a good overview of a particular process or machine. Information relating to the electrical and mechanical needs of the application is also provided. Any application is multi-disciplined. The engineer, programmer, or technician must be able to look at the big picture of the application. The soft logic package and the ability to control out of a PC-based environment are only one part of making the application a successful one. These applications highlight some of the specific areas and issues to be addressed. They can be issues relating to the computers, data acquisition, mechanics of the system, electrical needs, physical environments, and so on. Obviously, the application note is not all-inclusive but rather is an overview. Use these application notes as guides and as references to apply soft logic controls to your application.

PID Loop Control

One of the most common applications of soft logic controls in industry is the PID loop. The programmable logic controller has often been called upon to perform more extensive calculations to control the process. Monitoring, manipulating, and turning I/O on and off are the primary job of the PLC. However, as processes and machines have gotten more sophisticated and have been asked to deliver maximum performance, it is now expected that the PLC will be more of an overall process and multiple-process controller. The same functionality is asked of the soft logic system. If the PC-based controller can handle the extra requirement within, maybe by adding a module or two, then other devices (another motor, bigger tank, longer dryer, more sensors, etc.) won't have to be added. If a sensor can be added and the feedback directed into the PC for evaluation, then the process might be more accurately controlled, and thus more elaborate and expensive modifications to the process can be averted. It is still true that the fewer components in a system, the more reliable that system is. The more interconnecting cable and wire that exist between multiple devices, the more likely that data transmission and signal errors can occur. A PC-based controller is in order here.

The PC can used as a set point, or PID (proportional, integral, derivative) loop controller. As a matter of fact, today's PC-based systems are expected to have PID capability, the software, and predefined function blocks to perform it and must be able to have the flexibility to perform variations of the algorithm. And there are plenty of variations of PID. There are PI control loops. There are interactive and non-interactive PID loops. Some are adaptive, which means the controller can make additional corrections, above and beyond the set PID loop changes, as the process warrants. These can involve gain changes to the overall system. The *gain* of any system is defined as the ratio of the system's output signal to its input signal. This can be seen in Fig. 12-1. Full discussion of PID loop control is beyond the scope of this book. Refer to the Bibliography at the end of the book for additional sources which cover the subject more completely.

A PID loop is just that: a closed-loop system that receives feedback from some device and compares that feedback with a reference, or set point, for the process which it is controlling. Figure 12-2 depicts a typical temperature control system utilizing PID loop control. Often not all three components of the PID loop are incorporated in the actual control scheme. For example, a control signal output to a device which is proportional to the sum of the error signal and the set point is the P portion of PID. The control signal is directly correcting for any deviation seen in the process. This is often called PID control, but in actuality it is simply P, or proportional, control. For a given action there is a proportional reaction by the system's controller.

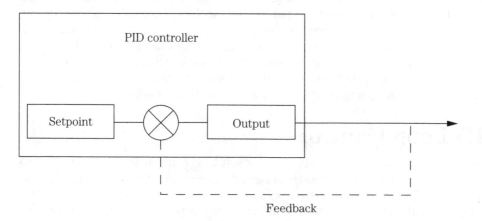

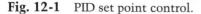

Fig. 12-1   PID set point control.

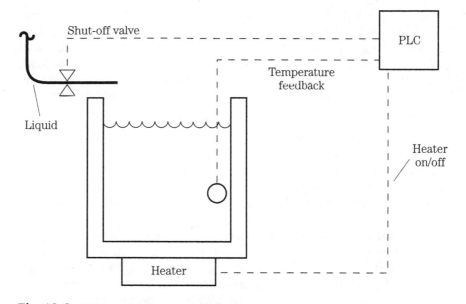

Fig. 12-2   PID temperature control.

Likewise, the I portion of the loop control is the integral of the error signal with respect to the set point. This is where a good understanding of calculus comes into play. Integrals take time into account. Values are reset through a corrective control loop during a period of time in this type of control. This looping is dependent on the severity of the deviation to the set point and the processor's capability. Some systems can employ both the P and I portions of the PID control scheme.

Last, the D portion of the PID loop is the derivative. A derivative is a change to, or derivation of, the resultant. This loop is more concerned with rate of change in the deviation. Similar in some ways to the integral loop, controller scanning and the frequency of the deviation become major components of the equation. Once again, this portion of the PID loop can be coupled with only the P portion when the application dictates. This is referred to as a PD control loop

PID control can be as simple as shutting off a valve when a desired temperature is met or as complicated as instantaneously correcting a machine's motor's speed, inertia, and torque as a material builds on a roll at high speeds. An important facet of PID control is how fast, in milliseconds, or even microseconds, it takes to go the entire loop. This is a function of the microprocessor speed, the source of the data (and how fast the transmission is), and how well the program and calculation methodology are laid out. Sometimes high-frequency filters are needed to keep PID signals true because any deviations to these signals can be perceived as major fluctuations in a sensitive, high-response, and high-resolution control scheme.

Soft Logic Applications

Throughout this book we have looked at the basic elements of PC-based control systems. Once working together, these elements provide for successful (usually if applied correctly) applications and accolades for the engineers who apply them. Getting there is not always that simple. A lot of work is involved, and there are many long nights spent trying to get a system to respond as it was intended. As PC-based controllers become more powerful and software becomes more plentiful, those more challenging applications will be pursued. Some, where even the thought of a PC on that type of a machine was unheard of in the past, are now done routinely. PC-based general applications can include some of the following:

- Material handling: transfer lines, conveying systems, parts handling, counting, sorting, automatic storage and retrieval, loading, and unloading
- Temperature control systems: monitor and control of a process's temperature; mixing, cooling, and heating of liquids
- Machine tools: CNCs, direct NC, grinders, saws, milling, drills, presses, welders
- Pressure control systems: pumping stations, air handling systems
- Conveyors/run-out tables: starting/stopping, counting, coordinating
- Robots: servomotor loop control, pass/fail, parts insertion, gantry
- SCADA systems: many data acquisition schemes, SQC, SPC, ISO 9000
- Assembly machines: automatic insertion, pick and place, fastening
- Energy management: HVAC, air balancing, cooling towers, chillers
- Work cell control: robots, storage, retrieval, staging
- Molding/casting: temperature and pressure control, mixing, drying, painting
- Furnaces/boilers: blower and burner control, induced-draft, and forced-draft fans
- Mining: conveyors, pumps, safety monitors, weighing systems
- Packaging: incoming/outgoing materials, weighing, sorting, bar-coding
- Power plants: brownout avoidance (switching), cooling, temperature
- Food processing: batch processing, weighing, packaging
- Petrochemical: valve and piping control, instrumentation, safety monitors
- Transportation: tracking, switching, dispatching, item handling
- Telecommunications: switching, logging, line checking, polling
- Aerospace: airplane manufacturing, air traffic control, parts tracing
- Metals: hot/cold mill control, gauging, raw material received

This PC-based list is not all-inclusive, and it will continue to grow. It goes on because plants are tired of being "locked in" to an expensive, captive proprietary PLC system. They need flexibility, and PC-based controllers are becoming extremely diverse. Computers and microprocessors are so prevalent that everyone and practically every business are getting into the act, using the high-technology machines to do or help do the work for them. Add-on, plug-and-play modules are more capable of doing local processing and freeing the soft logic processor for other functions. This diversification creates solutions and new advances. Thus this competition makes the PC-based control product's vendor base become more reliability-conscious and hastens the product's maturity. This all adds to the betterment of industry and the people who keep it going!

Following are some selected application examples utilizing PC-based technology to solve an application problem.

Extruder

Possible user:
Plastic film manufacturer; film packager

Scope of application (Fig. 12-3):
Extruders are made up of a control section, die section, encased screw system, motor, and often a gearbox. Extruders typically have several control requirements. A plasticized material is forced through an extruder die while being heated to form a specific cross section or shape. Besides controlling the main extruder motor, temperatures and pressures have to be monitored.

Specific concerns:
Since the extruder has many facets to it, a dedicated PC-based controller is required. The extruder immediately links to other sections of the process. Casting rolls and cooling rolls are prime examples. The soft logic will have to connect to these sections, monitor many I/O points, and control a DC or AC vector motor through a wide speed range. Full torque is required at these low speeds, and to compound matters no noticeable pulsing or interruptions can be tolerated from the drive's output to the motor. Speed regulation has to be extremely tight. Any pulsing will have an effect on the material. It can mark the material, make it too thin or too thick, and an interruption can break the flow of material altogether. Thus a high-integrity speed command from the PC is needed. Two other phases of control required from the PC seek to know when the extruder temperature is hot enough to begin extruding and to "watch" the extruded shape coming out. If it breaks or is too thin or too thick, then the system must be stopped and corrected.

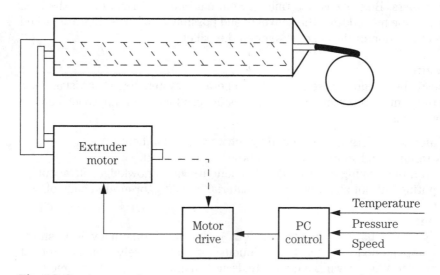

Fig. 12-3   An extruder system.

PC-based components used:

Traditionally, these applications have been done with PLCs and nonregenerative DC drives and motors. The DC motor's higher level of rotor inertia helps the motor to ride through load changes and to run smoothly at low speeds. However, AC flux vector drives have been able to perform well in these extruder applications. An industrial, rack-mounted computer has to used due to the harsher environment. An industrial touch screen display was also employed so that line operators could use a central point for data entry and collection.

Benefits:

Since a PC-based system was implemented, all kinds of data were collected. This data included temperature and pressure information at predetermined time intervals along with motor speeds and currents. This information allowed the quality control people in the plant to have electronic reports which could follow the run of product throughout the plant and outside. Additionally, the motor data allowed for trending charts to predict failures such as could be related to bearing problems and alerted maintenance personnel. Even with the lower-maintenance AC vector drive package, attention has to be given to these matters. The soft logic system is well suited to do this.

Gantry Robot Control*

Possible users:

All types of manufacturers.

Scope of application:

Focus on the process instead of program development. A major systems integrator provides gantry cranes that pick boxes from multiple conveyors and stack the boxes onto pallets. Box size is determined from bar code information on the box. The boxes must be moved from the conveyor and possibly rotated as they are placed at the correct position in the current layer on the pallet.

Problem:

Previously the integrator used a real-time operating system and C or Visual Basic to develop the control and user interface for custom products. This approach had the following problems:

- Product delivery time was limited by software development time.
- Only rarely could software between products be reused.
- The staff performing software development are very knowledgeable about computing but not about hardware, material handling, or motion control.

Solution:

By using the visual logic controller (VLC), the development cycle is shortened. The company no longer has to continuously invent and reinvent the product environment. The VLC provides a complete design, maintenance, and runtime envi-

* Courtesy of Steeplechase Software, Inc.

ronment for control and MMI. By utilizing the VLC, the control engineer can focus on implementing the features and functions of the robot instead of on programming.

Using the VLC as a tool, the designer is able to reuse MMI screens, programs, and subroutines from previous designs to allow further reductions in development time. To enable the robots to support a variety of different products being stacked on the pallets, stacking information is downloaded to the control program as a recipe. For the different products being taken from the conveyor lines and the different pallets being stacked, the recipe changes. From the positioning information in the recipe table, the robot gets path and position information to move a box from a conveyor to the correct position and orientation on the pallet.

Even though the mechanical details and the user interface of each machine produced by the OEM vary from machine to machine, through the use of the VLC, the company has been able to replicate additional cranes being controlled from the same VLC controller by reusing previously designed flowcharts.

Benefits:
Development cycle is reduced. (See Fig. 12-4.) MMI screens, programs, and subroutines from previous designs are made available for reuse. The capability to use cranes from different manufacturers is added.

Building Automation System

Possible user:
Commercial or property management facilities with a lighting, heating, and cooling system requirement.

Scope of application:
These applications are mainly for energy savings. As can be seen in Fig. 12-5, this heating, ventilating, and air conditioning (HVAC) system utilizes a PC to automate,

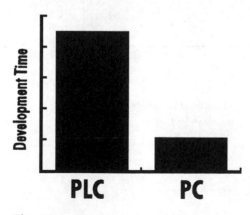

Fig. 12-4   Gantry robot control. Development cycles were greatly reduced using PC-based control. (Steeplechase Software, Inc.)

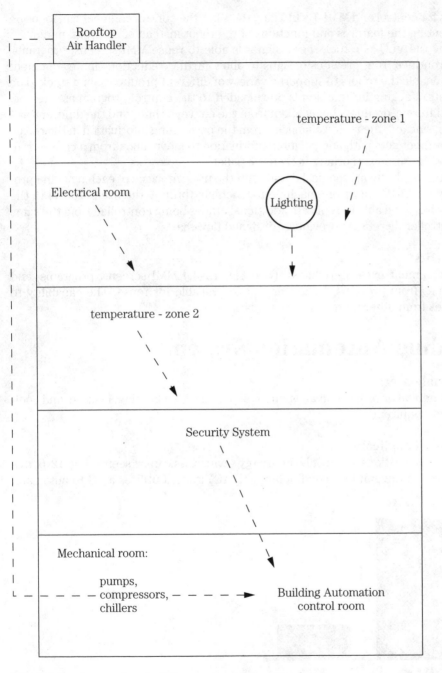

Fig. 12-5   A complete building automation control system.

monitor, and control many functions within a building. The building automation control PC is the nerve center of the building. The heating and cooling of the building are controlled in different zones and at different times of day. Variable-frequency drives are employed to give maximum energy savings on supply and return air fans. The lighting system is also part of the building automation system.

Specific concerns:

In many instances, a building is automated and revamped because it has old "energy-wasting" equipment in place. Being able to link and connect to existing components is always welcome, in order to keep costs down. A PC-based system with the appropriate interface modules is well suited for these kinds of applications. PID loop control is also a major requirement as many facilities have variable-air-volume (VAV) systems in place.

Benefits:

Obviously the energy savings will be the most critical for justifying a PC-based system. But many times it is necessary to collect real data to prove that the energy savings is being seen daily. The best scenario is to collect on-line data relative to actual kilowatthours and costs. Reusing AC motors and installing AC drives are also cost-effective on many of the fans and even on some pumps and compressors. All these devices can tie directly into the building automation soft logic package.

Fan and pump applications, energy savings, and soft logic systems:

Soft logic systems are ideally suited for building and HVAC energy management. Turning motors on and off which run pumps and fans is one approach, but utilizing electronic drives to slow the operation when loading is low is an even better approach. Bringing the I/O and sensors back to the PC, which in most instances does not have to be industrially hardened, and letting the soft logic take control are key. However, it is important to have a basic understanding of the laws of physics which apply to those fans and pumps being controlled.

Cooling towers, dryers, and other fan systems all move air or other gases. Air has different characteristics when cool from when hot. Likewise, the gas has to be treated differently when under pressure. In addition, horsepowers and speeds have specific relationships, or laws. These relationships are often referred to the *affinity laws*. Attention must be given to these laws whenever a variable-speed device such as an electronic drive is used. A simple equation for calculating the horsepower of a simple fan or blower is

$$\text{Horsepower (Hp)} = \frac{\text{cubic feet per minute (ft}^3/\text{min)} \times \text{pressure (lb/in}^2)}{33,000 \times \text{efficiency}}$$

This is a quick calculation for a system with normal temperature and pressure characteristics. However, horsepowers and motor speeds have distinct relationships in fan applications. For centrifugal or variable-torque situations, the affinity laws can apply. They are described as follows:

1. The flow in a system is a proportional relationship to speed, whether increasing or decreasing.

2. The speed in a given system increases by a square function as the pressure increases.
3. The speed increases in a given system increases by a cube function relative to the horsepower increases, and vice versa.

The affinity laws mean simply this: A fan's characteristics will follow these curves for flow, pressure, and horsepower. If a change is made to one or the other, then one must be willing to make the necessary changes to the rest of the system to get the performance desired. This can mean installing larger motors, changing base speeds, or changing gear ratios.

In pumping applications it is necessary to size a given motor for a certain flow rate (gallons per minute, gal/min) and a certain pressure (or head, ft). The equation is

$$Hp = \frac{gal/min \times head\ (ft) \times specific\ gravity\ of\ liquid}{3960 \times efficiency\ of\ pump}$$

where 3960 is a horsepower constant. Also the head pressure, in feet, is equal to 2.31 lb/in^2. The specific gravity of water has a value of 1 at normal atmospheric pressure and warmer temperatures (70 to 80°F). This value will change according to the temperature and pressure. These factors have to be considered whenever one is sizing a drive and motor for a pumping application. Also, many other nonwater liquids have different specific gravities. Some common liquids and their specific gravities are shown in Table 12-1.

TABLE 12-1. Various Specific Gravities for Common Liquids (English System of Units at 14.7 psia and 77°F)

Liquid	Specific gravity
Acetone	0.787
Alcohol, ethyl	0.787
Alcohol, methyl	0.789
Alcohol, propyl	0.802
Ammonia	0.826
Benzene	0.876
Carbon tetrachloride	1.590
Castor oil	0.960
Ethylene glycol	1.100
Fuel oil, heavy	0.906
Fuel oil, medium	0.852
Gasoline	0.721
Glycerine	1.263
Kerosene	0.823
Linseed oil	0.930
Mercury	13.60
Propane	0.495
Seawater	1.030
Turpentine	0.870
Water	1.000

Sludge Separation*

Possible user:
Municipal wastewater treatment facility.

Scope of application:
Integrating systems with a single programming language. Several engineers involved in planning, integrating, and deploying municipal sludge/sewage treatment facilities analyzed the available components to automate this process in search of a more efficient and more productive opportunity. (See Fig. 12-6).

Specific concerns:
Existing technology offered limited options for preparing and moving this water, other than to collect it, separate the sludge in a storage facility, and prepare the wastewater for shipment to another location for further processing. This process requires coverage of a significant geographical area. It requires digester/drying equipment for water collection and separation, a loading facility, and a very large site where the sludge can be dispersed for drying. Once the sludge has dried, it is removed and placed in another landfill waste site. This process takes between 6 and 9 months to complete, at which time most of the waste is usable.

Equipment used:
Utilizing the flexible, PC-based architecture of the visual logic controller, engineers were able to use state-of-the-art processing equipment, such as the latest valves, sensors, and dryers, to efficiently and effectively integrate the process and create a powerful, cost-saving solution. The VLC's flowchart programming language and its real-time (iRMX) control engine provided an integrated solution. With a single programming language, the many different pieces of equipment and components were easily integrated from the same control platform.

During development, the engineers used the real-time control program's simulation capabilities to verify and test the operation of specific components. This enabled them to complete control program testing months prior to equipment installation.

The new integrated system effectively provides a way to produce EPA-approved biosolids, eliminating odors and vector attraction. This system greatly reduces waste volume. The end product is now 95 percent dry, optimizing storage and reducing transportation costs. Site requirements are reduced by up to 75 percent.

Benefits:
The major benefit of this system is that it takes previously unusable by-products and produces environmentally friendly fertilizer of exceptional quality. The system enables the company to recover its operating costs through the sale of finished products. This system is very easily integrated as a turnkey retrofit project in existing plants. It is modular, fully automated, and ideally suited for communities of up to 50,000 inhabitants. A single programming language provided easy integration of

* Courtesy of Steeplechase Software, Inc.

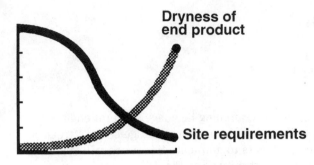

Fig. 12-6   Sludge separation—municipal
wastewater treatment facility. (Steeplechase Software, Inc.)

components and equipment. Simulation programs were used to verify and test operation of specific components. The end product was 95 percent drier, optimizing storage and reducing transportation costs.

Single Centrifugal Pump with Bypass

Possible users:
Water/wastewater facility; commercial and industrial facilities.

Scope of application:
Most radial-flow, or centrifugal, pumps have similar components and operate in much the same manner. The basic components can be seen in Fig. 12-7: an electric motor, a pump casing which houses the impeller, and associated seals. The centrifugal pump generally moves high volumes of fluid at low pressures. A drive placed on a pump motor to reduce the motor speed, which reduces the flow, is now a common occurrence. Because the pump system must have the capability to always run, a line bypass method is usually installed with the drive (on AC systems only). This can be seen in Fig. 12-8. The control of the pump rests with the PC-based controller. Soft logic allows for the monitoring of flows, levels, or pressures, whichever means of pump control the application requires. This is a generic pump application, not defining the reason for the speed control of the pump motor.

Equipment used:
Most pump installations will use an AC motor, thus making the drive an AC variable-frequency type. However, there may be some remote installations which use DC power, and therefore a DC motor is in place.

Specific concerns:
In level control, a sensor must provide a signal to turn the pump on or off. This can be a simple contact telling the PC to start the drive or starter. Likewise, a signal (either analog or discrete) is required to control the pressure, temperature, or flow of a fluid into a tank. These signals have to find their way into the PC, without noise, to provide the soft logic application and perhaps an internal PID loop to adjust the

speed of the pump. Additionally, data on incoming and outgoing temperatures or pressures can be obtained for the SCADA system of the plant.

Benefits:

The benefits are safe control of a tank's level, the energy savings, and the data acquisition. Instead of using valves and vanes in the system, the AC drive controls the flow. Another benefit is the ability to run full speed via the bypass system, determined by the PC in the event of a drive failure.

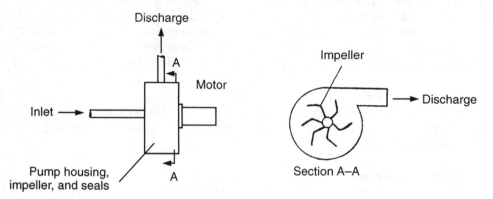

Fig. 12-7   Components of a centrifugal pump.

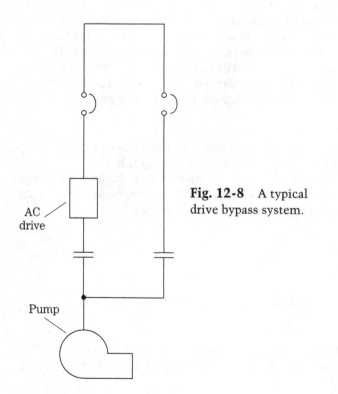

Fig. 12-8   A typical drive bypass system.

Parallel Pumps with Synchronous Transfer

Possible users:
Water/wastewater facility; commercial and industrial facilities.

Scope of application:
To optimize the motor and drive equipment available for a variable-flow pump system. This may entail running multiple pump motors from one drive and maintaining the ability to run at full, constant speed in the event the drive fails. In addition, the flexibility of sequencing pumps based on demand and alternating pumps to equalize wear should be inherent with the drive control system. All the sequencing and the optimization of the pump motors are determined by the PC-based controller.

Equipment used:
A PC with I/O mounted near the pumps in a NEMA 4/12 enclosure. Also AC drives and AC motors are used. Complex bypass schemes, contactors, and control logic are a part of the package.

Specific concerns:
Several configurations for parallel pump systems can be developed. However, there will be cost and complication issues to address as more functionality is expected from a particular system. For instance, the simplex drive and motor system from Fig. 12-9 with its bypass scheme was fairly "simple." Adding a motor and another drive to the system, we have now developed a double simplex pump system. This is shown in Fig. 12-10. Control logic is required specific to when contactors close and open. However, this time there is one less drive, but there are still two pump motors. The PC-based controller is in charge at this point. Some installations use the drive to bring the first motor up to line speed (60 Hz) and, once matched, switch it over to the 60-Hz line and then pick up the second motor based on demand (synchronous transfer).

Benefits:
The PC-based controller selects the pump motor to run, thus equalizing motor wear. It keeps track of the hours logged for each pump motor. It also can bring a pump motor up from a soft start to full speed and transfer it to the line; this keeps overall costs lower because there is one less electronic drive component. The bypass system allows for operation whenever the drive is out of service.

Cooling Tower

Possible user:
Any facility having the need to cool recirculated water.

Scope of application:
Based on the temperature of the water, the cooling tower fan will cycle on. This fan motor drives a fan blade which pulls high volumes of air through warm water, thus cooling it. (See Fig. 12-11.)

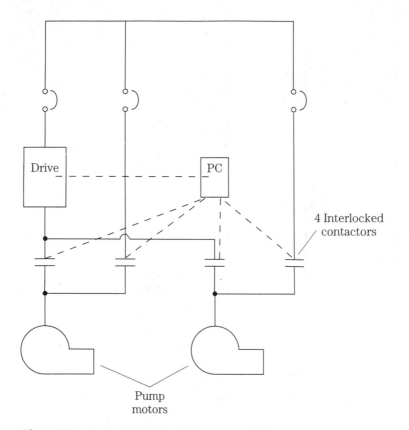

Fig. 12-9   A simplex drive bypass system.

Equipment used:

A soft logic system complete with a PI (proportional-integral) loop function block will control operation relative to a temperature set point.

Specific concerns:

Resonant frequencies are possible with such a fan installation. The fan motor, fan blade, motor, and coupling are usually substantial. Any vibration can be amplified to the point at which bearings, shafts, and couplings can fail. To avoid this vibration, a vibration sensor is mounted at the fan's mechanical system. This feedback will be monitored by the PC. Additionally, whenever there is condition in which the fan motor and blade are commanded (or drive has tripped) to coast to a stop, the fan can keep rotating for several minutes. Most AC drives have the capability to catch the spinning load and reaccelerate the motor to its requested speed. The PC-based controller will accomplish this by leaving the run and enable signal to the AC drive along with a speed command signal. Thus the drive will know what it's supposed to do.

Benefits:

By cycling motors in a multiple-cooling-tower scheme, even motor wear and eventual longer life can be achieved. Lighter loading will not require that all the cooling

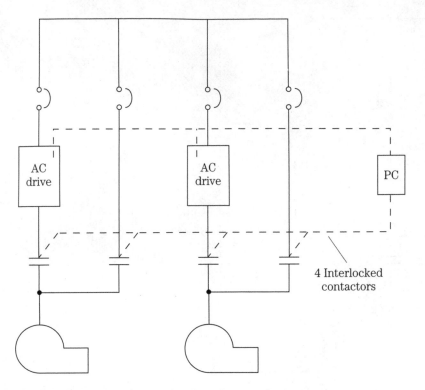

Fig. 12-10   A double simplex drive bypass system.

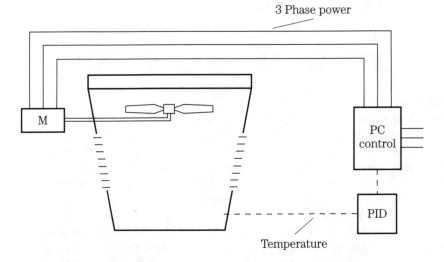

Fig. 12-11   A cooling tower system.

towers be operational. Multiple cooling tower fans can be set up to be controlled from one central PC. Depending on loads and the time of year, the PC can pull optimum performance out of the motor, drive, fan, or sensor system.

Roll Grinder

Possible users:
Steel and aluminum mills of all sizes.

Scope of application:
Rolling mills use several rolls in the process. Rolling steel, aluminum, or any other metal into thinner, finished sheet product is a process that is hard on the rolls themselves. They literally get beat up and chipped and lose their finish. Thus these work rolls and finishing rolls must come out of service and be reground to a finish worthy of getting them back into service (only to get beat up again). The drives which control the speed of the carriage, headstock, and grinding wheel (see Fig. 12-12) must be capable of reliability and performance to quickly return a roll to service with finishes sometimes as glossy as a mirror!

Equipment used:
The overall machine controller must be capable of scanning a high number of I/O. Coolant pumps, lubrication pumps, and safety interlocks have to be on or in place before the machine can run. Additionally, the PC will have to perform some minor coordinated motion control. The roll grinder is not doing any real position control, but all the speeds of the three motors have to be somewhat synchronized to one another. Traditionally, DC motors and DC drives have played the dominant role in roll grinder applications. Today's digital DC drives are capable of excellent speed and torque regulation. However, AC flux vector drives are also capable of the same speed and torque regulation needed in a roll grinder application. Also, some high-performance and high-cost roll grinders are driven by coordinated servo amplifiers and servomotors. This can be an expensive solution to an application easily tackled by a PC-based controller and some limit switches, some I/O, and some drives with motors.

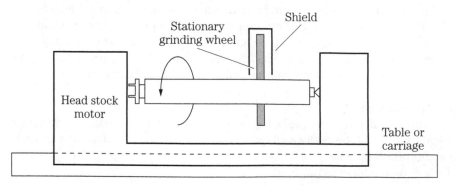

Fig. 12-12   Roll grinder.

Specific concerns:

No motion is allowed until all I/O safe conditions are met. The soft logic controls when motion begins. The operator will set the speed desired for each motor. The grinding wheel is a high-inertia load. It requires 150 to 200 percent torque for starting. Likewise, it needs regeneration or dynamic braking to stop quickly. All the drives have to function in a coordinated manner. If one is out of synchronization with any other, then "chatter" marks can appear on the roll and it will have to be ground again. Routing of feedback wiring is important. Since there is a traversing component to the grinder, the feedback wiring has to be routed through flexible conduit, in a track system, or in a trough. This can potentially lead to broken wires or to interference from high-voltage wires.

Benefits:

Using a PC in place of a full-blown servo control system is very cost-effective. The expensive servo system allows for extensive recipes and data collection, but so does the PC. In fact, the PC is better suited for the SCADA system, recipes, and keeping track of the roll being ground. Also in some instances the data on the particular roll ground must be plotted or printed out. This is definitely a function better handled by a PC. The use of AC, DC, or any other type of drive should give the operator very good speed control. This speed control, coupled with the individual drive's performance in torque regulation, means fewer passes should be required to grind a roll. Thus more rolls can be ground in a day, and the finishes should also be smoother.

Shipping Line*

Possible users:
Electronics manufacturers and assemblers.

Scope of application:

Meeting aggressive design and installation schedules while improving performance. A global electronics manufacturer needed to overhaul its shipping operations to deal with increased capacity. At the same time, the customer's information systems department was implementing a new, Windows-based order fulfillment system. The challenge was to design and implement a shipping conveyor system that could handle greater volume in less time and provide real-time data exchange with the new order management system, which links product selection, order entry, pricing, production scheduling, processing, shipping, and billing functions.

Specific concerns:

Since this installation was replacing an existing, already overtaxed system, it was critical that the job be performed quickly. For the customer, there was no turning back and no acceptable backup system to get products shipped. An aggressive schedule for completion was required.

* Courtesy of Steeplechase Software, Inc.

Equipment used:

The open nature of a PC-based architecture enables the visual logic controller to link the shipping line control system to the order management network through a simple RS-232 link. The VLC replaces existing PLCs and operator interface panels as well as interfaces to an I/O bus network that enables the customer to take advantage of I/O diagnostics. With these diagnostic capabilities, the VLC's MMI pinpoints problems for operators with error messages and graphical displays that enable them to handle line errors quickly and personally to improve uptime and output.

For instance, as seen in Fig. 12-13, VLC's MMI screen alerts operators to faults, such as a jam on a line. Operators view graphics and messages to see where a problem is and to find out whether a conveyor is running or stopped, when a conveyor is at maximum supply, and so on. The interface also provides diagnostic messages for all the line's sensors, valves, and motors. With the touch screen, users can ask the system to define problems to determine whether the problem is simply a predictive maintenance issue that needs scheduling before it causes downtime or needs immediate attention.

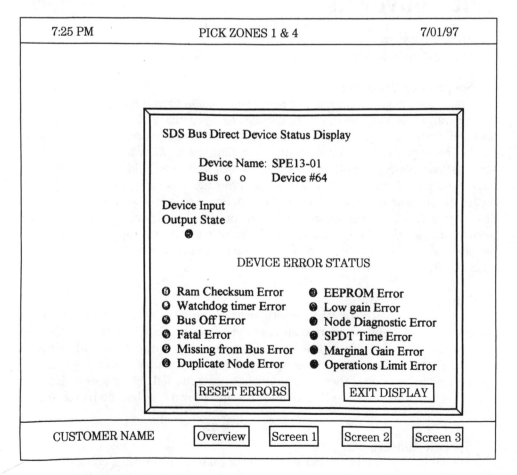

Fig. 12-13 Shipping line MMI screen.

Even though the control engineer assigned to the project had never worked with flowcharts before, the intuitive nature of the language enabled him to develop all the flowcharts for the 1000-foot line in 18 days. With VLC's real-time simulation capabilities, the engineer was able to test the control system designed from his own facilities so as not to disrupt the customer's shipping operation prior to installation.

Complete installation and system checkout took 282 worker-hours as opposed to the 650 worker-hours estimated for installation alone on a standard, hard-wired solution. Within 8 days, working 8 to 10 hours per day, a team of four finished the installation.

Benefits:

Intuitive flowcharts result in faster design time. Easy-to-use diagnostics provide process information. Predictive maintenance decreases downtime.

Belt Conveyors

Possible users:

Coal and mining facilities; food and beverage plants.

Scope of application:

Conveyors, being comprised of many rolls (some driven and others as idlers) and a continuous belt, are the main vehicles to move material from one location to another. They have to run fast or slow, fully loaded and empty. Therefore, there can be many methods of running and controlling them. Many mechanical systems such as variable-pitch pulleys, fluid couplings, and even eddy-current clutches have been used for years. Many conveyors are single-speed types utilizing a gearbox to get the low resultant speed at the belt. Some conveyor systems have a more elaborate control scheme. There can be one or more conveyors slaved to a master, perhaps to drop a smooth, consistent layer of material on top of another. This becomes a master-slave motion control application and is well suited for a PC-based controller.

Equipment used:

Servo motion control systems are overkill unless the conveyor has to be matched in speed and position to another factory machine. Even then a PC-based system has the capability to link with other electronic devices and other microprocessors in the plant. They can control hundreds of points of I/O, and synchronizing the motors to one another is done by outputting ratioed analog speed signals to the appropriate motors. See Fig. 12-14 for a breakdown of a belt conveyor system with PC.

Specific concerns:

The location of the PC is critical. Often the material riding on a conveyor belt is dusty and dirty. Some belts run outside. Therefore, the PC and associated I/O will

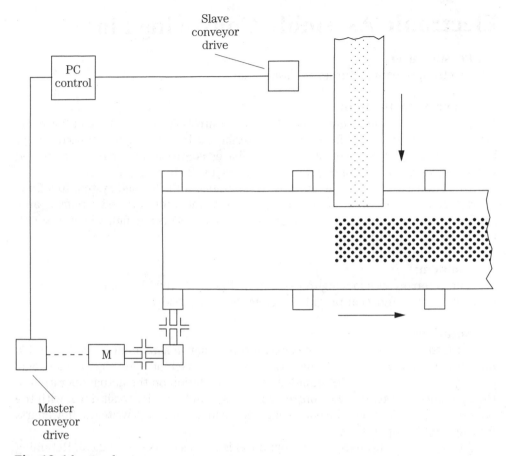

Fig. 12-14   Dual conveyor system.

have to be placed in enclosures suitable for the environment. Aside from that, the control scheme is fairly straightforward. Linking to other electronic devices is necessary in belt conveyor applications. Besides starting and stopping, overhauling conditions of the belt may need to be monitored. If this condition happens, then a mechanical brake may have to be turned on by the PC. Routing of the analog speed signal should be given close attention in order to prevent nuisance and intermittent trips. Incoming power should be isolated by a constant-voltage transformer so that voltage highs and lows to the PC can be minimized

Benefits:

The PC used in this application is a good choice because there is more I/O control than motion control. The motion control is relatively simple: The AC and DC drives provide excellent speed regulation; and as long as the speeds are not too low, torque regulation should not be an issue. The inherent soft-starting capabilities of the AC drives are actually displacing many reduced-voltage starters these days. If the motor is inaccessible, then a low-maintenance motor such as the AC induction type is excellent.

Electronic Assembly Conveying Line*

Possible user:
Electronics manufacturers and assemblers.

Scope of application:
A 24-h conversion from PLC to PC-based control. Through the use of flowchart programming and a graphical-operator interface, a PLC-controlled printed-circuit board conveying line was converted to a PC-based control installation with animated visual images and a host of diagnostic visuals in just 24 h.

A printed-circuit board manufacturer upgraded a PLC-based system to a flow-chart-based PC control system. The application transports printed-circuit boards from two assembly stations to two test areas. Empty pallets and faulty boards are returned to the two test areas.

Problem:
The company was looking to replace the PLC system with an easier-to-use PC-based control system that provided system-level diagnostics.

Solution:
With the picture used as the basis for the human-machine interface in hand, a pair of control engineers sat down to retrofit the machine. The PLC ladder logic didn't provide very much information or documentation on the actual operation of the machine. As a result, the control engineers found it easier to sit down with the operator who understood the conveying system in detail and to write the flowcharts for the machine operation.

Because the flowchart is the program, this process was very logical. Retaining only the list of I/O devices and part of the tag database, the sequence of events was defined. The control engineers split the machine into groups of sequences and decided priorities. Then they saved each completed and debugged routine. Twelve hours later, all the sequences were written and running. "We were so confident that we told the early shift to run the machine and note any problems," relayed one of the engineers. "Subsequent changes were minor and few."

The following day, they connected the MMI to the control program and brought device-specific diagnostic information from the sensors and actuators on Honeywell's Smart Distributed I/O System directly to the screen. This involved adding a few MMI-only routines to the flowchart control program and some diagnostics.

Eleven hours later, the pair had an animated visual image of the machine that indicates pallet positions, on/off status of the stop gates, and worded indication of how pallets are being coded at the relevant locations on the conveyor. Device diagnostics and error messages also are now visible to the operators, who can see everything that's happening in their operations from the PC and can respond as needed.

* Courtesy of Steeplechase Software, Inc.

This was the first PC-based control application for both engineers involved in the program. According to the lead engineer, "It was a tough sell, [I was] very skeptical about the robustness of a PC-based control engine. Once I witnessed the VLC's real-time programming in a real-time control environment, I knew it was the way forward. Under traditional programming environments, flowchart diagrams must be translated into a list of statements to suit the selected control platform. With the VLC, the flow-chart is the program. It saves you all the trouble."

Benefits:

PLC system converted to PC-based control in 24 hrs. System-level diagnostics meet customer's demand for easier-to-use control. Device diagnostics and error messages empower line operators.

Mixers

Possible users:

Paint and resin facilities; tire and rubber plants; chemical plants.

Scope of applications:

This has to be defined per the individual mixer. As was shown with the possible user list with this application, mixers can differ, and so can their control requirements. Driven loads can vary from light (liquid mixers) to medium (slurry and dough mixers) to heavy (solids and Banbury-type mixers). Others, such as powder and sand mixers or screw-type mixers, have hard-to-start loads. Thus, the scope of the application can be to provide the right amount of materials to be mixed, monitor temperatures, and time a particular batch, as in a batch process. A typical mixer is similar to a blender and is shown in Fig. 12-15.

Equipment used:

A rack-mounted PC, a soft logic package capable of 150 tags (I/O), temperature and pressure sensors, and some servo valves. For the medium- and heavy-duty mixer applications, DC drives and motors are a good choice. Their ride-through capability during severe load changes and the 200 percent plus torque when necessary are good for mixers with hefty service factors. Volts-per-hertz AC drives are excellent choices for light-duty mixers.

Specific concerns:

Batch processes require many functions from a PC-based controller. Having recipe information to control the amounts and types of materials to be added to the mix is paramount. Extensive databases need to be resident, or else a network must be in place for downloads and uploads. Shutting valves on and off can control the flow of material into a mixing tank, but the ability to adjust a valve by a servo valve amplifier is better. Temperatures, pressures, and flows have to be watched. The batch is also a timer function, and the PC must do this well also. Beyond the process control aspects of the application, safety is critical. Monitoring the entire process to protect the workers and the mix is required from the PC.

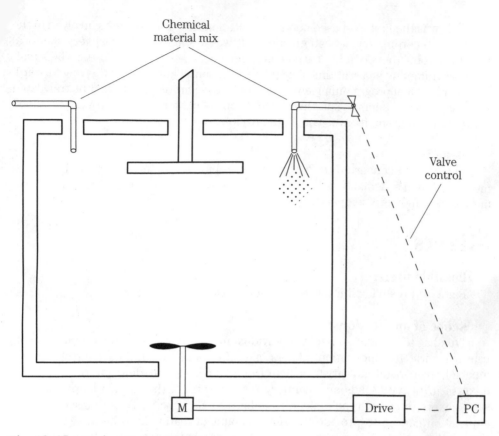

Fig. 12-15 Banbury intensive mixer system.

Benefits:

The PC-based system is ideal for this application. As changes are made to the batch-mixing process, the flexibility of the soft logic package will become apparent. Adding or deleting I/O is a breeze. Changing the application program will not take days and require a specialist programmer. Spare parts for the computer are also readily available, not from the inventory of the plant (an added expense) but from the local computer supply store down the street!

Batch Centrifuge

Possible users:

Sugar manufacturers; pharmaceutical companies.

Scope of application:

A batch centrifuge is made up of a basket where material resides, a motor assembly, and controls. The basket is a high-inertia, cylindrical component which must accelerate extremely fast to very high speeds to separate the liquid from the solids. The solids collect on the outer wall of the centrifuge basket and are later scraped off with a mechanical knife. The motor assembly commonly is mounted vertical to the basket; however, horizontal mounts and belting arrangements are often used. The controls include a master controller and motor drive control. The profile of a typical speed-versus-time curve is shown in Fig. 12-16. Preset speeds were loaded into the PC. It was able to change the centrifuge speeds based on a timer function. The soft logic application software, ideally suited for a batch-type process, was able to change the analog output, the drive's speed reference, to set the correct basket speeds.

Equipment used:

A enclosure housing racks of I/O, a rack-mounted MMI, an electronic drive, and the peripherals as needed. A PC suitable for its location is installed (it can be located away from the centrifuge, if possible). A batch centrifuge system will have many similarities to a batch-mixing process (valves, limit switches, temperature, pressure sensing, etc.). But it is a different machine altogether. The centrifuge basket spins at several thousand revolutions per minute, thus extra safety features have to be built in. The AC drives with an extra power bridge to furnish regeneration, for use in stopping and reversing, have been used along with inherently regenerative current-source inverters. Due to the high cycle rate of batch centrifuges, dynamic braking is not a good option for stopping. Dynamic brake resistors would get much too hot, perhaps melt.

Specific concerns:

The PC directs the motor drive controller as to the speeds and directions required of it. The drive has to accelerate in virtual current limit without tripping off-line. The same is true when stopping the centrifuge as any extra time in the cycle reduces the number of batches run in a given day. The drive must be capable of reversing in order to discharge the solid material, and tight speed regulation

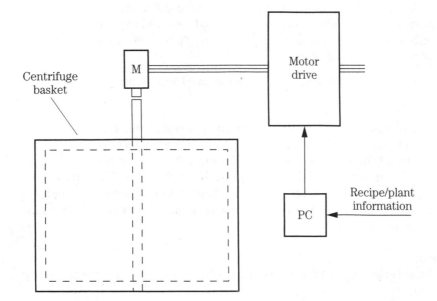

Fig. 12-16 A batch centrifuge.

at low speeds is required here. And since the centrifuge basket is spinning at extremely fast speeds, there has to be a built-in means of safely handling high-speed emergencies and basket runaways.

Benefits:

The PC can contain an extensive database with numerous recipes for the various batches. A single PC can actually control several centrifuges, thus minimizing up-front hardware. Many times there are several centrifuges in a lineup, and the PC must get data to and from a host computer system. The communication abilities of a PC and the ability to provide instant printouts of information are also attractive.

Assembly Transfer Line*

Possible users:
Automotive plants.

Scope of application:
Simplifying programming and debugging with flowcharts. The use of flowchart programming greatly simplifies the programming and debugging of a transfer line in an assembly application.

On an assembly line, workpieces are moved from one station to the next. At each station, an operation or group of operations is performed on the workpiece. In terms of the control system, there are several important considerations:

- From a control standpoint, each station's work is unrelated to the operations performed at all other stations.
- The workpiece must be moved from one station to the next.
- Workpieces must be inducted onto the line and removed from the line.
- If something goes wrong at one station or during a transfer, some of or all the other stations may be affected.

Flowchart programming makes it easier to manage these issues.

Problem:
The customer was looking for a way to create a modular transfer line. See Fig. 12-17. As product changes are released, the customer must quickly modify the assembly process to assemble the new product. This usually involves adding new stations and/or replacing existing stations on the transfer line. The PLC and ladder logic-based solution was too inflexible. Product changes required days or weeks of programming. This resulted in the customer's being unable to move quickly to introduce improvements to the product.

Solution:
The PC-based solution with flowchart programming now provides the flexibility that was lacking.

* Courtesy of Steeplechase Software, Inc.

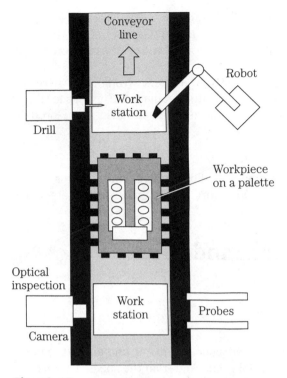

Fig. 12-17   Automotive transfer line. (Steeplechase Software, Inc.)

Each flowchart is an independent program that executes in parallel with the other flowcharts. Each station's behavior is programmed independently of that of all other stations. If a station must be replaced, it is a simple matter to:

1. Create and test the new station's programming at a separate location. This avoids any disruption to the current operation while the new station is being developed.
2. When the new station is ready, the customer simply removes the flowcharts that control the old station and replaces them with the flowcharts for the new station.

Flowchart programming supports and encourages the use of subprograms to capture reusable engineering effort. Common activities, such as hand-off sequence or a workpiece-clamping sequence, are coded as subprograms and used many times.

The overall design of the control system is rational and easily understood. Since independent pieces of the line are treated independently by the control system, it is easy for the designer to document which programs go with which function. There is no opportunity for one station's logic to corrupt another station's logic.

In addition to an abundance of added flexibility, the system designers found that they could easily add diagnostics to the line. The functional separation that enables modular flexibility also provides a natural platform for diagnostics. Since everything is already in its own cell of control, the additional logic to detect that something has gone wrong is unnecessary.

Once the system has detected a problem, the power of the PC comes into play. The problem is reported from the control engine up into Windows. Then the operator interface displays a diagnostic picture, including a text description of the problem.

This alerts the machine operator to exactly what went wrong and where the problem occurred. The display also gives the operator detailed instructions for fixing the problem. Without any help from the control engineer, the machine is brought back to a running condition.

Benefits:

Flowcharts simplify system programming and debugging. Subprograms enable capture of reusable engineering effort. Operators are empowered to detect line problems without engineering intervention.

Presses—Drill, Punch, and Brick

Possible users:

Metal fabricators; brick manufacturers.

Scope of application:

In metal applications, a punch press is fed a sheet of metal, and either the metal is sheared to a length or a piece of the metal is knocked from the sheet. This is done by striking the metal sheet with a very high-pressure tool punch against a die. This pressure is developed usually by the interaction of a large flywheel. This can be seen in Fig. 12-18. The motors being controlled in a press could be the feed motor, uncoiler motor, and one for the flywheel (this electric motor must be capable of high accelerating and running torques). Since an incredible amount of force is brought down against the metal to shear or punch it, the safety of the human operators is very important. Light curtains and clear-to-punch interlocks must be built into the PC's control circuit.

Equipment used:

A hardened PC, due to the vibration, shock, and typical dirty atmosphere around a metal punch press, is required. The I/O must be mounted and enclosed near the machine. An encoder or proximity switch is needed along with an internal counter to count pulses, in order to feed the exact amount of metal into the press. Control of all the motors, on or off, and the ability to change their acceleration and deceleration rates from the PC is necessary.

Specific concerns:

Safety is the most important concern. Second to safety is the need to feed the precise amount of material into the press block. If this is off by a small amount, then the piece punched may be of no value and have to be scrapped. Additionally, if an operator sees that the feed amount is wrong, he or she might elect to reach into the press to make an adjustment (don't do this) and risk injury. Feeding the right amount actually can eliminate a safety issue.

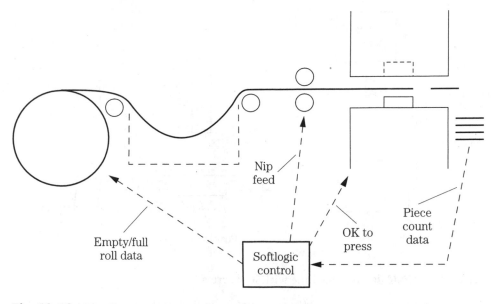

Fig. 12-18   Punch press.

Benefits:

The PC can perform many of, if not all, the functions needed by this application. Counting pulses from encoders or switches, keeping track of pieces punched per hour, and the ability to change feed lengths are some of those functions. Since the PC is a high-response, digital device, consistent and precision work can be performed. The PC is also well suited to interface with other presses on the plant floor as well as any out-feed equipment. The AC motors are welcome in these ambient environments because they have no brushes. Presses notoriously are run in dirty, dusty conditions, and DC motors tend to be maintenance problems.

Machine Tool/CNC

Possible user:

Any precision machine tool or parts manufacturer.

Scope of application:

To control the coordinated motion of a machine and utilize existing M codes and G codes from a variation of the RS-274D standard. A lead screw converts rotary motion to linear motion (see Fig. 12-19). This linear motion normally has to be controlled to very exacting tolerances. Most positioning-type applications will incorporate high-precision lead screws and recirculating ball bearing nuts to achieve high accuracies. Spindle motors are also asked to be controlled by the PC along with coolant and lubrication pump motors.

Equipment used:

Typically, servo drives and servomotors have been used. With their encoder or resolver feedback, they will be able to hold positioning tolerances down to a fraction

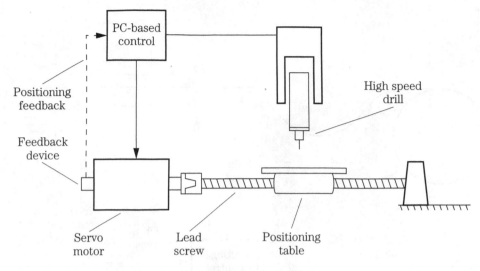

Fig. 12-19   CNC drilling machine with lead screw.

of a micrometer (0.000040 in). Stepper motors and closed-loop stepper controllers can also perform well in lead screw applications. A PC-based motion control system will provide the same degree of performance by using the same feedback devices and even the same motors and amplifiers, if so desired. A dual-axis or encoder interface board will be required to solve the motion control loops.

Specific concerns:

Since positioning accuracy is the goal in these types of applications, many external factors can affect performance of the drive control. A sound mechanical system is paramount. A flexible coupling should be used between the motor and lead screw to provide a certain amount of damping. This will also help with premature bearing failure at the feedback device due to misalignment. Hysteresis, or the motor's tendency to resist a change in direction, is another concern when repeated reversals are required.

Benefits:

The PC will allow many different parts to be made on the same machine and avoid time-consuming retooling. Data for different parts can be stored on the hard drive and implemented when required. The PC will also act as the traffic cop to watch over all the other discrete and analog I/O while the motion card(s) is (are) doing its (their) thing. The lead screw, or sometimes called a *ball screw* because of its ball bearings and ball nut assembly, is an excellent choice for controlling position in compact and confined spaces. High-precision screws with preloaded ball nuts are available, and with today's positioning controls, accuracies well below a micrometer can be achieved.

Glass Furnace, Shuttle, and Quench Line

Possible user:

Glass windshield manufacturer.

Scope of application: (Fig. 12-20)

A method was required to exactly match the line speed of a conveyor carrying windshields with that of a shuttle with vacuum grippers which transfers the windshields to a second conveyor. This meant that a photocell, triggered when sensing the leading edge of the windshield, needed to send an output to a controller. Meanwhile the conveyor line is still traveling at a fixed speed. Also the shuttle, once picking up the glass, must accelerate to the next conveyor, decelerate, and match the second conveyor's speed. The shuttle has to perform this task several times per hour.

Specific concerns:

How to time the arrival of the shuttle, precisely match the speed of the conveyor, and pick up the glass windshield without any damage to the glass piece. All this is prompted by a photocell signal.

Equipment used:

Servo positioning drives and a coordinated PC controller will be used. The drives control both the conveyor and the shuttle, so speed matching is easy. The problem is to detect the edge of the glass and match the shuttle speed to the glass speed on the conveyor.

A mode in the PC controller will be used to achieve the capability of interrupting the program with the photocell input. When the photocell is triggered by the edge of the glass, the soft logic controller stores the position of the glass on the conveyor (within 1 ms) so the shuttle can pick it up. It does this by reading the resolver count from the servomotor. Up to 10 values (position, absolute, etc.) can be automatically stored in the first in, first out (FIFO) stack without program intervention. The data can be read out of the axis's FIFO as needed. The operating system of the controller also has to be able to handle three direct inputs as interrupts to the processor. These are mainly used for ends of travel and the home switch. In a conveyor line such as this, the end-of-travel function is useless. Therefore, the photocell output went directly to the PC interface card as an interrupt input and thus guaranteed a maximum of 1-ms update time.

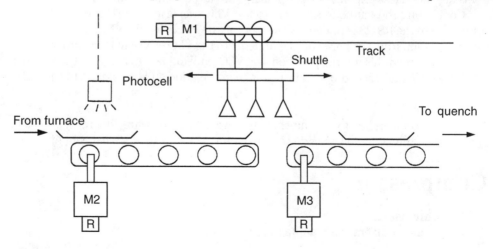

Fig. 12-20   Glass furnace.

Benefits:

By cutting down the time required to determine motor shaft position, the customer was able to run the conveyor line at the fastest speeds possible. This function also ensured that the glass windshield would not be marked or damaged.

Automated Storage and Retrieval System*

Possible users:

End users requiring material handling equipment.

Scope of application:

Integrating mainframe computer data with plant floor control systems. The automated storage and retrieval system (ASRS) consists of a series of trays that store material in a "buffer zone" until requested by the manufacturing execution system (MES). Each tray and storage location is identified by a unique bar-code number. The tray and location numbers are fed into the MES. When material is requested, the MES downloads the information to the storage system, and the tray is retrieved from the correct bin. The MES communicates via TCP/IP over Ethernet.

Problem:

Using a traditional PLC solution would require specialized hardware for both the bar-code scanners and the Ethernet connection. This would drive up the system cost significantly.

Solution:

The OEM decided to use the visual logic controller because of its ease of connectivity to commercial networks. The solution involves utilizing off-the-shelf hardware and software. An Ethernet communication card, and Microsoft's TCP/IP driver and Visual Basic communicate with the mainframe computer (MES). See Fig. 12-21. These items are much less expensive than similar systems used in conjunction with PLCs.

Connecting the bar-code scanners to the VLC was also easy. The scanners were connected to the RS-232 communication port on the PC. Using the VLC's RS-232 driver, the information from the bar-code is scanned into the VLC. A Visual Basic program was developed to read this information from the VLC via Windows' dynamic data exchange (DDE). The Visual Basic program formats the information and transfers it to the MES.

Benefits:

Eased connectivity to off-the-shelf hardware and software, decreased cost of system components, and bar-code scanned data transfers to MES are benefits.

Compressor

Possible user:

HVAC and refrigeration manufacturers.

---

* Courtesy of Steeplechase Software, Inc.

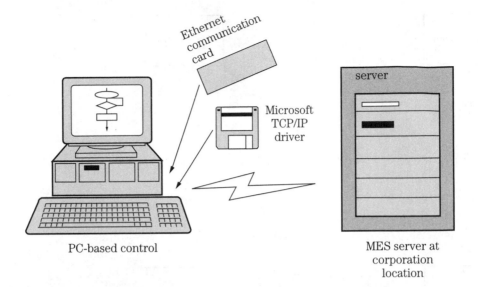

Ethernet communication card

Microsoft TCP/IP driver

server

PC-based control

MES server at corporation location

Fig. 12-21   Automated storage and retrieval system. Factory floor data is transferred to corporate MES. (Steeplechase Software, Inc.)

Scope of application:

A typical refrigeration system consists of four major components: a condenser, evaporator, heat exchanger, and compressor, as illustrated in Fig. 12-22. The compressor drives the whole system. A refrigerant is changed to a gas under pressure. It exchanges heat that it picks up along the way and condenses back into a liquid, and the cycle starts over. The compressor is actually a motorized pump which initiates the flow and pressure. It can be controlled by a soft logic system. The PC-based controller will also control the condenser, evaporator, and heat exchanger in the system.

Equipment used:

A PC-based controller is a good choice for many reasons. First, the loading varies in the refrigeration system depending on whether it is summer or winter. The PC can aid in determining seasonal requirements. Also, the PC can be an office-grade package as it should not be exposed to the outside elements and harsh environments. It will most likely reside in an office or control room somewhere. Its capabilities will allow it to monitor many I/O points and the multiple facets of the compressor/HVAC system.

Benefits:

The PC-based control for monitoring the I/O and the control of any electronic drives in the system is an extra benefit to the end user. Typically, a PC had to be used in the HVAC system for data collection, alarm detection, and monitoring. Graphics and screens sent to a color monitor were resident in the PC. Therefore, additional control out of the PC for everything else is a pleasant extra resource. This should make the justification practical and be very cost-effective also.

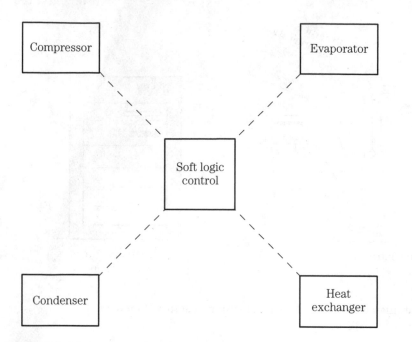

Fig. 12-22 A compressor system.

Box Palletizer

Possible user:
Any manufacturer whose product is boxed, stacked, and shipped.

Scope of application:
A manufacturer of particleboard furniture needs a means of stacking individual, boxed pieces as they come off the production line. In this particular case, the application called for fast movement (for increased piece count) and accurate positioning. One problem was that every box that came off the feed conveyor had a different size and weight. Most of the time, multiple pieces would be similar in size and weight.

The customer required that the motion controller be simple and inexpensive. Only two axes of motion had to be controlled, but both had to be coordinated. The customer also requested that the controller be such that his staff could write the actual motion programs.

Specific concerns:
Specific concerns: Different sizes and weights of boxes. Many times a teach type system is available with servo controls. However, when physical coordinates change due to different products, the motion program can be written such that calculations are done by the controller's microprocessor, and the corresponding position commands can be executed. Many users want a servo system that they can understand, program easily, and troubleshoot. Typically, the terms *servo systems* and *easily programmed* are not to be used in the same sentence. The servo is usually programmed

by the servo supplier or system integrator. Thus the proprietary trap is engaged again. A PC-based system is easily programmed.

Equipment used:

Since two servomotors had to be coordinated, a PC-based controller with an open architecture was selected. With its built-in power supply, input/output capability, diagnostics, and troubleshooting, a PC was a logical choice. This choice also minimized components. All that was required besides the PC-based controller was two servomotors, two PWM drives, a two-axis motion interface card, and the necessary cables. See Fig. 12-23.

Given that the customer wanted to do his own programming, all the motion functions, I/O functions, arithmetic calculations, and screen commands could be entered by the customer. The off-line development software was invaluable because the program could be simulated so that different size and weight boxes could be handled upon setup. The operator simply entered the box dimensions into the custom screens of the program, and the controller automatically calculated the position to move either the y or z axis in order to pick up or drop off a box. The vacuum grippers which secured the box were triggered on and off by the input/output functions of the controller.

Benefits:

This type of control made it possible to automate a portion of the manufacturing line. Previously, the boxes had to be handled physically by an employee. Sizing the servomotors for the heaviest box also allowed tremendous flexibility. In the future, more servomotors and drives can be easily added to the system simply by adding plug-in cards.

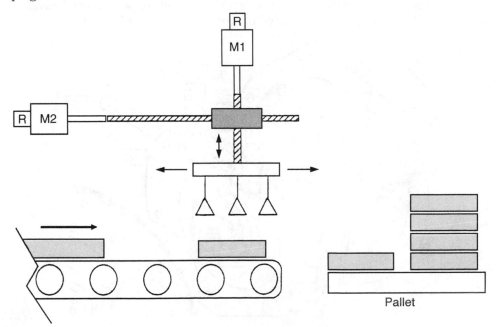

Fig. 12-23 Box palletizer.

Many applications end up having to utilize an existing special motor or have to incorporate a special control algorithm. Often the special motor is a real challenge. Wound rotor motors, two-speed motors, and synchronous motors are often considered as recipients of an AC drive's output. This is possible in most instances; however, certain accommodations must be made. For instance, a two-speed motor has two windings: a high-speed winding and a low-speed winding. To maximize the usefulness of an AC drive, the motor should be set up to only run on the high-speed winding, thus allowing for a volts-per-hertz curve all the way from zero to full speed. Likewise, a wound rotor motor has to have its slip rings tied together in order to make it accept an AC drive as a controller. These are considerations which will come up from time to time as more existing motors are reused.

Hot Spotting and Hyperlinking

Possible user:
Larger manufacturer of complex products containing thousands of parts.

Scope of application:
These applications are computer-aided engineering (CAE) operations. They link the design phase of the manufacturing process with the MRP and plant, assembly, and machine levels. Soft logic systems are used in conjunction with this level of information management. Hot spotting allows for the graphical highlighting of individual components of an image. The graphical highlight is then stored as a transparent layer of data, to be used later as needed. Figure 12-24 shows a drawing with distinct parts of the assembly fully labeled and numbered, allowing those individual parts to be identified, linked, and traced to other product parts families.

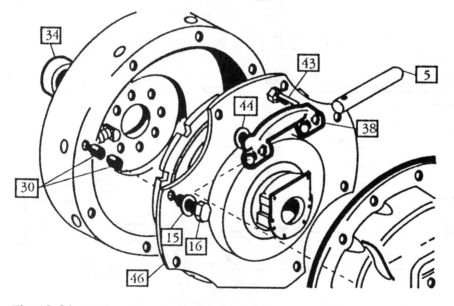

Fig. 12-24   Hot spotting a component within an assembly.

Specific concerns:
A solid, reliable method of exchanging this data throughout the process is required.

Equipment used:
Both hardware and software products make these applications work. A powerful, flexible soft logic package will be resident on the plant floor at an industrial computer station while a CAD package will be resident on a PC in the engineering department. A variation of a DDE package can be incorporated as required.

Benefits:
By setting up the parts libraries this way, the designer can link similar parts data with other product files. This method of linking throughout a part family is called *hyperlinking*. Design and processing times are greatly reduced, and the designer has much more flexibility.

Residential and Entertainment Applications

As the soft logic industry broadens and the packages become more affordable, new uses for the PC-based control are emerging. Intelligent systems in newer homes are controlling electrical outlets, heating and cooling systems, entertainment, security, and other household components. Additionally within other nonmanufacturing industries, PC-based control is also gaining prominence. Entertainers and television programmers have been using versions of soft logic technology for years. Now, with the PC being on the order of a commodity, smaller companies can employ their use in utilizing the soft logic for entertaining and presentation purposes. Two examples of these emerging soft logic follow.

Intelligent House Control

Possible user:
Any homeowner (new-home construction mainly).

Scope of application:
To automate a residence's heating and cooling systems and lighting; integrate the security system; make electrical outlets in the house programmable; and tie any and all communication devices into the package.

Specific concerns:
Most notably, except in an existing house in which pulling wire is going to be easy, most of these applications would be destined for new construction. The cost of an intelligent residential package can also reach 10 to 15 percent of a $250,000 home. Thus, its not for everyone, yet. However, with so many households

containing one or more PCs, the probability of adding onto one of those PCs is very good. This "add-on" concept of I/O boards in the home has to be refined, and it will be.

Equipment used:

As seen in Fig. 12-25, a central processing unit (the PC) is used in conjunction with a data entry/display unit. Specially equipped, smart outlet boxes must be installed and properly wired with cable which carries the bundles of wire necessary for low-voltage control, communications, and 115-V AC power. Add in the "smart-house" ready appliances, audio and video devices, and security products, and the system is nearly complete. Energy management components must be added, and the house is now automated!

Benefits:

Enables selection of which outlets should deliver power to an appliance, when, and for how long. This is practical for security reasons (lights on whenever occupants are away) and for convenience (to make coffee in the morning). Additionally, adjust the heating and cooling system as demanded by thermostat(s) and to separate the house into zones for ultimate temperature control. Linking the home

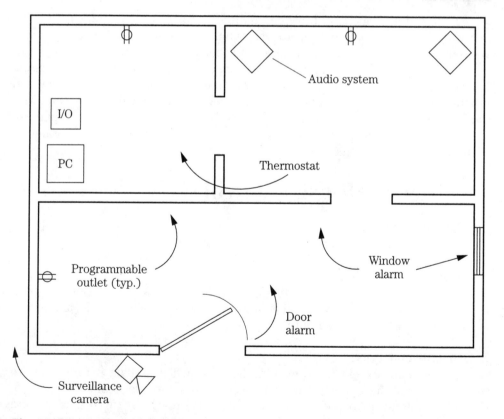

Fig. 12-25 An intelligent house system.

security system into a PC can allow for automatic telephoning of the police department and fire company, even while the occupant is away.

Automated Presentation and Entertainment

Possible users:
Sales and marketing executives; professional entertainers.

Scope of application:
To provide the tools necessary to "spice up" and automate a presentation. Everyone is looking for an edge these days, and with many presenters already traveling with a laptop and some version of Windows, this application will emerge quickly. Tying into the PC some extra hardware (to be controlled) and an interface card will allow many presenters to enhance their presentations. Trade shows and seminars are already media for these types of presentations.

Specific concerns:
Extra costs presently are an obstacle, although justification can be found in increased business or enjoyment from the presentation, which results in repeated opportunities (sometimes hard to measure). As costs of hardware and soft logic software continue to come down due to competition, more and more smaller concerns will be able to afford the package. Making the whole package, hardwarewise, more portable will also play an important role.

Equipment used:
A demonstration of a particular vacuum cleaner company's products will consist of the actual vacuum cleaner and an I/O module which acts as the interface to start and stop the commanded vacuums from a PC. Various lights can be controlled, also, thus making the presentation more appealing. A sound system for special effects can be incorporated.

Benefits:
The traditional in-house demonstration of the vacuum cleaner can be duplicated off-site (not in the home) at a mall, shopping center, etc. The possibilities are endless and are limited only by the creativeness of the system programmer. All presentations can be enhanced to a level that the presenter will be remembered vividly.

Conclusions

PC-based control has been tried on probably every one of these applications in the past. Using DOS-based, 8- or 16-bit machines, some creative interface cards, and some old programming languages, engineers were able to accomplish a sort of PC-based control. The end result or performance may not have been that which was desired or intended, but the effort was made. Those efforts have actually been the precursors to today's soft logic packages. As with anything else, why reinvent the wheel? Today's soft logic packages are well tuned and flexible enough to do those applications. They are easy to use and now have many ways to interface to other pieces of equipment. Additionally, other equipment is now being designed with soft logic in mind for interconnectability. The ultimate goal is to make control systems reliable enough, easy to use, and flexible. In doing this, the plant operators, process engineers, and managers can concentrate on the real issues within their manufacturing plant—to make product!

13
CHAPTER

PC-Based Factory
Control of Tomorrow

The first order of business will be to prove the soft logic systems in hard real-time environments. Along with this will be the success stories having to be told, over and over. To get believers, converts, and those who say "it can't be done" to specify a PC-based controller over a PLC is going to take time. Repeated successes and fewer "hard-drive" crashes will provide the story line for industry to accept this technology and run with it. After all, who bought the first PLC? Were there any skeptics to the PLC technology, especially in the beginning stages of that product's life? The PLC had to prove itself, and to this day it, like all computer controls, has to constantly prove its reliability. Time helps bring these kinds of products to fruition. They become more bulletproof and reliable, and other manufacturers of peripheral products help out by making their products compatible with the leading-edge controllers.

As has been mentioned, there is not enough history yet on PCs fully duplicating the PLC's real-time operating system for critical applications. The PLC has risen to such a level of product satisfaction and reliability that end users trust it and can expect it to last during all types of control oddities. They expect the same from a PC, and the technology is getting there. It is only a matter of time until most controller hardware starts to look alike. Presently, all controllers share certain key elements: They have one or more microprocessors on board, carry some memory, are software-driven, connect to the outside world somehow, and are powered by electricity. Thus, there will exist only a handful of ways to package all those similar items in the same box in the future. As a matter of prediction, if the microprocessor and controls technologies continue to strive toward smaller and smaller footprints, that will force all the control and computer products of this class to end up in virtually the same size box. So much more will be done with software that it will be incredible. Gone will be add-on modules and cumbersome pieces of hardware, thus causing all that "computer and control stuff" to go into a 6 in $\times$ 6 in $\times$ 6 in box (imagine that)! A graphical depiction is shown in Fig. 13-1. By default, all manufacturers' control products

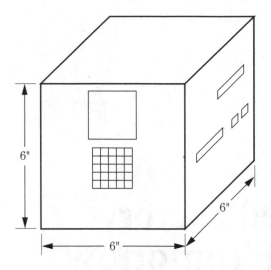

Fig. 13-1   The all-encompassing,
universal box—The computer/controller.

will have to look alike (only the colors and logos will be different). Obviously, this is an oversimplified prediction, but one that is very plausible!

Factory controls of the future will also be further removed from the machine and process. This is not to say that the controller hardware won't be physically at the machine, but more high-speed and integrity-laden communication schemes will allow users to have a lot of control from their desks or even their homes. It is not too far-fetched to troubleshoot and fix a machine over the telephone lines now; as a matter of fact, this is done in a number of applications all over the world. Expect more of this in the future.

Soft logic or PC-based control, which name will win out? Maybe both. Factory automation in the future will definitely have elements of each within it. New operating systems 10 years down the road will be so bulletproof that PLCs could potentially be all but forgotten. Imagine how fast the microprocessor clock speeds will be—perhaps 6.4 GHz or even faster! Memory and hard-drive space will be so affordable that monster programs unheard of in and on the factory floor will be commonplace on devices as simple as a thermometer. This is the future of factory control. Soft logic and PC-based control are only part of it!

Other elements on the factory floor will affect or be affected by PC-based control. Remote control technology should continue to change for the better. Interfacing to the PC and the soft logic system will, perhaps someday, utilize digital cellular technology instead of wires. The use of fuzzy logic systems and neural networks will increase. Decision making on the factory floor will go beyond on/off states. Even the Internet will mostly work its way onto the factory floor. It is conceivable for a machine operator at the machine's PC-based controller whenever a particular component goes bad. The operator could have the means to get on-line support via the Internet, to view an on-line manual, or to order a replacement part in an emergency breakdown. The possibilities are going to be endless.

Remote Controls

The term *remote control* can mean many things to many people. In its most basic sense, remote control implies that the process or machine operation is in the hands of a person who can affect that operation from elsewhere. As seen in Fig. 13-2, a remote control system can come in many forms. It can be a remote operator station at the machine. It can be a slave remote control to the main operator console down the line. It can be a wireless handheld controller such as that for overhead cranes. The premise is that the controller is not mounted on the machine, therefore it is a remote control.

There can be wires routed to and from the controller station, and then again it can be a wireless system. Wireless remote control will become more reliable in the future, and thus it should see greater use on the factory floor. Handheld terminals will be utilized to send and receive data. From the factory floor to the company mainframe, information will be able to flow, hopefully without interruptions. Likewise, data will be transmitted to the factory floor via some wireless method with instructions for the machine. Wireless remote controls will be extremely useful in physical locations where wire-type transmissions are not even possible (ocean, deserts, mountains). This a saga from the wireless factory of the future (or is it today?): Lucy, the president of XYZ Company, wants a part count from the machine in her plant which makes widgets. She may have to increase the quantity to satisfy an order she's just been made aware of. The problem is that Lucy is climbing Mt. Hood

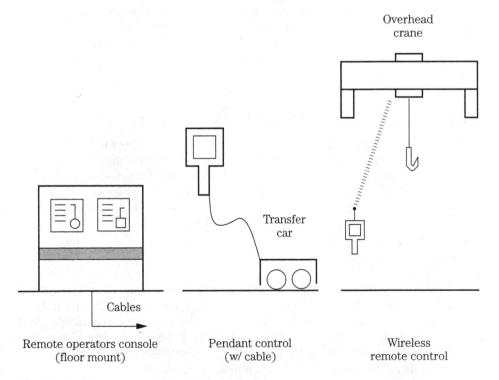

Fig. 13-2 Remote control techniques.

in Oregon, and the plant is in San Francisco. With her wireless transmitter/receiver, she will dial into the plant's computer system, enter her password, and log on. She'll enter the address of the widget machine and get on-line information. Her question will be answered, and she will key in data which will be accepted by the machine's controller. She will disconnect and continue climbing, knowing that the order will be filled. A phone call would accomplish the same thing except that there could be human intervention, which is what Lucy was trying to avoid. The possibilities are going to be endless.

The Internet

The previous example of a remote control application from afar is not too far-fetched whenever we factor into the equation the *Internet.* The Internet has taken the world by storm, and no one knows exactly where it will lead. As a manufacturing and production tool, its use is just being tested. Users presently are more often utilizing it for fun and entertainment, some electronic mail, and research. As more people use it and as more manufacturers see its potential, the Internet will grow in scope. It's not too far-reaching to see an entire factory's processes and machines on-line. All microprocessor-based equipment could be downloaded to a Web site, and a separate page could be dedicated to each machine. Virtually anybody could view a read-only page on a particular machine or process. Of course, we wouldn't want proprietary information out there, nor would we want people to be able to change things. However, an on-line plant tour could occur on the Internet complete with sound and moving pictures. All that would be missing would be the smell of machine oil and having to dodge a tow motor or two. Salespeople could make sales calls to a plant without even physically being there. The power of the Internet is not even 10 percent unleashed.

Fuzzy Logic and Neural Networks

While fuzzy logic and neural networks are not going to be the future of control, they do offer greater potential to the PC-based control environment. As we have found, PC-based controls are good at input and output manipulation, and soft logic is the essence of this behavior. Fuzzy logic influences the behavior of a system, in part controlled by chemical, mechanical, or electrical means. It does this by changing inputs and outputs in that system according to a rule or set of rules that model how the system operates. To oversimplify: A fuzzy logic control scheme takes a mathematical model (which can be proved with truth tables and facts) and replaces it with a *fuzzy model.* This fuzzy model is best described as a superset of boolean algebra, and it is used often in PID loop control (taking the output of the system and comparing it to the desired set point, then making a correction). Conventional PC-based control systems utilize a mathematical model which defines a relationship that transforms the requested state and measured state of the system into inputs that will alter the future state of the system's outputs. The problem with this type of control is that it usually assumes that the system is linear. As the system increases in complexity, it becomes harder to formulate the mathematical model. Thus the fuzzy logic system replaces the mathematical model with several smaller elements. The fuzzy logic controller combines these smaller elements into a whole and makes an inference about what the system's output should be, as it models linguistic expressions that have nonbinary truth values.

Fuzzy logic and control seem to be mutually exclusive. Just the word *fuzzy* conjures up notions of uncertainty. Logic implies yes or no, on or off. So this superset of conventional logic has been expanded to handle the concept of "partial truth." A *definite maybe* is now possible in using the AND and OR operations in a logic diagram. Fuzzy logic moves from the discrete I/O state to a continuous form—nonlinearity is the norm. This type of control has been around for decades and has been used in high-end mathematics modeling. In the last few years, fuzzy control systems have worked their way into advanced, linear (and nonlinear) process control applications. Other applications include pattern recognition (used in advanced machine vision systems), operations research, and data analysis (high-end trending). With more and more power furnished to the PC-based controller, fuzzy systems used in signal processing and automatic control will continue to evolve. Get out those advanced calculus books!

Neural networks, on the other hand, move us toward the field of artificial intelligence. With neural nets the properties of nonsymbolic information processing are explored. Whereas conventional controls work on the premise of linear functions, nonlinear and neural go hand in hand. Neural networks are hard to define. These networks have many lesser processors with their own memory. These units are connected by communication channels which carry numeric information. The units only process the data local to them and their respective I/O (their own little world). By utilizing several parallel processors and throughputting large amounts of data, some interesting output can be acquired. The neural network also attempts to simulate the brain and its activities. As is associated with artificial intelligence, neural nets operate in a "training" or teach mode. In this way systems can be taught functionality that they can use or repeat later. Again, the use of these types of higher-end systems, especially in process control, is going to gain in prominence.

Conclusions

PCs will continue to proliferate. Their name, *personal computers*, is going to outgrow its original definition. In factory automation, process control, and motion control there is an interest in and willingness to explore PC-based controls. Now, the PC industry should ready itself for another hardware explosion. Just as the PC has worked its way into millions of households, it will work its way onto thousands of factory floors in the next few years. Hardware configurations and footprints may have to change. We know that the software will! It already has by virtue of the soft logic packages out there.

Soft logic is really more than a "soft" real-time system. The words coin the merger of two industrial disciplines: *soft*ware and programmable *logic* control. These are two general terms that are used in a substantial sense to increase productivity and to help automate the world around us.

The new technologies emerging such as virtual reality, superconductivity, and digital communications will allow for tougher applications to be tried. Virtual reality will allow for the full simulation of applications without having to risk physical injury or damage machines and waste materials. Concepts and ideas can be explored via this technology, while the soft logic software designers sit in the wings waiting to make their next move! Superconductivity and superconducting materials could enhance electrical transmissions and communications by a quantum leap. Transmission speeds deemed impossible will be possible. Clock speeds of processors are already going to double every year or so. Imagine what superconductors will do to these speeds! The average computer system, instead of being outdated the day that it is purchased, will be outdated the *hour* after it is bought.

As for communications, the changes can be seen everywhere around us. Wireless and cellular systems abound. Analog systems are being replaced by new, digital systems. All types of smart devices and machines are manufactured with connectivity in mind. Whether in the home, office, or factory, the need to link to another device for some function is now a requirement. No longer is it acceptable to operate as a stand-alone system. Too many other devices connect, so will yours. These open architectures are going to be around for several years to come.

Which came first, the open architecture or the soft logic package? This is a good question not in need of an answer but rather in need of applications. Industry wants these types of solutions. Industry needs these types of solutions. Exploiting software and hardware systems in whatever manner someone so desires is a computer enthusiast's dream. Many past experiences have turned these exploitations into nightmares and have left lasting impressions on plant personnel. Their feeling is, "No! Not me this time!" Being left with a mix-and-match system of proprietary components, none really made for the other and all having their specific software (plus the software programmer is in Maui, now), has made industry wary of new controls. But these soft logic controls are different. They incorporate tried-and-true technology with application experience into an operating system which can handle the task. The industrial user now has the ability to select the "best-available equipment" for the job. Mix and match doesn't have the problems associated with it that it once had. Time and success will prove this. Besides, industry gets what industry wants.

If soft logic isn't the answer, then look for industry to lean to another technology for solutions. It won't tolerate inept, half-hearted approaches to very real manufacturing processes. Many `will even stick with the tried-and-true technology—they know that'll work. That's the nice thing about industry. Give it a solution that works well, and you've made a friend for life. Likewise, if the application is a bust, you better get out of town! Look for soft logic and PC-based controls to make a lot of friends and to stick. This technology may even get better. Stay tuned!

Bibliography and Further Reading

Bewley, L. E.: *Travelling Waves on Transmission Systems*, 2d ed., John Wiley & Sons, New York, 1951.

Boylestad, Robert L.: *Introductory Circuit Analysis*, 5th ed., Charles E. Merrill, Columbus, OH, 1982.

DC Motors, Speed Controls, Servo Systems, Electrocraft Corporation, Hopkins, MN, 1980.

Dulin, John J., Victor Veley, and John Gilbert: *Electronic Communications*, TAB Books, Blue Ridge Summit, PA, 1990.

Early, Murray, and Caloggero: *National Electrical Code Handbook*, 5th ed., National Fire Protection Association, Quincy, MA, 1990.

Fitzgerald, A. E., D. Kingsley, Jr., and A. Kusko: *Electric Machinery: The Processes, Devices, and Systems of Electro-Mechanical Energy Conversion*, 3d ed., Institute of Electrical and Electronics Engineers, New York, 1971.

Gottlieb, Irving M.: *Power Supplies, Switching Regulators, Inverters, and Converters*, 2d ed., TAB/McGraw-Hill, Blue Ridge Summit, PA, 1994.

Horn, Veley, and Gilbert: *Electronic Communications*, TAB Books, Blue Ridge Summit, PA, 1990.

IEEE Guide for Harmonic Control and Reactive Compensation of Static Power Converters, IEEE Standards 519-1981 and 519-1992, IEEE, New York, 1981 and 1992.

Karl-Heinz, John: *Programming with IEC 1131-3*, Tiegelkamp, Germany, 1995.

Lowden, Eric: *Practical Transformer Design Handbook*, 2d ed., McGraw-Hill, Blue Ridge Summit, PA, 1989.

Spitzer, David W.: *Variable Speed Drives—Principles and Applications for Energy Cost Savings*, 2d ed., Instrument Society of America, 1990, New York.

Steeplechase Software, Inc.: *PC-Based Control and Flow Chart Programming: The Handbook for Replacing PLCs on the Factory Floor*, Ann Arbor, MI, 1997.

Tomal, Daniel R., and Neal S. Widmer: *Electronic Troubleshooting,* 1st ed., TAB Books, Blue Ridge Summit, PA, 1993.

Underwriters Laboratories: *UL/ANSI Standard #508: Industrial Control Equipment,* Northbrook, IL, May 1994.

Williams, B. W., *Power Electronics: Devices, Drives, Applications, and Passive Components,* 2d ed.

Wisnosky, Dennis E.: *Softlogic: Overcoming Funnel Vision,* Wizdom Controls, Naperville, IL, 1996.

Common Acronyms

AC	Alternating current
A/D	Analog-to-digital
AE	Applications or automation engineer
AFD	Adjustable-frequency drive
AGV	Automatic guided vehicle
AI	Artificial intelligence
ALU	Arithmetic logic unit
AM	Amplitude-modulated
ANSI	American National Standards Institute
AOTF	Acousto-optic tunable filter
ASCII	American Standard Code for Information Interchange
ASD	Adjustable-speed drive
ASIC	Application-specific integrated circuit
AT	Advanced technology
ATDM	Asynchronous time-division multiplexing
ATG	Automatic tank gauge
ATM	Asynchronous transfer mode
AUI	Attached unit interface
BASIC	Beginner's All-purpose Symbolic Instruction Code
BBS	Bulletin board system
BCD	Bit or binary-coded decimal
BE	Back end
BiCMOS	Bipolar complementary metal-oxide semiconductor
BIL	Basic impulse level
BIOS	Basic input/output system
BJT	Bipolar junction transfer
BNC	Bayonet nut connector
BPS	Bits per second
BSC	Binary synchronous communications
BTU	British thermal unit

CAD	Computer-aided drafting
CADD	Computer-aided drafting and design
CAE	Computer-aided engineering
	Common-access method (committee);
CAM	Computer-aided manufacturing;
	Content-addressable memory
CASE	Computer-aided software engineering
CCD	Charge-coupled device
CD-ROM	Compact disk read-only memory
CF	Carrier frequency
CFC	Chlorofluorocarbon
CGA	Color graphics adapter
CHEMFET	Chemical field effect transistor
CIM	Computer-integrated manufacturing
CIP	Clean in place
CISC	Complex instruction set computer
CMOS	Complementary metal-oxide semiconductor
CNC	Computerized numerical control
COBOL	Common business-oriented language
CP/M	Control program/monitor
CPI	Clocks per instruction
CPU	Central processing unit
CR	Carriage return
CRQ	Command response queue
CRT	Cathode-ray tube
CS	Chip select
CSMA	Carrier sense multiple access
CSMA/CD	Carrier sense multiple access with collision detect
CSR	Command status register
CT	Current transformer
CTS	Clear to send
D/A	Digital-to-analog
DAS	Data acquisition system
DAT	Digital audio tape
DC	Direct current
DCD	Data carrier detect
DCE	Data circuit-terminating equipment
DCS	Distributed control system
DD	Double density
DDE	Dynamic data exchange
DES	Data encryption standard
DID	Direct-inward dial
DIN	Deutsche Industrie norm
DIP	Dual-in-line package
DIS	Draft International Standard
DLL	Dynamic link library

DMA	Direct memory access
DNC	Direct numerical control
DOS	Disk operating system
DP	Differential pressure
DPDT	Double-pole double-throw
DPE	Data parity error
DPM	Digital panel meter
DRAM	Dynamic random-access memory
DS	Double-sided
DSP	Digital signal processor
DSR	Data set ready
DTC	Data terminal controller
DTE	Data terminating equipment
DTMF	Dual-tone multifrequency
DTR	Data terminal ready
EBCDIC	Extended Binary-Coded Decimal Interchange Code
ECC	Error correction code
ECU	EISA configuration utility
EEPROM	Electrically erasable programmable read-only memory
EGA	Enhanced graphics array
EIA	Electronic Industries Association
EISA	Enhanced industry standard architecture
EMF	Electromotive force
EMI	Electromagnetic interference
EMS	Expanded memory specification
EOF	End of file
EOL	End of line
EPROM	Erasable programmable read-only memory
ESD	Electrostatic discharge
ESDI	Enhanced small devices interface
EXE	Executive or executable
FAT	File allocation table
FBD	Function block diagram
FCC	Federal Communications Commission
FDD	Floppy disk drive
FDDI	Fiber distributed data interference
FDM	Frequency-division multiplexing
FDX	Full-duplex transmission
FE	Front end
FEP	Front-end processor
FET	Field-effect transistor
FF	Form feed
FIFO	First-in, first-out
FILO	First-in, last-out (same as LIFO)
FLA	Full-load amperage
FLC	Full-load current

FM	Frequency modulation
FPGA	Field programming gate array
FPU	Floating-point unit
FRU	Field-replaceable unit
FSF	Free Software Foundation
FSK	Frequency shift keying
FTP	File transfer program
GAS	Gallium arsenide
GIGO	Garbage in, garbage out
GPIB	General-purpose interface bus
GUI	Graphical-user interface
HCFC	Hydrochlorofluorocarbon
HD	High density
HDD	Hard disk drive
HDX	Half-duplex transmission
HFS	Hierarchical file system
HMI	Human-machine interface
HP	Horsepower
HPFS	High-performance file system
HVAC	Heating, ventilating, and air conditioning
I/O	Input/output
I/P	Current-to-pressure
IBM	International Business Machines Corp.
IC	Integrated circuit
ID	Inside diameter
IDE	Integrated Device Electronics
IEEE	Institute of Electrical and Electronics Engineers
IGBT	Insulated gate bipolar transistor
IL	Instruction list
IMP	Interface message processor
IP	Internet protocol
IPC	Interprocess communication
IR	Infrared or current resistance (drop)
IRQ	Interrupt request
ISA	Instrument Society of America
ISO	International Standards Organization
JIT	Just-in-time (manufacturing)
KVA	Kilovoltamperes
KVAR	Kilovoltamperes reactive
LAN	Local-area network
LBA	Linear block array
LCD	Liquid-crystal display
LCL	Lower control limit
LD	Ladder diagram
LED	Light-emitting diode
LF	Line feed

LRU	Least-recently used
LSB	Least-significant bit
LSI	Large-scale integration
LUN	Logical unit number
LVDT	Linear variation differential transformer
MAN	Metropolitan-area network
MAP	Manufacturing applications protocol
MB/Mb	Megabytes/bits
MBR	Master boot record
MCC	Motor control center or metal-clad cable
MCGA	Multicolor graphics array
MCM	Multichip module
MFM	Modified frequency modulated
MG	Motor generator
MHz	Megahertz
MICR	Magnetic-ink character recognition
MIL-STD	Military standard
MIPS	Million instructions per second
MIS	Manufacturing information system
MISD	Multiple-instruction single-data
MMU	Memory management unit
MODEM	Modulator-demodulator
MOPS	Millions of operations per second
MOS	Metal-oxide semiconductor
MOSFET	Metal-oxide semiconductor field-effect transistor
MOV	Metal-oxide varistor
MP	Multiprocessor
MPP	Massively parallel processor
MRP	Manufacturing resource program
MSB	Most-significant bit
MS-DOS	Microsoft disk operating system
MSI	Medium-scale integration
MTBF	Mean time between failures
MTTD	Mean time to detect
MTTF	Mean time to fail
NBS	National Bureau of Standards
NC	Numerical control; normally closed
NEMA	National Electrical Manufacturers Association
NFS	Network file system
NMOS	Negatively doped metal-oxide semiconductor
NO	Normally open
NOP	No operation
NVRAM	Nonvolatile random-access memory
OCR	Object character recognition
OD	Outside diameter
ODI	Open datalink interface

OEM	Original equipment manufacturer
OMAC	Open, modular architecture control
OS	Operating system
OSF	Open Software Foundation
OSI	Open systems interconnect
P/I	Pressure-to-current
PB	Proportional band
PB	Pushbutton
PBX	Private branch eXtender
PC	Personal computer; programmable controller
PCB	Printed-circuit board
PCI	Peripheral component interconnect
PCM	Pulse-code modulation
PCMCIA	Personal Computer Memory Card International Association
PD	Positive displacement
PE	Professional engineer
PE	Processor element
PF	Power factor
PGA	Pin grid array
PI/O	Programmed input/output
PIC	Programmable interrupt controller
PID	Proportional-integral-derivative loop
PIV	Peak impulse voltage
PLA	Programmable logic array
PLC	Programmable logic controller
PLCC	Plastic-leaded chip carrier
PLL	Phase-locked loop
PM	Preventive maintenance
PMOS	Positively doped metal-oxide semiconductor
POC	Price of conformance
PONC	Price of nonconformance
POS	Point of sale
POST	Power-on self-test
PPP	Point-to-point protocol
PQFP	Plastic quad-flatpack
PROM	Programmable read-only memory
PT	Potential transformer
PWM	Pulse-width-modulated
QA	Quality assurance
QAM	Quadrature amplitude modulation
QC	Quality control
QF	Quad-flatpack
QIC	Quarter-inch cartridge
R&D	Research and development
RAM	Random-access memory
RAMDAC	Random-access memory digital-to-analog converter

RCC	Routing control center
RF	Radio frequency
RGB	Red, green, blue
RFC	Request for comments
RFI	Radio-frequency interference
RH	Relative humidity
RLL	Run-length-limited
RMM	Read mostly memory (same as EPROM)
RMS	Root mean square
RMW	Read, modify, write
ROI	Return on investment
ROM	Read-only memory
RPC	Remote procedure call
rpm	Revolutions per minute
RS232	Return signal 232
RTC	Real-time clock
RTD	Resistance-temperature detector
RTS	Request to send
SAM	Sequential-access memory
SCADA	Supervisory control and data acquisition
SCR	Silicone-controlled rectifier
SCSI	Small computer systems interface
SD	Single density
SDLC	Synchronous data link control
SE	Systems engineer; SoftLogic Engineer
SFC	Sequential function chart
SG	Specific gravity
SIMD	Single-instruction multiple-data
SIMM	Single in-line memory module
SIPP	Single in-line pinned package
SISD	Single-instruction single-data
SMD	Surface-mounted device
SMT	Surface-mount technology
SNA	System network architecture
SNR	Signal-to-noise ratio
SPC	Statistical process control
SPDT	Single-pole double-throw
SPT	Sectors per track
SRAM	Static random-access memory
SQC	Statistical quality control
SQE	Signal quality error
SRAM	Static random-access memory
SS	Single-sided
ST	Structured text
SVGA	Super video graphics array
T/C	Thermocouple

TCP	Transmission control protocol
TDM	Time-division multiplexing
THD	Total harmonic distortion
TIA	Telecommunication Industry Association
TLB	Translation-lookaside buffer
TOP	Technical office protocol
TPI	Tracks per inch
TTL	Transistor-transistor logic
UART	Universal asynchronous receiver/transmitter
UCL	Upper control limit
UDFB	User-defined function block
UHF	Ultrahigh-frequency
UMB	Upper memory block
UPC	Universal Product Code
UPS	Uninterruptible power supply
UTP	Unshielded twisted pair
UUCP	Unix-to-Unix copy program
UV	Ultraviolet
VCR	Video cassette recorder
VDM	Video display monitor
VESA	Video Enhanced Standards Association
VFD	Variable-frequency drive
VGA	Video graphics array/adapter
VHF	Very high-frequency
VLB	VESA local bus
VLF	Very low-frequency
VLSI	Very large-scale integration
VM	Virtual memory
VME	Versa module Eurocard; virtual memory executive
VRAM	Video random-access memory
VSD	Variable-speed drive
WAN	Wide-area network
WATS	Wide-area telephone service
WIP	Work in progress
WS	Wait state
XGA	eXtended graphics array
XOR	eXclusive OR
XT	eXtended technology

Note: For acronyms of organizations (ASME, IEEE, NEMA, etc.), see Chap. 5.

Index

About the Author

Robert Carrow (Harmony, PA) is a professional mechanical engineer with extensive experience in the electronics industries. He is the author of *The Technician's Guide to Industrial Electronics* and *Electronic Drives*.